The Effectiveness of International Environmental Regimes

Global Environmental Accord: Strategies for Sustainability and Institutional Innovation
Nazli Choucri, editor

Global Accord: Environmental Challenges and International Responses
Nazli Choucri, editor

Institutions for the Earth: Sources of Effective International Environmental Protection
Peter M. Haas, Robert O. Keohane, and Marc A. Levy, editors

Intentional Oil Pollution at Sea: Environmental Policy and Treaty Compliance
Ronald B. Mitchell

Institutions for Environmental Aid: Pitfalls and Promise
Robert O. Keohane and Marc A. Levy, editors

Global Governance: Drawing Insights from the Environmental Experience
Oran R. Young, editor

The Struggle for Accountability: The World Bank, NGOs, and Grassroots Movements
Jonathan A. Fox and L. David Brown

The Implementation and Effectiveness of International Environmental Commitments: Theory and Practice
David G. Victor, Kal Raustiala, and Eugene Skolnikoff, editors

Global Environmental Diplomacy: Negotiating Environmental Agreements for the World, 1973–1992
Mostafa K. Tolba with Iwona Rummel Bulska

The Greening of Sovereignty in World Politics
Karen T. Litfin, editor

Engaging Countries: Strengthening Compliance with International Environmental Accords
Edith Brown Weiss and Harold K. Jacobson, editors

The Effectiveness of International Environmental Regimes: Causal Connections and Behavioral Mechanisms
Oran R. Young, editor

The Effectiveness of International Environmental Regimes
Causal Connections and Behavioral Mechanisms

edited by Oran R. Young

The MIT Press
Cambridge, Massachusetts
London, England

This book was set in Sabon by Achorn Graphic Services, Inc.

Printed and bound in the United States of America.

Library of Congress Cataloging-in-Publication Data

The effectiveness of international environmental regimes : causal connections and behavioral mechanisms / edited by Oran R. Young.
    p.   cm. — (Global environmental accords)
  Includes bibliographical references and index.
    ISBN 0-262-24042-4 (cloth : alk. paper). — ISBN 0-262-74023-0 (pbk. : alk. paper)
    1. Environmental law, International.   2. Transboundary pollution—Law and legislation.   3. Environmental policy—International cooperation.
  I. Young, Oran R.   II. Series.
  K3585.4.E34   1999
  341.7′62—dc21   99-11114
                                                                          CIP

For Leonard Rieser
as a small contribution to the growing residue

Contents

Series Foreword   ix
Preface   xi
Contributors   xv

1 The Effectiveness of International Environmental Regimes   1
Oran R. Young and Marc A. Levy (with the assistance of Gail Osherenko)

2 International Vessel-Source Oil Pollution   33
Ronald Mitchell, Moira L. McConnell, Alexei Roginko, and Ann Barrett

3 The Barents Sea Fisheries   91
Olav Schram Stokke, Lee G. Anderson, and Natalia Mirovitskaya

4 Acid Rain in Europe and North America   155
Don Munton, Marvin Soroos, Elena Nikitina, and Marc A. Levy

5 Regime Effectiveness: Taking Stock   249
Oran R. Young (with the assistance of the project team)

Appendix: Notes on Methodology   281
References   289
Index   315

Series Foreword

A new recognition of profound interconnections between social and natural systems is challenging conventional constructs as well as the policy predispositions informed by them. Our current intellectual challenge is to develop the analytical and theoretical underpinnings crucial to our understanding of the relationships between the two systems. Our policy challenge is to identify and implement effective decision-making approaches to managing the global environment.

The Series on Global Environmental Accord adopts an integrated perspective on national, international, cross-border, and cross-jurisdictional problems, priorities, and purposes. It examines the sources and consequences of social transactions as these relate to environmental conditions and concerns. Our goal is to make a contribution to both the intellectual and the policy endeavors.

Preface

The research project whose findings are reported in this book began in 1991 with the support of a generous grant from the Ford Foundation that made possible the formation of a large, multinational research team and the development of a common research protocol designed to guide work on the effectiveness of international environmental regimes over a period of several years. Altogether fifteen researchers from five countries participated in the project and made available their knowledge not only to the development of the case studies but also to the formulation of the theoretical analysis of the determinants of regime effectiveness. Work began with an interactive process that culminated in a workshop held at Dartmouth College during the fall of 1991 at which the team reached agreement on the structure and content of a design for a large-scale collaborative research project on the effectiveness of international regimes. Subsequent workshops intended to assess progress and to engage in face-to-face discussions on both substantive and methodological issues about the project took place at Dartmouth during the fall of 1992 and at North Carolina State University in Raleigh during the fall of 1993. The passage of a considerable period of time between the last of these workshops and the completion of the final text of this book is testimony to the complexities of the subject we have chosen to study as well as to the complications involved in reaching closure among the members of a large, multinational research team.

When this project began, students of international regimes were still preoccupied to a large extent with puzzles relating to the formation of international regimes. They were seeking, for example, to sort out the relative importance of power, interests, and ideas as forces guiding the efforts of actors in international society to form regimes as mechanisms for solving collective-action problems.[1] Since then, we have witnessed a gathering interest among students of international regimes in questions about effectiveness or the factors that explain why some regimes are more successful than others in solving the problems that lead actors to create them. Some of the resultant work—like the 1993 volume edited by Peter Haas, Robert Keohane, and Marc Levy[2]—is notable for its role in framing the research agenda and providing initial clues to fruitful avenues for those concerned with this agenda to pursue. Other contributions—like the projects coordinated by Harold Jacobson and Edith Brown Weiss, by David Victor, and by Kenneth Hanf and Arild Underdal[3]—have opened up the subject of the implementation of international commitments in domestic legal and political systems, or what many now think of as the domestication of international agreements.

Two projects—this one and a parallel effort by another research team coordinated by Edward Miles and Arild Underdal[4]—have endeavored to tackle the question of effectiveness directly, seeking in the process to solve problems involving operationalization, measurement, and causal inference. This project features three in-depth but largely qualitative case studies based on a common research design and extensive interaction among researchers working on the individual cases. The Miles–Underdal project, by contrast, deals with a larger number of cases and seeks to develop quantitative measures that can be used to test propositions about the determinants of effectiveness using the procedures of variation-finding analysis. Also slated for publication by MIT Press, the volume reporting on the results of that project should join this book in providing a good sense of the current state of the art in research on the effectiveness of international regimes.

This project has been intertwined with the larger effort of the scientific community to understand effectiveness since its inception. The "regimes summit," designed as a consultation among leaders in the field of regime analysis and hosted by Dartmouth in November 1991, followed immediately on the first workshop of this project's research team and played a constructive role in the development of the project's research protocol.[5]

The project figured prominently in the September 1994 Workshop on Compliance with International Environmental Accords, which was funded by the United Nations University, organized by the Institute on International Environmental Governance at Dartmouth, and hosted by the University of Barcelona in Spain.[6] The analytic structure of the project also provided inspiration in the development of the International Regimes Database under the auspices of the project on Implementation and Effectiveness of International Environmental Commitments organized and funded by the International Institute for Applied Systems Analysis in Austria.[7] Today, this stream of work is at the center of a Concerted Action on the Effectiveness of International Environmental Agreements funded by the European Union.[8]

It is a pleasure to record a number of debts of gratitude to those who played critical roles at one time or another during the life of this project. The essential financial support came from the Ford Foundation under the terms of grants #890-0042-2/890-0042-3. Yet it is also important to emphasize that the home institutions of various members of the research team allowed—and encouraged—them to devote time and energy to this project. Special thanks are due as well to the John Sloan Dickey Center for International Understanding at Dartmouth for supporting my work on the project and providing support for the Institute of Arctic Studies which served as the administrative home for the project during its entire lifetime.

Although she appears in a minor role in the table of contents, Gail Osherenko played an essential part in managing the project during its early phases; her ideas also had a constructive influence on the project's conceptualization of effectiveness. Don Munton, who joined the project after it was already underway, deserves special thanks for his efforts to bring the case study on acid rain to closure. Konrad von Moltke has been a constructive critic throughout; he joined me as the co-organizer of the Barcelona Workshop in 1994. Nicki Maynard, who has served as the office manager of the Institute of Arctic Studies throughout the lifetime of this project, has provided essential support not only in making the necessary logistical arrangements but also in handling all the complications of moving draft after draft of the individual chapters of this book around the world from one computer to another by electronic means. Last, but by no means least, I want to offer my sincere thanks to all the members of the multinational research team who worked together both to hammer out a common research design for this project and to apply it systematically to a series of important cases.

Notes

1. Andreas Hasenclever, Peter Mayer, and Volker Rittberger, *Theories of International Regimes*. Cambridge: Cambridge University Press, 1997.

2. Peter M. Haas, Robert O. Keohane, and Marc A. Levy, *Institutions for the Earth: Sources of Effective International Environmental Protection*. Cambridge: MIT Press, 1993.

3. Edith Brown Weiss and Harold K. Jacobson, *Engaging Countries: Strengthening Compliance with International Environmental Accords*. Cambridge: MIT Press, 1998; David G. Victor, Kal Raustiala, and Eugene B. Skolnikoff, *The Implementation and Effectiveness of International Environmental Commitments*. Cambridge: MIT Press, 1998; and Kenneth Hanf and Arild Underdal, *The Domestic Basis of International Environmental Agreements*. Aldershot: Ashgate, forthcoming.

4. Edward Miles et al., *Explaining Regime Effectiveness: Confronting Theory with Evidence*. Cambridge: MIT Press, forthcoming.

5. "Regimes Summit," workshop report dated 2 December 1991 and circulated by the Institute of Arctic Studies at Dartmouth College.

6. Oran R. Young and Konrad von Moltke, "The Consequences of International Environmental Regimes: Report from the Barcelona Workshop," *International Environmental Affairs*, 6 (1994), 348–370.

7. Helmut Breitmeier, Marc A. Levy, Oran R. Young, and Michael Zürn, "International Regimes Database (IRD): Data Protocol," IIASA WP-96-154, December 1996.

8. Funded in 1997, this concerted action will organize a series of meetings among scientists working in this area over a three-year period.

Contributors

Lee G. Anderson is professor of economics and marine policy at the College of Marine Studies of the University of Delaware.

Ann Barrett is an employee relations officer with the Nova Scotia Government Employees Union.

Marc A. Levy is lead project scientist for the Socioeconomic Data and Applications Center (SEDAC) at CIESIN within the Columbia University Earth Institute.

Moira L. McConnell is professor of law and director of the Marine and Environmental Law Programme at the Dalhousie University School of Law.

Natalia Mirovitskaya is a senior research fellow of the Institute of World Economy and International Relations (IMEMO) in Moscow and a fellow of the Nicholas School of the Environment at Duke University.

Ronald V. Mitchell is assistant professor of political science at the University of Oregon.

Don Munton is professor of international studies at the University of Northern British Columbia.

Elena Nikitina is a senior research fellow of the Institute of World Economy and International Relations (IMEMO) in Moscow.

Gail Osherenko is a senior fellow of the Institute of Arctic Studies at Dartmouth College.

Alexei Roginko is a research fellow of the Institute of World Economy and International Relations (IMEMO) in Moscow.

Marvin Soroos is professor of political science at North Carolina State University.

Olav Schram Stokke is a senior research fellow of international environmental governance and research director of the Fridtjof Nansen Institute in Oslo.

Oran R. Young is professor of environmental studies and director of the Institute on International Environmental Governance at Dartmouth College.

1

The Effectiveness of International Environmental Regimes

Oran R. Young and Marc A. Levy
(*with the assistance of Gail Osherenko*)

Why are some international environmental regimes more successful than others in solving the problems that motivate their establishment? More modestly, why do some environmental regimes have a greater impact than others on the behavior of those whose actions have given rise to the relevant problems? To pose these questions is to launch an enquiry into the effectiveness of institutional arrangements in international society. A regime that channels behavior in such a way as to eliminate or substantially ameliorate the problem that led to its creation is an effective regime. A regime that has little behavioral impact, by contrast, is an ineffective regime. As these observations imply, the concept of effectiveness as applied to international institutions defines a continuous variable. Regimes can range along a continuum from ineffectual arrangements, which wind up as dead letters, to highly effective arrangements, which produce quick and decisive solutions to the problems at hand.

All international environmental regimes are "social institutions consisting of agreed upon principles, norms, rules, procedures, and programs that govern the interactions of actors in specific issue areas."[1] It would be pointless therefore to speak of regimes that have no behavioral consequences whatsoever.[2] Yet nothing in this formulation is inconsistent with the empirical observation that regimes differ greatly in terms of their effectiveness. Some institutional arrangements score higher than others in effectiveness by virtually any measure. More commonly, some individual regimes are more effective than others with regard to some criteria, and many regimes work better during some stages of their life cycles than others.

The Antarctic Treaty System, a successful example, has proven remarkably effective since its creation in the 1950s in preventing the hardening of jurisdictional claims in the south polar region and in keeping this region open to entry for nationals of all the participating states who desire to engage in scientific research and other permissible activities. This regime has also proven flexible enough to adapt to significant changes in the Antarctic agenda and in the composition of its own membership without any serious loss of effectiveness. The ozone regime that emerged during the 1980s, another successful example, has produced striking results regarding the problem of phasing out the production and consumption of chlorofluorocarbons (CFCs) and a number of other chemicals that migrate into the stratosphere and destroy ozone molecules in the upper atmosphere. Despite its initial success, however, this regime now faces real challenges that arise from difficulties in implementing its provisions in key developing countries and the emergence of black markets in some of the relevant chemicals (Parson and Greene 1995; French 1997). There is no denying, by contrast, that many international fisheries regimes have failed to restrict harvesting practices, leading again and again to severe depletions of important fish stocks (Peterson 1993). Some of the most far-reaching efforts to overcome these failures (for example, granting coastal states management authority in extensive fishery conservation zones covering waters adjacent to their coasts), moreover, have served only to shift the locus of this problem rather than to solve it.

How can we explain such differences in the effectiveness of international environmental regimes? The search for an answer to this question raises a series of more focused questions. How exactly do international institutions operate to influence behavior and, in the process, to solve problems? How much of the variance in the behavior of individual actors and in collective outcomes at the international level can we reasonably attribute to the operation of institutional arrangements in contrast to other driving forces—like material conditions and ideas—at work in international society? How do institutions interact with other social drivers to determine the character of collective outcomes at the international level? What analytic tools are available to help shed light on these complex, typically contingent relationships? Although the last decade has witnessed a striking growth of interest in international regimes in the United States and beyond,[3] we remain unable to answer these central questions in a convincing fashion. Many regime analysts, concerned mainly with processes of regime formation, simply do not address them. Others, whose thinking reflects in-depth knowledge of individual regimes, propose answers that fail to generalize to a broader range of cases.

Even more disturbing are the difficulties that those who tackle these questions regularly encounter in moving beyond measures of association to demonstrate causal connections between the operation of institutional arrangements and their apparent effects and, in the process, answering the arguments of critics who see international institutions as mere epiphenomena (Strange 1983; Mearsheimer 1994–1995). The research reported in this book belongs to a gathering movement intended to remedy this situation.[4] Its distinguishing feature is the idea that transcending sterile debates about the effectiveness of international regimes requires a sustained effort to probe the behavioral mechanisms or pathways through which institutions affect the behavior of actors and, through them, the outcomes of interactive behavior at the international level. Only by investigating the sources of behavior can we specify the conditions under which regimes are likely to prove effective and present arguments that are not vulnerable to charges that the relationships reported are little more than spurious correlations. We do not claim to have produced a set of empirically tested generalizations about the sources of regime effectiveness that are valid across a range of issue areas. Our contribution lies in the specification and application of models designed to illuminate the sources of actor behavior and in detailed studies of a set of environmental cases chosen as vehicles for probing the relevance of these models to actual behavior governed by the operation of international regimes.

The Meaning of Effectiveness

Effectiveness is a matter of the contributions that institutions make to solving the problems that motivate actors to invest the time and energy needed to create them. On closer examination, however, effectiveness emerges as an elusive concept. It can mean a number of different things, and some of its meanings require difficult normative, scientific, and historical judgments.

Problem-Solving Approach

International regimes commonly emerge in response to particular problems—environmental deterioration, escalating tariffs, border conflicts. The most intuitively appealing sense of effectiveness centers on the degree to which a regime eliminates or alleviates the problem that prompts its creation. Yet this definition presents practical problems that are sometimes severe. The social systems that are the focus of international regimes (as well as the natural systems within which they operate) are typically complex. Longitudinal data on the evolution of these systems, moreover, are frequently inconsistent or nonexistent. As a result, it is often difficult to ascribe observed changes in these systems to the operation of international regimes. The difficulties are compounded by the fact that most problems serious enough to justify the creation of an international regime motivate actors to pursue solutions through a variety of initiatives, including some that do not involve the regime directly. What looks like an effective regime, measured in terms of problem solving, might merely be an irrelevant sideshow. Accordingly, the intuitive elegance of this definition, which directs our attention to the substantive bottom line, can become the source of its own limitations because it is so hard to apply meaningfully.

Legal Approach

A legal definition of effectiveness might hold that the measure of a regime's effectiveness is the degree to which contractual obligations are met—rules are complied with, policies changed, programs initiated, and so forth. Like the idea of problem solving, this legal view has a firm grip on our intuition. As opposed to the problem-solving definition, the legal approach provides for relatively straightforward measurement because effectiveness is defined in terms of obligations written into treaty language. But this operational clarity comes at a price. A regime can be effective in a legal sense without doing much to solve the problem that led to its creation. In some cases, regimes generate significant positive effects beyond the terms of the contractual obligations involved. In other cases, legally defined effectiveness may even generate perverse substantive outcomes.

Economic Approach

An economic definition of effectiveness would incorporate the legal definition and add an efficiency criterion. Economists want to know not only whether a regime generates the right outcome but also whether it does so at the least cost. Other things being equal, less costly adjustments are more effective. This approach has the same attractions and weaknesses as the problem-solving definition; it has strong intuitive appeal but poses great difficulties in application. Measurements of efficiency require either empirical observations of alternative regimes or calculations based on theoretical models that do not abstract away determinants of efficiency that are critical in practice. In the domain in which international regimes operate, the former are generally absent and the latter too restrictive to generate reliable guides. When we assess a given institutional arrangement for solving or managing an international problem, we are seldom able to determine how efficient it is.

Normative Approach

It is also possible to think about effectiveness in terms of normative principles, such as fairness or justice, stewardship, participation, and so forth. Few analysts place such normative constructs at the center of their definitions of effectiveness, though many incorporate them more loosely. Equating effectiveness with the achievement of such values presents measurement problems that are severe, without promising comparable analytic rewards. Although assessing the normative consequences of international regimes is undoubtedly a worthwhile endeavor, it is more appropriate to treat this exercise as a matter of evaluation rather than as part of an effort to improve causal understanding.

Political Approach

A political definition treats regimes as directed at particular international problems and conceives of these problems as functions of specific constellations of actors, interests, and institutions or what we call behavioral complexes in this project. Effective regimes cause changes in the behavior of actors, in the interests of actors, or in the policies and performance of institutions in ways that contribute to positive management of the targeted problem. Such a definition does not exclude consideration of whether problems get solved, compliance is high or low, or normative goals are met. It merely insists that such claims focus on how behavioral changes, attributable to the operation of a regime, are responsible for the improved environment. In thinking of the purposes for which regimes are established, we have in mind broad problem-oriented goals rather than specific action-oriented goals. In most cases, the purpose is unambiguous. The objective of the 1985 Vienna Convention and the 1987 Montreal Protocol is to protect the ozone layer; the objective of the 1992 Framework Convention on Climate Change and the 1997 Kyoto Protocol is to stabilize greenhouse gases at a level that will "prevent dangerous anthropogenic interference with the climate system." Effectiveness in a political sense means spurring action toward achieving these objectives. Specific regulatory rules, protocols, and operational targets are means to these ends rather than ends in themselves. A notable consequence of this definition is that compliance is not granted a privileged conceptual position. Activities that move the system in the right direction, even if they fall short of full compliance, are signs of effectiveness. Likewise, institutions that goad members to undertake measures that go beyond what is required for compliance are considered more effective than those that only elicit the minimum behavioral change required.

Because international regimes are political institutions, we regard some variant of the political definition as a necessary component of the study of institutional effectiveness. In the absence of perverse exogenous effects, regimes that are effective in the political sense will also be effective in the problem-solving sense. Political effectiveness, however, has no necessary connection to either the legal or the economic sense of the term. A politically effective regime might be highly inefficient or produce low levels of compliance. In the case studies reported in this volume, we seek to demonstrate the behavioral impacts of regimes and through such impacts the contributions of institutional arrangements to problem solving at the international level.

Introduction to the Cases

The cases we have chosen for in-depth study in our analysis of the effectiveness of international regimes all involve institutional arrangements that address environmental problems and have been in place long enough to compile track records that can be evaluated systematically. But they differ in a number of important respects. The oil pollution regime is a global arrangement that includes a large number of members but focuses on a set of concerns that is limited in functional terms. The fisheries regime for the Barents Sea is a bilateral arrangement that operates in a setting in which there is significant disagreement about the delimitation of jurisdictional boundaries. The case study of air pollution encompasses two distinct regimes, a regional arrangement covering transboundary fluxes of several pollutants in Europe, which includes the United States and Canada as members, and a bilateral Canadian–American regime focusing on acid precipitation in North America.

Two of these regimes—the arrangements dealing with vessel-source oil pollution and the long-range transport of airborne pollutants in Europe—have been subjected to intensive analysis. Several members of the research team working on this project have been prominent among those who have undertaken this research. We regard this as a source of strength for the present study. Our purpose here is to subject individual regimes, including those that are familiar from previous accounts, to a rigorous effort to understand the behavioral pathways that account for the extent to which they have proven effective in solving problems or, more generally, are influencing the behavior of their subjects. The measure of our accomplishment will lie in our ability to generate new insights about the causal mechanisms through which these—and any other—regimes succeed in affecting the content of collective outcomes in international society.

Oil Pollution

Problems that arise from intentional discharges of oil by tankers cleaning their cargo tanks or using empty tanks to hold sea water as ballast first came to the attention of the international community in the 1920s (M'Gonigle and Zacher 1979; Mitchell 1994). Following several unsuccessful attempts, thirty-two countries prodded by the United Kingdom reached agreement on the terms of an international convention (known as OILPOL) in this area in 1954. The centerpiece of this agreement was a set of discharge standards that required tanker owner/operators to adhere to well-defined rules regarding the discharge of oil in conjunction with tanker operations in a variety of prohibited zones. This regime was subsequently restructured in an effort led by the United States that culminated in an international convention (known as MARPOL) adopted originally in 1973 and substantially amended in 1978. As revised under the terms of MARPOL, the regime covering intentional discharges of oil grants additional authority to port and coastal states and moves toward a system of equipment standards and the provision of reception facilities in ports in contrast to discharge standards. Although individual states have assumed much of the responsibility for implementing the oil pollution regime, the International Maritime Organization (IMO) provides administrative support for this arrangement at the international level. Widely regarded as relatively unsuccessful in its initial version, this regime has proven much more effective during the period following the move toward equipment standards. In exploring the factors that account for this evolution, the case study set forth at length in chapter 2 reveals a number of interesting insights about the factors that lead to success or failure in efforts to solve international problems through the creation and operation of institutional arrangements.

Barents Sea Fisheries
The Norwegian–Russian regime for the fisheries of the Barents Sea owes its origins to the combination of a desire to avoid serious conflict in a strategically sensitive area, marked by jurisdictional disagreements, and an enhanced opportunity for coastal states to create fisheries regimes as a result of the acceptance of broad fishery conservation zones (and ultimately exclusive economic zones or EEZs) in coastal waters during the 1970s (Stokke and Hoel 1991). Embedded in a series of three distinct agreements dating from 1975, 1976, and 1978, this bilateral regime sets forth procedures for managing shared stocks of cod, haddock, and capelin; provides a means to allow fishing to continue in an orderly fashion in the disputed area of the central Barents Sea, and establishes a Mixed Fisheries Commission to administer this arrangement and create a framework for cooperation in the area on an ongoing basis. In some ways, this regime has been remarkably successful. It has served to manage the unresolved jurisdictional dispute between Norway and Russia, and it has regulated fishing activities in the region through periods involving economic recession and political turmoil and transformation in Russia. By itself, however, the regime cannot ensure the health of a number of major fish stocks in the area,[5] and it does not encompass provisions to deal with

emerging threats to the Barents Sea fisheries that arise from activities like the dumping of radioactive contaminants in the Barents and Kara Seas by Soviet (now Russian) agencies and the development of hydrocarbon reserves in the area. Our case study of this regime, reported at length in chapter 3, helps to delineate the domain of effects that need to be considered in thinking about the performance of international regimes, and it explores the methods most suitable for tracking the causal pathways leading to different effects.

Transboundary Air Pollution
The third case study has a dual focus. It emphasizes the regime established under the terms of the 1979 Geneva Convention on Long-Range Transboundary Air Pollution (LRTAP) and its subsequent protocols on sulfur dioxide (1985), nitrogen oxides (1988), volatile organic compounds (1991), sulfur dioxide, again (1994), and persistent organic pollutants (1998) supplemented by an account of experience with the regime grounded in the 1980 U.S.-Canada Memorandum of Intent and now articulated in the North American Air Quality Agreement of 1991 (Levy 1993; Munton forthcoming). The LRTAP arrangement diverges from our common view of institutions in that it does not lay down many clearcut rules or behavioral prescriptions. Rather, it establishes a joint mechanism for improving knowledge regarding the phenomenon of acid rain and encourages member countries to make quite general pledges (for example, a 30 percent reduction of sulfur emissions by a specified date) on the understanding that each government will be free to fulfill these pledges in any way it sees fit. Although this may appear to many as a rather inauspicious beginning, the LRTAP regime has set in motion an evolving institutional arrangement that is taken seriously by most governments today and appears to have had a noticeable impact on policymaking in a number of member states. As reported in chapter 4, this case study is revealing for what it tells about the capacity of international institutions to enmesh actors in evolving practices, even when they do not appear to have strong teeth in conventional regulatory terms. For its part, the North American arrangement offers an interesting contrast on a number of dimensions (for example, number of participants). Overall, it has also generated fewer beneficial effects.

The Domain of Effects

How wide should we cast our net in the search for impacts or consequences of international environmental regimes? Given the web of interdependencies operative in international society, it is easy to envision regimes producing ripple effects across both space and time, so that individual regimes may be seen as initiating chain reactions whose impacts are felt far and wide. Yet trying to track down all these effects is clearly an impossible task for those working on individual cases. It is also unnecessary in order to reach meaningful conclusions about the effectiveness of international regimes. In practical terms, then, we need guidelines to direct our attention to the principal effects of regimes and to ensure that the individual case studies are constructed in a manner that facilitates comparisons among them. In dealing with this issue, we have found it useful to differentiate three dimensions of effects: (1) effects within the behavioral complex (that is, the constellation of actors, interests, and interactions centered on a specific issue or issue area) and effects external to the behavioral complex, (2) direct and indirect effects, and (3) effects that help to solve a problem and effects that make it worse. These dimensions of effectiveness obviously intersect with one another. But the ways in which the dimensions intersect is less important at this stage than the notion that each dimension is worthy of attention and that within each dimension there are logical areas to emphasize more than others.

Because our conception of effectiveness is multidimensional, we do not devote any appreciable effort to constructing measures of effectiveness that are fully comparable across these cases. The goal of this project is not to attach a particular value to each regime on a universal scale or index of effectiveness, but rather to understand the full range of significant effects that each regime is responsible for and to deepen our understanding of the mechanisms by which regimes produce these effects.

Internal and External Effects

Although regimes are sometimes treated as self-contained arrangements, it is important to bear in mind that each regime is embedded in an identifiable behavioral complex. Because regimes are designed to help solve problems that arise within specific behavioral complexes, it makes sense to look first and foremost for regime effects occurring within the relevant complex. We look, for instance, at emission levels of power plants in the acid rain regime, tanker operations under the MARPOL rules, and fishing fleet behavior in the Barents Sea. If the regime affects any of these things, it has had an effect within the behavioral complex in which it is embedded. The relevant test for discerning an impact of this type is to ask whether the regime affects the management of the problem that motivated its creation by inducing changes in the behavior of states and other actors whose behavior is directly involved in the relevant behavioral complex.

Regimes can also have effects outside the issue areas in which they are embedded. These are commonly unforeseen and generally unintended consequences flowing from the operation of institutional arrangements. They are much like what economists lump under the heading of externalities in their efforts to understand the operation of exchange systems based on more or less well-defined structures of property rights. As economists often point out, side effects can be positive as well as negative. The added costs of incorporating new technologies to control sulfur dioxide emissions to reduce acid rain, for instance, could increase incentives to develop new energy sources, which would not only play a role in reducing transboundary air pollution but also help to alleviate the greenhouse effect by reducing our dependence on fossil fuels. That said, however, the side effects of interest in our study of international regimes typically fall into the category of negative externalities. For the most part, they have more in common with the problems arising in domestic societies from the shift to tall smokestacks as a response to clean air regulations than with the gains arising from a hypothetical development of some new energy source.

A few examples relating to cases here may help to pin down the category of external effects. Thus, the phasing out of third-party fishing in the Barents Sea not only affected the fishing complex in that area but it also affected other fisheries as displaced fishers sought new opportunities to ply their trade elsewhere. The geographical limits of the LRTAP regime appear to have produced effects far to the east in Siberia by generating incentives for Soviet–Russian policymakers and managers to move some production facilities eastward instead of shifting to cleaner technologies.

It appears to be the case also that the oil pollution regime has deflected attention from the larger question of land-based marine pollution both by focusing on vessel-source discharges and by relying on organizational arrangements, like the International Maritime Organization, possessing little capacity or incentive to take up the problem of land-based pollution.

Clearly, the primary focus of our case studies is and ought to be on effects unfolding within the relevant behavioral complexes. Nevertheless, because effects outside the issue area are often of substantive importance, we cannot ignore them in putting together these case studies. In the chapters reporting on the individual cases, we seek to identify and describe the principal external effects, though we do not strive for the same level of methodological rigor as we do for effects internal to the behavioral complex.

Direct and Indirect Effects

The question of whether a regime's effects are direct or indirect is a matter of the length of the causal chain connecting the regime to the behavior in question. Direct effects are linked by short causal chains, indirect effects by longer ones. In most cases, direct effects center around behavior involving compliance with regime rules and participation in programmatic activities. A few examples drawn from our cases will lend substance to what should be an intuitively easy point to grasp. In the case of acid rain, we want to know whether transboundary fluxes of airborne pollutants have declined due to the operation of the regime as well as whether affected lakes and forests have shown signs of recovery. In the case of oil pollution, we want to know whether the quantity of oil entering marine systems as a result of intentional discharges has declined and—a more difficult point—whether the level of these discharges is lower than it would have been if the regime had not come into being. In the fisheries case, we want to know if levels of fish catches are dropping or otherwise coming closer to optimal levels and if such changes are leading to a recovery in the relevant fish stocks. In all these cases, the regime's effectiveness is a function of direct reductions in environmental stresses that are attributable to observation of regime rules and procedures.

This measure of effectiveness requires examination of compliance records, a process that is straightforward conceptually but not necessarily easy to carry out under the conditions obtaining in individual cases. Thus, we want to track compliance records regarding the standards for discharging oil at sea as well as the equipment standards applying to the construction of new oil tankers. Similarly, we want to know how well the parties have complied with the annual quotas or total allowable catch limits established for fishing in the Barents Sea (which is quite different from questions regarding the abatement of the problem of stock depletions in the area).

Yet the category of direct effects encompasses more than just compliance. Actions that fall short of compliance, go beyond it, or have nothing to do with specific rules can be important direct effects of a regime. A switch to some alternative mode of production or new transportation system would fall into this category of direct effects. This would include, for example, some investments in production facilities for HCFCs that are attributable to the developing ozone regime, though these investments do not appear in compliance reports on the phasing out of CFCs. Similarly, some moves to replace coal and oil with natural gas as a source of energy constitute a response to new rules relating to pollution control, though they do not show up in statistics that focus on the movement of airborne pollutants. The essential point here is to identify behavioral responses that can be linked directly to the operation of a regime but are not easily captured in data relating to the abatement of the initial problem or compliance with regime rules. In some cases, effects of this sort will be among the most important consequences flowing from the formation and operation of international environmental regimes.

Indirect effects of a regime are responses that are causally connected to a regime's rules or activities, but with considerably more intervening factors between regime features and reductions in environmental stress. They may contribute to broader streams of events that affect the character of international society over a period of time. At the extreme, they are like the proverbial butterfly in China, whose beating wings cause dramatic perturbations in weather on the other side of the planet. Effects as distant as these from the regime need not preoccupy us in this project. In many instances, however, indirect effects are somewhat less removed. The direct effects we identify will in some cases touch off chain reactions leading to indirect effects that ripple through a larger system. A switch from coal or oil to natural gas, for example, may increase the demand for a new set of technologies and lead to significant shifts in investment and employment patterns. Similarly, a move to deemphasize fossil fuels may heighten interest in nuclear energy and raise concerns about the health and safety consequences of increased reliance on nuclear technology. Alternatively, such a move may trigger a growing interest in various unconventional energy sources and increase pressures on governments to promote the development of these sources through public action.

Many of the interesting indirect effects operate through an impact on environmental politics, either within the regime's issue area or in other areas. Regimes can play a role in setting the agenda for future deliberations, initiating dynamic processes that lead to institutional evolution, and, more broadly, influencing the way we think about large-scale environmental problems. None of these effects directly reduces stress on the environment, but they may be instrumental in actions that reduce stresses later on. Interestingly, these effects can occur quite apart from the success or failure of a regime in solving the initial problem. In some cases, failure may actually serve to trigger these indirect effects. The activities of the Environmental Monitoring and Evaluation Programme (EMEP), for example, appear to have played a role in setting the agenda for efforts to develop new protocols within the LRTAP framework and in developing the increasingly influential approach to pollution problems associated with the concept of critical loads. The failure of the initial approach based on discharge standards appears to have been a factor in the decision to introduce equipment standards in the effort to curb discharges of oil. The problems plaguing efforts to manage fisheries, with little attention to the dynamics of large marine ecosystems of which they are a part, have undoubtedly provided a stimulus for the introduction of thinking about whole ecosystems when dealing with marine resources.[6] This category of indirect effects appears important in all our cases; we therefore endeavor to address them explicitly in analyzing the impacts or consequences of these regimes.

Good and Bad Effects

Any given effect a regime has, whether internal to the behavioral complex of the regime or external to it, whether direct or indirect, will fall somewhere on a continuum running from helping to solve an environmental

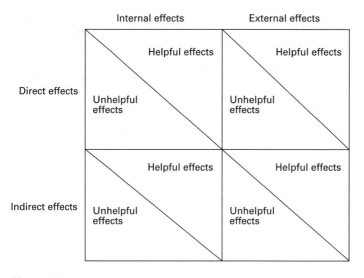

Figure 1.1
Domains of regime effects

problem at one extreme to making it worse at the other. "Good" and "bad" are shorthand labels for these extremes; they do not signify moral judgments, but rather distinguish effects that make a problem easier to manage from those that make it harder to manage. The good effects of regimes normally attract the most attention, since they are the ones that a regime's framers either intended or seek to take credit for after the fact. As many of the examples of external effects discussed above indicate, however, a regime can easily have effects that make problems more difficult to solve. We have tried to remain alert to such effects in conducting these case studies.

Integrating these three distinct dimensions, we can map the domain of effects onto a space with eight cells, as shown in figure 1.1. The cell of greatest interest to this project is the one containing direct effects that are internal to a behavioral complex and help make a problem easier to solve. We aim for a high degree of comprehensiveness in identifying these effects and in explaining the behavioral pathways leading to them. For effects that fall in the other seven cells, we must exercise some discrimination. Although there are good reasons for looking at all of them in gaining a complete understanding of each case, we report only those that appear especially pertinent in the following chapters. The factors that make such effects pertinent vary from case to case and effect to effect. We do not undertake thorough causal explanations for these other types of effects, unless those working on a particular case believe strongly that such attention is warranted.

Measuring Effectiveness

A major complication affecting efforts to measure the effectiveness of international regimes arises from the fact that it is necessary to make causal inferences to say anything about levels of effectiveness or variations in these levels under a variety of conditions. The danger of spurious correlations is ever present in this realm. Suppose, for instance, that we observe the adoption of new rules requiring the installation of segregated ballast tanks (SBT) and crude oil washing (COW) technologies in oil tankers and we subsequently observe that these technologies are in fact being installed. Can we confidently assert that the oil pollution regime is having an effect in this regard? Not necessarily. The shipping companies may have concluded that it was cost effective for them to adopt these technologies, quite apart from any pressure arising from the development of international rules. Or it may be that a dominant state decided to bring pressure to bear in this area without reference to the international rules or code of conduct. Similar comments are in order about transboundary fluxes of airborne pollutants. Reductions in transboundary fluxes of sulfur dioxide or nitrogen oxides could well be a consequence of political deals engineered by key states or, more broadly, shifting ideas about links between pollution and human health in contrast to the operation of the LRTAP regime.

It follows that measuring effectiveness is a more complex and demanding task than, say, measuring the frequency of wars, the distribution of resources that constitute bases of power in the material sense, or even the level of interdependence in international society. Because effectiveness is our dependent variable—the phenomenon we wish to explain—this is a serious problem. What can we do to solve or at least to alleviate this problem in the interests of making progress toward deepening our understanding of the roles that institutions play in international society?

Clearly, we cannot expect to find litmus tests or "smoking guns" that will allow us to construct a simple index of effectiveness. Even so, we are not helpless in the face of this problem. A number of techniques of analysis are available that we can bring to bear in sorting out true effects of international regimes from mere spurious correlations. Where regimes do have consequences, such techniques can help pinpoint their effects by controlling for the impacts of other factors and indicating how events would have unfolded differently in the absence of these institutional arrangements. We have made use of two distinct types of techniques for these purposes, one centering on natural or quasi-experiments and the other featuring thought experiments.

Natural or Quasi-experiments
Because we cannot conduct laboratory experiments involving international regimes and the number of truly comparable cases is normally too small to allow for the use of standard statistical procedures, we are clearly at a disadvantage in our efforts to measure effectiveness. We face a problem much like that confronting those who seek to understand major episodes of biological extinctions in the earth's history or long-term changes in the earth's climate system. But as these comparisons suggest, there are techniques of analysis that can help us deal with this problem. In the first instance, we can make use of natural or quasi-experiments by exploring comparisons across different issue areas or over time within a single evolving regime in such a way as to take advantage of variation on the independent variable.[7] This involves examining situations that are broadly comparable except for the presence or absence of a regime or, alternatively, situations that remain largely unchanged over time except for alterations in the character of the prevailing regime. The case of oil pollution before and after the introduction of equipment standards is a striking case in point. So also is the case of LRTAP in the Soviet Union (now Russia) where the regime's provisions cover the area west of the Urals but do not apply to the rest of the country. If the two distinct institutional configurations correspond closely with observable differences in behavior, we can infer that there is a good chance that these developments are attributable to the institutional variable. Given the nature of such experiments, it is important not to overestimate the significance of the

inferences drawn. Observed differences in outcomes may well be results of concomitant but unnoticed variations across our cases in factors other than the institutional variable. Even so, this is an exercise well worth pursuing as one means of separating institutional effects from behavioral changes driven by other forces.

Thought Experiments

To complement the findings derivable from natural experiments, we also employ what various writers have characterized as thought experiments. Specifically, we turn to what has become known in the recent international relations literature as the method of counterfactuals.[8] This technique involves a rigorous effort to reconstruct the flow of events as it would have unfolded in the absence of some key factor (for example, a particular international code of conduct or regime). What would have happened, for example, if those responsible for the oil pollution regime had not shifted from discharge standards to equipment requirements? How would the problem of transboundary air pollution in Europe have evolved if the players had not seized the opportunity afforded by the creation of the Conference on Security and Cooperation in Europe (CSCE) and the lull in the Cold War to reach agreement on the terms of the Geneva Convention of 1979? It is apparent that this sort of analysis can become sloppy and ultimately lose its value in the hands of careless analysts. The keys to success here involve framing counterfactuals as precisely as possible and zeroing in on the behavior of key actors at critical junctures. This typically requires looking at decision-making processes within individual regime members, focusing on important branching points where events might have taken a different turn, and asking "what path would have been followed if the regime had not been present?" The efforts of those studying the acid rain case to account for the responses of a few key states (for example, the United Kingdom and the Soviet Union) to the introduction of the Geneva Convention of 1979 and the subsequent LRTAP protocols exemplify the sort of procedures that are likely to work in this connection.

Although no single procedure can be expected to yield definitive measures of the effectiveness of international regimes, the value of this analytic tool kit is considerable, especially when the individual techniques are used in combination. By way of illustration, consider the challenge of demonstrating that LRTAP played a role in causing the Soviet Union to reduce sulfur emissions in the western part of its territory during the 1980s. The fact that the Soviet Union was bound by the sulfur dioxide protocol west of the Urals, but not to the east of that line, sets up a natural experiment concerning differences between the presence or absence of a regime and Soviet behavior (in this case, shifting dirty industries east and clean ones west as well as retrofitting some dirty industries in the west). By itself, this experiment tells us that the regime probably mattered, though it does not explain why it mattered. The use of counterfactuals helps us to pinpoint these connections more precisely. What would have happened, for instance, if there had been no link to détente and the CSCE process, but only an environmental agreement pure and simple? Such a question would lead us to examine the decision-making process in more detail, looking for evidence of high-level concerns linked to broader relations with the West. It might also lead us to seek out additional natural experiments. For example, we could compare LRTAP with an environmental regime that the Soviets participated in without a clear connection to détente—perhaps the Baltic Sea arrangement. If the Soviets tended to be less responsive to such an arrangement than they were to LRTAP, this would add evidence for a claim that the LRTAP commitments influenced Soviet behavior through linkage to détente.

Behavioral Pathways

Measuring the effectiveness of regimes and, in the process, demonstrating that regimes matter is an essential step in understanding the role of institutional arrangements as determinants of collective outcomes in international society. Without some capacity to measure levels of effectiveness, we cannot make any additional progress toward understanding the sources of institutional effectiveness in international society. But the conclusion that regimes do matter and that there is considerable variance from case to case in levels of institutional effectiveness does not tell us how regimes operate to produce the effects in question. If we are to lay to rest the doubts of the skeptics, gain deeper insights into the roles institutions play as determinants of collective outcomes, and develop knowledge that is usable by those responsible for designing or adjusting regimes to deal with a variety of future problems, it is critical to move on to an exploration of the pathways through which institutions produce results. Because regimes always generate their effects by influencing the behavior of actors involved in the relevant issue areas, we focus in the case studies on the behavioral pathways or mechanisms through which institutions produce effects.

International environmental regimes virtually always constitute elements of multifaceted and dynamic behavioral complexes with a variety of political, economic, technological, and social changes taking place around them. As a result, studies of the pathways leading to regime effects have often fallen prey to one or both of the following pitfalls. Many studies attempt to impose order on complex realities by assuming (usually implicitly) that a single behavioral mechanism is adequate to explain all the causal links in question. This tack is unsatisfying not only because preliminary evidence suggests the operation of a number of behavioral mechanisms but also and more fundamentally because it appears that distinct mechanisms often interact with one another in important ways. This makes it difficult to understand a single mechanism in isolation from the others. This problem goes well beyond the common error of interpreting an unjustifiably wide range of behavior as falling under a single behavioral mechanism selected for emphasis, while neglecting equally promising alternatives.

Studies that succeed in avoiding this trap frequently go to the other extreme, trying to remain faithful to the richness and nuances of specific cases by neglecting to use models treated as analytic tools that social scientists have devised to pinpoint the sources of behavior. This is also a mistake, because social science models can help us identify effects of regimes that might otherwise go unnoticed in purely descriptive accounts. This is especially so for effects that are either not understood by the participants themselves or internalized so deeply that they are not discussed in a way that would make them apparent to an observer engaged in a purely descriptive effort.

To avoid these common pitfalls and, in the process, to reach conclusions of interest to those responsible for designing international regimes, it is necessary to study the roots or sources of the behavior of the members of regimes as well as important actors operating under the auspices of regime members. This is where our project can make its most important contribution to understanding the role of institutions—in contrast to material conditions and ideas—as driving forces at the international level. Rather than endeavoring to frame conventional hypotheses that seek to identify necessary or sufficient conditions for regimes to have an effect, we have chosen to formulate a set of behavioral models that can help us identify and explain the pathways through which regimes affect collective outcomes and, in the process, account for variations in the levels of effectiveness achieved by different regimes. Unlike prior efforts that have sought to identify behavioral mechanisms from an examination of specific cases (Haas, Keohane, and Levy 1993), here we frame a set of models that appear important on theoretical grounds and then turn to the case studies to assess the relevance and relative importance of the behavioral mechanisms associated with each of the models under real-world conditions.

What differentiates these models from one another is the specific mechanism each highlights as the generative source of behavior on the part of the states and other actors—intergovernmental organizations, nongovernmental organizations, corporations, and even individuals—whose behavior contributes to outcomes in the issue areas under consideration. The models are analytic constructs not intended to be mutually exclusive. It is possible, indeed common, for the same behavior to be a product of several distinct mechanisms operating together. Our objective, therefore, is not to reach conclusions concerning whether the individual models of behavior are right or wrong. Rather, we ask how much of the behavior of central importance to success or failure in problem solving in our cases can be accounted for by each of these models of the forces that give rise to behavior. Under what conditions are the various behavioral mechanisms likely to come into play as significant determinants of behavior? How do the mechanisms interact with one another? What can we learn about how regimes work by looking at the mechanisms comprehensively that others have missed by using more piecemeal approaches?

We begin with two models that treat actors as unitary and rational—at least in the bounded sense—utility maximizers (Ostrom 1998). These familiar models allow us to explore a suite of the most common arguments regarding the impact of institutions on the behavior of various actors. We then proceed to alter the assumptions of these models in the interests of examining several additional behavioral pathways. The next three models relax the assumption of rational utility maximizing behavior. This makes it possible to consider a range of behavioral pathways involving such things as norm-driven behavior, social learning, and the operation of social roles. Finally, we relax the assumption relating to unitary actors. This allows us to look at ways in which international institutions figure in the internal politics of actors and, in the process, affect the external behavior of the actors in international society.

Regimes as Utility Modifiers

The causal mechanism underlying this model is one that most of us find familiar and easy—perhaps too easy—to incorporate into our thinking about regimes. It states that actors are self-interested utility maximizers whose behavior will be guided by institutional arrangements to the extent that they alter the costs and benefits individual actors attach to well-defined options. We need not worry about the identity and the role premises of actors or wrestle with such matters as the impact of social norms. We can simply ask how specific rules and regime activities will influence the costs and benefits that established actors factor into their utilitarian calculus. This may not be easy to do in practice. Producers of chemicals, for example, have encountered difficulties in making decisions about investing in production facilities for HCFCs, in part because they have found it hard to foresee how the rules of the ozone regime will evolve over time. Similar comments are in order about some of the chemicals implicated in transboundary air pollution. But in many cases, the utilitarian implications of new rules and regime activities are relatively clear-cut. There can be no doubt, for instance, that the costs of trying to avoid the use of SBT and COW technologies have risen sharply with the establishment of rules spelling out equipment standards as part of the oil pollution regime. Much the same can be said of efforts to resist rules calling for a phaseout of CFCs under the terms of the ozone regime. Whatever the complications of computing the costs and benefits associated with particular options, however, the causal mechanism at work here is clear enough. Actors possessing well-defined utility functions alter their behavior if and when social practices make it worth their while to do so.

Regimes as Enhancers of Cooperation

Although this model also assumes unitary actors and rests on utilitarian premises, we separate it out for individual treatment here because it directs attention to the collective-action problems that are widely viewed among students of international relations as important obstacles to the achievement of sustained cooperation. There are many circumstances under which rational actors engaged in interactive decision making fail to reap joint gains or to avoid joint losses due to the effects of strategic behavior (Ostrom 1990; Ostrom, Gardner, and Walker 1994). Regimes, on this account, emerge as mechanisms for alleviating these problems and allowing the participants to achieve collective outcomes that lie closer to the Pareto frontier (Sandler 1997). Because collective-action problems take a variety of forms, regimes created to alleviate these problems can affect behavior in a number of ways (Oye 1986; Axelrod and Keohane 1986). They may, for example, serve to mitigate fears of cheating through measures designed to increase the transparency of the behavior of relevant actors. They may reduce incentives to defect either by sanctioning violators or by lengthening the shadow of the future on the issues in question. Or they may simply reduce transaction costs by making it unnecessary to cope with the consequences of strategic behavior again and again in the same issue area. But the basic point remains the same. In this model, regimes affect behavior by mitigating the collective-action problems that stand as barriers to the realization of joint gains otherwise available to parties engaged in interactive decision making. Much of the recent literature on international regimes has proceeded on the assumption that this is the principal function of social institutions.[9] One of our goals is to reexamine this assumption in the interest of differentiating among the distinct causal pathways through which regimes affect outcomes in international society.

Regimes as Bestowers of Authority

We turn next to several behavioral pathways that come into focus once the utilitarian emphasis on calculations of benefits and costs is set aside. The basic premise of the first of the resultant models is that social norms rooted in considerations of legitimacy or authoritativeness often guide the behavior of individuals and collective entities alike.[10] This pathway suggests that those who regard the rules and other provisions of regimes as legitimate or authoritative will often comply with their requirements without engaging in detailed calculations of the benefits and costs of doing so (Franck 1990). In the case of individuals, such behavior is apt to be a product of socialization. Most people are taught to act in certain ways because it is the right and proper thing to do or because it is the law, rather than because it is in their self-interest to do so. For the most part, people are likely to respond in this way when they feel that prescriptions are legitimate or backed by social norms that deserve their respect. Those who have escaped the grip of the resultant "habit of obedience" and who routinely question authority are the exceptions in most social settings.[11] When we come to collective entities, on the other hand, the behavior this model points to is apt to be influenced by processes involving internalization or routinization as well as by socialization. Public agencies charged with the implementation of regimes commonly come to treat the performance of this task as part of their organizational mission to be pursued without constant questioning of the broader consequences flowing from the rules in question and defended in dealings with other agencies pursuing distinct missions of their own. In both cases, however, it is the normative status or the authoritativeness of regime rules and activities that triggers the behavioral response rather than some calculation of the anticipated benefits and costs associated with different options available to decision makers. Those who think in utilitarian, much less realist or neorealist, terms may find it hard to believe that behavior of this sort is prevalent at the international level, whatever its status in domestic society (Keohane 1986). But we are convinced that it would be a mistake to rule out this source of behavior in examining the causal mechanisms that account for the effects of international regimes.

Regimes as Learning Facilitators

Institutions, in this model, achieve their effects by initiating processes that give rise to individual and, especially, social learning.[12] The learning in question can take the form of new perspectives on the nature of a particular problem to be solved, new ideas about measures likely to prove effective in solving the problem at hand, new insights into the process of implementing these measures, or new solution concepts for larger classes of problems to which the specific case belongs. The route to such learning may lead through the generation of new facts that reduce uncertainty or produce a more accurate picture of the specific issues at stake, through the development of new intellectual capital pertaining to identifiable categories of problems, or through a reassessment of roles and values leading to the redefinition of actor interests.[13] The evidence suggests, for example, that the LRTAP regime has played a role not only in enhancing our understanding of the mechanisms at work in long-range air pollution but also in energizing a broader process of consciousness raising about the importance of the impacts of air pollution on human health and natural systems. Similarly, many who argue that the climate convention is an important milestone base their case on the expectation that the convention will accelerate a learning process that enhances the willingness of members to agree to more substantial restraints on emissions of greenhouse gases over time. The actual processes through which learning occurs are not well understood. Thus, we need to improve our grasp of the roles of individual leaders, groups of experts, and what have recently been described as epistemic communities in the learning process.[14] The essential point of this model is clear. It spotlights the roles that regimes play in changing factual information, prevailing discourses, and even values and, in the process, altering the motive forces that give rise to the behavior of individuals and collective entities active in the issue areas covered by these institutions.

Regimes as Role Definers

Yet another nonutilitarian pathway emphasizes the fact that regimes sometimes operate at the constitutive level, shaping the identities (and therefore the interests) of actors and, in the process, influencing the way actors behave as occupants of the roles to which they are assigned. Most of us are accustomed to thinking in contractarian terms, treating actors and their interests as given, then proceeding to analyze the bargaining processes through which such actors endeavor to hammer out the terms of social contracts. But it is perfectly possible to turn this analysis on its head and look at the ways in which institutions operate to define roles and allocate them among participants (Wendt 1992). In fact, actors regularly take on new roles under the terms of institutional arrangements, even when their basic identities are well established prior to the emergence of the rules in question. Consider the striking changes in the roles that flag, coastal, and port states play under the new law of the sea and, more specifically, the rules relating to Exclusive Economic Zones and marine pollution as cases in point. The enhanced role of coastal states helped Norway and Russia phase out third-party fishing in the Barents Sea in a relatively noncoercive manner, and the growing strength of coastal and port states in contrast to flag states appears to be a factor of some significance in the case of oil pollution. The redefinition of old roles or the creation of new roles may in turn reflect the evolution of underlying ideas regarding environmental matters. But the causal mechanism associated with this model directs our attention to sources of behavior that lie behind or beneath the sorts of factors identified in utilitarian arguments.

Regimes as Agents of Internal Realignments

We come, finally, to a model that relaxes the unitary actor assumption. What distinguishes this behavioral pathway from the others is its emphasis on the proposition that both the members of international environmental regimes and others active in the relevant behavioral complexes need not be treated as unitary actors. It often helps to approach corporations and environmental organizations as well as states as collective entities, composed of a number of groups seeking to promote their own concerns, by propounding distinctive conceptions of the collective interest or, in the case of states, the national interest.[15] Regimes, on this account, affect behavior by creating new constituencies or shifting the balance among factions or subgroups vying for influence within individual states or other actors. In the simplest cases, the establishment of a regime gives some of those involved in a behavioral complex new ammunition to use in their dealings with others. Green organizations, for example, can argue that it will be politically costly for a government to violate or simply ignore rules relating to the discharge of oil or transboundary fluxes of airborne pollutants because it will spark domestic opposition and tarnish a state's reputation for living up to its commitments in the eyes of the other members of international society. Beyond this, regimes may play some role in restructuring the alignment of domestic groups that endeavor to influence a government's behavior or factions that seek to redirect a corporation's behavior. Environmental concerns, like air and water pollution, sometimes give rise to unusual alliances that link factions located on the conservative and progressive ends of the political spectrum. In the specific case of transboundary air pollution in Europe, the creation and operation of LRTAP owes much to an alliance between environmentalists and those concerned with bringing about a period of détente in the Cold War. The advent of equipment standards under MARPOL in the oil pollution regime has clearly affected the relative strength of various constituencies that seek to influence the actions of tanker owners and operators. Whatever the details surrounding individual regimes, this model tells us to look to the internal dynamics of states or other collective entities to explain when and to what extent regimes are likely to prove effective.

To round out this initial effort to differentiate among behavioral pathways, we reemphasize that regimes may affect the behavior of relevant actors either directly or indirectly. Our first thought in understanding the effectiveness of regimes is to look for direct effects. Thus, the introduction of equipment standards for oil tankers had immediate consequences for the actions of ship owners and operators. The setting of allowable catch levels for commercially harvested species in the Barents Sea has direct implications for Norwegian and Russian fishers. But the behavioral impacts of regimes often involve pathways that are more circuitous in nature but no less real. The creation of a highly visible regime can have an enabling effect in the sense of leading over time to the emergence of an associated community of governmental and nongovernmental actors that becomes a powerful pressure group dedicated to the achievement of the regime's goals. A regime can become a focal point for the activities of nonstate actors that act as watchdogs on key prescriptions and, in the process, increase the transparency of the behavior of regime members. A regime can also encourage the growth of intellectual capital that leads to a new understanding of the problem and subsequently to a concerted effort to restructure the regime itself. In the case studies reported here, we endeavor to move beyond a naive perspective on effectiveness, developing instead a sophisticated approach that allows for tracing important behavioral pathways through several steps.

Putting this account of different behavioral pathways into perspective, we return to our original point. Our goal is not to determine whether individual models are right or wrong. Rather, we seek to shed light on the conditions under which specific causal mechanisms are likely to come into play as well as on the interplay among causal mechanisms operating within the same behavioral complex. The objective is to move over time toward the development of propositions regarding the distinctive roles played by different causal mechanisms. Some observers have suggested, for example, that the bestowal of authority is particularly important as a determinant of behavior in political-legal systems that are open or democratic, that the encouragement of learning is critical in situations where there is a high degree of uncertainty about the nature of the problem to be solved, and that solving collective-action problems looms large in cases where the incentives to defect are great and the shadow of the future is short. Many other propositions of this sort are possible and worthy of systematic study. To the extent that we succeed in framing and refining a body of propositions of this nature, the conclusions we reach here will be of interest to those responsible for designing institutions to deal with the large-scale environmental problems looming ahead. Those individuals will be able to make use of this knowledge to improve the fit between the problems to be solved and the regimes they create to deal with them.

Generalizability

Because this study does not seek to test a set of theoretically derived hypotheses against evidence drawn from a study of actual cases, the issue of generalizability does not arise here in the same way that it does in more conventional empirical analyses. We are concerned with understanding behavioral pathways and exploring how they work in practice rather than with establishing the relative significance of different pathways in some global sense. Nonetheless, we cannot ignore the question of the extent to which our case studies are representative of some larger universe of institutional arrangements. If our cases were judged to be outliers or all examples of a particular subset of international regimes, the findings we reach could be criticized as applying only to special cases and lacking in generality. What can we say about the representativeness of the cases we examine in depth in the following chapters?

With respect to the domain of environmental regimes, at least, we believe our cases are sufficiently diverse to provide general insights into the nature of the various behavioral mechanisms and the conditions under which they operate. The cases range from bilateral arrangements through regional arrangements and on to global arrangements featuring large numbers of members. Similarly, they encompass issues that involve living resources and pollutants entering both marine and atmospheric systems. What is more, these cases include situations in which the problem is a direct result of goal-directed behavior (e.g., overfishing) and in which the problem is an inadvertent byproduct of behavior directed toward other ends (e.g., transboundary air pollution). None of this is sufficient to prove in some formal sense that our cases constitute a representative sample. But these observations do make it clear that the cases cover a relatively diverse group of environmental regimes.

Beyond this lies the question of the extent to which we can generalize our conclusions to the larger universe of international regimes dealing with a variety of issue areas. There are, of course, certain respects in which environmental problems are distinctive. They are often treated as issues of lesser political significance than security or economic issues, and they commonly feature relatively high levels of uncertainty about important aspects of the problems to be solved. Even so, environmental cases raise many of the same underlying concerns that arise in connection with other categories of institutional arrangements (Young 1997). The relative significance of utilitarian calculations and nonutilitarian sources of behavior, for instance, is a matter that cuts across a wide range of issue areas. So, too, is the issue of the role of various internal political processes that come into focus when we drop the assumption that the members of international regimes can be modeled as unitary actors. A measure of caution is in order about the application of our findings to the workings of regimes that are not environmental in character. Yet we believe that much of what we have to say applies across issue areas, and we hope that others will pick up the challenge of assessing the role of various behavioral pathways in determining the effectiveness of regimes dealing with economic and security issues.

Plan of the Case Studies

Finally, we offer some notes on the ground rules applying to the development and presentation of the individual case studies. Each case study begins with an account of the relevant behavioral complex, including an account of the problem or problems to be solved, the stakeholders and their interests and resources, and the principal attributes of the regime established to deal with these matters. Although the articulation of this fact pattern is an essential step in analyzing each case, it is important to get through this phase as quickly as possible to get at the challenging issues involved in the study of effectiveness.

The central component of each case study consists of a causal narrative that details the effects produced by the regime in question and seeks to identify causal connections between the relevant behavior and the operation of the regime. Each case study tells a convincing story about the consequences flowing from the regime rather than going through a more mechanical process of listing effects one after another and repeatedly deploying the methods we have identified to verify the connections between the regime and its effects. But these stories or narrative accounts must be constructed with care and precision. Our intent is to preserve the narrative style, while leaving the reader in no doubt about the evidence supporting the conclusions reached.

The final and crucial segment of each case study is devoted to a systematic assessment of the inferences to be drawn from that case about the behavioral models we have articulated in designing the overall project. Because these models have been identified and briefly described in this introductory chapter, there is no need to recapitulate them in the reports on the cases. Rather, the case studies seek to arrive at conclusions framed in terms of the models. The overall conclusions of our project—reported in chapter 5—have been determined, in large measure, by what the case studies have turned up and what the teams working on the individual cases have found to be important and interesting.

To ensure comparability, we have agreed that the authors of each case study will address a common set of core questions in the final substantive sections of their chapters:

• Which or which combination of causal mechanisms is at work?

• What features or conditions of the case account for the roles played by the various causal mechanisms?

• In what ways do the operation of individual causal mechanisms appear to depend on interactions with other mechanisms (for example, do changes in benefit/cost calculations depend on altered role definitions)?

• Are there surprising or otherwise interesting ways in which the causal mechanisms operate in the case compared to what social science models would lead us to expect?

Since we expect that the results of our efforts to answer these questions will constitute the principal contribution of this project, each case study seeks to respond to these questions from the point of view of the individual case. The final chapter returns to these issues in a comparative mode, setting forth the overall conclusions of the project and discussing the implications of these findings for future research on the effectiveness of international regimes.

Notes

1. Levy, Young, and Zürn 1995, 274.

2. As Levy, Young, and Zürn (1995, 272) put it, "[w]e do not think it makes sense to use the term 'regime' in the absence of a minimum degree of formalization and a minimum degree of convergence of expectations." But this view is entirely compatible with the observation that regimes vary greatly in their behavioral impacts, much less their ability to solve problems.

3. For helpful surveys of the burgeoning literature, see Rittberger 1993 and Levy, Young, and Zürn 1995.

4. See, among others, Young 1989; Haas 1989; Young 1992; Rosenau and Czempiel 1992; Haas, Keohane, and Levy 1993; Young 1994; Keohane and Levy 1996; Underdal 1998; Weiss and Jacobson 1998, Victor, Raustiala, and Skolnikoff 1998; and Hanf and Underdal forthcoming.

5. For a discussion of recent trends in Barents Sea fish stocks, see Hoel 1994.

6. On the concept of large marine ecosystems or LMEs, see Sherman 1992.

7. For a general account of such procedures, see Campbell and Stanley 1966.

8. On the rising interest in this method among students of international relations, see Fearon 1991, Biersteker 1993, and Tetlock and Belkin 1996.

9. For a particularly influential example, see Keohane 1984.

10. For a review of literature contributing to the recent revival of interest in the role of norms among students of international relations, see Raymond 1997.

11. For a classic account of the "habit of obedience," see Hart 1961.

12. Social learning has recently become a focus of interest for numerous students of international relations. Notable among these are the members of the social learning project led by William Clark at Harvard University. For helpful published accounts, see Nye 1987 and E. Haas 1990.

13. For a variety of perspectives reflecting the renewed interest in the role of ideas among students of international relations, see Goldstein and Keohane 1993.

14. See Young 1991 on the role of leaders and Haas 1993 on the idea of epistemic communities.

15. On the idea of two-level games in this connection, see Putnam 1988.

2

International Vessel-Source Oil Pollution

Ronald Mitchell, Moira L. McConnell, Alexei Roginko, and Ann Barrett

Forty-five Years of Oil Pollution Control

Over the past four decades, the international regime seeking to control intentional discharges of oil has undergone dramatic changes. In 1954, concern that oil intentionally discharged from ships was causing environmental and aesthetic harm led thirty-two nations to negotiate the International Convention for the Prevention of Pollution of the Sea by Oil (OILPOL), which was the first treaty to address marine pollution of any sort (OILPOL 54, 1954). Addressed exclusively to reducing coastal oil pollution, the treaty required tanker operators to discharge waste oil far from shore or into the port reception facilities which it required governments to ensure were available. In the regime's first ten years of existence, few governments made any effort to induce operators to change their behavior and most operators ignored the treaty's provisions.

In 1998, a substantially revised International Convention for the Prevention of Pollution from Ships (MARPOL) imposes far stricter limits on all marine and many atmospheric pollutants carried or produced by ships (MARPOL 73/78, 1978). Rules now ban all oil discharges and require all tankers to carry pollution-reduction equipment. Governments and other actors (classification societies, insurance companies, shipbuilders) have extensive programs to monitor and prevent tankers from operating without such equipment. Almost all tankers now have the required equipment, although some operators still make illegal discharges. Total oil discharges appear to have decreased significantly even as total oil transported by sea has increased dramatically.

Much, though not all, of the dramatic change over the past 45 years can be attributed to a regime that learned from initial failures and developed regulatory structures that took advantage of the authority accorded to it, especially by nongovernmental actors, to identify those inclined to violate the regime and prevent them from doing so. Even governments and nonstate actors that opposed the regime's rules during negotiation used the rules, once adopted, to judge the behavior of tanker owners and tanker operators. In this way, the regime altered the opportunities and incentives for violating its proscriptions. Over time, the regime created a legally and behaviorally effective regulatory system (see chapter 1) that also has made progress toward ecological effectiveness in improving the marine environment.

This case study critically evaluates whether the regime can account for these significant changes in treaty rules, monitoring, and behavior, and environmental improvement. It begins by describing the behavioral complex of the environmental problem, the actors involved, and the regime. The chapter then evaluates whether the major changes in the behavioral complex were caused by the regime or by exogenous factors. The chapter concludes by clarifying which of the regime's causal mechanisms best fit the process by which the regime effected such changes.

Behavioral Complex

Why would a ship or tanker intentionally discharge oil at sea? A small fraction of cargo remains in a ship's tanks as clingage after cargo delivery. Two standard practices led to clingage being mixed with seawater during ballast voyages. First, tankers filled empty cargo tanks with seawater as ballast to stabilize the tanker. Second, tankers cleaned their tanks with seawater before receiving more oil. Captains discharged the resultant oil and water mixtures (or "slops") at sea prior to arrival in port. Although clingage is only a small fraction of total cargo, a 100,000-ton tanker could discharge 300 to 500 tons of oil per voyage. Given thousands of tanker voyages per year, such discharges quickly accumulated into a major environmental problem. In the early 1950s, tankers were transporting 250 million tons of oil by sea annually and discharging some 300,000

Table 2.1
Input of oil into the sea

Year of estimate	Million metric tons per year		
	1971	1980	1989
Transportation			
Tanker operations	1.080	0.700	0.159
Dry-docking	0.250	0.030	0.004
Terminal operations	0.003	0.020	0.030
Bilge and fuel oils	0.500	0.300	0.253
Accidents	0.300	0.420	0.121
Scrappings	no est.	no est.	0.003
Subtotal	2.133	1.470	0.569
Offshore production	0.080	0.050	no est.
Municipal and industrial wastes and runoff	2.700	1.180	no est.
Natural sources	0.600	0.250	no est.
Atmosphere—emissions fallout	0.600	0.300	no est.
Total	6.113	3.250	0.569
Discharge from tanker operations	1.080	0.700	0.159
Crude traded	1,100	1,319	1,097
Discharge as percent of crude trade	0.098	0.053	0.015

Sources: MEPC 1990c; National Academy of Sciences 1975; National Academy of Sciences and National Research Council 1985.

tons of that into the oceans.[1] Increased transportation of crude oil by sea has led to subsequent estimates of intentional discharges ranging up to five million tons per year (McKenzie 1978; National Academy of Sciences and Council 1985; Pritchard 1978; Wardley-Smith 1983).

Accidents and discharges of bilge oil by nontankers constitute other sources of ship-generated oil pollution. Municipal and industrial wastes and runoff also contribute significantly to ocean oil pollution (see table 2.1). In the 1950s, experts considered intentional discharges as the major source of ocean oil pollution, with other sources representing only a "small part" of the problem (United Kingdom 1953, 9). More recent estimates indicate oil from intentional discharges, despite increases in oil transport, has decreased far more rapidly than from other sources and now constitutes far less of the total.

As an extremely visible pollutant, oil often raises environmental concerns because of its aesthetic impact, even though biological impacts have proved difficult to identify. Scientific understanding of how oil affects the marine environment has developed slowly. Major tanker accidents cause immediate catastrophic biological damage in localized areas, but appear to have few wider and longer-term effects (GESAMP 1990, 2; National Academy of Sciences and Council 1985, 489). Concerns over intentional discharges have been more contentious. Until the 1960s, many scientists and regulators believed that oil persisted indefinitely in the marine environment (Kirby 1965; Pritchard 1987, 19; United Kingdom 1953, 7). This view was contested by studies, some conducted as early as the 1920s, that showed evaporation, decomposition, and bacterial action made oil "unobjectionable" over time (Kirby 1968, 210; Sutton 1964, 9). Intentional discharges that do not dissipate before they reach shore, however, kill seabirds by inhibiting the insulation of their feathers and causing internal damage when ingested. Recurring exposure to such discharges also appears to pose long-term threats to fish, shellfish, and other marine life in coastal zones along major shipping lanes (Camphuysen 1989; National Academy of Sciences and Council 1985; Patin 1979, 22–23).

Traditional international law has viewed the oceans as a global commons from which no state may be excluded. Like any public good, creating a clean ocean requires that a regime overcome free-riding problems. But oil pollution also constitutes an externality. In this case, the concentrated few who can provide for the public good (and must incur costs in so doing) do not benefit from it, while the diffuse many who benefit from a cleaner environment cannot provide it. Unlike a fisher, even after accounting for long-term interests, an oil transporter has no economic incentives to reduce pollution. The cleaner ocean is only a "good" at the socially aggregate level (Mitchell 1999). Ensuring that oil transporters reduce their discharges therefore poses particularly difficult problems that require an imposed order, at least vis-à-vis the polluter (Young 1983).

International efforts to regulate oil pollution have arisen from the interplay of several sets of actors: publics and nongovernmental organizations (NGOs) in a few activist coastal states pushing for international controls to reduce oil pollution, affected industries lobbying to avoid the costs of regulation, governments seeking to reconcile pressures at a national and international level, and intergovernmental organizations seeking to foster negotiation and implementation of international agreements.

Unlike acid rain (see chapter 4), science has rarely placed the issue of oil pollution on the international agenda. Even without clear evidence of environmental harm, oiled seabirds and soiled beaches from frequent intentional discharges and from large, dramatic accidental spills have usually been the stimulus for calls for action. Most studies have justified action based on the costs of cleanup, decreased tourism, and deaths of birds (GESAMP 1990, 2; United Kingdom 1953, 2; United Kingdom 1981).

NGOs have also wielded less influence than in many other environmental problems. Domestic NGOs did pressure the British and U.S. governments to take leadership positions on intentional oil pollution control. From the 1920s through the early 1960s, campaigns by the Royal Society for the Protection of Birds (RSPB) and complaints from resort owners and local cleanup authorities focused on the small but continuous problems of oil from intentional discharges (Pritchard 1987, 12–13; United Kingdom 1953, 1–2). In the 1950s and 1960s, the British Advisory Committee on Oil Pollution of the Sea (ACOPS) sponsored several conferences that drew international attention and produced proposals for amendments to international agreements. The Committee on Law and Social Policy brought pressure on the United States in the 1970s to take action. In general, however, oil pollution has not been a major focus of NGO activism.

Rather, growing tanker traffic and increased environmentalism strengthened general public concern. Widespread media coverage of accidents led to calls in Europe and the United States for international regulation of intentional as well as accidental discharges (Cowley 1988, 3). The 1967 Torrey Canyon disaster—though not the first major tanker accident[2]—initiated a "'we-must-be-seen-to-do-something' syndrome," prompting amendments to OILPOL in 1969 and 1971 and the 1973 MARPOL Conference (O'Neil 1990, 2). Thirteen tanker accidents (including eight near the United States) during the winter of 1976–1977 prompted the 1978 Tanker Safety and Pollution Prevention Conference. The Amoco Cadiz accident in 1978 prompted negotiation of a European Memorandum of Understanding (MOU) to enhance pollution enforcement. The European MOU—and four more-recent MOUs in other regions (Plaza 1997)—involve intergovernmental agreements to cooperate in inspecting and enforcing existing International Maritime Organization (IMO) regulations, without promulgating additional ones. These regional organizations work closely with the IMO and are considered as part of the IMO regime in this analysis.

Two groups transport oil: oil companies and independent tanker owners. Many tankers register in developing states, such as Liberia and Panama. Major oil companies based in the United States and United Kingdom directly own and operate one-third of the world's tankers, control many more through long-term charters, and own the oil transported in both. Independents, based mainly in Norway, Sweden, Denmark, and Greece, own and operate the remainder but do not own the oil they transport. Not surprisingly, then, these groups differ in their preference for conserving oil by reducing intentional discharges. The equipment and operational costs of reducing discharges falls on tanker operators but the benefits of less wasted oil accrue to cargo owners. The economic incentives of oil companies to reduce the discharges of the cargo they own coincide with environmental goals whenever oil prices are high enough to offset recovery costs. By contrast, charter agreements generally pay independents for oil loaded rather than oil delivered, thus passing through few incentives to conserve oil.

Being fewer in number, oil companies have organized—through the International Chamber of Shipping, the Independent Tanker Owners Association (INTERTANKO), and Oil Companies International Marine Forum (OCIMF)—and influenced international rules more readily than independents. Oil companies supported international rules whenever such rules promised to derail unilateral U.K. or U.S. rules that threatened their competitive advantage. Among independents, the absence of a similar unilateral threat at home has produced resistance to most international regulation. Indeed, some analysts interpreted U.S. initiatives as aimed at achieving competitive advantage by excluding tankers bearing "undesirable" flags, putting smaller companies out of business with equipment retrofit costs, and providing work for stagnant shipyards (Glazov 1979, 278; Moguilevkin 1982, 194; Primakov 1986, 314).

Oil transportation also involves relatively small numbers of shipyards, classification societies, and insurers. Tankers are ordered directly from shipyards as new ships or bought used from previous owners. Industry-created classification societies, such as Lloyds of London and Det Norske Veritas, inspect and classify vessels to ensure conformance with specified criteria that generally reflect relevant international requirements. Insurance costs, in turn, depend on classification. The economic interlinkage of these actors in the oil transportation industry creates an infrastructure rich in information about tankers and their operators.

Any state's interest in and ability to control oil pollution depends on several factors. State positions depend on the political strength of environmentally concerned activists and publics relative to oil transportation interests. Developing states often lack strong environmental constituencies pushing for environmental control because other welfare issues assume greater national priority. Accidents near developing states have generally not led those states to push for greater pollution control. Traditional international law gave flag states exclusive jurisdiction to prescribe and enforce law over vessels registered in that state. Port and coastal states had to weigh the benefits of increasing their rights against the precedents it established in other issue areas, especially during periods when the Law of the Sea negotiations were occurring.

A state's ability to threaten unilateral legislation and to enforce international rules depended on its position in world oil markets. The United States and United Kingdom could prompt international action through credible threats of unilateral action because major oil companies were based there. Coastal states experiencing oil pollution could not act on their incentives to regulate and sanction it because they lacked legal jurisdiction over tankers flagged in other states. In contrast, flag states had the authority to detect and prosecute discharge violations but lacked incentives to do so. For example, 15 to 30 percent of all tankers register in Liberia which, being located off major transportation routes, receives little coastal pollution and has few incentives to regulate it. Similarly, oil exporting states could monitor compliance with rules regulating maximum discharges during the ballast voyage, tank inspections, and provision of reception facility but lacked incentives to do so. Importers and exporters of oil can monitor equipment, certification, and record-keeping rules, and importers that experience pollution also have incentives to do so.

The oil pollution regime has developed through action at diplomatic conferences and within an international organization. The OILPOL Conference of 1954 established the Inter-Governmental Maritime Consultative Organization (IMCO) as a specialized U.N. agency. IMCO had a mandate to address all international shipping issues, including safety, working conditions, loadlines, and pollution. In 1982, IMCO was renamed, but not fundamentally restructured, as the International Maritime Organization (IMO). IMCO organized diplomatic conferences in 1962, 1973, and 1978. Amendments have also been negotiated within IMCO subcommittees. Creation of the Marine Environment Protection Committee (MEPC) as a full committee accompanied procedures for "tacit acceptance" of MEPC amendments that automatically enter into force unless more than one-third of the parties object.

Intentional oil discharges have remained the exclusive purview of IMO and MEPC. Regional organizations have consistently elected not to establish standards that differ from IMO rules. States and nonstate actors such as classification societies view IMO as the sole legitimate source for international shipping regulation.

Since its inception in 1954, the regime has maintained the constant goal "to take action by common agreement to prevent pollution of the sea by oil discharged from ships" (OILPOL 54, 1954). The MARPOL agreement currently in force still calls for "the complete elimination of intentional pollution of the marine environment by oil and other harmful substances" (MARPOL 73/78, 1978). This superficial consistency in goals, however, overlooks two deep changes in the regime: a broadening of its goals and a dramatic improvement to its regulatory structure that allowed it to achieve the goals it set for itself.

From its inception, this regime has been regulative in nature. The regime has followed a strategy of adopting the most restrictive rules possible given political constraints, allowing a period for actors to implement them, and revising the rules to reflect experience with earlier rules whenever politically feasible. Nonregulative strategies, e.g., technical and financial assistance, education, scientific and technical research programs, were possible but have played only minor roles in the regime. Unlike acid precipitation (see chapter 4), negotiators considered oil pollution's sources and deleterious aesthetic, if not environmental, impacts to be obvious. Unlike fisheries (see chapter 3), setting oil pollution standards did not require feedback on the environmental health of the ecosystem. Fixed rules, including a ban, could be entertained because oil pollution was an unnecessary externality. Rules could restrict the means without restricting the level of the environmentally harmful activity. Unlike in a fishery, the goals of immediate economic growth and long-term environmental protection could be met simultaneously, albeit at some expense. Negotiators could aspire to design rules that fixed, rather than processes that managed, the problem. Steady progress has been made at promulgating rules that covered more pollutants, had a better chance of achieving regime goals if actors complied with them, and were likely to lead actors to comply.

The 1973 MARPOL agreement defined the environmental problem in far broader terms than had the 1954 OILPOL agreement. MARPOL strengthened OILPOL's rules on discharges, added expensive equipment standards and restrictions to reduce accidental pollution, and incorporated annexes to address four other vessel-source pollutants. Since then, the MEPC has continued to broaden the regime's scope, regulating air pollutants from ships, noxious solid substances, and organism-contaminated ballast water.

Three Distinct Subregimes

The following discussion provides brief histories of the regime's three subregimes that have sought to limit discharges in designated zones, and subsequently, oceanwide; to require equipment that reduced the oil-water mixtures created; and to provide alternative means of oil-water disposal.

The Discharge Standards Subregime   After unsuccessful negotiations to regulate intentional discharges in 1926 and 1935, attention to the problem resurfaced in the early 1950s, driven largely by domestic concerns within the United Kingdom. In 1953, a British panel recommended the government impose strict discharge limits on U.K.-registered ships and host an international conference. The British convened the OILPOL Conference in 1954. The resultant agreement sought to reduce coastal pollution by requiring tankers to refrain from discharges within "prohibition zones" extending fifty miles off the coast of member states. The logic was that discharges mixed with enough water and made far enough from shore would dissipate before causing coastal pollution. The agreement allowed discharges below 100 parts of oil per million parts of water (ppm) within even these prohibition zones.

Amendments in 1962 extended these zones to 100 miles for several countries and, more significantly, prohibited new tankers from exceeding the 100 ppm limit anywhere in the ocean (OILPOL 54/62, 1962). This latter rule was the first to require any tankers to reduce, rather than merely redistribute, their discharges. Although existing tankers could comply simply by discharging outside prohibited zones, new tankers would need equipment that could measure oil content if they were to even appear to comply. This implicit equipment requirement prompted British-based Shell Oil to develop the Load on Top (LOT) method to reduce discharges by combining deballasting and tank-cleaning slops in a single tank, discharging water from underneath the oil as it separated out, and recovering the remaining oil by combining and delivering it with the next load of cargo. LOT required more time and effort from tanker operators than did discharging, but benefited oil companies by reducing wasted cargo and allowing tankers to address pollution concerns without buying new equipment. Unfortunately, although the total discharges of a tanker using LOT would decline, the oil content of its discharges would often exceed the 100 ppm standard unless it also installed expensive oil content monitors. Oil companies, therefore, lobbied for a revised standard that would legalize LOT.

The 1969 amendments, which took effect in 1978, did legalize LOT but also—over the objections of oil companies—expanded the 1962 principle of reducing discharges to all tankers, new and existing. Within coastal zones, tankers could discharge only "clean ballast" that produced "no visible traces of oil" (OILPOL 54/69 1969). Outside these zones, tankers had to keep the rate of discharge below 60 liters of oil per mile (l/m) and the amount discharged per voyage below 1/15,000ᵗʰ of a tanker's cargo capacity. These new standards could all be measured with equipment that tankers already had on board. In 1973, MARPOL incorporated all existing discharge standards and tightened the total discharge limit to $1/30,000^{th}$ of cargo capacity for new tankers. These discharge standards took effect when the MARPOL Convention and its 1978 Protocol (MARPOL 73/78 1978) entered into force in 1983 with a minor reduction in the legal rate of discharge to 30 l/m in 1993 (Anonymous 1993).

All these regulations targeted the actions of tanker operators and relied on deterrence to influence behavior. Detecting violations of the 100 ppm and 60 l/m limits entailed costly wide-area naval or aerial surveillance or port inspection of oil record books in which captains were to record all discharges, whether illegal or not. The clean ballast provision remedied the problem that violations of the 100 ppm and 60 l/m criteria could not be independently verified. The total discharge provision went further by allowing port inspections to identify violations by confirming that essentially all expected slops were still on board. Because tankers only produce slops on the ballast voyage, however, only oil loading ports could conduct such inspections. If they did so, international law required they turn over prosecution and penalization to the ship's flag state. The 1962 and 1969 amendments developed clauses requiring states to detect, prosecute, and stiffly penalize discharge violations in an effort to improve enforcement.

The Equipment Standards Subregime By the early 1970s, the United States had grown concerned that compliance with the 1962 discharge standards in force at the time was "spotty, at best," and doubted industry claims that compliance with the 1969 amendments would be significantly higher (M'Gonigle and Zacher 1979, 227–228). Increasing environmental concern had already prompted Congress to pass legislation in 1972 requiring all American tankers and all tankers entering American ports to install segregated ballast tanks (SBT) and double hulls unless other nations accepted comparable international rules. SBT involves configuring a portion of a tanker's tanks and piping so it never carries oil, thus eliminating the oil and water mixtures created by traditional ballasting. SBT-equipped tankers generated far fewer slops than a comparable tanker practicing no pollution control, and their ability to reduce discharges was roughly equivalent to that of a tanker complying with the discharge standards. In response to the American threat, IMCO convened the MARPOL conference in 1973, which promulgated the first requirements for equipment to reduce the amount of slops a tanker generated. Several countries accepted the United States' argument that the monitoring, enforcement, and compliance problems of discharge standards could not be remedied through further refinement; more fundamental changes were needed. Garnering reluctant support from American oil companies seeking to avert unilateral regulations, the United States modified its proposal to require only large tankers built after 1979 to install SBT. This modification ignored the many small tankers and allowed a long phase-in period before it applied even to all large tankers, but it constituted a proposal most countries could support.

By 1977, growing environmentalism at home again forced the U.S. government to place intentional oil pollution on the international agenda. A spate of accidents led President Carter to propose requiring all existing ships to retrofit with SBT and double hulls. As in 1972, the United States also threatened unilateral action if international rules did not meet its concerns. IMCO convened the 1978 Tanker Safety and Pollution Prevention Conference. Having concluded from the 1973 MARPOL negotiations that new equipment requirements were inevitable, oil companies and maritime states developed and proposed crude oil washing (COW) as an alternative to SBT. Spraying down tanks with crude oil during delivery (rather than water during ballast voyages) increased cargo delivered while reducing waste oil. The 1978 protocol produced a compromise between the industry and American positions. It required all ships, large and small, built after 1982 to install both SBT and COW, but allowed older ships to retrofit with either option. Once an owner installed COW or SBT, that tanker's captain (even if unconcerned about pollution) would discharge fewer slops. The environmental promise of the 1978 Protocol lay in requiring all tankers—new and existing, large and small—to retrofit with at least one of the technologies.

Equipment regulations provided the foundation for a subregime based on a more effective strategy that would prevent, rather than deter, violations (Mitchell 1996; Reiss 1984). Responsibility for compliance shifted from tanker captains to tanker owners, and the site of violation shifted from the open ocean to the shipyard. MARPOL required flag state surveyors, or classification societies nominated by them, to conduct surveys during construction and retrofit, then periodically thereafter. Classification societies often have both a greater capacity and greater incentives to conduct surveys than do flag states. Inspectors would certify equipment compliance via an International Oil Pollution Prevention (IOPP) certificate (MARPOL 73/78 1978, Annex I, Regulation 4). Port states could then, under MARPOL, verify that required equipment was on board and operating properly. These inspections piggybacked on existing classification society and government inspections for safety, customs, and other domestic and international regulations.[3]

Equipment rules induced compliance in two ways. Although a tanker captain faced no constraints in discharging illegally, a tanker buyer needed cooperation from a builder, a classification society, and an insurer to get a tanker built without the required equipment. These actors had few incentives to assist in such violations. Thus, even buying a noncompliant tanker became next to impossible. This aspect of the regime was reinforced by a tanker owner's knowledge at the time of construction that resale of an illegal tanker would be lower because it would have access to fewer oil markets. Thus, equipment standards were harder and less attractive for tanker owners to violate, reducing the subsequent need for programs to monitor and enforce.

MARPOL also created the structure needed to make such regulations work. The convention explicitly authorized port states to bar noncompliant ships from their ports or detain them until they no longer posed "an unreasonable threat of harm to the marine environment" (MARPOL 73/78 1978, Art. 5(2)). Developed port states, which were significantly more environmentally concerned, could monitor and respond to equipment violations without the assistance or approval of reluctant flag states.[4] The ease of identifying violations and linking them to violators, coupled with the authority to detain tankers or bar them from entry, if caught in violation, provided a strong deterrent, reinforcing the elements of the compliance system that prevented violation in the first place. Notably, this deterrent threat has rarely been used in response to an equipment violation.

The Reception Facility Subregime   Although LOT, SBT, and COW all reduced the quantity of slops that a tanker needed to discharge, in many circumstances tankers still generated some slops that could not be discharged within treaty limits. Addressing this required oil-loading ports to provide reception facilities as an alternative to disposal at sea. The 1954 convention required that states "ensure provision" of reception facilities for nontankers in "major" ports, but it allowed each state to define which ports these were (OILPOL 54 1954, Art. VIII). Facilities for tankers were recommended but not required. The United States and Liberia both did not ratify the convention because of this article, objecting to making governments responsible for the costs of providing facilities (Okidi 1978, 33). The 1962 conference reflected these concerns, rejecting proposals for tighter obligations and rewriting the article, requiring only that governments "take all appropriate measures to promote provision" and recommending that industry provide reception facilities "as a matter of urgency" (OILPOL 54/62 1962).

In 1973, MARPOL reverted to the requirement that states "ensure provision" of reception facilities, expanding its application to both nontanker and tanker ports, as well as clearly defining such ports. These facilities had to avoid causing delay to tankers using them. IMO designated "special areas" for greater environmental protection and established more stringent requirements for them, including requirements that states ensure reception facilities in ports in the Mediterranean, Black, and Baltic Seas special areas by 1 January 1977 regardless of when the treaty entered into force, in other special areas "as soon as practicable," and elsewhere within one year of the treaty's entry into force (MARPOL 73/78 1978, Annex I, Regulations 10 and 12).[5] Many states have interpreted the language that governments must "ensure the provision" rather than "provide" reception facilities as requiring oil companies and port authorities, not governments, to pay for the facilities (M'Gonigle and Zacher 1979, 116). This language papered over what has become a continuing debate over whether governments or industry must provide facilities.

Making reception facilities available in more ports was necessary, but by no means sufficient, to assure fewer discharges. Even adequately sized and efficient facilities involved additional time and expense in port for a tanker operator compared to discharging at sea. Requiring facilities in more ports and on a designated timetable in special areas represented improvements. Unfortunately, MARPOL was signed and ratified by only four of the thirteen Organization of Petroleum Exporting Countries (OPEC) states where facilities were most needed.

To encourage ports to provide facilities, IMO has periodically surveyed existing facilities and studied the need for facilities in particular regions, but it has made few efforts to fund facilities where needed or to sanction governments that failed to ensure their provision (Anonymous 1996). Although OILPOL and MARPOL encouraged captains to report inadequate facilities to IMO through their governments, few such reports have been submitted.

Causal Narrative

The regime has clearly experienced considerable change over the past four decades. Do improvements in the rules and the shape of the rules reflect the regime's influence or simply exogenous changes in the interests of powerful actors? Did any of the regime's rules, especially those aimed at altering tanker operators' and tanker owners' behavior, have their intended effects? Did behavior change, and, for those changes that did occur, was the regime responsible? This section depicts "snapshots" of the behavioral complex to identify such changes and assess their causes. This regime's concern with compliance makes it appropriate to evaluate the regime predominantly on legal effectiveness, but the following section also evaluates the regime with respect to the other definitions of effectiveness delineated in chapter 1.

Environmental Improvement

Despite empirical obstacles, one can assess the environmental or problem-solving effectiveness of the intentional oil pollution regime with some confidence. In the 1950s and 1960s, estimates suggested that a typical tanker discharged 0.4 to 0.5 percent of each voyage's cargo as slops, producing a world total of about 1 million tons per year (IMCO 1965, 6; Moss 1963; National Academy of Sciences 1975). A later National Academy of Sciences' study estimated the total was down to 750 thousand tons per year, despite significantly higher tanker traffic, and reestimated in 1989 that this figure was down to 159 thousand tons per year (MEPC 1990c; National Academy of Sciences and National Research Council

1985). Estimates of the percent of transported crude discharged at sea also declined from an estimated 0.4 percent in the 1960s to 0.098 percent in 1971, to 0.053 percent in 1980, and to 0.015 percent in 1989 (table 2.1). Other independent estimates made between 1960 and 1990 confirm a consensus that intentional oil pollution decreased over time, especially after MARPOL's signature in 1973.

Such estimates, however, must be treated with caution. Most rely on assumed rates of oil clingage to tanks, actual tanker traffic levels, and judgments regarding how oil companies and independent tankers were discharging their waste oil. Trends can reflect changes in analytic assumptions as much as, if not more than, changes in the real environment.[6] Although experts have traditionally underestimated intentional discharges and overestimated improvements, intentional discharges—both in total quantity and per ton transported—have most likely decreased (Khristenko 1983, 24).

Data on environmental quality do lend some support to the view that discharges have decreased. Data from the U.S. Pollution Incident Reporting System for 1973 through 1986 show major decreases in intentional discharges as a result of bilge pumping and other operations by tankers and nontankers, but only small declines in ballast discharges. Marine tar surveys show ship-source oil pollution decreasing between 1969 and 1980 (Holdway 1986; Smith and Knap 1985). Russian data indicate North Atlantic tar concentrations peaked in 1980, dropped in 1982, stabilized at low levels in 1983–1986, and increased slightly from 1986–1988 (Simonov 1984; Simonov and Orlova 1987; Simonov and Orlova 1989).

Many analysts have not only claimed that intentional discharges have declined, but have linked the decline to the OILPOL/MARPOL regime. As early as 1965, oil companies claimed that LOT had eliminated 60 percent of all intentional discharges (IMCO 1965, 6). The evidence of behavior change presented below also supports the conclusion that compliance with regime requirements decreased intentional discharges over time. By adopting LOT, many tankers undoubtedly reduced their average discharge, even if they violated specific limits on total discharges. The high level of compliance with MARPOL's equipment requirements and the reduced discharges when such equipment was used also suggest that total oil inputs declined. The continuing adoption of these technologies by the fleet should be producing further reductions. In 1990, one IMO official concluded that uncertainty regarding compliance levels meant that intentional discharges "could lie between 6 and 0.1 [million tons], but the author optimistically assumed that it would be much nearer to the latter" (Sasamura 1990, 3–6). A more impartial GESAMP study concluded that MARPOL "regulations have resulted in a major reduction of intentional pollution" (GESAMP 1990, 21).

These data clearly require cautious interpretation with respect to both trends in intentional discharges and assertions that the regime caused such trends. None of the data sources are individually robust. Taken together, however, environmental quality data, expert estimates, and compliance evidence reinforce arguments that oil pollution from vessels "is now less serious than it was a decade ago" (IMO 1989, 12). The data are consistent with a view that discharges have declined and that compliance with the regime's discharge and equipment standards account for some share of this. Because some tankers continue to discharge illegally, however, and because tankers are only one among many sources of oil pollution, environmental improvement proves hard to discern. Oil pollution remains a problem, but probably a smaller one than experienced previously. Without putting much faith in precise estimates of levels of intentional discharges, it appears that the regime has had some degree of problem-solving effectiveness, moving toward, if not completely achieving, the goal enshrined in OILPOL's preamble: "to prevent pollution of the sea by oil discharged from ships" (OILPOL 54 1954).

The poor quality of available data suggests one more conclusion. Given that this regime is one of the oldest environmental regimes and that it has had a consistent goal for over forty years, the lack of any program systematically to collect and analyze data on environmental quality is a distressing failure. Such a program would allow better evaluation of whether the regime was having its intended effect of solving the oil pollution problem. The studies cited here have involved ad hoc government or independent efforts that lack any of the coordination needed to make results comparable across studies and over time. As the long-range transboundary air pollution regime (see chapter 4) suggests, such programs are difficult to coordinate and are by no means sufficient to unambiguously identify trends in environmental quality or the causes of those trends. Collecting such data is a necessary first step, however, in evaluating whether the regime is helping to resolve and manage the problem that motivated its creation.

Scope and Stringency of Regulations

If the regime has had the strategic goal of reducing intentional discharges since its inception, it has sought to achieve this goal through the more immediate, tactical goals of

(1) increasing the activities regulated,
(2) developing rules that would improve the environment if complied with, and
(3) eliciting compliance with those rules.

In 1954, OILPOL rules dealt exclusively with intentional oil pollution from vessels and achieved only low levels of compliance. Even had compliance levels been higher, these rules would not have significantly mitigated the environmental problem. By 1998, the regime regulated intentional discharges from offshore oil rigs, accidental spills from tankers, most other hazardous cargo, as well as sewage, garbage, and most air pollutants produced by ships. Compliance is now higher than in 1954 and more likely to produce the desired environmental improvement.

Can the regime take credit for the change between these two snapshots? Certainly most of the impetus to expand the scope of regulations came from exogenous forces, not from processes set in motion by the regime. Governmental and industry agreements on liability for and responses to accidental spills were negotiated only in the wake of disasters such as the Torrey Canyon and Exxon Valdez.[7] MARPOL included non-oil pollutants in response to growing environmental concern, especially in the United States. In almost every case, new regulations were responses to external stimuli, such as major accidents and threats of unilateral U.S. action, not to IMO initiatives or activism.

The regime facilitated regulation of these new arenas. As new problems arose, the lower transaction costs of negotiating new agreements within a single, existing forum had obvious advantages (Keohane 1984). The international nature of the shipping industry and of oil pollution made a single forum useful. Furthermore, both governments and industry preferred unified rules to a patchwork of regional and unilateral measures. Although such exogenous interests may explain why IMO has exercised "sole proprietorship" over these issues, they do not explain the speed and shape of regulatory progress. MARPOL preparation and negotiation of stringent standards on five major categories of pollution took less than two years. Requirements for equipment to reduce oil dispersed during accidents and limiting air pollution from ships were quickly adopted as minor amendments to MARPOL. In contrast, LRTAP (see chapter 4) has taken years to negotiate each of its protocols on individual air pollutants. The speed of negotiation suggests that MARPOL benefited from the structure and diplomatic experience gained in negotiations of OILPOL and its amendments. Placing OILPOL under a UN specialized agency responsible for all maritime issues created the experience, expertise, and legitimacy needed to justify regulating all vessel-source pollutants within the same regime. Indeed, this single framework provides a striking contrast with the separate regimes for acid precipitation, stratospheric ozone protection, and climate change, or the species-specific approaches to fisheries (see chapters 3 and 4, Peterson 1993).

A single legitimate forum also averted unilateral and regional remedies. The United Kingdom in 1953 and the United States in 1972 and 1977 were ready and able to take unilateral action, but refrained from doing so after less stringent international rules were adopted. European states channeled their concern over oil pollution after the 1978 Amoco Cadiz disaster into an agreement to more rigorously enforce existing IMO regulations instead of, as one might have expected, into more stringent tanker requirements. Latin American, Asian and Pacific, Caribbean, and Mediterranean states have channeled environmental concern into enforcing existing MARPOL standards rather than promulgating new ones (Plaza 1997). Thus, the regime has made cooperation far easier to negotiate and implement than if these countries were faced with having to develop new international agreements. It appears highly unlikely that such nested enforcement regimes as now exist, or such comprehensive regulation of air pollution from ships (which contributes only a small share to the global problem), would have developed at all in the absence of the existing regime.

The regime's standards have also increased in stringency over four decades. Even assuming perfect compliance, the 1954 rules required only that tankers discharge farther from shore. The 1962 rules limiting discharges throughout the ocean would have taken decades to have environmental effects as they applied only to new tankers. The 1969 limits on total discharges corrected this by requiring all tankers to reduce discharges effective upon entry of the rules into force. MARPOL's restrictions on new tankers limited total discharges still further for new tankers. And the rules also improved the likelihood of enforcement and compliance. Even a conscientious captain could not monitor compliance with the 1954 and 1962 limits, because the technology needed to measure oil content at 100 ppm did not yet exist. Detecting violations required sighting large and blatant spills or the unlikely possibility of port inspectors identifying a crew that had incriminated itself by logging its illegal discharges in the Oil Record Book (ORB). The 1969 "no visible trace" rule facilitated detection of violations by ships and aircraft, although linking detected slicks with the responsible tanker remained a problem. The total discharge rule went further and made it possible for oil loading states to unambiguously identify violations and their perpetrators through in-port inspections.[8]

MARPOL continued this trend toward more stringent regulation. MARPOL's 1973 requirements for equipment on large new tankers cost industry more than discharge standards and also improved environmental protection by increasing the likelihood of industry compliance. The 1978 protocol extended these rules to all tankers. MARPOL also set fixed dates for industry compliance with provisions concerning equipment and reception facilities. Few states entered the 1973 and 1978 negotiations supporting SBT requirements, and powerful states including Japan and France actively opposed their adoption. States that were home to large independent fleets—Denmark, Germany, Greece, Norway, and Sweden—opposed SBT requirements in 1973. Even when, in 1978, they supported SBT retrofits as a means of reducing global tanker capacity and increasing transportation prices, they had no incentives to actually apply those requirements to their own tankers. Laggard states accepted these more stringent rules because they involved few immediate costs and because of U.S. threats of even costlier unilateral requirements. More stringent rules clearly depended on these threats but the United States would have been less successful at getting other countries to accept such regulations. If, counterfactually, no regime had existed, laggard states would have accepted unilateral action as unpreventable but unfortunate, and they would have been unlikely to adopt such regulations themselves. The regime thus altered their perception of their alternatives: laggards accepted regulations more stringent than they desired as a quid pro quo for activist states to forego even more stringent unilateral measures.

Did this increasing stringency merely reflect increasing public concern or hegemonic pressures? This appears unlikely, as the rules adopted have been more stringent than many governments or industry would have adopted unilaterally. Even the rather weak 1954 rules exceeded what most countries would have done otherwise. The United States believed its own rules had obviated the need for international action (International Conference on Pollution of the Sea by Oil 1954, 4). Denmark, France, Japan, Norway, Sweden, and most developing states also opposed regulation as unnecessary (Pritchard 1987, 98–99; United Nations 1956). The 1962 amendments were accepted despite the opposition of oil and shipping companies and of the United States, Japan, Norway, and the Netherlands (M'Gonigle and Zacher 1979, 95–96). The 1969 amendments to apply more stringent discharge limits to all tankers were accepted even though few states had similar legislation pending and despite calls by Shell to eliminate OILPOL's requirements altogether in favor of voluntary industry adoption of LOT (Kirby 1968). The regime allowed the United Kingdom and the United States to induce far more states to incorporate stringent regulations into national law than would have been possible through unilateral action or diplomatic pressure outside the regime forum.

Lastly, the regime established rules that no state could have promulgated unilaterally. International law limited state jurisdiction over territorial seas out to three miles, and OILPOL regulated actions of foreign tankers out to fifty miles. International law gave flag states the exclusive right to inspect a ship's tanks; the 1969 amendments established this right for port states. International law forbade detaining foreign tankers for pollution violations, while MARPOL established the right to do so. International legal norms consistently inhibited states from taking unilateral action considered to infringe on other states' sovereignty, yet MARPOL made such actions possible.

The regime has had negative effects as well. Pollution control regulations are now so numerous that tanker operators find it difficult to know which rules apply to them. The regime has tended to overregulate, restricting pollutants from ships even in cases in which ships constitute a minor portion of the problem. One may even fault the regime for underregulating the land-based sources that constitute the primary share of marine pollution. These sources have been addressed through a piecemeal approach that leaves many pollutants uncontrolled in some regions. From an economic perspective, the regime has not achieved ecological improvement as efficiently as possible, resorting to inefficient command-and-control approaches while rarely determining whether the benefits of control exceed the costs.

In summary, the regime provided a forum within which the preferences of dominant states and the pressures resulting from dramatic tanker accidents and larger environmental concerns produced international regulations broader in scope, more stringent, more rapidly adopted, and acceptable to more states than if those same preferences and pressures had operated without the benefit of the regime. The regime could not have achieved these changes without pressures from dominant states and publics, but neither would those pressures have produced such extensive regulation without the regime.

Eliciting Behavior Change: Deterrence, Prevention, and Compliance

Differences among the discharge, equipment, and reception facility subregimes offer an opportunity to evaluate the relative effectiveness of their methods of eliciting behavior change (see chapter 1). Equipment standards led tanker owners to install expensive equipment despite its costs, classification societies and flag state governments to adopt new standards for monitoring ships, and some port state governments to detain noncompliant tankers. In contrast, the discharge and reception facility subregimes have been far less successful at eliciting new behaviors.

Discharge Standards   In 1954, most tankers could and did discharge oil slops wherever their captains saw fit. By 1998, although rules constrained the rate, location, and amounts of legal discharges, which appeared to have declined, intentional discharges remained common among some of the tankers that did not yet face equipment requirements. Various efforts to increase this subregime's influence failed to cause fundamental changes in the behavior of tanker operators. Why? Relying on a deterrence-based model of compliance, discharge standards required extensive and effective enforcement to alter tanker operators incentives, and hence their behavior.[9] Before tanker operators would adopt new ways of discharging their waste oil, governments would have to adopt policies that would detect, prosecute, and penalize noncompliant operators at rates sufficient to offset any gains from violation.

Under OILPOL's initial rules, government authorities could detect violations either by inspecting the oil record book or by aerial and naval surveillance. A 1961 IMCO survey, however, documented that the difficulty of conducting such inspections made them quite rare.[10] Not unexpectedly, states identified numerous reasons for the lack of enforcement. The oil record book relied on self-incrimination, could be easily falsified, and initially did not even require recording of the information relevant to identifying violations. Surveillance was costly, difficult at night and in high seas, and plagued by the low ratio of surveillance area to potential violation area.[11] Finally, most violations had to be referred to recalcitrant flag states for prosecution (Pritchard 1987).

The 1969 Amendments began to remedy these enforcement problems. Its "clean ballast" rule was hailed as a remedy to both detection and evidentiary problems, because "any sighting of a discharge from a tanker within fifty miles from land would be much more likely to be evidence of a contravention of the convention" (IMCO 1977, Annex, Par. 5). MARPOL went further and required states to practice "all appropriate and practicable measures of detection," and many developed states began aerial surveillance programs in the 1970s (Anonymous 1990b; Cowley 1990; McLoughlin and Forster 1982; MEPC 1978; Peet 1992, 11–12; Smit-Kroes 1988). The growth in government monitoring of discharge violations, however, appears unlikely to have been a response to international rules. Some monitoring began before the requirements took effect, others began more than five years after the requirements, and many were small and later discontinued (Collins 1987, 277). Almost all programs, including that of the United States, focused close to shore despite the 60 l/m limit on discharges beyond the fifty-mile zone. Aerial surveillance appears to have been more responsive to domestic environmental pressure than to international regulation.

The clean ballast and 60 l/m standards also did not remedy the difficulties of linking vessels to illegal discharges with evidence adequate for prosecution. The 1961 survey had shown that successful prosecutions almost always involved discharges in port, not at sea where evidence was far harder to collect (IMCO 1961). Port and coastal states still fail to refer more than one-third of all violations to flag states for lack of evidence, and one-fifth of the cases that have sufficient evidence are never prosecuted (Peet 1992, 14). Aerial surveillance photographs often fail to convince port state prosecutors to pursue a case, let alone prosecutors in flag states (Cowley 1990). Governments are not required to accept photographs of slicks as evidence of a violation, despite the clean ballast language (IJlstra 1989).

Even the total discharge standards failed to induce more enforcement because, although in-port inspections could now detect violations, initially only flag state officials and oil company representatives had the legal authority to conduct such inspections. The former were rarely present in a port of call and the latter had few incentives to report the results of such inspections. MARPOL remedied this by giving port states the right to inspect ships and their tanks (MARPOL 73/78 1978, Art. 6(2)). Since discharges could only be calculated after the ballast voyage, however, such inspections had to occur in oil loading states. Only four such states signed MARPOL, and no oil loading state had incentives to expend resources to keep other states' coasts clean, while placing their own ports at a competitive disadvantage relative to states with less burdensome inspections (Burke, Legatski, and Woodhead 1975, 126).[12] Total discharge limits failed because they placed new rights and obligations on governments that had little logical, and had shown little historical, incentive to undertake enforcement.

Prosecution of any discharge violations was rare because customary international law and OILPOL relied on the principle of flag state jurisdiction. States had to hand over evidence of violations outside their territorial seas to flag states who often were reluctant to prosecute their own tankers. For flag states, prosecution benefited others and entailed immediate costs and threats to revenues derived from ship registry fees. The 1961

IMCO survey revealed that flag states did not successfully prosecute any of the 128 violations referred to them. National reports to IMO show that, from 1967 to 1983, only 16 percent of referrals were successfully prosecuted by flag states and that this figure has decreased since MARPOL took effect in 1983 (Mitchell 1994, 163).

With such low detection and prosecution rates, deterring discharge violations required states to impose stiff penalties in the few cases of conviction. Indeed, treaty clauses and IMO resolutions have consistently tried to induce states to impose stiff penalties (MARPOL 73/78 1978, Art. 4(4); IMCO 1968; IMCO 1979; IMCO 1981; M'Gonigle and Zacher 1979, 222; U.S. Congress 1963, 40). Neither authorized nor imposed fines, however, have ever been high (M'Gonigle and Zacher 1979, 228; Mitchell 1994, 168–169).

Given these enforcement problems, it is not surprising to find that initially low levels of compliance have not improved. High quality time-series data on compliance are unavailable, but a wide array of evidence suggests that noncompliance with discharge standards was frequent early on and remains common. IMO experts and governments have often cited continuing discharge violations to justify their calls for greater enforcement effort (Anonymous 1990a, 12; MEPC 1989a; MEPC 1991d). Industry representatives admit that tankers frequently must violate discharge standards because governments fail to provide reception facilities and because charter arrangements often require tankers "to arrive with clean ballast at loading ports" (Anonymous 1990c; MEPC 1989b; MEPC 1991c). U.S. tanker crews have claimed that illegal discharges are "the norm on the high seas" (Curtis 1985, 707). German port authorities found that half of all tankers "were unable to declare where oil residues had gone" (Second International Conference on the Protection of the North Sea 1987, 14).

Specific data on compliance with the total discharge limits reinforce the conclusion that tankers frequently fail to comply with discharge standards. Reports to IMO of total detected violations and average detected violations per country have decreased since the 1969 Amendments entered into force in 1978 (see table 2.2). These data, however, include significant differences in the number of countries reporting and do not allow adjustment for the amount of enforcement effort involved. More

Table 2.2
Alleged violations of discharge provisions of OILPOL 1954/62/69 and MARPOL 73/78

Year	1975	1976	1977	1978	1979	1980	1981	1982	1983	1984	1985	1986	1987	1988	1989	1990
Number of reports of alleged discharge violations																
Port and coastal states reporting	3	4	4	7	10	13	5	NA	10	10	13	12	10	15	15	15
Reported violations	145	185	166	397	497	570	91	NA	87	185	199	191	113	163	181	125
Avg. violations per reporting country	48	46	42	57	50	44	18	NA	9	19	15	16	11	11	12	8
Number of reports of referrals of alleged discharge violations to flag states																
Countries reporting	1	1	2	4	6	8	1	1	10	10	12	12	8	12	13	13
Reported referrals	6	9	23	115	139	180	5	10	40	150	131	170	97	144	157	98
Avg. referrals per reporting country	6	9	12	29	23	23	5	10	4	15	11	14	12	12	12	8

Sources: Dempsey 1984, 487 and 511; Peet 1992, annexes 4, 5, and 11.

consistent data from ongoing Dutch surveillance programs and from oiled seabird surveys suggest that oil slicks detected in the North Sea have not decreased significantly since the early 1970s (Camphuysen 1989). States participating in the European Memorandum of Understanding have detected oil record book violations at a relatively constant 3 percent rate of all inspections since the early 1980s. There are still "many cases of unlawful discharges of oil into the sea" (Second International Conference on the Protection of the North Sea 1987, 14).

A 1976 Dutch survey found only sixteen of seventy tankers using Load on Top (MEPC 1976). A 1981 National Academy of Sciences study assumed that 50 percent of the world tanker fleet was violating the $1/15,000^{th}$ limit (MEPC 1981). Although they updated this figure in 1989 to 80 to 85 percent compliance, they supplied no supporting evidence for their greater optimism (MEPC 1990c, 15). Several studies have found that tankers discharged far fewer slops at reception facilities than they were estimated to generate (den Boer, Havinga, Hazelhorst, Holsink, Meijer, Splint, van Spronsen, and Zwijnenberg 1987; Vanhaecke 1990). Even oil company surveys in the 1970s found "a long-suspected indifferent compliance by LOT tankers"; one-third of them were not using LOT at all and another third were using it poorly (M'Gonigle and Zacher 1979, 110–111; Pritchard 1987, 214). Oil company tankers had reduced their discharges significantly by 1975 but were still averaging three times the legal limit of $1/15,000^{th}$ while independent tankers were discharging thirty times this limit (U.S. Congress 1980, 5). The timing of discharge reductions that did occur, however, and the fact that oil company tankers—who owned the cargo—changed their behavior far more than independents—for whom pollution reduction involved only costs—suggests that the behavior was responding to increasing oil prices in 1973 rather than entry into force of OILPOL requirements in 1978.

This evidence suggests the discharge subregime has not significantly changed tanker operator behavior. Attempts to make the subregime more effective have consistently failed to induce the desired behavioral changes by either governments or nonstate actors.

Reception Facilities   Most developed states today have many more facilities to receive oil wastes than they did in 1954. Many of these ports still lack adequate facilities, however, and most ports in developing states lack, or have inadequate, facilities. Especially disturbing is the absence of facilities in ports in oil-loading states and in special areas where reception facilities are most needed. If the discharge subregime illustrates a case in which initial ineffectiveness led to numerous, if unsuccessful, efforts to improve subregime rules, provisions on reception facilities illustrate a case in which states have been reluctant to agree on any measures that had a chance of making the subregime effective. The reception facility subregime has explicitly rejected sanctions for noncompliance and positive incentives for compliance, relying exclusively on the stigma of public knowledge of noncompliance to induce behavioral change. The subregime has largely failed, however, to establish the system needed to implement even such a minimal strategy.

The subregime has consistently faced a conflict between the need for efficient reception facilities as a viable alternative to discharging at sea and the unwillingness of governments to incur the costs of providing such facilities. Initially, reception facility requirements did not clarify whether governments or industry were responsible for providing them.[13] Even MARPOL language that specified dates for ensuring provision of reception facilities failed to specify who must provide them. Tanker owners and operators continue to contend that providing facilities is a government, not industry, responsibility (MEPC 1983a; MEPC 1989c).

The system established to induce provision of facilities also reflected the lack of commitment to ensuring their provision. This subregime relied on a system of national self-reporting that consistently failed to identify ports that lacked adequate facilities. Irregular compilations of national responses to surveys by the UN, IMCO, and IMO have been published in formats that help tanker captains identify and use reception facilities in ports that have them. The publications do not, however, assess the adequacy of facilities to meet tanker demand without undue delay, as required by the treaty, nor do they identify ports without facilities. In short, the system fails to identify any noncompliant ports. Recognizing this, amendments in 1962 and provisions in MARPOL required that governments annually identify noncompliant ports in other countries (OILPOL 54/62 1962, Art. VIII). While the reporting system for ports providing facilities evoked relatively high numbers of responses but did not identify noncompliant ports, the reporting system for ports with inadequate facilities has produced very few responses. Before the late 1970s, not a single report was received. A 1984 survey of inadequate facilities received responses from only twenty-five countries (Sasamura 1984, 10–11). Between 1985 and 1992, only four of the seventy-five responses to IMO's required annual implementation reports have contained any information on inadequate facilities.

Reliance on government reporting clearly failed to identify ports lacking, or having inadequate, facilities. Independent evidence demonstrates that this nonreporting, whether intentional or not, masked significant noncompliance. The International Chamber of Shipping (ICS) surveyed ship masters in 1983, 1985, and 1990, and it found numerous ports where reception facilities were absent, had limited capacity, were costly to use, or involved long delays (MEPC 1983b; MEPC 1985; MEPC 1990d). As recently as 1996, the International Association of Independent Tanker Owners (INTERTANKO) was producing similar information while noting that the information "should have been made available" to IMO by governments and that "many countries, industrialized as well as developing, are in breach of MARPOL by having oil ports which do not provide these essential facilities" (MEPC 1996). IMO and various regional organizations have also identified ports in need of facilities, especially ports in special areas and in developing states (Montfort 1984; Placci 1984; Sadler and King 1990). The difference between the government reporting system and these other efforts confirm that governments have neither the incentives nor ability to check up on reception facilities in other countries' ports. Tanker operators have the ability to identify noncompliant ports; however, they "are reluctant to risk losing the goodwill of a harbour authority by making an adverse report on the reception facilities" (Hambling 1984). The obvious means of getting such information to IMO involved offering anonymity. Yet, governments had no incentive to offer such anonymity since doing so required them to put their credibility at risk when forwarding information provided by tanker operators. In contrast, shipping companies incur unnecessary costs when their ships enter ports with inadequate facilities, costs that led them, through the International Chamber of Shipping surveys, to offer anonymity to those reporting such facilities.

Even had noncompliant ports been identified, no response system existed to induce compliance. When ICS surveys or regional studies identified noncompliant ports, neither positive nor negative responses ensued. Early on, governments recognized that ports might not provide facilities because they could not afford, or had no incentives to incur, the costs involved.[14] Moreover, although states that would incur these costs could fund facilities from oil revenues or port charges, they have few incentives to do so (Regional Marine Pollution Emergency Response Centre for the Mediterranean Sea 1991). Various proposals have been made to have developed states fund facility construction, including imposing an international tax on oil imports (MEPC 1977), but the MEPC has yet to adopt any such program.[15] Developed countries have often failed to fund facilities in their own ports and have been unwilling to finance them in developing countries.[16] IMCO/IMO has hosted seminars to increase understanding of cheaper ways to provide reception facilities. After forty years, however, it seems unlikely that developed states will finance the compliance of developing states, as they have done with other environmental treaties (Keohane and Levy 1996).

IMO's rejection of positive incentives for providing reception facilities has been paralleled by a failure to sanction ports for not providing them. Some governments have penalized their own port authorities for not providing facilities, but none have sanctioned other ports or governments for failing to do so (Davison 1984; Hambling 1984; Powles 1984, 156–157). Governments have the ability but lack incentives to sanction one another for failing to make facilities available; in contrast, shipping interests have incentives but lack the authority "to penalize ports that neglect their obligations" (MEPC 1989c). IMO regularly exhorts countries to provide more and better facilities but has never blacklisted or otherwise shamed noncompliant countries. In short, the subregime has done a poor job of identifying ports lacking adequate facilities, and it has failed to fund or sanction, or get others to fund or sanction, governments whose ports lack facilities.

The costs of facility provision and the absence of deterrents or incentives to incur those costs predict low compliance levels. The regime nevertheless may have increased the number of available facilities. In 1935, only seven of thirty-four states had port reception facilities (Pritchard

1987, 60–61). Table 2.3 summarizes data from IMCO/IMO surveys between 1956 and 1990 on the fraction of ports reported without facilities.[17] Most new facilities are in developed countries. Organization for Economic Cooperation and Development (OECD) countries, including the United States, have increased their number of facilities, number of ports with facilities, and percentage of ports with facilities. The sharp increase between 1973 and 1980 reflects reporting on more ports, installation of some new facilities, and the relabeling of some existing facilities. In contrast, OPEC oil loading states and other non-OECD have not provided the reception facilities needed to foster tanker compliance with discharge standards. Independent studies have estimated that 8 percent of U.S. ports and 18 percent of other OECD ports lack reception facilities, while 44 percent of non-OPEC, non-OECD states and 62 percent of OPEC states lack reception facilities (Sadler and King 1990).

Table 2.4 shows that reception facilities have been provided only, at best, by developed states. The oil exporting regions and special areas that MARPOL designated as most in need of environmental protection have few, if any, facilities. MARPOL established a January 1977 deadline for provision of facilities in the special areas of the Baltic, Black, and Mediterranean Seas but this deadline had no noticeable influence on behavior. The Red Sea, Persian Gulf, and Gulf of Aden special areas—which were to provide facilities "as soon as possible"—remain unimplemented twenty years after MARPOL was signed precisely because reception facilities remain unavailable.

The U.S. experience demonstrates how the regime influenced provision of reception facilities in developed states. Under OILPOL, the United States strongly opposed international calls for governments to provide reception facilities. Few facilities were added before 1960, and no new facilities were "constructed between 1962 and 1967" (Okidi 1978, 33). While negotiating MARPOL in 1973, a more environmentally concerned United States pushed for more stringent facility requirements but still left it to oil reclamation companies to provide them (Okidi 1978, 33). By the time MARPOL took effect in 1983, the United States explicitly required port authorities and terminal operators to provide facilities; more importantly, it required the Coast Guard to certify facilities as adequate and prohibited tankers from entering uncertified ports (Davison 1984,

Table 2.3
IMO surveys on reception facilities in port

Year Source	1956 IMO	1964 IMO	1973/1976 IMO	1980/1984 IMO	1990 IMO	1990 SADLER
All reporting countries (No. of)						
Countries reporting	40	31	27	40	37	129
Ports	162	189	353	508	993	478
RFs	402	475	654	847	1,765	NA
Ports without RFs	37	31	37	22	104	151
Percent of ports without RFs	22.8	16.4	10.5	4.3	10.5	31.6
United States (No. of)						
Ports	14	14	55	39	325	49
RFs	217	232	266	59	948	NA
Ports without RFs	0	0	0	0	36	4
Percent of ports without RFs	0.0	0.0	0.0	0.0	11.1	8.2
OECD (non-U.S.) countries (No. of)						
Countries reporting	19	18	17	18	18	22
Ports	121	149	260	390	575	212
RFs	169	217	345	635	739	NA
Ports without RFs	27	22	36	14	48	38
Percent of ports without RFs	22.3	14.8	13.8	3.6	8.3	17.9

OPEC countries (No. of)						
Countries reporting	3	1	1	2	1	13
Ports	9	0	4	2	1	76
RFs	8	0	4	1	0	NA
Ports without RFs	1	0	0	1	1	47
Percent of ports without RFs	11.1	NA	0.0	50.0	100.0	61.8
Non-OPEC/non-OECD countries (No. of)						
Countries reporting	17	11	8	19	17	93
Ports	18	26	34	77	92	141
RFs	8	26	39	152	78	NA
Ports without RFs	9	9	1	7	19	62
Percent of ports without RFs	50.0	34.6	2.9	9.1	20.7	44.0

Sources: IMCO 1964; IMCO 1973; IMCO 1976; IMCO 1980; IMO 1984; MEPC 1990b; Sadler and King 1990; United Nations 1956.

Table 2.4
Reception facilities in ports bordering special areas

Year Source	1956 IMO	1964 IMO	1973/1976 IMO	1979 MED	1980/1984 IMO	1984 MED	1988 MED	1990 IMO	1990 SADLER
Special area countries (No. of)									
Countries reporting	15	11	12	—	16	—	—	16	41
Ports	43	79	139	—	246	—	—	304	204
RFs	30	70	153	—	413	—	—	381	NA
Ports without RFs	25	20	25	—	6	—	—	18	63
Percent of ports without RFs	58	25	18	—	2	—	—	6	31
Nonspecial area countries (No. of)									
Countries reporting	25	20	15	—	24	—	—	21	88
Ports	119	110	214	—	262	—	—	689	274
RFs	372	405	501	—	434	—	—	1,384	NA
Ports without RFs	12	11	12	—	16	—	—	86	88
Percent of ports without RFs	10	10	6	—	6	—	—	13	32
Mediterranean countries (No. of)									
Countries reporting	9	5	5	16	8	11	7	8	17
Ports	32	50	52	79	67	59	46	97	103
RFs	20	32	66	NA	84	NA	NA	145	NA
Ports without RFs	22	18	3	16	6	16	10	17	29
Percent of ports without RFs	69	36	6	20	9	27	22	18	28

Sources: IMCO 1964; IMCO 1973; IMCO 1976; IMCO 1980; IMO 1984; MEPC 1990b; MEPC 1979; Placci 1984; Sadler and King 1990; United Nations 1956.

47 and 65). These stringent domestic rules might have been instituted even in the absence of MARPOL, but the regime's ongoing pressures undoubtedly helped to channel the expressions of more inchoate domestic pressures for environmental protection into specific policy actions.

Although governments have provided fewer facilities than desired and their actions surely reflect growing concern over marine pollution, treaty requirements and ongoing MEPC discussions regarding the need for reception facilities appear to have helped motivate financially capable and environmentally concerned states to provide them. Unfortunately, these same requirements and discussions appear to have had little, if any, impact on those developing or oil-loading states where reception facilities are most needed. The subregime established requirements for the provision of facilities that have become more specific over time, but never established an enforcement or compliance-management strategy to dramatically alter the behavior of the most important actors.

Equipment Standards   In 1954, no tankers had separate tanks for seawater ballast nor did any tankers use crude oil to clean their tanks after delivery. Since 1982, every new tanker built has come with both technologies already installed and earlier tankers have been retrofitted with at least one of the technologies. Most classification societies, insurers, and port authorities have made evidence of these pollution-reduction technologies a prerequisite to being classified, being insured, and being allowed into port. Much, although not all, of this dramatic change in the structure of the tanker fleet can be attributed to the direct influence of this third subregime's effective management of compliance through encouraging compliance and preventing violation rather than through enforcement efforts designed to deter violation.

Requiring flag state and classification society inspectors to issue IOPP certificates and port state inspectors to check equipment against those certificates involved monitoring that readily fit the standard operating procedures of actors in the oil transportation industry. IMO and MOU data document that the IOPP certificate discrepancy rate was less than 10 percent immediately after MARPOL entered into force, and dropped to below 3 percent within a few years. These data confirm not only that most flag states and classification societies were issuing certificates but that IOPP/equipment verification quickly became part of the standard inspections of many developed states. Although classification societies have incentives to certify ships that do not meet MARPOL standards, these are countered by port state inspections and the involvement of some governments in the certification process.[18]

These actors would not have undertaken such efforts to monitor pollution equipment were it not for MARPOL's requirements: none of these actors checked for pollution control equipment prior to the MARPOL requirements, nor would they have done so if only a few activist states had adopted such requirements. Unlike aerial surveillance, adding pollution prevention criteria required only small changes and added only marginal costs to surveys and inspections already being conducted for safety and customs reasons. Also unlike naval or aerial surveillance, certification and inspection programs could be comprehensive, making it highly likely that illegally equipped tankers would be identified. These factors produced the surprising result that nine European states that opposed the 1973 and 1978 proposals requiring SBT were, by 1984, actively engaged and committed to inspecting IOPP certificates and SBT equipment. Other states have added pollution equipment to in-port inspections and begun establishing inspection agreements modeled on the European MOU (Anonymous 1993; Secretariat of the Memorandum of Understanding on Port State Control 1992). These monitoring efforts would not have arisen without MARPOL. Consider an alternative possibility in which European states, for example, sought to cooperate to enforce a varied array of domestic oil pollution regulations. Doing so would have been far more difficult without MARPOL's international system of IOPP certificates and equipment requirements. The equipment subregime thus succeeded in inducing monitoring not by placing requirements on those who would be reluctant to monitor them, but by providing rules that fit easily and cheaply into existing surveillance activities targeted at nonpollution policy concerns, such as safety and customs.

The equipment regime also facilitated information gathering and evaluation of the regime. Governments could more easily report on equipment enforcement than on discharge or facility enforcement. Annual government reports to IMO contain no data on ship or aerial surveillance efforts—such information is not even requested—but do contain data on equipment and certificate inspection efforts. Most countries, however, do not report to IMO at all. In contrast, the MOU reporting system has proved remarkably successful. Member states input daily inspection results to a central computer by modem or telex. Since 1982, all fourteen member states have reported most, if not all, of their annual inspections to the MOU, while less than half have provided annual enforcement reports to IMO (Mitchell 1994, 178–179). The European MOU database facilitated enforcement by allowing states to avoid reinspections and to focus inspections on tankers with recent deficiencies. The European MOU reassured states that they were not enforcing alone, helped states deploy enforcement resources more effectively, and focused attention on enforcement through regular meetings and reports. MARPOL's equipment standards provided a rule, compliance with which developed port states— that is, the states that had shown themselves to have incentives to conduct oil pollution enforcement—could monitor inexpensively and effectively.

Theoretically, by requiring states to respond to noncompliant tankers, either by detaining or barring them from port, MARPOL's equipment subregime made sanctions more likely and more potent. Port states were more likely to use these administrative sanctions because they eliminated the long delays common to legal proceedings, relied on less stringent standards of evidence, did not rely on prosecution by the flag state, and imposed "opportunity" costs on tanker owners (that is, lost business opportunities) far greater than the usual fines imposed. Thus, enforcement by even a few oil importing states put the noncompliant tanker owner at risk of detention or of the even more costly consequence of foregoing those oil markets altogether. In practice, however, very few states have detained tankers. Between 1984 and 1990, only seven states reported having ever detained a ship for MARPOL-related reasons.[19] Most states clearly do not feel obligated by MARPOL's requirement to detain tankers that threaten the marine environment. Those states that have detained ships, however, only began doing so after MARPOL took effect. We can exclude the possibility that domestic environmental pressures would have led these states to begin using detention even in the absence of MARPOL, as fines imposed for discharge violations stayed constant over this same period (Dempsey 1984; Peet 1992). Thus, detention provided a potent legal option for states that were inclined to enforce, but it created few new incentives or behaviors among states not so inclined.

The equipment subregime's response system was redundant, creating obstacles to buying a noncompliant tanker in the first place—because most classification societies would not classify and most insurers would not insure such a ship—and reinforcing these obstacles with the threat that, if one did own a noncompliant ship, it would be difficult to use it. These legal pressures for compliance were offset by economic pressures for noncompliance. SBT increased a tanker's capital costs by 5 percent and reduced its cargo-carrying capacity, with some minor offsetting benefits in reduced time spent in port (Waters, Heaver, and Verrier 1980, 124–25). In contrast, the capital and maintenance costs of COW were far less than those of SBT and these costs were offset by the capacity to deliver a higher percentage of cargo loaded. Comparisons of the three available technologies estimated LOT as saving $17,000 per voyage, COW as saving $9,000 per voyage, and SBT as costing $1,500 per voyage (Cummins, Logue, Tollison, and Willett 1975; Pearson 1975; Waters, Heaver, and Verrier 1980, 124–25).

Industry positions reinforce this assessment of the relative economic merits of each approach. Oil companies and shipping interests resisted SBT requirements until U.S. unilateralism made some regulation inevitable, oil companies pushed COW in 1978 as a more economical alternative than SBT,[20] and shippers have more recently opposed broadening the application of SBT requirements to older ships on economic grounds (Bergmeijer 1990, 13; MEPC 1991b; M'Gonigle and Zacher 1979, 134). As representatives of Shell and Lloyds noted in 1990, "left to himself, no owner will, understandably, wish to be placed at a commercial disadvantage to his competitors by introducing segregated ballast on his ships if the whole industry is not doing likewise" (Osborne and Ferguson 1990, 62). Indeed, some analysts in 1978 were predicting that compliance would be lower with COW requirements than with discharge standards and that "the degree of compliance with this new [SBT] requirement may be negligible" (Okidi 1978, 34).

Compliance patterns contradict such predictions based on economics, thereby confirming that SBT adoption was a response to MARPOL while

COW was a response to both economic and legal factors. Many oil companies installed COW before MARPOL required it, installed COW instead of SBT on all tankers allowed to do so, and pressed for COW's installation by independents (Drewry Shipping Consultants 1985, 21; Gray 1978, 12 and 92; MEPC 1981, 11; M'Gonigle and Zacher 1979, 262; Osborne and Ferguson 1990, 62; Waters, Heaver, and Verrier 1980, 95). Although COW was preferable to SBT, given the lower cost and greater future flexibility of LOT, tanker operators should have preferred LOT and hence deferred or refrained from installing COW (Drewry Shipping Consultants 1985, 21; Waters, Heaver, and Verrier 1980, 95). Independents have also installed COW as required even though, as tanker owners and operators, they pay the costs of installing and operating COW while cargo owners reap the benefits.

Tankers appear to have installed the lowest cost alternative that met MARPOL's equipment requirements. Available data confirm that they have installed SBT only when required, but have done so despite its costs. Few tankers had installed SBT in 1973 but industry analysts soon found tanker owners beginning to build to the new international standards (Drewry Shipping Consultants, 1981 25; Zacher 1978, 208). Two research groups document that almost all tankers have met both the SBT and COW requirements. A 1981 analysis found that most tankers did not install these technologies before they were required to do so by MARPOL, and those that were retrofitting tended to install COW rather than SBT (Drewry Shipping Consultants 1981, 25). By 1991, however, 94 percent of tankers built prior to 1980 had installed SBT or COW as required, 98 percent of tankers built between 1980 and 1982 installed SBT as required, and 98 percent of those built after 1982 installed both SBT and COW as required (Clarkson Research Studies 1990; Mitchell 1994). Government and industry experts concur that virtually all new tankers required to have SBT do have it, despite its expense and lack of cost-effectiveness (Bergmeijer 1990, 13; MEPC 1990c, 8; Sasamura 1990; Second International Conference on the Protection of the North Sea 1987, 57). These high percentages clearly indicate that essentially all tankers, whether registered in nations that supported SBT during negotiation or not, are complying with MARPOL's requirements. Most experts view SBT compliance as motivated by legal concerns and COW compliance as motivated by economic concerns, an assessment reinforced by the fact that most older tankers, given the choice, have chosen to retrofit with COW rather than SBT (MEPC 1990c, 8; Mitchell 1994).

This evidence undercuts an economic explanation of SBT installations and suggests that they and, to a lesser extent, COW installations were motivated by MARPOL requirements. Two rival hypotheses other than economic incentives, however, might more plausibly explain SBT adoption: hegemonic pressures and public opinion. Despite claims by some analysts, SBT adoption cannot be attributed to U.S. hegemony (Grolin 1988). Certainly, U.S. threats in 1972 and 1977 motivated the incorporation of SBT requirements into MARPOL and the United States has required tankers to retrofit more quickly than MARPOL has (Drewry Shipping Consultants 1985, 11). But available evidence suggests that American action alone would not have produced the all-but-universal compliance observed. The United States has never wielded hegemony in world oil markets. The U.S. share of new tankers launched, tanker registries, and oil imports has always been below 20 percent (Mitchell 1994, 278–279).[21] Countries with larger shares of these markets opposed SBT requirements in many cases. Given its position in the oil transportation market, the United States could effectively control, at most, one-third of the world tanker market. To produce observed SBT rates, it would therefore have had to force other states unconcerned about oil pollution to legislate and enforce SBT requirements in the absence of international agreement, but no evidence exists that the United States brought such pressure to bear. Other states would not have required COW or SBT, and certainly not both, on new tankers in the absence of MARPOL. Thus, without MARPOL, we might well expect some adoption of SBT, perhaps on the order of 30 or maybe even 50 percent to ensure the oil industry access to the lucrative U.S. market. U.S. unilateral action alone, however, would appear unlikely to have produced the 98 percent SBT adoption rates observed.

Paths by which increasing public concern could have led tankers to install SBT and COW without MARPOL also seem implausible. Oil companies might have perceived some political benefits in reducing their discharges. As environmental consciousness grew, companies undoubtedly became more concerned about having intentional pollution soil their reputations as well as birds and beaches (Moss 1963, 46). Without MAR-POL's requirements, however, it appears unlikely that tanker operators would choose to "prove their environmental credentials" by adopting SBT, the most costly alternative for reducing intentional pollution. Public concern often tells actors to do something, but agreed-upon rules and laws provide an important standard and focus in deciding what to do.[22]

In summary, the equipment subregime has caused a dramatic behavioral change by tanker owners and by the government authorities and classification societies that monitor the behavior of these owners. While MARPOL could not have produced such changes without facilitating factors such as existing infrastructures for monitoring behavior, U.S. hegemonic pressures, and environmental concern, neither could these factors by themselves have produced the same change in behavior in the absence of internationally agreed-upon rules delineating specific equipment requirements and deadlines.

Analytic Assessment

Exactly how did the regime cause these changes in the behavioral complex? Using the causal pathways delineated in the first chapter, this section evaluates which ones proved important, which proved unimportant, and how much interplay there was between mechanisms.

Oil pollution control represents a hard case; adoption of stringent rules, enforcement of those rules, and compliance with those rules were all unlikely. Collective action theory predicts that the powerful and concentrated oil transportation industry would resist the imposition of large pollution control costs to provide diffuse, nonquantifiable benefits to the public at large (McGinnis and Ostrom 1992; Olson 1965; Snidal 1985). Yet, industry efforts to oppose international regulation have proved surprisingly unsuccessful at preventing progress toward broader and more stringent rules.

Given the theoretical disfavor of command-and-control regulation as inefficient, one would expect movement away from, rather than toward, adoption of equipment standards. Collective action theory would also predict more monitoring and enforcement of discharge standards than equipment standards. The benefits of conducting coastal surveillance for compliance with discharge standards could be limited to the enforcing country; in contrast, all coastal countries benefited from any government that conducted equipment inspections (Axelrod and Keohane 1986). Nor were the economically more efficient discharge standards inherently difficult to monitor. Analysts at the time proposed placing international inspectors on all tankers to achieve the same level of environmental improvement as equipment regulations at significantly less cost (Cummins, Logue, Tollison and Willett 1975; Pearson 1975). Yet, naval and aerial surveillance programs are few and small while national and regional efforts to conduct and improve port state inspections for equipment are widespread and increasing in number.

Finally, compliance with any oil pollution control was unlikely, especially with equipment requirements. Claims that oil pollution involves a "low incentives to defect" coordination game (Ausubel and Victor 1992) are contradicted by the observed noncompliance with discharge standards, clearly demonstrating the continuing incentives that tanker owners and operators have to violate the rules. To the extent compliance did occur, it should have been more common with the discharge standards because of the availability of a cheaper and more cost-effective technology—LOT—than the SBT or COW required by MARPOL.

Against this backdrop of forces making regime impact unlikely, stringent rules were adopted over objections of powerful interests, governments and nonstate actors have monitored and enforced less efficient and less privatizable rules, and tankers have complied with more expensive regulations while often violating cheaper ones. This section evaluates each of the causal pathways in turn to assess their ability to explain the experience of this regime.

The Regime as a Utility Modifier

Although the success of the regime as a whole has been mixed, much of the success the regime has had can be attributed to its success at modifying the utility that state and substate actors placed on different alternative behaviors. In particular, the equipment subregime proved more successful than the discharge and reception facility subregimes because it modified the utilities of tanker owners in ways that the other subregimes failed to do. The equipment subregime convinced tanker owners that the expected costs of violation, that is, the likelihood of being detected without the equipment and the cost of being barred from or detained in port in response, exceeded the economic benefits of not installing the equipment. Such an analysis suggests that the equipment subregime more effectively deterred violation than did the discharge or reception facility subregimes.

Closer examination shows, however, that the equipment subregime changed behavior by reducing opportunities to violate rather than reducing the expected utility of violation. If the equipment subregime's primary causal mechanism had involved deterrence, we should expect to see either frequent detention of tankers by states and high compliance rates or an absence of detention and ongoing violations. In fact, however, available evidence confirms that tankers complied with MARPOL's 1980 and 1982 equipment compliance schedule even though no state detained a single tanker prior to 1983 (Mitchell 1994, chapter 8).

The equipment subregime restructured the behavioral complex to remove the MARPOL compliance decision from the exclusive purview of a single entity. Unlike the autonomous decision making of a captain considering whether to discharge illegally or a government considering whether to install a reception facility, a tanker owner deciding whether to install SBT and COW needed the cooperation of a builder, a classification society, and an insurer in an admittedly illegal act. After MARPOL adopted equipment rules, even ordering a tanker without SBT and COW became difficult. Tankers complied with MARPOL's equipment rules because private transactions prevented them from doing otherwise. In effect, the equipment subregime altered tanker owner behavior by removing noncompliance from their choice set. This alteration, however, demonstrates the interplay of various causal mechanisms. The equipment subregime's success at changing choice sets stemmed from its ability to alter the roles played by classification societies, insurers, and builders and the ability to alter these roles stemmed, in turn, from these actors view of the subregime as a legitimate authority for international regulation.

We can attribute the contrast between the increasingly vigorous efforts of governments to inspect for equipment with the ongoing absence of surveillance for illegal discharges to the regime's altering of utilities.

States enforced the former because it was far more cost-effective, providing greater behavioral and environmental impact at lower cost because it involved only minor modification to existing port inspection programs. In contrast, even a government that expended the resources necessary for a large surveillance program had no assurance that discharges would be either detected or deterred. Equipment standards also increased enforcement by decreasing the cost and difficulty of imposing sanctions. Any port authority could detain a noncompliant tanker or bar it from port much more quickly and cheaply than they could prosecute, convict, and collect fines from a tanker caught discharging illegally. Even though few states have detained ships, those that did, including the United States, have controlled significant fractions of the oil import market. This led even Soviet ships—which could have been built, classified, and insured without required equipment—to comply because of the fear that they would be unable to trade outside the Soviet Union. Discharge standards relied on flag and oil-loading state governments with few incentives to expend resources to deter discharge violations. Both activist governments as well as classification societies, insurers and builders that could either prevent or deter equipment violations lacked any similar power to prevent or detect, penalize, and hence deter, discharge standards. In the case of governments, those uninterested in pollution control did not become enforcers, but rather those with exogenous interests in enforcement enforced the most cost-effective rules of the convention. In the case of nonstate actors, the acceptance of international rules as legitimate, even when undesirable, produced constraints on the behavior of the actors whose behavior the regime targeted.

The reception facility subregime proved especially weak at altering the utility governments attached to ensuring facilities were available. Even when tanker captains revealed noncompliance with requirements for reception facilities, governments had few incentives to, and rarely did, criticize other governments for such failures. Nor were options available to force compliance, and governments never seriously considered providing a collective funding mechanism to pay for their installation. The failure to provide reception facilities would tend to lead tankers to discharge just prior to entering port, oiling nearby beaches. States concerned about such discharges would provide their own facilities but had no incentive to pay for their provision elsewhere. Those not concerned about such discharges had no incentive to provide them. The current distribution of reception facilities—primarily in developed countries—reflects a coincidence of the interests and capacity to provide facilities similar to what one might well expect even absent any international regime of pollution control.

Taken together, the efforts of these actors either altered the choice sets or utilities of tanker owners to make equipment installation, while expensive, the behavior of choice. In contrast, such modification of utilities was simply less feasible with discharge and reception facility standards.

The Regime as an Enhancer of Cooperation

Utility modification played an important role in the regime's success at altering behavior. The ability of the regime to enhance cooperation has had little impact on state or tanker operator behavior but, instead, has largely been evident in the adoption of numerous regulations that one would not otherwise have expected to be adopted, or certainly not as rapidly as they were. The regime has generated progressively more stringent regulations by providing a ready-made forum that enhanced cooperation. The Marine Environment Protection Committee and its predecessors kept the attention of a body of experts focused on issues of marine pollution from ships. When exogenous forces, such as dramatic tanker accidents, a growing consensus for environmental protection, or unilateral regulatory threats from a powerful state arose, the regime provided the capacity to respond quickly and knowledgeably to channel such pressures into new policies. And new regulations could readily be added to the existing regime structure.[23] Activist states also regularly proposed amendments that would not otherwise have reached the international agenda, as evidenced in recent proposed amendments to regulate air pollution from ships. Enhancing cooperation among tanker owners and operators was unlikely to influence behavior, since these actors had few exogenous incentives to alter their behavior. The ease of cooperation, however, did facilitate and even encourage governments to promulgate more environmental regulations.

Proposals to broaden or strengthen regime rules, if backed by sufficient environmental concern, resonated with the regime's and MEPC's mandate and were adopted as new regulations. Since these rules were not revoked as environmental concern waned, the regime provided a one-way ratchet by which (1) stronger rules were adopted during periods of high issue salience, (2) regime norms of precedence and legitimacy prevented subsequent revocation or weakening, and (3) adoption of more effective rules prevented actors from simply ignoring the rules during periods of low issue salience. Proposals to retreat from existing environmental protection received little serious consideration.[24]

This causal pathway is not easily isolated. The institutional capability to facilitate cooperation would have gone unused if member states had not accorded the regime the legitimacy and authority to act as the only appropriate forum for international discussion of vessel-source pollution. IMO gained legitimacy over time by being responsive to both economic and environmental concerns, and because it had responsibility for all areas of international shipping, creating linkages that reduced incentives for parties to leave the table in response to regulations they opposed.

States have raised issues of vessel-source pollution in IMO for two reasons. First, all vessel-source pollution poses collective action problems that no state can solve alone. A state facing domestic political pressures to address such a problem must collaborate with others, but would have found this difficult had no regime existed. Second, governments facing domestic pressures to address pollution generally face countervailing pressures against regulation by industries that seek to avoid being placed at a competitive disadvantage. As the experiences of the United Kingdom in the 1950s and 1960s and of the United States after the mid-1960s show, industries choosing between regulation and no regulation prefer the latter, but industries choosing between international regulation and unilateral regulation prefer the former. Given the structure of the incentives in this behavioral complex, the regime altered the ease with which states could achieve cooperative arrangements. The regime enhanced cooperation by reducing transaction costs that would otherwise have inhibited the frequent amendment and revision of regime rules. Indeed, without the regime, it would have been more difficult and more unlikely for more stringent and broader regulations to have been adopted.

In the absence of the 1954 OILPOL treaty, an international regime on intentional oil pollution or marine pollution certainly could have been created. The UN Conference on the Human Environment in 1972 and growing environmentalism in the 1970s, especially in the United States, would surely have produced some form of international marine pollution regulation. The preexisting regime for intentional oil pollution and the forum of the IMO for negotiation, however, made those efforts bear fruit much faster and produced more stringent and effective rules, thus avoiding pitfalls that would have plagued a new regime.

The one area in which the regime enhanced cooperation with impacts on behavior is in the realm of transparency (Mitchell 1998). Violations of equipment standards, moreso than of discharge or reception facility standards, were inherently transparent and were made more so by the explicit granting of survey and inspection rights to classification societies and port state governments. This transparency made accurate and comprehensive monitoring of a fleet's compliance far easier than it was with respect to discharge standards. The transparency also reassured each owner that others were complying. Conscientious operators who desired to comply with the discharge standards faced the classic free-rider fear that others would gain competitive advantage through undetected and unsanctioned violations, a fear not faced under the equipment standards because violations were so transparent.

The Regime as a Bestower of Authority
The regime's success at modifying utilities, particularly of tanker owners and operators, depended in large part on the authority and legitimacy accorded to the regime and its regulations. Thus, the regime's ability to influence behavior by modifying utilities depended, in part, on authority the regime already had within the maritime community. States' perceptions of IMO as the only authoritative voice in regulating maritime policy in general gave IMO rules on marine pollution more rapid and broader legitimacy in the shipping community. Counterfactually, a separate, strictly environmental secretariat administering OILPOL and MARPOL would probably have produced greater efforts to address marine pollution from sources other than vessels, particularly land-based sources, an important task that IMO has consistently considered as beyond its mandate. Such an organization, however, would have faced more industry resistance than did IMO in response to stringent rules because it would

have had less legitimacy with the industry, and the linkage with other maritime issues would have been reduced.

As already noted, classification societies based their classification criteria on IMO rules. Shipbuilders incorporated IMO rules into ship designs. This was true for all IMO requirements that addressed safety, labor, and other regulatory areas as well as pollution. The legitimacy accorded such rules folded into a routinization of behavior among classification societies and shipbuilders that created an institutional and market context in which noncompliance became less of an option. Insurers as well had few incentives to establish premiums along lines contrary to those established by international law.

The power of the regime as a bestower of authority is evident in the higher levels of port state control than of aerial surveillance. The European, Latin American, Asia-Pacific, and Carribean Memorandums of Understanding have all been agreements to increase port state inspections for violations of all IMO agreements. IMO rules facilitated and encouraged this "nested cooperation" by providing ready-made and legitimate rules that nations could agree to enforce without having to negotiate their content. Governments concerned about a problem find it difficult to enforce rules other than the existing international standards. Once a government became concerned about intentional oil pollution, it enforced MARPOL's rules. Had MARPOL's equipment provisions been developed outside of the IMO context, they might well not be so automatically included in the inspections mandated by these regional agreements.[25] The subregime did not cause reluctant states to institute inspection procedures but it did structure what things they looked for in an inspection once exogenous factors led them to institute such a program. Governments found they could monitor and respond to equipment violations more easily than discharge violations or reception facility violations.

The Regime as a Learning Facilitator

Given the facilitation of learning that the Barents Sea and acid precipitation regimes have produced (see chapters 3 and 4), the oil pollution regime is remarkable for the lack of evidence of such a pathway of influence. Ideas and perceptions of the environmental problem have been driven by exogenous political and social forces that the regime has not, and probably could not have, created. The regime has sought to directly influence material conditions rather than to influence them through altering ideas (see chapter 1, figure 1.1). The regime has rarely collected data to identify trends in marine environmental health. The regime has not even sought to improve its economic effectiveness.[26]

The absence of changes in values and perceptions of the environmental problem is evident in the lack of much improvement beyond that required by the regime's explicit rules. Nothing like LRTAP's "overcompliance" is evident (see chapter 4). The regime failed to internalize a concern for the marine environment, as evident in the unwillingness of existing tankers to install SBT technology when not required and the continuing violation of discharge standards.

The regime has, indirectly, induced oil companies to develop and promote processes and technologies that met the environmental goal of reducing oil pollution while reducing costs. Oil companies only developed and promoted the 1950s-era LOT procedure in response to the 1962 amendments requiring equipment on all tankers unless pollution was reduced. Similarly, they began touting the environmental benefits of COW, though developed in the late 1960s, only after MARPOL required SBT on large new tankers. Thus, regulation induced technological developments that led to enhanced ecological effectiveness. In contrast to the LRTAP story, however, learning has been largely limited to developing solutions rather than understanding the problem and has largely reflected indirect efforts to reduce the costs of regulatory compliance.

Although the regime has not moved toward better understanding of the problem, it has learned from experience with past operation of the regime to produce more effective regulations. Put in the causal language of this volume, a regime initially focused on intentional oil pollution has developed rules that (1) applied to more sources of oil and other marine pollutants, (2) promised greater environmental protection if industry complied, and (3) were more likely to be enforced and obeyed.[27] Although the power of unilateral threats by activist states explains the fact of regime progress, the past experience with the regime explains the shape of that progress. Consider the counterfactual: without evidence that tanker operators were often disregarding discharge standards, pressures for oil pollution control would have been unlikely to lead to strict equipment regulations. Even if stricter controls were adopted, the command and control approach of equipment standards would have been an unlikely first step. Acceptance of such a regulatory approach depended on the knowledge that less costly and more efficient operational approaches had failed to achieve results. Regime learning is also evident in MARPOL's detention provisions, specified compliance dates for SBT installation and reception facility provision, and provisions for tacit acceptance of amendments, all of which sought to remedy failures of earlier treaty provisions.

The Regime as a Role Definer
Little, if any, of this regime's success can be attributed to a process of defining actors' roles. The oil pollution regime has taken advantage of the incentives of actors in existing roles, rather than defining those roles. The regime played on existing relationships, interests, and standard operating procedures among classification societies, insurers, and shipbuilders to transform them into regime monitors and enforcers with powers that differed from and, in many ways, exceeded those of governments. Classification societies, for example, have more access to information about tankers than governments do, but must build reputations for high standards to recruit new business. At the same time, neither classification societies nor insurers had to change their behavior significantly to support the subregime.

The discharge and reception facility subregimes proved highly ineffective at redefining states' roles. The regime failed to convince oil loading states to conduct the inspections needed to monitor the total discharge limits of 1969. Governments have proved remarkably reluctant to assume the role of reception facility providers in their own countries, let alone the role of reception facility financier in developing countries. The regime also tried, without success, to induce flag states and oil-loading states to enforce discharge provisions. Flag states and oil-loading states would not enforce aggressively enough to deter discharge violations. Yet, jealous guarding of flag state sovereignty prevented the regime from bestowing those responsibilities on port or coastal states.

Modifying the roles of classification societies allowed the regime to avoid encroaching on flag state jurisdiction and sovereignty while skirting the problems raised by the lack of resources in many flag states with large tanker registries. Equipment standards succeeded by giving monitoring duties to classification societies, who incorporated such standards into their inspections, not because of a conscious calculation of the benefits of these provisions, nor from any fear of penalties for not doing so, but because most classification societies' inspection standards match international law as a matter of course and standard operating procedures. For them, agreed-upon international rules set a standard, deviation from which required explanation.[28] In turn, insurance companies decided whether to insure a ship based on its being classified. MARPOL essentially "deputized" classification societies and insurers to monitor and enforce its equipment standards.

The Regime as a Source of Internal Realignment

The oil pollution regime's effectiveness also owes little to inducing domestic political realignments. In activist states, like the United Kingdom early on and the United States more recently, the regime provided politicians facing domestic pressure for marine pollution control with an alternative to unilateral regulation. International policies could achieve better environmental protection and the attendant political benefits without imposing economic costs on domestic industries. For oil companies in such countries, the regime provided a forum whose existence could be pointed to as a reason not to impose unilateral domestic regulation but, failing that, provided a second chance to shape shipping regulations. Oil companies proposed and supported COW and SBT because they provided economic benefits relative to existing alternatives. Yet, economics alone would not have lead them to support international requirements, as evident in their consistent resistance to mandate these techniques. Only in the context of threats of unilateral action and an environmental regime that was promulgating increasingly stringent regulations did industry see international regulation as an attractive alternative.

In nonactivist states, the regime appears to have had little influence over domestic political alignments. Most governments enforced IMO rules over time because the regime provided an available and authoritative guideline for enforcement in response to growing environmental concern at home rather than because the regime prompted that growing environmental concern. Exogenous factors, rather than the regime, prompted governments to want to "look green." Once this concern developed, the regime's rules had the legitimacy necessary to make them one of the standards against which "looking green" was assessed.

Overall Assessment

This regime's successes and failures demonstrate an interplay of several of the six causal mechanisms proposed (see chapter 1). The regime enhanced cooperation by providing a forum that made promulgating regulations to combat vessel-source marine pollution easier and quicker. Although the regime did not "bestow" authority, it did use the legitimacy and authority that states and nonstate actors accorded it to develop international regulations. The regime eventually developed equipment regulations that succeeded at modifying the utilities of tanker owners and, thereby, tanker operators after earlier discharge regulations had failed in the effort to influence tanker operators directly. The regime did not so much "define" roles for different actors as it took advantage of the regime-compatible incentives of relevant actors' existing roles. The regime showed some learning in devising new regulations and strategies for implementation, but the pathways of learning facilitation, role defining, and internal realignment contribute far less to our understanding of the success of the oil pollution regime than those involving utility, authority, and roles.

Attempting to analyze the regime within the structure of the six causal pathways of this volume also points up some difficulties with the framework. The equipment subregime operated primarily by changing the alternatives available to tanker owners by taking advantage of the existing roles and procedures of classification societies, who adopted the regime's rules into their standard inspection programs because they saw these rules as authoritative. The resultant unwillingness of builders, classification societies, and insurers to assist an owner interested in building and operating a noncompliant tanker essentially removed the option of buying such a tanker. This pathway can be viewed as modifying tanker owners' utilities. This case suggests, however, that there may be some value in distinguishing between regimes that raise the costs of an option so that it is not chosen from those which effectively remove the option from the available choices.[29] A secondary, supporting pathway for the regime provided authoritative, but low-cost, methods of implementing the agreement, thereby facilitating effective monitoring and sanctioning by governments inclined to do so. The effectiveness of the equipment subregime relative to the discharge subregime reflects the lessons learned by the regime from the failure of many efforts to improve the discharge subregime.

Several characteristics of the behavioral complex appear to have conditioned the success of this regime. In some ways, this complex limited regime effectiveness. The ability of oil companies to resist stringent regulation and the weakness of public concern in most states before the 1970s clearly slowed regime progress. The deference given to flag states under international ocean law hobbled and delayed efforts by those few states concerned with intentional oil pollution to gain the legal authority needed to combat it.

In other respects, however, the behavioral complex fostered regime success. Progress made when strong concern arose in powerful states, such as the United Kingdom and the United States, would not have occurred had strong concern arisen among developing states. Because oil pollution involves private international trade, the opportunities for inducing behavioral change were greater than they are in other issue areas. Imagine if all tankers were government-owned: equipment violations would have been more prevalent because transporting governments would have been more likely than industries to consider international rules as infringements on their sovereignty and enforcing governments would have been more wary about detaining noncompliant tankers. Market characteristics such as the private information infrastructures of classification societies and insurers also proved crucial to the effectiveness of MARPOL's equipment requirements, but are not paralleled in many other issue areas. The fact that tanker accidents produce high-visibility, catalytic political events also made regulatory progress easier than it would have been otherwise. The short-lived outcries following catastrophic accidents have placed the issue on the international agenda with enough force to override objections by powerful states like France and Japan.

Finally and fortunately, IMO's relatively slow pace of progress toward effective regulation does not appear to have irrevocably harmed the marine environment. As has been noted in regard to depletion of the stratospheric ozone layer, a regime that appears quite effective at changing behavior may be created too late to prevent the environmental damage that motivated its creation (Parson 1993). The ocean has absorbed and biodegraded significantly more oil than the world's population to date has discharged, allowing time for the regime to learn how to become more effective.

Conclusions

Has the intentional oil pollution control regime been effective? Yes and no. On the positive side, despite a slow start, the regime adopted quite effective rules in MARPOL 73/78. MARPOL has restructured the tanker fleet so that it is far less likely to discharge oil intentionally. The new regulations led classification societies, insurers, port state governments, and tanker owners to undertake actions they would not have undertaken in the absence of the regime. The regime can take some credit for increasing the number of reception facilities available today and for expanding its regulations to include accidental oil spills, oil platforms, and a wide array of other marine and air pollutants from ships. The regime has been most effective when targeting the actions of nonstate actors in ways that take account of the existing incentives and abilities of governments and corporations. Progress, when it has occurred, has required the coupling of pressures from powerful states with evaluation of previous experience to direct efforts toward successful new policies.

On the negative side, for three decades the regime relied on discharge standards that remained largely ineffective at altering tanker operations. This ineffectiveness resulted from poor choices of policy strategies as well as from constraints imposed by the larger regime of ocean law that circumscribed the roles of port, coastal, and flag states. The limitation of IMO's regulatory mandate to ships has undoubtedly delayed attention to land-based and other sources of ocean pollution. Even today, reception facilities remain uncommon in precisely the areas where they are most needed—special areas and oil-loading states. Reporting on enforcement, compliance, and environmental quality also remain poor.

This case highlights two concluding insights about how regimes influence behavior. First, the case has brought to light an important variant of the causal mechanism of regimes modifying utilities, namely that regimes also can alter the alternatives available to actors. Regimes can act to prevent violations of their provisions as well as to deter such violations. Regimes, during negotiation, can also structure debate about alternative policies to exclude those that backtrack while facilitating discussion of those that move the regime forward. Second, the case has highlighted that regimes often influence behavior through a complex of causal mechanisms rather than a single one. The experience in vessel-source oil pollution cautions that accurately understanding how a regime achieved its aims requires careful attention to the variety of potential causal pathways to assess how much influence each has, and how the different causal pathways interact to contribute to regime success.

Notes

The authors would like to thank four anonymous reviewers as well as Oran Young, Gail Osherenko, and the other authors in this volume for invaluable assistance and suggested improvements to earlier drafts of this chapter. We also want to thank Michelle Sieff for her helpful research during the early stages of the writing.

Ronald Mitchell is an assistant professor of political science at the University of Oregon. He can be contacted at rmitchel@oregon.uoregon.edu.

Moira McConnell is a professor of law at Dalhousie Law School and is director of Dalhousie Law School's Marine Environmental Law Programme. She is also a member of the Negotiation and Conflict Management Programme. She can be contacted at mmcconnell@kilcom1.ucis.dal.ca.

Alexei Roginko is a research associate with the Institute of World Economy and International Relations, Russian Academy of Sciences. He can be contacted at alexeir@netfinity.cig.ru.

Ann Barrett has been an attorney with the Nova Scotia Government Employees Union since 1996. Prior to that she was an attorney in private practice in Halifax, Nova Scotia. She can be contacted at annb@nsgeu.ns.ca.

1. These figures adjust James E. Moss's 1963 estimate to account for the smaller amount of oil transported in 1953 (Moss 1963, 51; Pritchard 1987, 76).

2. Norway had seen a major oil spill in 1958 (Kirby 1968, 217). Many "fairly large-scale oil pollution incidents" in 1960 prompted U.K. research on cleanup methods (Wardley-Smith 1969, 27). One survey reported 91 tanker groundings and 200 collisions between June 1964 and April 1967 (Kirby 1968, 218).

3. Further improvements to enforcement were opposed by maritime states, including the Soviet bloc, European states, and flags of convenience, who sought to protect free navigation and developing states who sought to strengthen their rights as coastal states in the Law of the Sea Conference (M'Gonigle and Zacher 1979, 233).

4. Many port states added pollution control equipment to normal inspection procedures and began coordinating inspections with other countries, even though they specifically refrained from cooperating to detect discharge violations. Flag states accepted port states barring their ships from port or detaining them because such administrative sanctions did not directly infringe on flag state legal prerogatives.

5. A "special area" involves IMO-designated areas deserving special environmental protection, and facing more stringent pollution control requirements.

6. As one example, estimates of discharges from tanker operations decreased 35 percent between the National Academy of Sciences' 1971 and 1980 estimates, but even larger decreases occurred in their estimates of offshore production (38 percent), municipal waste and runoff (56 percent), atmospheric fallout (50 percent), and even natural sources (58 percent).

7. These include private industry conventions—The Tanker Owners Voluntary Agreement Concerning Liability for Oil Pollution (TOVALOP 1969), and the Contract Regarding an Interim Supplement to Tanker Liability for Oil Pollution (CRISTAL 1971)—and intergovernmental conventions—the International Convention Relating to Intervention on the High Seas in Cases of Oil Pollution Casualties (1969) and its 1973 protocol, the International Convention on Civil Liability for Oil Pollution Damage (1969) and its 1976 protocol, the International Convention on the Establishment of an International Fund for Compensation for Oil Pollution Damage (1971) and its 1984 protocol, and the International Convention on Oil Pollution Preparedness and Response (1990).

8. Given the average slop generated by a tanker, authorities could assume any tanker returning for a new load of cargo with completely clean tanks had discharged slops in excess of the 1/15,000th limit.

9. As early as 1926, experts had noted that enforcing discharge standards was simultaneously difficult and essential (IMCO 1977; Pritchard 1987, 23).

10. Although states had detected 705 violations, 80 percent were within three miles of shore, despite the agreed upon fifty-mile zone, and most of the enforcement effort came from just two states, Britain and Germany (IMCO 1961).

11. Authorities could not even assess a discharge's oil content after it entered the ocean and so had to forego prosecution of all cases that did not clearly involve discharges well in excess of the 100 ppm standard.

12. Germany is the only state to report having referred violations to a flag state based on the absence of "proof of the whereabouts" of oil wastes (MEPC 1990a, MEPC 1991a).

13. Some states rejected even weak language requiring states to "ensure the provision" of reception facilities because they did not want to assume "any financial

responsibility" for building and operating such facilities (Okidi 1978, 33; U.S. Congress 1963, 19; Pritchard 1987, 128).

14. Analysts have estimated costs at $3 to $20 million per facility, $140 million for needed Mediterranean facilities, and over $500 million for all developing countries (Montfort 1984, 249; Placci 1984, 296–302; UN 1992).

15. In 1984, European states had only begun "looking into the possibility of eventual financial support for the development of reception facilities" (MEPC 1984). By 1996, IMO had yet to do more than urge member states to submit proposals for "financing schemes for reception facilities" (Anonymous 1996).

16. The IMCO secretary-general responded to a Tunisian request for assistance by reminding "delegations that the financial burden for the installation of facilities should be borne by the countries concerned" (MEPC 1980).

17. Systematic analyses of the complex and often inconsistent IMCO/IMO data are difficult. Available figures probably overestimate the percentage of ports with reception facilities. U.S. statistics are isolated to prevent its 1990 report of major increases in numbers of ports and facilities from skewing the data. Other countries have also changed the detail of reporting over time—e.g., Norway reported on nine ports in 1963, four ports in 1973, twenty-two ports in 1980, and ninety-six ports in 1990—but have never identified a port that lacked reception facilities.

18. The committees of shipowners that run classification societies have a vested interest in ensuring that their vessels are not kept out of operation by unfavorable reports (M'Gonigle and Zacher 1979, 331).

19. Most states have done so only rarely, and only states with traditions of rigorous enforcement—the United States, United Kingdom, and Germany—have used detention often.

20. Mandatory and immediate SBT retrofitting made economic sense for independent tanker owners in Greece and Scandinavia who were hardest hit by the tanker market slump after 1973's oil price rise: it would have helped reactivate much of their laid-up tanker tonnage by reducing the active fleet's capacity by 10 to 25 percent (M'Gonigle and Zacher 1979, 123 and 135). Most oil company fleets remained fully employed during this period and, not surprisingly, opposed calls for retrofitting as being unnecessary and expensive.

21. Indeed, the U.S. share of new tankers launched and tanker registries was both low and declining at the time the United States became concerned over oil pollution.

22. Whatever the impact of these public pressures, they would have had almost no impact on independent tanker operators who had little public reputation to lose (Drewry Shipping Consultants 1981, 35).

23. For example, MARPOL controlled intentional pollution from offshore oil rigs simply by defining them into the regime as a form of vessel, an unlikely outcome in the absence of an existing set of regulations for vessels.

24. For example, a 1960s oil industry proposal to replace mandatory discharge rules with voluntary industry use of LOT was rejected in favor of even stricter

constraints on discharges, and such a proposal has never surfaced again (Kirby 1968). Similarly, actors who opposed all equipment requirements in 1973 restrained themselves to calls for requiring COW instead of SBT in 1978, and even then they were forced to accept both technologies on new tankers.

25. As with classification societies, governments appear to have decided to enforce all IMO treaty provisions that can be inspected through in-port procedures, rather than to enforce only those provisions they supported during negotiation.

26. Indeed, at least one analyst has argued that the regime has been inefficient, too costly, and has expended too many resources for too few environmental benefits (Pearson 1975).

27. For example, the United Kingdom's 1962 proposal for an oceanwide discharge ban on all new tankers could have been accepted only in the context of existing zonal prohibitions on all tankers. The 1969 requirement for total discharge limits was a conscious, if unsuccessful, attempt to "fix" the increasingly obvious difficulties of monitoring existing discharge rules. The United States' 1973 proposals for equipment requirements directly responded to the failure of OILPOL's discharge standards. The 1977 Carter Initiatives merely extended existing SBT requirements from new tankers to all tankers.

28. Although some inspections might well certify ships not meeting these standards, the baseline inspection included and complied with them.

29. For example, the nonproliferation regime's technology denial program seeks, however unsuccessfully, to *prevent* states from acquiring nuclear weapons because, at least in cases such as Iraq, it appears that *deterring* states from doing so would be unlikely to succeed (Mitchell 1997).

3

The Barents Sea Fisheries

Olav Schram Stokke, Lee G. Anderson, and Natalia Mirovitskaya

Introduction

This chapter will assess the effectiveness of the Barents Sea fisheries regime. We are particularly interested in identifying institutional features and behavioral processes that have contributed to its effectiveness or lack thereof. The core of the Barents Sea regime is formed by its specification of rights, rules, and recognized practices for making collective decisions. Prior to 1977, the areas in question were international waters beyond 12 miles, and most of the fishery resources were subject to multilateral management. The introduction of 200-mile exclusive economic zones (EEZ) by Norway and the Soviet Union restricted considerably the membership of the regime. A joint Soviet–Norwegian, and later Russo–Norwegian, Fisheries Commission makes authoritative recommendations on operational restrictions and quota allocations. A point we shall return to, this is in line with the 1982 Law of the Sea Convention (UNLOSC), signed but not ratified by both countries.

As elaborated in chapter 1, we shall address regime effectiveness along two dimensions: behavioral impact and solutions to the problem that the regime was set up to address. These two dimensions are closely connected: the only way regimes can contribute to problem solving is by affecting the behavior of actors who are relevant to the problem. That problem must be specified in depth in each given case. Here, this is done by delineating the fundamental problems of fisheries management, propped up by the stated and some nonstated regime goals; in the Barents Sea fisheries context, this yields a discussion focusing on jurisdiction, conservation, and allocation.

A systematic analysis requires a solid data base. Until recently, due to the potential military relevance of the fishery complex, no official Soviet information was made publicly available on employment, capital investment, number and gross tonnage of vessels, and composition of fishing fleets. Although the Barents Sea fisheries is among the key industries of Murmansk County, as late as 1990 an analytical review of the regional economic situation failed to provide detailed data on it. The longstanding tradition of secrecy on the polar ocean activities of the Soviet Union was not broken until August 1991. A large part of the files of the Committee of Fisheries are still closed, but we are now able to get information on the case from regional sources. But while publicly available, the reliability of Russian data are quite low due to the economic difficulties and the fluid structure of management and administration.

In the next section, we present the behavioral complex addressed by this fisheries regime, including key actors and the challenges they face in managing the Barents Sea resources. Then we lay out the core elements of the bilateral fisheries regime and specify in greater detail the problems it is meant to address. In section three we assess the effectiveness of the regime by bringing out the extent to which and how it helps solving those problems; and section four relates this causal analysis to the set of pathways and mechanisms laid out in chapter 1. Indeed, the significant changes that have occurred in the status of the stocks targeted by the regime, the relatively long period of its existence, and the highly radical changes that have occurred in the Russian behavioral complex in later years join to make the Barents Sea case a suitable ground for specifying and judging hypotheses about the effectiveness of international regimes.

Problems of Fisheries Management in the Barents Sea

The Barents Sea is among the most biologically productive oceans in the world—and it is also quite vulnerable. Sea-water temperatures are low, which slows down evaporation processes and may serve to reduce the bacteriological degeneration of pollutants. And there are extreme fluctuations in light intensity. Variation in the water inflow from the Atlantic impose continual shifts in temperatures and ice extension. The sea's ecosystems are quite simple, in that there are few organisms on each link of the chain, so the disruption of one may have serious implications for the rest of the system. All considered, the sea's marine environment is highly unstable and the ecosystems, extending into the adjacent Norwegian Sea, are marked by huge fluctuations, especially at higher trophic levels. The major commercial ground fisheries target cod, haddock, and saithe, while the pelagic fisheries take Norwegian spring-spawning herring, capelin, and blue whiting.

The Behavioral Complex

Although the Barents Sea fisheries complex is simpler than in many other ocean areas, since the harvest is largely taken by two states only, a complicating feature is the fact that the area is extremely sensitive militarily. This is due to the importance of nuclear submarines deployed in northern waters for the maintenance of the strategic deterrence throughout the Cold War period. One consequence of this sensitivity is helpful to fisheries management, namely that both coastal states have been eager to avoid unnecessary political tension in the area. Three other circumstances should also be noted when delineating the challenge of fisheries management of the Barents Sea stocks. Parts of the maritime areas in question are disputed among the two coastal states. Second, fisheries remain cornerstone industries both in northern Norway and in northwest Russia. And third, in both countries the fisheries industries are well organized into the management process itself. We shall elaborate on these points further before defining more closely the nature of the problems addressed by the Barents Sea fisheries regime.

Norway and Russia have still not settled their disagreement over whether the marine delimitation should follow a line of equidistance or the sector line, the latter supported by the Russian side. At stake is a disputed area of some 155,000 square kilometers where fishing grounds are rich and the prospects for finding petroleum quite good.[1] Because of the link in international law between the accepted exercise of management authority and the strengthening of jurisdictional claims, this dispute is hampering resource management in the Barents Sea. Another jurisdictional problem concerns the EEZ around Svalbard. This issue is rooted in a long-standing and contested claim on the part of the Soviet Union, and later Russia, that it is entitled to a privileged status among the signatories to the 1920 Svalbard Treaty; that treaty gives sovereignty over Svalbard to Norway with some specified limitations.[2] Norway argues that there is nothing in the treaty to suggest that Norway does not have unilateral management authority on Svalbard, only an obligation not to discriminate against foreigners in certain issue areas. Furthermore, Norway claims that this obligation is limited to the onshore areas and territorial waters and does not concern the EEZ (Churchill and Ulfstein 1992). For its part, the Soviet Union never recognized Norway's right to establish unilaterally a management zone around Svalbard and most other signatory states have also filed reservations. This is why Norway has implemented only a nondiscriminatory fisheries protection zone in the area, although it claims an EEZ. Cautious not to act in a way that would acknowledge Norwegian authority in the area, Moscow has prohibited Soviet and later Russian fishermen from reporting their catches in the Svalbard zone to Norwegian authorities. Nor do they sign inspection papers. This has made every Soviet and Russian trawler inspected in the zone a formal lawbreaker and they receive due warnings from the Norwegian Coast Guard.

Yet another unsettled jurisdictional issue relates to the small pocket of high seas found inbetween the Norwegian and Russian exclusive economic zones. Since 1991, vessels from various third countries have been targeting cod in this so-called Loophole. The fraction of the stock found in the Loophole is very low and most of those third countries have no historic record of fishing in the area. Both Norwegian and Russian authorities have expressed concern over the growth of unregulated fishing in the area, and at the 1993 commission meeting they agreed to increase their presence in the area in terms of control vessels. Third parties such as Greenland, the Faroe Islands and the European Communities have, after bilateral negotiations with Norway, agreed to stay away from the Loophole, whereas states such as Iceland are currently under political pressure from both Norway and Russia to do so. The dispute has been embedded in the international process of establishing clearer rules for the management of stocks in high seas areas, which culminated with the 1995 United Nations Fish Stocks Agreement.[3]

Another important feature of the behavior complex is the regional economic significance of the fisheries sector. In northern Norway, the fisheries industry still accounts for somewhere between 5 and 10 percent of employment; and in the county of Finnmark, as much as two-thirds of the industrial employment is found in the fisheries (Hersoug 1992, 235). While only one-tenth of the Norwegian population lives in these northern parts, roughly half of the 27,000 active fishermen do. Almost 90 percent of the catch is exported, and in export value, fisheries products is the third biggest item in Norway; only the petroleum and metallurgical industries are bigger exporters (*Statistisk årbok* 1992, 269–73). In northwest Russia, too, and especially in the Kola peninsula, the fishing industry forms the backbone of the economy. Throughout the Soviet period, immense capital infusions were aimed at developing and modernizing the overall national marine power, considered to be of vital strategic importance. In the early 1990s, the Soviet fisheries complex accounted for some 30 percent of the total value of industrial production in the area and for 20 percent of the industrial labor force (Luzin 1992); these figures do not include support functions such as the building and maintenance of vessels. Some 80,000 were employed by the fisheries association Sevryba (North Fish), which at that time organized most of the fisheries industry in the northern Soviet region (Davidsen 1992, 72). Of these, roughly 30,000 were working on vessels, many in distant waters. Sevryba catches reached 1.6 million tons in 1990, and more than 90 percent of the production was exported to other regions of the country or abroad (Luzin 1992). The subsequent domestic food shortage and growing problems of access to other fishing grounds further enhanced the significance of the Barents Sea fisheries for the northwest Russian economy. In Arkhangelsk, fisheries play a far more modest role, and there they also rely more on distant waters than does the Murmansk fleet.

Although there are some notable differences between Norway and Russia regarding the structure of the fisheries industries in the north, both countries have a tradition of considerable involvement of industrial actors in the decision-making process of managing fisheries resources. For most of the period under scrutiny, the Soviet Ministry of Fisheries was the principal orchestrator of five regional fisheries combines.[4] One of these was Sevryba which, on the assumption that economic efficiency is enhanced by concentration, included the fishing industries of Murmansk and Arkhangelsk counties as well as the republic of Karelia.[5] A highly complex and vertically integrated organization, Sevryba was dominated by four rather independent branches: the two vessel fleet organizations Tralflot and Murmanrybprom, largely operating trawlers; Sevrybkholod-flot, with shipyards, transportation vessels, and tankers; and one unit supplying various onshore functions, including port services, processing plants, and construction works. The northern fisheries complex used to be a miniature of the Soviet command-and-control system. All activities of its branches from stock surveys to retail stores were planned, regulated, and reviewed from above. While not exclusive, the role of the Fisheries Ministry in drawing up the main parameters of industry development was momentous. Sevryba was essentially one of the tools in this centralized structure and hence was governed in line with ministry priorities. Vessels and equipment were purchased by the state and provided to the industry free of charge; hence, these costs were not included in cost of production. Research activities and technical improvements were planned from above and financed from the state budget. Thus, the industry on the whole worked in a rather artificial economic climate in which product prices were only vaguely related to the actual costs of production.

Since 1990, the structure of Russian fisheries has undergone radical changes. In accordance with the Law on State Enterprise all economic functions were transferred to the company level; and in 1992 Sevryba was privatized and registered as a joint-stock company owned by its component organizations. Most parts of the huge northern fishery complex were turned into private concerns held by stockholders (Baskakov 1993). Once a key actor in all aspect of the industry, the Committee on Fisheries now concentrates primarily on a management framework (Korelsky 1993). In the last years of the Soviet Union, the State Committee on the Environment had tried to take over regulatory and control functions in the fisheries sector. But while a 1989 internal arrangement assigned some licensing and control functions to that agency, this action had little impact and the established fisheries bureaucracy was soon back in charge formally (Nikitina and Pearse 1992, 374). While it is currently in a state of flux, the regulatory process retains a high degree of integration between the industry and the fisheries bureaucracy. Sevryba was and continues to be a stable participant at commission meetings. Quotas and other restrictions agreed to at joint commission meetings are scrutinized by a regional corporative body, the Technical-Scientific Fisheries Council, which prepares recommendations for the Fisheries Committee on distribution of quotas.[6] Over the past few years, regional authorities in northwest Russia have strengthened their position in the management process, primarily at the cost of Sevryba but also of the Fisheries Committee in Moscow. Thus, since 1994, regional management councils in Murmansk, Arkhangelsk and Karelia prepare recommendations on company-level quota distribution, but Sevryba plays an important role even at this level (Hønneland 1998, 60).

As to monitoring such regulations, report-based surveillance is two tiered. Larger vessels are obliged to report daily to the Polar Research Institute of Fishery and Oceanography (PINRO) in Murmansk, as well as to a ministerial research and statistical department in Moscow, VNIRO.[7] Small- and medium-sized vessels report catches to Murmanrybvod, the local arm of a committee department that passes it onto VNIRO which summarizes catch and production figures. In theory, this has permitted cross-checking of catch and processing figures. It should be recalled, however, that for most of the regime period, the harvesting fleets and the processing units were organized within one single, tightly integrated organization, Sevryba. Beyond this, regular inspections are performed by Murmanrybvod and, since 1993, the Military Boundary Guard, which is taking a growing interest in conducting compliance control activities in the Barents Sea. Indeed, according to a 1997 presidential decree, the Boundary Guard is now primarily responsible for these functions; however, the implementation of this decree remains to be seen.

Regarding the Norwegian fishing industry, three conflicting lines should be noted, all built into the heterogeneous Norway's Fisherman Association. This organization represents the fishing industry in annual negotiations with the authorities over government support and other issues. A first dividing line is between the cod and herring fisheries, and conflicting issues include the distribution of governmental support and the balance between ground fish and capelin quotas, which are competitive because the former feeds on the latter. After the appearance of EEZs, another dimension was added because access for the herring sector to traditional fishing grounds in the North Sea is being traded for groundfish quotas in the Barents Sea. The second conflict, relevant especially to the cod fisheries, goes between trawlers and vessels using conventional gear like the handnet and longline. To some extent, this conflict overlaps with the third line of conflict, which divides the northern fishermen from those operating out of west Norway. The western industry dominates the pelagic fisheries, including herring and capelin, as well as the offshore factory trawler segment. For its part, the northern industry controls a large part of the inshore trawler fleet supplying local processors,[8] but small- and medium-sized vessels using conventional gear make up its largest component. While their share has varied, the coastal fishers have on average taken two-thirds of Norway's arctic cod harvest in the Barents Sea (Hersoug and Hoel 1992, 53).

Just like in Russia, there is a high degree of porosity between industry and bureaucracy in the Norwegian regulatory process. Before the annual negotiations with Russia, there is a consultation phase with affected organizations, research institutions, and administrative bodies. After the commission meeting, transformation of its recommendations into Norwegian regulations starts in the Regulation Council, an advisory body to the Fisheries Directorate, which proposes operational restrictions and the allocation of quotas to different vessel and gear types.[9] Along with the recommendation of the Fisheries Directorate, this action forms the basis for the final decision on the regulative system for each fishery, normally made by the Fisheries Ministry.

In Norway, the key bodies responsible for compliance control are the Coast Guard, the Fisheries Directorate Control Division, and the fishermen's sales organizations. The latter are obliged to compile reports from processing plants and send them to the Fisheries Directorate which may then cross-check with the catch reports of the vessels, sent weekly by factory trawlers and upon port call for smaller vessels. Weekly reporting by factory vessels was introduced in 1991 and sharpened the existing reporting procedure. Whenever they begin or end a fishing run, they must report current inventories. In addition, all vessels must keep updated catch logbooks, the accuracy of which is controlled by onsite inspections, in offshore waters conducted largely by the Coast Guard.

In summary, a territorial dispute between the two coastal states is a complicating feature of fisheries management in the Barents Sea. In both the Russian and the Norwegian north, the fisheries industry forms a backbone of the economies and industry participation in bureaucratic decision making is extensive. In these tight corporative systems, scientists, bureaucrats, and fishermen interact on a regular basis and they are all evaluated by roughly the same criteria, i.e., the health of stocks and industries as measured by the most recent production figures. In such a situation, it can be quite tempting to allow pressure for sustained harvesting levels to influence regulatory decisions (Engesæter 1993, 86).

The Bilateral Fisheries Regime

In the mid-1970s, the Barents Sea fisheries regime replaced a wider, regional regime based in the Northeast Atlantic Fisheries Convention as the appropriate means for management of stocks in the Barents Sea.[10] The bilateral fisheries relations between the two coastal states, however, were already extensively developed. More than fifty years earlier, under a Soviet policy of colonizing northern territories, a number of concession treaties had provided Norwegian companies with practically exclusive foreign hunting rights in Russian territorial waters. These concessions, which promoted the development of friendly and cooperative relations between Norway and the young Soviet state, were terminated in the early 1930s with the beginning of the Stalinist period. A new start began in the 1950s as Soviet policy was oriented toward rapid development of oceans activities and economic development in the north. A series of intergovernmental agreements institutionalized the renewed cooperation in research and exploitation of the Barents Sea's resources.[11]

Three bilateral agreements between the Soviet Union and Norway form the basis of the Barents Sea fisheries regime.[12] The preamble of the 1975 Framework Agreement stresses the need for conservation, rational utilization, and the building of good relations between the two nations.[13] Of particular interest is the passage that special emphasis will be placed on scientific investigations and the coordination of such investigations when managing marine resources. The Joint Fisheries Commission, set up by Article III, is the institutional hub of the regime. It meets annually and makes consensual recommendations on total quotas of the three shared stocks: cod, haddock, and capelin. Moreover, the commission makes recommendations about the distribution of quotas among the parties, the share to be allocated to third countries, as well as operational restrictions such as geographical distribution of catches, mesh size, and minimum size regulations, and closed periods. Although the negotiations are closed to the public, quite detailed protocols are made available in the wake of commission meetings and the attitude toward media on the substance of the negotiations is generally quite open. The commission is also instrumental in coordinating scientific research among institutions in the two countries. And as provided for in Article II, the commission has recently served to stimulate the emergence of cooperative relations in areas such as industrial cooperation among harvesting companies and processors in the two countries and the exchange of catching and selection technologies (Stokke 1992). Sensitivity to the disputed nature of parts of the Agreement Area is shown in Article V, which states that nothing in this agreement will affect the status of rights or claims held by the contracting parties regarding fisheries jurisdiction in the area. When the Norwegian Storting, or parliament, passed the agreement, it was eager to emphasize this article.[14]

In support of this framework, the 1976 Mutual Access Agreement expands the geographic area of cooperation to fit the subsequent Norwegian 200-mile EEZ declaration and paves the procedural ground for reciprocal fishing.[15] Within agreed-upon quotas, beyond 12 miles, and subject to coastal state rules and licensing, this agreement permits fishing in waters under the jurisdiction of the other nation. Finally, the 1978 Grey Zone Agreement produces a system of enforcement in the disputed part of the Barents Sea.[16] This is achieved by acknowledging parallel jurisdiction in a zone that includes the area under dispute. Both parties license national and third-party vessels operating in this zone, enforcement being exercised by the government that has issued the license, thus avoiding situations where Norwegian fishermen are subject to Soviet inspections in waters claimed by Norway and vice versa.

Although Soviet authorities have often referred to the regime as performing joint management of the ecologically integral stocks (Zilanov 1988), the Norwegians insist that, formally, it is a harmonization regime since the joint commission is endowed with recommendatory powers only. Although these recommendations are more or less automatically adopted by the national governments, the latter are free to set up stricter rules independent of the other pertaining to their own part of the ecosystem. This bilateral fisheries regime is nested in a set of wider regimes, organizations and interstate relations. While rather vague and unfinished regarding shared fish stocks, the 1982 United Nations Law of the Sea Convention (UNLOSC) confirms both the coastal state privilege and the obligation to set up cooperative institutions to conduct rational management of shared stocks.[17] Even before the convention entered into force, these features were generally seen to have entered into the body of international customary law. Furthermore, producing coordinated knowledge is nested in the broader work within the International Council for the Exploration of the Sea (ICES), a multilateral institution that has served as a coordinating vehicle on Atlantic marine research since the turn of the century. And Norwegian–Soviet relations in the fisheries sector have also been embedded in the wider framework of international relations in the region, which have changed much during the past decade from a conflict-embedded low in the early 1980s over the era of Soviet perestroika and East-West thaw to the present largely optimistic and cautiously cooperative situation.[18]

Specifying the Problem: Jurisdiction and Management

We have seen that the agreements underlying the bilateral regime revolve around two general aspects of resource management: the jurisdictional basis for regulation and compliance control activities, and the need to balance the concerns for conservation and utilization. In this section we shall establish more precise criteria for evaluating the effectiveness of the Barents Sea fisheries regime.

Jurisdictional concerns were essential from the outset in that the bilateral regime is a response to the emerging consensus, during the negotiations of the Law of the Sea Convention, on extended coastal state jurisdictions. The framework agreement was negotiated as a part of a package that included Soviet consent to Norwegian trawl-free zones beyond twelve nautical miles (Churchill and Ulfstein 1992, 93). This consent of traditional user states was seen as essential to Norway because of a recent verdict in the International Court of Justice that went against Iceland's unilateralist procedure in establishing its extended fishery zone.[19] In recent years, the external jurisdictional problem has revolved around the Loophole, a high-seas enclave in the Barents Sea. Whereas the internal problem stems from the perception that the design of the regime might interfere with the delimitation talks of the two coastal states, which have been an ongoing issue since 1974. In short, the jurisdictional aspect of the problem addressed by the regime is partly to gain acceptance for a phase-out of third countries, initially from the EEZs and more recently from the international waters adjacent to them, and partly to meet the requirements of fisheries management in the disputed area of the Barents Sea without affecting the legal status of the competing claims to juridiction in these waters.

At a general level, the second major problem addressed by the Barents Sea regime is balancing conservation and utilization; this requires management of the fisheries activity due to the lack of individual control of fish resources. If all individuals have open access to stocks, their incentives may cause a race for the fish, which can cause inefficiencies and waste in the current period, and can lead to stock depletions in the future. Essentially, the goal of fisheries management is to allow for proper use of fish stocks over time. The key phrases of this definition are "proper use" and "over time." Proper use has to do with how much and what types of products are produced, who produces them, and how the gains from production are distributed. The over-time element derives from the renewable nature of fish stocks. The amount of catch in any period can affect the amounts that will be available for harvest in the future. Therefore the decision to produce a certain amount in a given period should be made taking into account the needs of the future as well as the needs of the present. As will be seen below, this is the crux of evaluating the effectiveness of fisheries regimes. It will be useful here to discuss the two aspects of fisheries management separately in more detail.

Consider first the over time, or conservation problem, centering on the size of catch and not its distribution. When addressing this problem, fisheries managers must face the inherent variability of the resource and the difficulty of obtaining knowledge about the population dynamics of the resources. They also need to determine a trade-off ratio between catch today and catch in the future. This intertemporal use problem is made even more difficult by the fact of scientific uncertainty. If the exact amount and timing of increased stock productivity that will result from a reduction in catch are known, people have a basis for determining if the gains are worth the current self-determined deprivations. In the real world of fisheries management, however, things are not so clear cut. There can be large fluctuations in stock size that may be independent of current catch levels. Further, the cost of obtaining and evaluating data to determine the current and likely future status of the stock, with or without changes in the catch levels, is high and the accuracy of the estimates and forecasts is less than perfect. Therefore the cost of increasing current catch levels and the benefits of current harvest reductions, in terms of future stock potential, are difficult to ascertain.

The problems of uncertainty and over time trade-offs are clearly intertwined. Individuals, groups and regional development authorities with concrete needs, such as being able to pay the boat mortgage or to improve regional employment, may not be convinced that the stocks are in as bad a shape as scientists say, or that proposed cut-backs will have any bearing on future stock productivity. In the Barents Sea, it is a regular phenomenon that fisheries organizations question the scientific basis of estimating stocks in periods of strict regulation (Sagdahl 1992, 78–9). In general, when the degree of uncertainty is high, it can be tempting for policymakers to apply a pick-and-choose strategy among scientific results, stressing only those which are congruent with their perceived self-interest. Thus, as elaborated below, it is typical that the dispute between Norway and Russia over the proper trawl mesh size in the cod fishery is argued in terms of scientific uncertainty or even dissensus about the mortality rate of fish that escape the trawl mesh.

Even with a specified catch level for a given year, it is still necessary to determine how it is to be taken and by whom and what final products will be produced. The political reality is that this allocative problem is most often seen in distributive terms. For example, should the harvest be taken by offshore trawlers or by the coastal fleet of smaller, less mobile vessels? The answer to this question is of obvious importance to members of the respective segments of the industry. The problem can have another dimension if one area of the country or one type of gear has few alternative employment possibilities, or if, as in the case of Norway, there are regional development goals that can be mobilized by subsectors desiring preferential access to annual allowable catches. A regular conflict issue in Norwegian fisheries politics is the competitive relationship between northern and western fleets.

In theory the most desirable allocation should be chosen according to a society's preferences and notions of fairness and equity. In reality, however, it is often determined by the relative bargaining power of the various interest groups in the fisheries management decision process. While a complete analysis of such bargaining is beyond the scope of this discussion, it will be useful to highlight one aspect with particular relevance to the evaluation of fisheries management regimes. For analytical purposes only, the conservation and allocation issues have been discussed separately. In reality, of course, they are highly related and these two aspects of fisheries management are often determined simultaneously. Different regulation schemes, even if designed to achieve the same catch level, will probably have different distributional implications. For instance, closed seasons may affect various parts of the fleet differently depending on their ability to fish in the open season. If the fish are generally located further off shore during the open season, smaller, less seaworthy boats may be at a disadvantage. In short, because various interest groups tend to favor the types of regulation measures that give them a bigger share of the catch, the range of bargaining points over distribution can sometimes extend to conservation issues. Given the bargaining strengths of the various groups, the negotiated regulation program may not be capable of adequately dealing with conservation issues. In the Barents Sea, for example, Norway generally favors high total quotas in the cod fisheries, combined with strict gear regulations, because this is the least costly regulation technique, given the comparatively large average size of ground fish in the Norwegian zone. The situation is different for Russia, as we shall see.

Another aspect of this is the perceived ability of interest groups to maintain their relative bargaining power. To the extent that strong interest groups feel they can maintain their power over time, there will be incentives to consider conservation issues. A proposal for reduced catches in the present to increase catch potential in the future may be appealing because interest groups are relatively sure that when distribution issues are addressed in the future, they will receive an increase in harvest that will compensate for their current reduction. On the other hand, when relative bargaining powers are perceived as unstable, the interest groups might argue against proposals that will lead to a certain decrease in current catch and an uncertain change in future catch. In the Barents Sea, this is currently an issue since the fishery in the high seas Loophole is perceived by Norwegian and Russian fishers as evidence that the fruits of their restraint in the past are being harvested by others.[20]

Another reason why allocation and conservation matters become mixed is that the bargainers may agree to sidestep conservation needs to increase the possibility of agreement. If the recommended catch levels are low and all interest groups have similar bargaining power, an increase in the catch for one group must result in a decrease in the catch of another. These bargaining conflicts can be, and often are, reduced by agreeing to an allowable catch that is larger than recommended. We shall return to this issue below.

Until now the discussion has been somewhat abstract. Good management is proper use through time, and decisions on intertemporal use must be made based on time preferences and uncertain relationships between harvest today and stock size tomorrow. It is a big step from this formulation of the fisheries management problem to setting up a program that can make it operational in the real world. Note that while the focus of a management agency has been compartmentalized for ease of description, many if not all of these issues are interrelated.

A prerequisite for a management agency is a scientific unit to perform the necessary data collection and analyses to determine stock conditions and critical parameters of the population dynamics of the relevant stocks. In the Barents Sea, this function has largely been filled by the Norwegian Institute of Marine Research (IMR) and PINRO in Murmansk, although in recent years other research institutions have become involved as well. Although this assignment involves a certain amount of basic scientific work, it is also necessary to have the ability to provide assessments and answer questions concerning the likely effects of various harvest levels and regulation techniques used to achieve them.[21] These tasks are particularly difficult at the international level. It is usually the case that for science to be credible, there must be input from all parties involved, which even in the most open circumstances can be difficult to achieve. The research organizations may be located at great distances from each other, they may use different approaches or techniques, and may have different types of research vessels or lack access to compatible computers. In other instances the scientists of one country may, or may be perceived to, knowingly produce false or misleading results that support a nation's bargaining position. Either way, the scientific basis for management is eroded.

A procedure for selecting the desired levels of harvest in any period of time is also required. In the Barents Sea, the central mechanism in this respect is the bilateral Fisheries Commission. The commission must interpret and balance the biological and social concerns, then turn them into a system of regulations that, given the existing industry structure and the agency's enforcement capability, will cause the catch of the fishing fleet to remain within the desired range. This is particularly difficult when more than one country or political entity is involved.[22] First, there will probably be a larger number of interests among which the access to the resource must be divided. Second, and more important, there may be a lower acceptance of others as credible claimants and this may affect the intransigence of the actors. For example, while fishermen from Finnmark may agree that residents of southern Norway have a right to fish off their coasts, they may view Russian fishermen with a jaundiced eye and may dismiss claims from third-party states out of hand. The possibilities of legitimate bargaining with these groups and the possibility of reaching agreement will vary inversely with the perception of the validity of the groups' claims. This problem can be compounded if the nations have different preferences about the value of fish today versus fish tomorrow and about what is a fair and equitable distribution of fish within and among countries. Third, states often find themselves in a classical collective action problem: the impact of costly restraint on stocks on the part of one coastal state can easily be destroyed if the other state, the industry of which feeds on the same stock, fails to introduce similar measures. The dynamics here are that, unless one party is reasonably sure that the other will do the same, it will likely be reluctant to introduce restrictions on its own industry.

Determining which set of regulations will do the desired job and getting them implemented are only the first two steps. It is also necessary to institute a monitoring and enforcement system to ensure that the participants actually comply. The participants must believe there is a reasonable chance that deviant behavior will be detected and that the punishment will outweigh any potential benefits of cheating.[23] In the Barents Sea, the individual coastal states reserve the right to enforce any rules against their own citizens within their respective areas of jurisdiction. If one state is skeptical of the desire or ability of another to enforce regulations against its citizens, that state may be reluctant to enforce the same regulations against its own citizens. Similarly, if industry participants think that the rules are not being effectively enforced in other countries, they will be less likely to comply themselves. Just as with regulations, states may find themselves in a serious collective action problem when addressing compliance control.

In summary, we have seen that the conditions of fisheries management in the Barents Sea are: (1) disputed authority over parts of the geographic area covered by the regime; (2) lack of individual ownership of the resource implying externalities of costs and individual incentives to take more than collectively rational; and (3) uncertainty and often dissensus about the consequences of given levels of fishing. Hence, the jurisdictional problem addressed by the Barents Sea regime is to gain acceptance for the phase out of third countries and to implement a fisheries management system in disputed waters without seriously undermining competing territorial claims. As for the fisheries management problem, three practical tasks are especially salient and will serve as operational criteria for management effectiveness: the generation of high-quality scientific results that are relevant to management decisions, the ability to create regulations that take into account this knowledge when balancing conservation and allocation concerns, and a level of compliance control that can ensure these rules are adherred to.

Causal Narrative: The Management Regime at Work

Following the approach elaborated in chapter 1, we shall analyze the effectiveness of the Barents Sea regime by determining, first, the extent to which the various problems outlined above are solved and, second, the causal significance of the regime for this level of problem solving. We shall note the six causal pathways, or mechanisms, that inform the effectiveness analysis throughout this volume: in general, the regime may modify behavior relevant to the problem by affecting calculation of utility, alleviating collective action problems, bestowing authority, facilitating learning, assigning new roles to actors, or affecting the domestic alignment patterns in member states.

Solving the Jurisdictional Problem?

Regarding the problem of jurisdiction over third parties, the regime proved quite effective in its early phase. Previously, only the foremost among a large group of user states in the Barents Sea, the introduction of EEZs, and the subsequent development of the bilateral regime gave Norway and the Soviet Union more or less exclusive management authority in these waters. The regime, however, was not the key explanation for this. When assessing changes in the status of the problem addressed by the regime, the relevant contrast is not the situation prior to the establishment of the regime but what the situation would have looked like today without it. The counterfactual comparison would be a situation where Norway and the Soviet Union were in charge of their own EEZ but without the bilateral institutions in place. The phase-out of third countries was negotiated in sets of negotiations separate from those establishing the bilateral regime, and the only regime features that reflect these negotiations are the provisions dealing with regulation and inspection of third-country vessels. On a reciprocal basis, the United Kingdom and Iceland were assured continued, albeit geographically more limited, access to specific fisheries after a transition period of ten years. All other countries were phased out after only three years and without any extension after this sunset period.[24] The restricted nature of the bilateral regime has implied that a greater share of the fish is left to the coastal states for distribution among themselves, but none of this could have happened without the simultaneous impetus of the new Law of the Sea (UNLOSC 1982). Hence, the impact of the regime was to mobilize the authority of emerging customary law to legitimize phasing-out of third countries. Within a few years, the third-country share of the Barents Sea catch was cut by half to roughly 5 percent.[25]

More recently, the external jurisdiction problem has revolved not around EEZs but around the so-called Loophole, located in the international waters beyond those zones. This problem is hardly solved today: the third-party catch of arctic cod in these waters reached a peak in 1994 at roughly 60,000 metric tons;[26] since then, harvests have been lower but this is due to the lesser availability of fish, not reduced effort. Owned largely by Icelanders or Faroese,[27] some of the foreign fishing vessels operating here were registered in "open registers," flying flags-of-convenience and thus rendering less useful the traditional, diplomatic way of addressing the problem. Since 1995, however, Icelandic authorities have encouraged the Loophole fleet to fly Icelandic flags to generate a presence in the area. Until now, the Russo-Norwegian regime has not been a significant factor in efforts to cope with the problem, beyond the fact that it allows both members to allocate a certain share of their quotas to third countries. This has been an implicit, but important way to dissuade third parties from engaging in the fishery. The fact that Greenland was given a small cod quota in Norwegian waters in a 1992 agreement—which simultaneously obliges Greenlandic authorities to keep total harvests, including that taken in high-seas areas, within this quota—was widely seen as evidence that acceptance of a coastal state role even beyond the EEZ had come at a price.[28] Eager not to form a precedent that might encourage others, Norwegian authorities had clearly stated that there is no relationship whatsoever between ongoing Greenlandic harvesting in the Loophole and allocation of quotas, and the agreement itself stresses the reciprocal nature of this allocation.[29] Nevertheless, both Norway and Russia are well aware of the possibility of using access to their own zones as a political instrument to control third-party harvesting in the high-seas areas adjacent to their EEZs. In every protocol since the 1992 meeting of the bilateral Russo-Norwegian commission, they have pledged to include a formulation similar to the one found in the Norwegian–Greenlandic agreement when drawing up quota arrangements with third parties.[30] In the case of vessels from the European Union, this inclination to quietly buy out challengers has been combined with diplomatic persuasion. In 1992, a few French and German vessels operated in the Loophole, and only left the area after Norwegian authorities put heavy pressure on both the commission and the flag states.[31]

Overall, the causal significance of the regime in addressing the Loophole problem has been limited. True, the track record of the regime—especially the fact that Barents Sea fish stocks are quite healthy compared to, for instance, those found in Icelandic waters—has been important for the legitimization of the hard line adopted by the coastal states toward newcomers. With the current high level of conflict, however, such arguments have not persuaded newcomers to respect the no-quota approach of Norway and Russia. On a more practical level, the commission has served to enhance policy harmonization among the coastal states. Since 1993, the Russian government has joined Norway in diplomatic efforts to pressure third parties, especially Iceland, to stop their nationals from engaging in harvesting in the Loophole.[32] This pressure has led to a reduction of industrial contacts between the northwest Russian and the Icelandic fisheries industries, including committee encouragement to put a stop to direct landings of cod in Iceland from Russian vessels.[33] Over the past few years contracts with *i.a.* Sevryba companies had been important to the processing industry in Iceland.[34] Similarly, Norway now prohibits landing there of vessels operating in international waters without a quota, and the country has even considered steps to prohibit Norwegian companies from serving such vessels.[35] Since the fleets operating in the Loophole are not tightly integrated with the Russian and Norwegian fishing industries, however, and since there are many nearby ports (e.g., on Iceland) that are delighted to accept fish from these vessels, such measures have so far had only limited effect.

As to whether the regime has actually solved the internal aspects of the jurisdictional problem—allowing fisheries management in the disputed areas of the Barents Sea without compromising the competing claims of the two coastal states—the jury is still out. The key regime component is the Grey Zone Agreement with its parallel systems of licensing and enforcement in the agreement area, which includes the disputed segment. Before the establishment of that zone, Norway and the Soviet Union were faced with basically three alternative policy options, none of which would have been very helpful in solving the jurisdictional problem. First, not to provoke the territorial jealousy of the other, both parties might have refrained from intrusive monitoring in the disputed area. In an increasingly regulated fishery, however, such a blind spot would have been quite intolerable, especially as fish have been plentiful in the disputed area in the period under discussion. Moreover, the parties would have had to abstain from the regulation and enforcement of third countries as well, which would be quite detrimental to the thrust of the emerging Law of the Sea. In consequence, coastal state fishers would have suffered and the health of the fish stocks would have been in jeopardy. Alternatively, one of the parties could have kept a low profile and left regulation and enforcement to the other. There is little doubt, however, that this would have seriously undermined the territorial claims of the restrained party. Indeed, the fear that without an agreement the Soviets might try to enforce regulations in the disputed area on their own was a real concern among key Norwegian decision makers.[36] Finally, both parties could have acted as if they were in charge of the disputed area and conducted both regulation and enforcement on all vessels in that area. As the Svalbard experience showed, however, Norwegian inspections of Soviet vessels in an area where Norwegian jurisdiction is not clear was likely to meet with opposition from the Soviet government. And this opposition would be even stronger when the Soviets had a claim of their own to the area. The same argument, although softened by the asymmetry in their power relationship, would be valid for Soviet inspections of Norwegian vessels. In both cases, there would be a considerable risk of embarrassing incidents leading to diplomatic activity and a possible escalation of conflict.

With the Grey Zone Agreement in place, agreed-upon management measures could be implemented and enforced without such risks; and also without one party having to accept enforcement activity from the other in waters claimed to be its own. Nevertheless, a deeply split Norwegian Storting, by only a slight majority, passed the Grey Zone Agreement after an unusually bitter debate. The opposition argued that the agreement was geographically biased by covering an area to the west of the disputed area far bigger than that to the east. It was also argued that it might give the Soviets expectations about joint management solutions in the Barents Sea on both fish and shelf resources.[37] If the critics of the Grey Zone Agreement were right when arguing that its geographical location strengthens the Soviet position, the regime would have failed to solve the problem of avoiding negative jurisdictional effects of fisheries management in the area. The fact that this temporary agreement has been renewed each year for nearly two decades without any debate, however, suggests that these effects, if present, are no longer seen as very significant.

Summing up, the jurisdictional part of the problem addressed by the Barents Sea regime has been solved to a considerable extent. Internally, the design of the regime has helped to decouple necessary regulation and compliance control from the contested territorial issue. And externally, while the role of the regime in helping coastal states reduce or remove third-party harvesting in the pocket of international waters in the Barents Sea has been rather limited, the regime was instrumental in realizing the potential, created by the evolving Law of the Sea, for coastal state privileges within the EEZs.

Solving the Management Problem?

In the Barents Sea, the state of the commercially most important stocks, as measured by spawning stock biomass, were in decline before the introduction of the bilateral regime, and this decline continued for roughly a decade. Figure 3.1 portrays the decline and recovery of the major commercial stocks in the Barents Sea ecosystem: cod, haddock, and capelin which are managed cooperatively by Norway and Russia, whereas saithe and herring are managed by Norway independently of the bilateral regime.

As shown, between 1980 and 1987, the major commercial species were in dramatic and continuous decline. The most conspicuous failure was that of capelin, which vanished completely in 1986. In economic terms, the decline of cod in the 1980s was the most painful, particularly among coastal fishermen in northern Norway. There is general agreement that the capelin collapse is by far the most important reason for the subsequent cod problems (Hamre 1991, 241). When the plankton-eating capelin disappeared, a crucial link was broken between the primary biological production in the Barents Sea and species such as cod or mammals. Nevertheless, two features of figure 3.1 are hard to reconcile with a portrayal of the regime as performing poorly in solving the conservation problem. First, the most significant commercial stocks recovered in the late 1980s. This is true both for cod and the plankton-eaters. While the resurgence of capelin in the early 1990s was short-lived, this was proba-

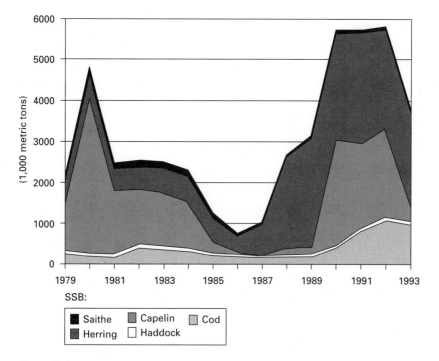

Figure 3.1
Spawning stock biomass (SSB) of shared and exclusive Norwegian stocks in the
Barents Sea. Source: *ICES Cooperative Research Report,* several volumes.

bly both caused and offset by a concomitant strengthening of the herring
stock. Second, exclusive Norwegian stocks like saithe, redfish, and herring, managed by Norway without the complications of international coordination, have not fared any better than the shared stocks.

With the caveat that the recent increase in the plancton-eater biomass
has been managed rather cautiously, these stock developments are closely
reflected in the Barents Sea harvests. Before 1977, the fluctuations of major species often occurred in an antiphase so that the over-all catches
remained stable. From then on, however, the decline in catches was wide
and unequivocal untill the general recovery, which began around 1990.
Figure 3.2 portrays catches of the most commercially significant Barents
Sea species in the period under investigation. Simultaneously, and partly
by implication, employment in the fishing industry has been dwindling

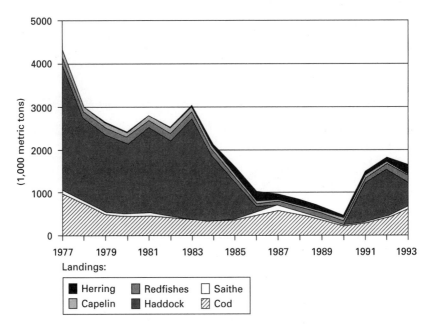

Figure 3.2
Commercial catches in the Barents Sea. Source: *ICES Cooperative Research Report,* several volumes.

in both coastal states during the past decade. This process is due not only to harvest levels but also to changes in technology and such factors as export market development and the size of government subsidies.

Thus, biological and socioeconomic indicators portray a well-known pattern of ups and downs and cannot support any firm conclusions on the problem-solving contributions of the bilateral management regime. In the study of fisheries management, moreover, there is growing appreciation that harvesting is only one among a number of factors affecting the status of stocks; indeed, it is frequently not even the most significant one. Changes in natural conditions, especially water temperature and salinity, can often have a considerable impact; and the same goes for much discussed but little understood interrelationships between various components in marine ecosystems. Such rival explanations for observed trends in the biomass, however, should not be used as excuses for what may appear as significant management failure during parts of the period under investigation. But they warn against basing an effectiveness analysis solely on aggregate outcomes, like the health of fish stocks or annual harvests. The causal leap between the operation of the regime and such success indicators is simply too long to support strong statements about causal impact. Especially with only one case, it is extremely difficult to give a plausible counterfactual account of what would have happened in the absence of the regime.

Thus, demonstrating that the Barents Sea fisheries regime has been instrumental in solving the conservation and allocation problem requires showing how it has affected behavior relevant to the stock situation and harvesting levels in the Barents Sea.

Eliciting Behavioral Change

Previously we showed that it is useful to distinguish three behavioral aspects of the management problem: generation of adequate knowledge about the health of the ecosystem and the impact of harvesting of various stocks; ensuring that available scientific knowledge is applied in establishing adequate regulations; and compliance control, including monitoring to assess adherence to the regulations as well as imposition of sanctions on violators. Here we will look more closely at how the regime has affected performance along those three dimensions.

Generation of Knowledge   The principal task of scientific investigations in fisheries management is to identify and convey to managers and fishermen the over-time and social trade-offs that are involved in given management programs. The regime has affected this practice in basically three ways: facilitating coordination of research effort, enhancing its financial basis, and restricting the set of research organizations involved.

Broadly speaking, the emergence of the regime has not led to dramatic shifts in how fisheries investigations are planned or conducted and how the results are imputed into the process. Rather, the regime appears to have supported and stimulated activities that were already under way in the Barents Sea. Even prior to the regime, scientists in each country were called upon to make recommendations on quotas and operational restrictions, and they cooperated closely through ICES. Initiated in 1956 (Zilanov et al. 1991), nongovernmental collaboration between Norway's

IMR and the Soviet PINRO grew steadily in scope and intensity. Previously confined to exchange of information on national research efforts, the cooperation gradually expanded to joint research programs and joint surveys (Børsting and Stokke 1995). Regular research symposia are being held and there is growing harmonization of methodology and modeling.

The significance of the regime for this growing collaboration is partly to provide a framework that facilitates regular interaction among scientists and partly to place scientific investigation close to the center of the decision-making process. In turn, the division of labor realized through collaborative survey programs and joint cruises enables the IMR and PINRO to pool scarce resources. This has been particularly useful because of the complementary resources of these institutes: the Murmansk institute has commanded relatively more manpower and vessels than that of the Norwegians, whereas the latter is considerably better endowed in terms of computerized data-processing. Moreover, the collaboration has permitted both parties to base their stock assessments on data from the entire ecosystem. A prerequisite for making effective use of this opportunity is that equipment is compatible and data are collected in the same way by all participants. Intercalibration of methods and equipment has been a constant concern in the joint programs and also in the scientific symposia throughout the 1980s (Hoel 1993). Thus, partly because these scientific organizations have been strong in different areas, and partly because of their intercalibration efforts, cooperation has enhanced their capacity to produce policy-relevant knowledge.

This bilateral scientific coordination is nested in the wider, longstanding cooperation within ICES, and the exchange of catch reports and scientific data would probably have occurred even in the absence of the bilateral fisheries regime. Indeed, Norway's data on Soviet and Russian catches in the Svalbard zone are acquired through the ICES framework and not via the bilateral commission.[38] Still, the Russo-Norwegian scientific cooperation runs far deeper than what is usual in ICES and also forms the core of the various ICES working groups on arctic stocks. In 1997, however, despite efforts of Russian fisheries authorities, Norwegian research vessels were denied access to the Russian zone, a decision widely perceived as originating in naval quarters.[39] The year before, a similar change of attitude had struck the bilateral joint research program on measurement of nuclear contamination in the Barents and Kara Seas.[40] In the spring of 1998, a permit was finally granted to the Norwegian fisheries scientists but only to a northern part of the zone where fish are scarce and the research gains moderate.[41] While helpful, well-established fisheries science networks are no guarantee against obstruction from other sectors. The paradox, however, is that problems such as these were not encountered in the fisheries area throughout the 1980s when the general bilateral relations were far less cooperative.

Beyond the acceptance of military authorities, fisheries-independent investigations based on surveys, increasingly important today (Sahrhage 1989), require substantial financial resources. This shows another way in which the regime has affected the generation of scientific knowledge. By giving the departmental scientific organizations prominent places in the decision-making process, the regime has made it easier for these organizations to extract funding from state authorities and hence finance sustained efforts in stock monitoring and assessment. As we shall see, this was especially visible in the first few years after the disruption of the Soviet Union. Both the framework agreement and the subsequent practice of the joint commission have served to regularize the request and supply of policy-relevant information on the status of fishery stocks. Because scientific evidence forms such a crucial part of the discussions, and because positions on contentious issues must be presented in at least apparently neutral, scientific language, it becomes a matter of routine for bureaucracies and industry organizations to require concrete and practical information on all matters related to the abundance and distribution of stocks. In turn, the scientific organizations become accustomed to having to answer such questions, with clear consequences for the way they balance basic and applied research.

It is a common feature of international regimes that they imply scientific commitments in need of budgetary counterparts. Both Norway and the former Soviet Union have traditionally financed and administratively subordinated scientific activities to the fisheries bureaucracies.[42] The Norwegian IMR has had stable political and financial surroundings. While the institute loosened its ties to the fisheries bureaucracy in the late 1980s, the budget of the IMR has continued to grow steadily. Investment in research vessels and equipment has been substantial and the number of cruise days allocated to the Barents Sea stock assessment has remained stable since the mid-1980s at roughly 40 percent of the IMR total.[43] In contrast, Soviet budgets for fisheries science were cut in the 1980s, partly as a result of reduced incomes from the fisheries. The economic reforms brought severe financial constraints on institutions relying on state funds and, in the late 1980s, the departmental institutions PINRO and VNIRO had to close down several hydrobiological laboratories (Matishov 1989, 18). The financial responsibility for PINRO was gradually shifted from the ministry to the industry association Sevryba. While tight institutional links among science, ministry, and industry were certainly nothing new in the Soviet context, the change nevertheless implied a shift of emphasis toward more practical, supportive fish-finding tasks. Investigations with no ready commercial value for harvesting activities were given lower priority than before. For the 1993 season, the costs of a two-month cruise for one vessel, including vessel hire, crew, external services, and overhead, was estimated by PINRO to range between 31 and 34 million rubles, at that time roughly USD 70,000;[44] and both crew and bunkering required hard currency. Sevrybpromrazvedka,[45] a fleet operator who also conducts fisheries research for Sevryba companies, has reportedly been forced to cut the number of annual research trips from a previous 240 to only 34 in 1994.[46] Similarly, around the turn of the decade, PINRO's hired staff was cut by almost half,[47] and worries grew among Norwegian scientists that bunkering problems could jeopardize PINRO's contribution to the joint research program.[48] Since 1993, PINRO has been assigned quotas of cod and haddock to finance noncommissioned work,[49] but these quotas were considerably lower in 1994 than the year before (Hønneland 1994, 21).

In this period of financial strain, the bilateral regime appears to have played a quite productive role. Norwegian authorities have granted considerable additional funds to maintain and strengthen IMR ties with PINRO. A clearly expressed motive was to ensure continuity in terms of personnel, equipment, and quality in the lines of activity that are seen as particularly useful to the stable monitoring of the Barents Sea ecosystem.[50] There is little doubt that well-developed contacts among these institutions enhanced the perception that those funds would be used in a manner conducive to management objectives in the Barents Sea. The support has been used to upgrade PINRO computer systems and also to finance broader interaction among researchers from the two institutes to further harmonize methodologies.[51] The research director of PINRO even argues that partly due to Norwegian support, especially on the equipment side, the quality of Russian research effort in the Barents Sea has increased.[52] Today this appears to be an over assessment, especially considering the drop in the number of Russian research cruises and the recent impediments to coordinated surveys. Rather, the regime has somewhat softened the transition for the northwest Russian fisheries research apparatus from the Soviet period to the present market-oriented situation.

The impact of the regime on scientific activity is not unambiguous, moreover, for there may be a dark side to the focal position of departmental fisheries scientists in the management process. It is a frequent feature of international environmental regimes that they serve to strengthen the position of some subsections in the behavioral complex at the expense of others. In Russia today, and in Norway as well, other fisheries research organizations are trying to get a bigger share of the research funds available in this area (Hoel 1993). In Norway, environmental organizations such as the Norwegian Foundation for the Protection of Nature and Greenpeace have emerged as vociferous critics of the high quota line of the joint commission.

In the Soviet Union, by contrast, criticism came primarily from other scientific quarters. It is helpful to regard this scientific cooperation through the prism of how Soviet scientific policy was formed. All research activities in the Barents Sea were planned, financed, and controlled by an Arctic Commission of the Council of Ministers. The results were considered to be of strategic importance and were either kept secret or given very limited dissemination. There was a practical ban on all scientific publications with the word "arctic" in them. Even as recently as 1990, publication of data was severely restricted, and the developments of fisheries in the north was given in percentages (Anon. 1990a). At that time, PINRO publications and the results of Soviet-Norwegian symposia were the only widely available sources of information on Barents Sea resources in the Soviet Union. But PINRO was not the only Soviet institution working on the Barents Sea living resources. Marine biological research in these waters was also conducted by three research institutes under the Academy of Sciences—the Institute of Oceanology, the Institute of Zoology, and the Murmansk Institute of Marine Biology (MMBI). Researchers in these institutions complained that until the late 1980s they were not allowed to openly raise their concern over resource depletion and were restricted in their contacts with foreign scientists (Matishov 1992).[53]

A related question associated with giving certain scientific organizations a primary place in regime processes is whether this affects their adaptiveness to the changing research frontier. Especially in the last years of the Soviet Union, the bilateral regime in general and PINRO in particular were heavily criticized by scientists from competing institutes for failing to take seriously the challenge of multispecies modeling in the Barents Sea. This challenge has been a major theme in scientific debate, nation-state practice, and international agreements for some fifteen years. It is hardly accurate to claim, however, that the scientific organizations operating within the bilateral regime have been oblivious to the multispecies perspective. On the contrary, multispecies research has proceeded particularly far in the Barents Sea (Tjelmeland 1992), partly because of the simplicity of the ecosystem and partly because considerable resources have been put into a cooperative, ambitious multispecies modeling program focusing on relationships among mammals, capelin, and cod. The core of this program is the collection of stomachs of predator species, which is conducted in compatible ways by IMR and PINRO (Tjelmeland 1988, 7). Despite this attention to species interactions, however, current models are still far from being well developed to form the basis for fine-tuned management decisions from year to year. For the time being, the simplicity and more limited time horizon of single stock models make them better suited for regular management questions (Jørgensen 1993, 20). The only significant application of multispecies science in the Barents Sea is that the role of capelin as a food base for major ground-fish species has formed part of the reason for cautious management of this stock during the 1990s. Knowledge of species interaction may also have encouraged the Norwegian subsidy of the taking of seals and whales in the Barents Sea (Hoel 1994, 122).

The point that functionally specific regimes may also harbor narrowness and rigidity may be relevant not only for scientific priorities but also more broadly for the understanding of the problem addressed and the issues perceived as weighty in the decision-making process. To some extent, the bilateral fisheries regime confirms the corporative segmentation in both national fisheries management systems, implying, for instance, that regulatory decisions are reached in comparative isolation from wider environmental management in the region. To some extent, the parties are mindful of this problem. Vital management tasks were for a short period assigned to the State Committee on the Environment before being returned to the Fisheries Ministry; and the Norwegian Regulation Council, basic to the implementation of the regime, includes an environmental agency and has given observer status to a nongovernmental green umbrella organization. Nevertheless, these are quite recent and not very consequential developments, and they cannot alter the impression of two decision systems dominated by the perspective of the fisheries sector proper. Within that sector, the regime is inclusive, but there is reluctance to involve nonfisheries interests. On the other hand, conditions are quite beneficial for a greater degree of integretion of fisheries and broader environmental concerns. At the fact-finding level, the key scientific organizations in the fisheries area, IMR and PINRO, are also the most relevant national institutions for marine environmental monitoring in the Barents Sea. At a political level, in a Russo–Norwegian Environmental Commission, the integration of various aspects of marine environmental management, including the impact on stocks of various pollutants in the Barents Sea, has been a salient concern in recent years (Stokke 1994).

Although some cooperation would have happened anyway through ICES, the bilateral regime has empowered departmental scientific organizations by embedding their cooperation in a firm administrative and political framework, routinizing their interaction with the bureaucrats and, as long as feasible, stabilizing the financial basis for investigations. To some extent this has happened at the expense of competing institutions and confirmed a sector-specific approach to fisheries management. We have seen, however, that the gradually tighter, cost-saving collaboration between research institutions in the two countries has been important for the emergence of multispecies science in the Barents Sea.

Regulation   The bilateral Barents Sea regime has facilitated generation of adequate fisheries regulations in four principal ways. The first, mobilization of scientific authority, has already been dealt with and is assured by the active involvement of scientific organizations in the preparation for as well as during commission meetings. While other types of inputs have a legitimate place as well, scientific advice serves as a focal point in the international regulatory negotiations. Second, on several regulatory matters the regime helps to remove negative issue linkages. One such instance was analyzed above in that the Grey Zone Agreement allows both Norway and Russia to proceed with regulation of harvesting activity in the disputed area of the Barents Sea without fearing negative side effects in the jurisdictional domain. Another instance, as we shall see, is the role of the Mutual Access Agreement in permitting a more rational pattern of harvesting the shared resource. Third, the regime draws political attention to deficiencies in regulatory practices; and fourth, it helps to soften certain highly conflicting matters among regime members. Before elaborating on these causal pathways, it is necessary to take a closer look at the evolving regulatory activities of the Barents Sea coastal states.

One indicator of whether states reflect in their management decision available knowledge about the trade-off between present and future consumption is the extent to which managers deviate from scientific recommendations in their quantitative regulations. It is a rather crude indicator, because political managers may differ from scientists in their view of the trade-off evaluation between present and future use of resources. Nevertheless, when scientific knowledge in an area is quite advanced and the scientific units are given as central a position in the process of regulation as they are in this regime, their advice is arguably a relevant yardstick.

Examining figure 3.3a, one might be struck by the fact that through the regime period, the managers appear, on average, to have followed quite closely the advice given by the marine scientists. In summing up the recommendations and quotas for the shared stocks in the period from 1977 to 1993, the two roughly balance each other for arctic cod and capelin; for arctic haddock, the deviation is somewhat higher at 12 percent, but this is still less than half the difference between recommendations and quotas for spring-spawning herring, which is managed by Norway alone.

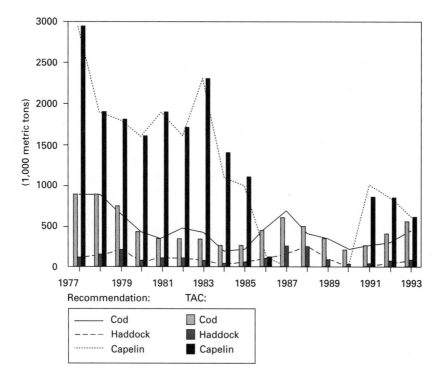

Figure 3.3a
ICES recommendations and Joint Commission decisions on total quotas for the
three shared stocks in the Barents Sea. Source: *ICES Cooperative Research Report,* several volumes.

Scrutinizing the figure somewhat more closely, however, one discovers
that although the average performance is good, there are some years
where the regulations have considerably exceeded what was recommended. The year 1984 stands out in this respect. The capelin quota was
set 27 percent higher than recommended, that for cod almost 50 percent
higher and for haddock the regulators doubled the quota advised by scientists. For all three of them, ICES had dramatically lowered its recommendations, compared with the preceding year, so these deviances are
not surprising. While the regulators did not follow the scientists all the
way they nevertheless cut the quota considerably from the preceding year,
and in the subsequent two years they narrowed and removed the gap
entirely although this continued to be very painful to the fishing industry.

The 1986 capelin quota was less than a tenth of what it had been two years earlier. Still, the capelin case is less impressive than the cod case, as in 1985 the industry had been unable to reach the capelin quota and there was wide appreciation that more problems lay ahead. For cod, the relative integrity of the regulators is demonstrated by the fact that they narrowed and then removed the gap between their quotas and the scientists' recommendations despite the fact that fishermen had been able to overfish the two preceding years' quotas by as much as 26 and 40 percent, respectively. When the scientists again promised fair weather for 1987, the parties nevertheless agreed to a slightly lower quota than that recommended by ICES.

Hence, regarding the shared stocks, it appears that the coastal states have been reasonably good at absorbing bad news from the scientists and transforming it into stricter regulations. As shown by comparing figures 3.3.a and b, moreover, there appears to be scarce systematic difference between the stocks subject to international negotiations and the exclusively Norwegian stocks, such as saithe, redfish, and spring-spawning herring. This is remarkable since the setting of low TACs on the shared stocks is far more demanding at the domestic political level because of the high commercial value of the shared stocks and their significance for settlement in the north. It is also often hypothesized that it is harder for international management bodies than for national ones to produce ecologically sound management since intractable distributional questions cannot be solved by command as in domestic systems. All considered, figures 3.3a and b portray the regime as being reasonably successful in terms of stimulating the coastal states to set quantitative regulations in only moderate excess of ICES recommendations.

The total quotas agreed to in the bilateral commission are turned into national rules of different types. In the Soviet Union, production plans were the common mechanism, whereas an important segment of the Norwegian fishery fleet—coastal vessels using conventional gear—has primarily been regulated by temporal closures.[54] When considering the adequacy of these various measures over time, it may be useful to consider the reported overfishing of various stocks in the Barents Sea, defined as aggregate landings having exceeded the total allowable catch.

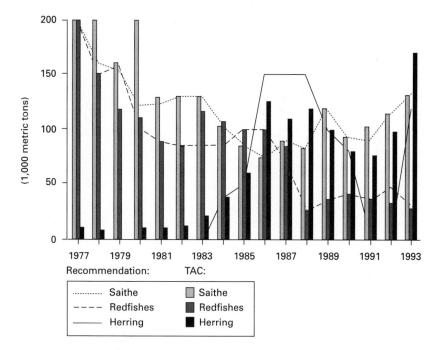

Figure 3.3b
ICES recommendations and Joint Commission decisions on total quotas for three exclusive Norwegian stocks in the Barents Sea. Sources: *ICES Cooperative Research Report*, several volumes.

Figure 3.4 compares the level of overfishing of quotas for the most valuable species regulated by the regime, arctic cod, with two exclusive stocks, saithe, and redfish. It is important to note that these are reported landings and do not necessarily reflect individual noncompliance of fishermen; rather, this type of information indicates whether the regulatory measures used to implement the quota agreement have been sufficient. Two features stand out in this figure. While there are some fluctuations, overfishing of cod has been insignificant since 1985, indicating that the national measures taken since that time are better tailored to keep the harvest within agreed upon levels. Second, cod, while far more significant in commercial value, largely follows the same ups and downs in terms of overfishing as the two nonregime species; and when it deviates, cod overfishing is lower. Both observations support the impression that the

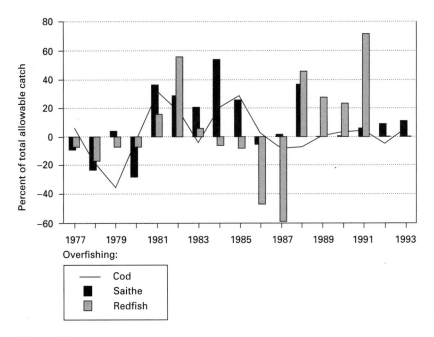

Figure 3.4
Overfishing of arctic cod, in percentage of TAC, as compared with that of exclusive Norwegian stocks. Source: *ICES Cooperative Research Report,* several volumes.

adequacy of the regulation measures taken under the regime has improved over time.

Thus, regulatory performance within the regime, whether measured by the extent to which members can agree on total quotas that reflect scientific recommendations or their ability to implement that agreement in adequate national rules, appears to be fairly high and furthermore improving over time. The effectiveness question, then, is to determine the significance of the bilateral fisheries regime for this situation. Let us inspect this causal question in some detail.

As shown above, an important aspect of the Barents Sea fisheries regime is that it sets up clear rules under which the two parties can license one another's vessels for operating in their respective EEZs. This is relevant both for exclusive and shared stocks. Each year the USSR, and later Russia, has been allowed to take roughly half of its ground-fish quotas in the Norwegian EEZ. Although this arrangement means more competition for the Norwegians, especially the coastal fishermen with limited operational range, it is widely recognized as rational because the fish are larger in this part of the ecosystem and it takes fewer individuals to fill the quota. Indeed, this was one of the major goals of the negotiators. When presenting the Mutual Access Agreement to the Norwegian Storting, the government noted, regarding arctic cod, that "optimal exploitation of the stocks requires that a rational division is found between catches of juvenile fish in the northern and eastern Barents Sea and those of fertile and spawning fish in the future Norwegian economic zone."[55]

This regime feature is important also because it provides the legal basis for a mutually beneficial quota exchange, in which Norway has received primarily cod, shrimp, and scallops in exchange for larger quantities of redfish, blue whiting, and sometimes herring.[56] Given the differences between the two states in fleet structure and reliance on ground-fish, such trading of fishing rights has cushioned the transition to the new coastal state regime and enabled a better utilization of both existing capital and the fisheries resources.[57] With the regime in place, this became part of a regulated and reciprocal practice, and the amount of cod the Soviets were allowed to take in Norwegian waters could be tailored to the needs of coastal fishermen, hence reducing potential anxiety in the northern fisheries communities. Also, as noted, the Mutual Access Agreement is very detailed in its elaboration of rights, rules, and procedures. The parties regarded the substance of the agreement to be potentially problematic and in need of unequivocal specification. As EEZs were quite new at the time and they clearly benefited the coastal states, it is not surprising that the two regime members were cautious about the kinds of practices they would agree to during the formative years. Although this was never a part of the official rationale for that specific agreement, the Norwegian foreign minister later stated in the Barents Sea context that as a result of increasing activity in the northern areas ". . . we must be both mentally and practically prepared for new episodes to occur . . ." and that it was ". . . important to have developed procedures and methods designed to prevent new episodes from leading to conflicts."[58] Thus, by specifying very clearly in the mutual access agreement conditions and procedures to be followed by both parties, the regime removed a set of potential risks that might otherwise have induced Norway to prevent Soviet vessels from taking parts of their quota in Norwegian waters.

One consequence of the regularity of commission meetings and the relatively high transparency of activities occurring within them is that political attention can be drawn to deficiencies in the regulatory efforts of the other, rendering leniency politically more costly at home and abroad. This is demonstrated by how Norway's substantial overfishing of cod in the early 1980s was handled within the regime. From the inception of the regime, Norwegian coastal fishers had been allowed to continue their operations with conventional gear like the handnet and longline, even after the quota had been taken. This provision was seen as a part of the compromise on how to divide the cod quota and was a great relief to coastal fishers in northern Norway. Moreover, the additional amounts of cod taken were expected to be moderate, thus not warranting serious concern. Before 1980, these expectations were proven right but then changes in the abundance of fish close to the coastline pushed Norwegian over fishing to levels ranging between 40 and 100 percent.[59]

The Soviet Union did not raise the issue until 1981, but from then on it expressed deep concern over the potential impact of the Norwegian practice.[60] The immediate Norwegian response was to introduce new regulations. Defending these measures in the Storting, the Norwegian Fisheries Minister pointed out that the Soviet side had attacked the conventional gear exemption and that, to retain it, overfishing must stay within reasonable bounds.[61] In 1983 both parties reached agreement, stating that fishing with conventional gear should be limited in accordance with the quotas and the stock situation. Following this, the conventional gear exemption provision was removed from the protocols and overfishing was gradually reduced. Importantly, there was no compensation for this substantial change in the user rights accorded by the regime (Stokke and Hoel 1991). It is highly probable that the regime, by focusing political attention on a concrete case of regulation failure and by allowing it to be dealt with in an institutional framework respected by both parties, had a role in moving the reluctant party to modify its behavior. It would definitely have been to Norway's advantage to keep the exemption, but the transparency of the system, combined with the fact that the coastal fleet operations now amounted to a downright violation of the spirit, if not the letter, of the regime, rendered it costly to insist on the previous provisions.

Yet another important function of the regime is to take out the conflictual heat of issues that might otherwise impede the development of regulations. To demonstrate this causal pathway, we shall focus on how the regime has enabled members to grapple with the two most divisive issues in the management of the Barents Sea fishery resources: how to divide the three shared fish stocks, and what operational measures to apply when regulating the harvesting pattern, that is, targeting different year-classes of fish.

Concerning the division of the shared stocks, even prior to the signing of the framework agreement in 1975, the parties had reached an understanding on an equal sharing of arctic cod and haddock for 1976; and this fixed key was confirmed two years later (Engesæter 1993). Unlike more mature sharing arrangements, such as those between Norway and the European Union based on stable or adjustable zonal attachment, the Barents Sea solution reflected partly historical fishing but predominantly a political need among the participants to agree on the issue. Zonal attachment was problematic to assess since the EEZ delimitation was and continues to be a matter of dispute; and there was inadequate knowledge about the biological distribution of the stock. Only in 1979 was the capelin division set, and the 60–40 percent solution in favor of Norway was a result of both historical catches and additional scientific input on stock abundance and migration (Engesæter 1993). The fact that the initial division of the shared stocks is not subject to negotiation at commission meetings means that the quota negotiations are not mired in difficult questions of distribution: the fixed keys provide a safety net or a fallback division if these negotiations should fail. As the parties can be confident about the share they will acquire, this year and in the future, they can concentrate on issues of conservation over time.

As to the second divisive issue, regulation of the harvesting pattern, some harmonization between the coastal states is important both for the adequacy of the measures and for the likelihood that they will be enforced. Without this, the impact of costly restraint on the part of one coastal state can easily be destroyed by the other. The matter causes conflicts because migration patterns make the average size of cod and haddock taken off the coast of Norway larger than that taken off of Russia. Norway prefers to see the stocks protected by large minimum mesh-size requirements because targeting bigger individuals is the best way to combine low fishing mortality and high total quotas, which is good for the fishing communities in the north. Predictably, the smaller mean size of the ground fish in the Soviet zone rendered this conservation measure less attractive to that country.

Here is how this contentious issue has been handled in the regime. While the question had been raised by Norway in 1978, the parties agreed in the 1980 commission meeting to use 125 mm as a minimum mesh size. ICES had strongly recommended a greater mesh-size expansion in 1979 and repeated its recommendation in the two subsequent years.[62] In response, Norway raised the mesh-size issue again in 1981 and then every year until 1988, advocating an enlargement to 135 mm in the whole ecosystem.[63] The Soviet argument against increased mesh size was that this is not the best way to avoid the taking of undersized fish. Soviet scientists argued instead that juvenile fish are usually killed in large-meshed trawl bags and far better protection is achieved by a combination of minimum size regulations and prompt area closures. Since the Soviets did not agree, Norway went along with a unilateral mesh enlargement for Norwegian vessels and for foreign vessels with Norwegian licence. The Soviet side objected to this unilateral measure in a note,[64] restated in the subsequent commission meeting,[65] but after that refrained from raising the issue again. Having paid lip-service to their principled view that all regulations should be conducted jointly, the Soviets later stated that the agreed measure was sufficient and they would retain it.[66] The vocabulary softened even further in 1989, when both parties admitted that they still disagreed on the mesh size but that unitary measures in the whole ecosystem were long-term goals.[67]

Although the laggard state has so far failed to implement the stricter measure proposed by the other, significant adaptation has taken place on the part of the Soviet Union and later Russia. The regime has not kept the Norwegian side from setting stricter standards in its own waters than those agreed to in the commission, so Soviet and later Russian vessels have been obliged to use this gear when operating in Norwegian waters.

Within their own zone, according to Russian sources, the Soviets intensified their use of area closures in the course of the mesh-size dispute. Indeed, Murmanrybvod, the Russian Coast Guard, exercises greater discretion in establishing area closures than its Norwegian counterpart (Davidsen et al. 1994, 24). Finally, urged by the joint commission, the scientific organizations were quick to respond to the needs for more knowledge concerning selection. Since 1981, the joint Norwegian–Soviet research program has included studies on this issue, first confined to mesh size but later taking a broader approach to the question of selection techniques. As the harvesting pattern debate moved from the highly politicized mesh-size question to an issue on which none of the parties was politically committed—namely a Norwegian proposal to introduce a new sorting grid in the shrimp and cod fisheries—the Soviet and later Russian regulatory response became far more positive. The two countries soon agreed to mandate such devices in the shrimp fishery and the Russians have signaled a willingness to introduce them in the cod fishery as well. One interpretation of this development is that the mesh-size dispute had been so heavily politicized and marked by such strong policy commitments that giving way on the issue was perceived as embarrassing to both sides. If credible reference can be made to new knowledge about the matter, however, especially when this knowledge has been established by one's own scientists, such embarrassment can be reduced. Thus, face-saving may have been one of the intended functions of this set of investigations, in addition to the task of clarifying the relative merits of various selection techniques.[68]

In summary, the regime has enhanced regulatory practices in the Barents Sea by mobilizing the authority of fisheries science in the decision-making process, by decoupling rules permitting reciprocal fishing from initial fears of political incidents or legal encroachment of coastal state authority, and by exposing inadequate regulations. It has also served to depoliticize conflicting aspects of regulation. In the case of the initial quota division of the three shared stocks, the fixed keys inherent in the regime have removed an issue from the annual agenda; and in the mesh-size dispute, the regime lessens the shadow of disagreement by permitting unilateral measures and helping members overcome their differences through scientific innovations, as well as providing acceptable ways for nations to make otherwise awkward shifts in their positions on the disputed matter.

Compliance control   Overfishing of allotted fishing quotas is a pervasive phenomenon everywhere, and neither Norway nor the former Soviet Union are exceptions in this respect. Compliance control is affected by the relative transparency ensured by the regime that, combined with the regularity of commission meetings, serves to render it more costly for the laggard state to continue practices that violate commitments accepted under the regime. Although such processes are difficult to measure and not unequivocal, both the prestige of marine biological science and the high degree of domestic involvement in the workings of the regime may serve to enhance the authority of the decisions made within it.

In mapping the evolving compliance control practices in the Barents Sea, and subsequently examining the significance of the regime for this, we shall focus on three aspects. The first indicator is geographic coverage. As shown above, a very significant change introduced by the regime is that inspections are now conducted on a regular basis in the disputed area of the Barents Sea, because the specifics of the Grey Zone Agreement serve to decouple these practices from the competing territorial claims. Although for each party the regime solves only half of the problem, as it allows enforcement only for vessels licensed by itself and gives no access whatsoever to the enforcement behavior of the other party, it has been instrumental in meeting part of the enforcement requirements in the disputed area.

Another indicator of the emerging enforcement practices is the number of Coast Guard inspections in the Barents Sea. This indicator is not wholly satisfactory because aggregate numbers tell nothing about thoroughness or the kind of violations that are targeted. Moreover, it would be a more precise measure of inspection intensity if we could adjust for changes in the number of fishing vessels operating in the area. On the other hand, because the trend in both countries has been toward fewer fishing vessels operating in the Barents Sea, the growth in the number of inspections per vessel is probably higher than indicated by the line in figure 3.5, which portrays the activity in the three northern zones where Norway claims management authority. These are the Norwegian EEZ,

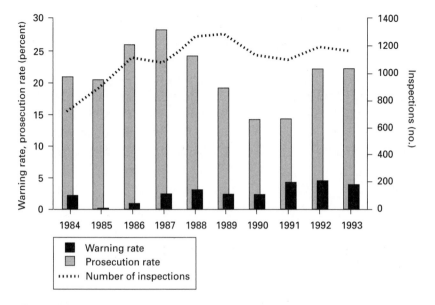

Figure 3.5
Inspections and violation rates in Norwegian waters. Source: Norwegian Coast
Guard materials.

including the Grey Zone, and the two indiscriminate fishery protection
zones around Svalbard and Jan Mayen. Comparable diachronic data for
the Soviet zone is not available. The figure shows a marked increase in
the number of inspections, beginning in 1984 and continuing until late
in the decade when it drops slightly. The strengthening of the Coast
Guard had been a high priority issue ever since the extension of Norway's
marine jurisdiction.

A third and more indirect indicator of efforts to enhance adherence
with regulations is also portrayed in figure 3.5. When we control for variations in the inconvenience of the rules, changes in the violation rate, or
the number of violations per inspection, assumably reflect changes in the
overall compliance control system, including appeals to solidarity, inclu-
sion of the industry in the management process, intrusive monitoring,
and the severity of sanctions imposed on violators.[69] In Norwegian waters, both domestic and foreign vessels have shown a stable and high
inclination to violate various kinds of regulations, especially reporting

procedures and mesh-size restrictions. Violations vary in severity, and figure 3.5 distinguishes between incidents in which the Coast Guard issues a warning, written or oral, and those in which legal prosecution is initiated; both violation rates are measured in percentage of Coast Guard inspections.[70] It might be expected that the growing frequency of inspection recorded above has rendered potential violators more careful, but this is only partly confirmed by figure 3.5. Over the past decade, the warning and prosecution rates combined have ranged between 20 and 30 percent. Two periods of extensive violation stand out in the figure. The first, between 1986 and 1988, might be explained by a rise in the inconvenience of regulations. Unlike the rest of the decade, the cod and haddock quotas during these years were set so high that fishers were actually unable to take them. For haddock, underfishing ranged between 40 and 60 percent. While this surely allieviates the inconvenience of quantitative restrictions, it dramatically boosts the incentive to break operational regulations like mesh-size rules and area or time closures. In its 1988 report, the Coast Guard confirmed that mesh-size violations and inadequate logbooks were the most frequent type occurring in the Norwegian zones that year. The rate of violations rose again in 1991, and as the figure shows, this latter increase comprised the more severe type of violation leading to legal prosecution. This second wave of violation probably reflects an actual decline in the compliance control performance rather than the conditions surrounding it. These problems were closely related to the dissolution of the integrated production system in the northwest Russian fisheries complex and the steep growth of direct landings of fish in foreign ports (Stokke 1992). The Soviet control system had largely been based on juxtaposition of catch reports from vessels and vessel-owners on the one hand, and reception reports from processing units on the other. When harvests were increasingly landed abroad, this control system became a paper tiger. ICES has estimated that underreporting of arctic cod was as high as 130,000 tons in 1992, or roughly 25 percent;[71] and Russian vessels are believed to be responsible for the lion's share of this. The Norwegian Coast Guard reported that by late April, as many severe violations had been revealed in the Norwegian EEZ as during the entire previous year, and Russian vessels were the most frequent violators.[72] A comprehensive report estimating levels of overfishing in the Barents Sea was produced by Norwegian authorities responsible for monitoring which concluded that predominantly Russian, but also Norwegian, Faroese and EU vessels had conducted substantial illegal fishing in 1992 and that uncertainty was particularly high for activities in the Russian EEZ.[73] According to the inspection director of Murmanrybvod, only 18 out of 154 licensed vessels were inspected even once in the course of 1992.[74] Claiming that the situation is now under control, the Russian commissioner later confirmed that Russian overfishing had reached very high levels that year.[75]

Official statistics would imply that the situation in Soviet waters was very different from that in the Norwegian part of the Barents Sea. Although for the entire Soviet EEZ, 7,306 inspections revealed 753 violations in 1989, none of the 118 Barents Sea inspections were reported to reveal violations of any kind.[76] The impression that Soviet vessels have been relatively rule abiding, especially in the 1980s, is supported by inspection reports from the Norwegian EEZ. While Soviet fishers were regularly caught throughout the 1980s violating the rules in this zone, they usually fared better than Norwegian and third-country vessels.[77] Nevertheless, in the Soviet system as well as the Norwegian, there have been clear incentives to take more than the allotted quota. Under the old production system, overfulfilling one's plan by 15 to 20 percent was rewarded by a 20 percent premium on wages for crew and captain.[78] True, as pointed out by Hønneland (1993, 145), in the Soviet context where merchandise was considerably scarcer than purchasing power, such rewards were not necessarily strong incentives to overfish quotas. If a captain failed to meet the production plans, however, his career opportunities would be seriously undermined. Before 1990 the captain would be personally responsible for fulfilling production tasks, and failure could lead to transfer to a less attractive vessel or denied participation in the highly profitable foreign expeditions. The captain might even be out of job, a phenomenon that was on the rise in the Soviet fishing industry during the 1980s. Moreover, there is little reason to believe that Soviet captains have behaved better in their own EEZ than in the Norwegian one, as fines used to be twenty times higher when the violations occurred in foreign zones.[79] And today the incentives to break quantitative or operational restrictions are much greater than under the former system, as direct landings in foreign ports yield substantial hard currency earnings.

Hence, especially in the waters under Norwegian jurisdiction, compliance control efforts have intensified during most of the regime period and, to some extent, this appears to have affected the rate of violation. Closely related to the transition from the Soviet Union to Russia, however, the overall Russian compliance control system has had problems in recent years adjusting to a large part of the harvest being landed abroad.

Turning now to the causal significance of the bilateral fisheries regime in affecting compliance control in the Barents Sea, there is little doubt that domestic enforcement institutions would have existed even in the absence of the international regime. They are set up primarily to meet domestic needs. And the most direct impact of the regime on the development of compliance control in the Barents Sea is that it has permitted monitoring and enforcement in its disputed parts. Beyond this, the regime affects compliance control practices in two principal ways: legitimization and embarrassment.

A case can be made for the view that the pattern of participation in the making of regulatory decisions in the Barents Sea fisheries regime affects the likelihood that they will be heeded by fishermen. There are several aspects of this, and to some extent they are intertwined. The regime has served to routinize certain types of activities in both countries that are relevant to management practices. Regulatory decisions are largely guided by a well developed, interactive scientific apparatus of quite high standing that serves to enhance their legitimacy. Presumably, this has been particularly significant in the latter part of the period under scrutiny when the messages from the scientists have been dismal. Another process-related feature that may enhance the standing of regime outputs is the institutional porosity in both member states among managers and industry. The key industry organizations, Sevryba and Norway's Fisherman Association, are prominent participants both in the preparatory process in their respective countries and at delegation meetings. As a result, they develop a considerable degree of competence concerning both the scientific underpinnings and the international regulations affecting the operations of their members, both of which may enhance their inclination to accept and abide by these regulations. Although there is also a danger to this inclusive aspect of the regime, in that it gives industry an opportunity to successfully press for short-term gains at the cost of over-time conservation, participation tends to enhance those prepared to carry out the decisions made.

The Barents Sea fisheries regime has also served to draw political attention toward inadequate implementation and enforcement practices, thus causing embarrassment. By ensuring a regular and publicly available set of standards, both scientific recommendations and administrative rules by which behavior can be evaluated, the regime serves to increase the general exposure of fisheries management to criticism and political pressure. In both countries, domestic criticism of the regime was mounting in the late 1980s, and critics were able to support their argument with comprehensive information generated within the regime on fishing behavior throughout the ecosystem. Moreover, the regime's bilateral character has rendered it harder for coastal states to ascribe inadequate management performance to general collective-action problems inherent in large-number management systems. While they can still blame the other member, the regime has boosted the accountability of the fisheries authorities in the two states.

The embarrassment pathway is also apparent in relations between the two coastal states, as seen above in the role of the regime in channeling dissatisfaction with Norwegian regulation of the coastal fleet. More recently the regime has served to add political energy in dealing with the growing Russian compliance control deficit noted above, thus increasing the political costs of lenient implementation. During the summer of 1992, a number of indications suggested that Faroe vessels fishing on Russian licences were substantially over fishing their quotas.[80] Norway raised the issue with the Russians, referring to the third-country quota agreed to in the annual negotiations[81] and the need for adequate control measures. Although the initial response was that Russian authorities had no evidence of illegal operations, a few weeks later the Faroese were thrown out of the Russian zone despite the fact that, in the meantime, they had bought additional quotas from Russian companies.[82]

Russian acknowledgment in the early 1990s that monitoring and enforcement were inadequate was immediately followed with a series of initiatives to enhance the level of coordination among compliance control authorities in the two countries. In 1993, a precursor to what is now a Permanent Committee on Management and Control prepared the following set of cooperative proposals that are currently being implemented:[83] (1) There is agreement to exchange reports on landings made by vessels of the other country, as well as inspection reports and to initiate direct lines of communication among inspection vessels from the two countries. This drastically reduces possibilities to operate with one set of figures in the logbook meant for foreign authorities, which may cross-check with actual inventory either in port or at sea, and another set for home authorities. (2) A system of observers on inspections of the other country is being tried out, both in ports and onboard vessels. Important for the jurisdictional decoupling characterizing the regime, these observers do not have any inspection competence of their own. (3) The two control bureaucracies have agreed to intensify their interaction to standardize routines and learn from solutions developed by the other; for this purpose, joint courses for inspectors are held. (4) Agreement has been reached on common conversion parameters when estimating the round fish correspondence to various processed products, which is important for passive control—an essential component in any monitoring system. (5) Finally, cooperation exists in the technology area on the development of a positional tracking system in the Barents Sea.[84]

Analytic Assessment: Pathways and Mechanisms

Using the terminology developed in chapter 1, this section will elaborate on the behavioral models and pathways invoked in the causal narrative of how the bilateral fisheries regime has helped its members cope with their jurisdictional and fisheries management problems in the Barents Sea.

The Regime as Utility Modifier

This mechanism, which highlights the role of the regime in altering the costs and benefits of various types of behavior, has been significant to the full range of management challenges faced in the Barents Sea. As to the internal jurisdictional problem, the Grey Zone part of the regime permits enforcement activity without compromising the competing jurisdictional claims in the area to the same extent as its most likely alternatives.

This it does by distinguishing between the agreement area and the disputed area, thus weakening the links between actual inspection and prosecution in the former and the accumulation of jurisdictional claims in the latter. Although the specifics of this particular agreement are unique, the more generic technique of shrouding the acts of authority inherent in fisheries management in a manner that is silently understood by all concerned is common to other regimes as well. One example is the evolving inspection system under the Convention for the Conservation of Antarctic Marine Living Resources (Stokke 1996). In the Barents Sea, just like in the Antarctic, one reason the coastal states have been willing to engage in such diversionary exercises is an eagerness to avoid high tension or conflicting situations in the region.

The regime has also modified actor incentives in the fishery research area by facilitating cost-saving coordination of investigations, especially through collaborative survey programs, thus rendering investments in scientific activities more attractive. A significant precondition for the ability of research institutes to mobilize the regime for funding purposes, however, has been the considerable value of the fisheries in the Barents Sea. When the harvest shrank after the capelin collapse in the mid-1980s, Soviet funding for scientific investigations began a downward turn that only accelerated with the dissolution of the Soviet Union. By contrast, in the far more stable Norwegian economic context, scientific activities have remained steady despite considerable fluctuations in the commercial value of the fisheries.

Facilitating cooperation by delinkage of problematic aspects has also been conducive to regulatory work under the regime. By specifying very clearly in the mutual access agreement the conditions and procedures to be followed by both parties when vessels operate in each other's zone, the regime eliminated potential risks of tension or embarrassing incidents that might otherwise have resulted from operation of, in particular, Soviet vessels in Norwegian waters. Because of the larger individual size of the cod taken off Norway, such access is rational from an economic point of view. The relevance of this regime feature in other geographical areas can be high, as both shared stocks and potentially tense interstate relations are frequent occurrences in world fisheries. The regime has also served to remove or soften the impact of manifest conflicting issues in the management process. In the question of mesh-size regulations, the regime has helped the coastal states turn a political issue into a scientific or even technical one.

Another way in which the regime affects the utilities associated with various regulatory practices in the Barents Sea stems from the fact that it only sets minimum standards for the coastal states. Although the latter have agreed to cooperate in fisheries matters, they retain significant rule-making autonomy in their own zones. The front-runner benefits stemming from this, including political credit for environmental responsibility, is evident in the dispute over mesh-size regulations. The regime did not stop Norway from launching stricter measures unilaterally in its own zones, implying more authoritative pressure on the other party to take similar steps. Of course, this is a double-edged sword. If a no-agreement situation is unattractive to both parties, this may enhance their flexibility in the negotiations. Young (1989) has pointed out that a sense of urgency can be stimulating for negotiators trying to hammer out acceptable compromises, as this will keep them from bickering over details. On the other hand, as the mesh-size dispute demonstrates, a harmonizing regime is far less vulnerable to conflicts in that regulation and enforcement do not grind to a halt while contentious issues are being settled. Thus, this feature of the regime alters the utility of front-runners in regulative matters and, conversely, allow some measure of embarrassment for laggards. In the case of Soviet dissatisfaction with Norwegian regulation of the coastal fleet in the early 1980s, embarrassment is also enhanced by the fact that the regime provides transparency regarding measures taken and a stable meeting point for representatives engaging in a discourse structured by certain clearly expressed principles, including conservation over time.

Embarrassment is a process affecting compliance control as well: the transparency ensured by the regime increases the exposure of its members to scrutiny, at home as well as abroad. Criticism of inadequate regulations has been voiced by various groups, both environmental and scientific, in Norway and the former Soviet Union, and these critics feed on the information made available through the regime. Commission meetings have been a forum for channeling dissatisfaction about inadequate Russian compliance control activity. Thus, in a regime that cannot itself implement and enforce agreed upon regulations, transparency can play a vital role in inducing the members to give life to the agreement, because it becomes embarrassing, and hence costly, to violate it. In the Soviet and Russian contexts, the conditions for this particular mechanism have improved considerably over the past few years. This is so partly because information has become more accessible and criticism of powerful institutions far more accepted, and partly because the late 1980s saw the emergence of an independent environmental movement in northwestern Russia.

The Regime as Enhancer of Cooperation

The perception exists among regime participants that the track record of their cooperation and the regularity of their meetings has served to enhance mutual confidence and understanding among researchers and managers in the two coastal states. These are important ingredients in any formula to overcome collective action problems. One instance is the mutual access arrangement, whose general attractiveness drops rapidly if one party doubts the sincerity of the regulation and enforcement practices of the other. If domestic enforcement is lenient and incentives to overfish are present, which they often are, fish taken in the zone of the other country will not necessarily be adequately balanced by reductions in a country's own waters. Since the dissolution of the Soviet Union, knowledge has been gained about scant restraint among fishers and inadequate compliance control of vessels licensed by Russia both in its own waters and the Grey Zone. This demonstrates that mutual access is only a practical regime feature if there is either a high degree of confidence in the regulation and enforcement practices of the other or considerable transparency regarding these practices. Previously, the transparency of enforcement practices was quite low in the bilateral fisheries regime, but because of an emerging coordination of compliance control efforts it is now on the increase.

A more tangible regime feature facilitating regulatory work is the set of fixed keys guiding the initial division of shared fish stocks, which has the impact of decoupling conservation matters from those related to allocation, reducing considerably the transaction costs associated with annual negotiations. In turn, this may benefit scientific cooperation as well. Since the quota division here, unlike the situation with some other agreements, is unrelated to changes in zonal attachment, there is no incentive to distort scientific findings to exaggerate the relative abundance in one's own waters. An important condition for agreeing to the fixed keys, however, was the fact that knowledge about zonal attachment was rather limited at the time they were agreed to; had this not been the case, such rough-and-ready measures would probably appear too arbitrary, despite the fact that they facilitate annual negotiations.

The Regime as Bestower of Authority

The authority mechanism has not loomed large in this analysis of the Barents Sea fisheries regime. While formally the regime is one of harmonization only, however, measures agreed to are in practice automatically translated into national rules. There is an interesting interplay, moreover, between utility modification and bestowal of authority in the processes in which Norway and Russia responded to criticism from each other on coastal fleet regulations and enforcement practices in their own zones.

As to compliance control, the regime confirms and borrows the prestige of fisheries science in the management process to enhance the authority of regime outputs. The inclusiveness of the regime of industry representatives might trigger the same mechanism by bringing together the scientific community and the organizations directly affected by regulations. Although this may enhance the legitimacy of the rules, the overall impact on management is ambiguous since participating industry groups often try to dilute regulative measures. The robustness of the authority mechanism is also at stake here, as an important condition for the applied scientific organizations to uphold their perceived integrity within close corporative systems is independency of industrial groups. Especially in Russia, over the past few years the burden of financing scientific activities in the Barents Sea has been substantially shifted from bureaucracy to industry.

The Regime as Role Definer

One of the key accomplishments of the regime appears to be that it operationalized in the Barents Sea context the emerging consensus during the Law of the Sea negotiations on extended coastal state jurisdiction, thus assigning radically new roles both to coastal and noncoastal states in the ocean belt between 12 and 200 nautical miles from the baselines. The upshot of this was rapidly declining third-party harvests in the Barents Sea. Almost any fisheries regime set up by Norway and the Soviet Union would have achieved this since both EEZs and the phasing out of third-country vessels was firmly nested in emerging customary law. And later on, when coastal state management of cod outside the EEZs was challenged by vessels operating in the Loophole of international waters in the Barents Sea, the role of the regime has been very limited.

Beyond the jurisdictional issues, role assignment has been particularly weighty for the generation and input of high-quality, impartial scientific advice in the management of Barents Sea living resources. A salient feature of the regime is the central role it has given to applied science, in both the texts underlying the regime and activities generated within it. This feature, in combination with the authority and learning mechanisms, has presumably enhanced the availability of funds for scientific investigations in the Barents Sea. The regime has made it routine for regulators to turn to particular scientific organizations with practical questions about management problems, and these organizations have gradually improved their ability to respond to such questions in a manner comprehensible and acceptable to the regulators. The likely budgetary impacts of this are further enhanced by the fact that a well-founded scientific basis is often mobilized by regulators to underscore the authority of the rules they agree to.

The Regime as Learning Facilitator

The regime has provided a testing ground for various contentious management solutions, including the parallel system of licensing and compliance control in the Grey Zone and the mutual access arrangement that, early on, was regarded with considerable caution by regime members. These arrangements have gradually grown into regular and uncontroversial practices that help balance the three regime objectives of delinking management from jurisdictional concerns, stock conservation, and efficient allocation of harvesting effort. More specifically, the bilateral regime has served as a transmission belt for fisheries research technologies, especially on the software side of stock modeling, and in recent years for harvesting technologies as well.

While the regime has generally supported scientific activities, it has at the same time accorded a privileged position to a small subset of largely departmental scientific organizations in providing knowledge about stock dynamics in the Barents Sea. Critics argue that this, and the fact that actors outside the fisheries sector—especially environmental organizations—have found it hard to gain access to the decision-making process, has served to confine the understanding of the problem dealt with in the Barents Sea and delayed the introduction of wider, ecosystemic considerations into management decisions. At the most general level, allocation of particular tasks to certain organizations implies accumulation of special experience and expertise that, over time, make the participation of those organizations in regime activities increasingly natural and even necessary. This situation may render decision making less open to competing views or perspectives and thus truncate the operation of another mechanism— that of learning. The very secretive nature of Soviet science on matters related to the fisheries industry, and the Arctic more generally, has strengthened such a tendency—until *glasnost* made it possible, or even opportune, to criticize the doings of establishment institutions. Beyond this, there is nothing unique about the Barents Sea in this regard as the assignment of special responsibilities to certain institutions is commonplace when particular competencies are required to solve problems. Acting as a counterforce to any such tendency toward secrecy or narrowing of perspective is the rather high degree of transparency ensured by the regime, because of its nestedness in ICES, concerning scientific activities and results. Also working against overspecialization is the fact that both the Norwegian and the Russian research institutes, which predominate in the mapping of stock dynamics, are also responsible for wider environmental studies in the Barents Sea. Hence, under the auspices of the regime, a comprehensive and cooperative multispecies modeling program was initiated rather early on; and to some extent this is already affecting regulative decisions, as evidenced in the conservative management of capelin in the early 1990s.

The Regime as Source of Internal Realignment

This mechanism, which highlights the significance of the regime in creating new constituencies and empowering some domestic groups at the expense of others, has played only a minor role in the management of

Barents Sea living resources. In both countries, the level of inclusiveness of various target groups is very high during preparatory stages and at commission meeting, whereas other groups with an expressed interest, such as environmental organizations, have not loomed large in regime-related activities. This is a reflection not of the regime, however, but of the weak position of the latter in domestic decision making on fisheries management. We have noted the brief intermezzo during the last years of the Soviet Union, in which an environmental agency was formally in charge of parts of the management tasks, and also the trend that environmental agencies and nongovernmental organizations have gradually increased their participation in the Norwegian corporative system in the fisheries area. Both of those processes, however, were domestic and not regime driven. Beyond the modest point that critics of management practices, especially in Russia, have utilized the information made available through the bilateral regime, the impact of the regime on domestic alignment patterns has been negligible.

Conclusion

Has the Barents Sea fisheries regime been effective in contributing substantially to the solution of the problems that gave rise to its formation? The problem addressed by this particular regime is two stranded. The sovereignty part of it has been to achieve consent for phasing out of third countries from the area and to get a fisheries management system up and running in the disputed parts of the Barents Sea without jeopardizing competing claims to sovereignty. And the fisheries management problem is essentially to strike an adequate trade-off between current and future use of the resource and to legitimize the allocation of that resource between various users among and within states.

Today, the internal part of the sovereignty problem has largely been solved, and the regime itself, particularly the Grey Zone Agreement, has played an important part by blurring the relationship between necessary regulatory and compliance control activities in the disputed area and the substantiation of sovereignty claims. Externally, however, while early on the regime was instrumental in realizing the potential created by the evolving Law of the Sea for coastal state privileges within the EEZs, the regime has failed to prevent or even reduce third-party harvesting activities in the high-seas areas beyond the economic zones. This is not surprising, as the legal nesting of coastal state authority was much weaker regarding high-seas fisheries. During the very period when the Loophole fisheries became an issue in the Barents Sea, the respective rights and obligations of coastal states and flag states in the management of straddling and highly migratory stocks were themselves made subject to global treaty negotiations under the United Nations.

The second strand of the problem addressed by the regime is fisheries management, or proper use of the resource over time. For most of the period in question, the state of fish stocks and industries has been far below desired levels. Still, the general health of the ecosystem has improved in recent years, and the three shared stocks managed within the regime have fared comparatively well, especially when considering the additional problems stemming from nonexclusive management. Limited knowledge about the relative impact of changes not related to the regime, such as temperature shifts, however, renders it difficult to decide only on this basis whether or not the bilateral regime itself has made a substantial difference. This is a generic problem of causal analysis and one that pertains also to the behavioral aspects of fisheries management examined in this chapter—scientific investigation, regulation, and compliance control. For these three, however, the causal leaps are shorter and the counterfactual reasoning involved in any single case study are more transparent. Analysis of these behavioral variables suggests that the regime has contributed positively to the environmental and socioeconomic situation in the region. It is likely that the situation would have been worse—perhaps considerably worse—in the absence of the regime.

On scientific investigations, in summary, the bilateral regime has clearly strengthened departmental research organizations by placing their cooperation in a firm framework, regularizing their interaction with decision makers, and boosting the financial basis for research activities. This has encouraged practical, applied research on the Barents Sea resources. While this may have happened at the expense of competing institutions and confirmed a sector-specific approach to management, the cost-efficient pooling of resources among scientists in the two countries has nevertheless furthered the growth of fairly advanced multispecies science in the Barents Sea. Whereas some level of cooperation would have been realized anyway through ICES, the regime has enhanced the generation of scientific knowledge about stock dynamics in the Barents Sea as well as the imputation of such knowledge into the management process.

As to the conversion of such knowledge into adequate regulation of harvesting, the bilateral regime has played a role in helping the coastal states overcome the two main dilemmas of fisheries management: the conservational one of choosing between present and future use, and the allocational one of deciding how and by whom the fish should be taken. By mobilizing the authority of fisheries science in periods of stock decline, and by providing a forum for embarrassment of inadequate regulations, the regime has fostered regulations that are steadily more in line with ICES recommendations and increasingly constrain harvesting activity. About the allocative dilemma, the regime has promoted a more rational employment of fishing by reducing fears that reciprocal fishing may lead to political incidents or undermine coastal state authority. It has also developed ways to depoliticize conflicting allocative issues, as shown by the fixed keys on the initial quota division of shared stocks, or the channeling of conflicting issues into the scientific apparatus by redefining them as primarily technical matters.

On the third task of fisheries management—compliance control—the regime has been partly successful. It has improved the geographic coverage of such activities by ensuring that licensing and inspection in the disputed part of the Barents Sea can occur in a way that touches only lightly on the sovereignty issue. Without the regime in place, such inspections would have been very difficult to achieve. On the other hand, transparency has remained limited as inspectors from either state can only enter vessels licensed by the country itself in the Grey Zone and inspectors do not have access to the zone of the other. To some extent, the prestige of marine biological science, and also the inclusive approach taken by the regime toward domestic industrial organizations, may have served to boost the authority of regulations, thus forming an independent part of the overall system of compliance enhancement in the Barents Sea. And the regularity of commission meetings, involving largely the same key people from one year to another, has made it more embarrassing for a laggard state in terms of compliance control, such as the Soviet Union and Russia in the early 1990s, to continue lenient enforcement of commitments taken on under the regime. Such processes, and the perception that both parties could gain from them, were important to the rapid advancement of coordination in the compliance control area since the dissolution of the Soviet Union, including exchange of inspection data and observers on inspecting vessels of the other.

Regarding the applicability of the Barents Sea experience to other management regimes, the conditions surrounding this regime, except for the last few years following the demise of the Soviet Union, have not been exceptional. True, the very high value of the Barents Sea fisheries makes it stand out somewhat, as does its geographic placement in the midst of the East-West military rivalry. But the impact of this setting has been neither very strong nor necessarily disruptive for fisheries management. To some extent, the shared view among regime members that tension should be avoided in this area has probably been conducive to reaching agreement on contested or difficult matters (Stokke and Tunander 1994). As to the very special conditions resulting from the political and economic reorganization of the former Soviet Union, it is important to note the continuity of the regime-generated processes emphasized here. While the profound changes in Russia posed new challenges to the management system, they also created new opportunities, as shown in the growing cooperation on this matter. But in either case, these changes have only amplified problems and practices that were already present in the bilateral management system.

At one level, then, lessons drawn from this case are related to the specific features of the management regime that have triggered the behavioral adaptation recorded here, relevant to the jurisdictional problem and fisheries management tasks. An account of these features would focus on, for instance, the diversionary provisions of the Grey Zone Agreement, the regularity of commission meetings, the centrality of the scientific institutions, the fixed keys, the transparency of the regime, and so forth. As we have tried to show, however, and as emphasized in chapter 1, these regime features are closely tied in with the contextual specifics of the case under scrutiny. Therefore, when considering the applicability of the findings in this case study to other contexts, such regime features must always be closely linked to the more generic behavioral mechanisms and causal pathways that we have brought out when assessing and explaining the effectiveness of the Barents Sea fisheries regime.

Notes

Very constructive comments received from Oran Young, Marc Levy, and the other contributors to this volume are appreciated as well as those from Steinar Andresen, Marius Hauge, Alf Håkon Hoel, Arvid Hylen, Geir Hønneland, Per Solemdal, Jon Birger Skjærseth, Arild Underdal, Davor Vidas, Jørgen Wettestad, and four anonymous reviewers.

Olav Schram Stokke is research director at the Fridtjof Nansen Institute, Norway, and can be contacted at Olav.S.Stokke@fni.no. Lee G. Anderson is professor of economics and marine policy at the College of Marine Studies, University of Delaware, and can be contacted at lgafish@UDel.Edu. Natalia Mirovitskaya is senior research fellow at the Institute of World Economy and International Relations, Russian Academy of Sciences; she is presently affiliated with Nicholas School of the Environment at Duke University, and can be contacted at nataliam@duke.edu.

1. Drilling in the Barents Sea has been very promising on the Russian side of the disputed area, but less so on the Norwegian side. Occurrences have been largely gas (Moe 1994).

2. Norway is obliged to keep Svalbard demilitarized, give nationals of any of the signatory states equal access to specified economic activity, and refrain from collecting higher taxes than required to cover the costs of administering the archipelago.

3. Agreement for the Implementation of the Provisions of the United Nations Convention on the Law of the Sea of 10 December 1982 relating to the Conservation and Management of Straddling Fish Stocks and Highly Migratory Fish Stocks (New York, 4 December 1995; adopted 4 August 1995), reproduced in *International Legal Materials*, Vol. 34, No. 6, 1995, 1547–1580.

4. Now the Committee of Fisheries of the Russian Federation, which forms a part of the Ministry of Agriculture.

5. Only a few thousand individuals are engaged in fishing and processing outside Sevryba, in the seven to eight fisheries *kolkhozes* (cooperatives) in Murmansk County (Castberg 1992, 21).

6. The council is composed of representatives from central fisheries and environmental bureaucracies, regional authorities, fisheries industry organizations and research institutions; it is chaired by the first deputy chairman of the Fisheries Committee.

7. Just like PINRO, VNIRO is represented in Russian delegations to ICES as well as the bilateral Russo-Norwegian Commission.

8. Report to the Storting (St.meld.) 58, 1991–92, 36–8.

9. Similarly to Russia's Northern Scientific Fisheries Council, the Norwegian Regulation Council includes representatives of the fishermen, the processing industry, trade unions, and central bureaucracies in the fisheries and environmental areas. In addition, the Norwegian Saami parliament is represented (Report to the Storting (St.meld.) 58 1991– 92, 73).

10. North-East Atlantic Fisheries Convention (London, 24 January 1959), *United Nation Treaty Series,* Vol. 486, 157.

11. These agreements concerned the regulation of sealing (1957), procedures for handling claims in connection with damage to fishing gear (1959), and reciprocal access in each other's fisheries zones (1962).

12. Russia is the legal successor of the Soviet Union in these agreements. Russia argues that the 1920 Svalbard Treaty is also a part of the Barents Sea regime, but this is denied by Norway.

13. Overenskomst mellom Regjeringen i Kongeriket Norge og Regjeringen i Unionen av Sovjetiske Sosialistiske Republikker om samarbeid innen fiskerinæringen (Moscow 11 April 1975, in force the same day), *Overenskomster med fremmede makter,* Oslo: Ministry of Foreign Affairs, 1975, 546–9.

14. Recommendation S. of the Standing Committee on Foreign Affairs and the Constitution (Innst. S.) 191, 1974–75.

15. Overenskomst mellom Regjeringen i Kongeriket Norge og Regjeringen i Unionen av Sovjetiske Sosialistiske Republikker om gjensidige fiskeriforbindelser (Moscow 15 October 1976, in force 21 April 1977), *Overenskomster med fremmede makter,* Oslo: Ministry of Foreign Affairs, 1977, 974–8.

16. Avtale mellom Norge og Sovjetunionen om en midlertidig praktisk ordning for fisket i et tilstøtende område i Barentshavet (Oslo 11 November 1977, provisional entry into force 11 January 1978, in force 27 April 1978), *Overenskomster med fremmede makter,* Oslo: Ministry of Foreign Affairs, 1977, 436–40. The "adjacent area," which is considerably larger than the disputed area, is commonly referred to as the Grey Zone.

17. Article 63 of *UNLOSC* states that shared fish stocks shall be managed cooperatively, and that coastal states ". . . shall seek, either directly or through appropriate subregional or regional organizations, to agree upon the measures necessary to coordinate and ensure the conservation and development of such stocks . . ."

18. For a broad presentation of the emerging cooperation in the Barents Region, with an emphasis on Russo-Norwegian relations, see Stokke and Tunander 1994.

19. Cfr. Fisheries Jurisdiction (United Kingdom v. Iceland; Federal Republic of Germany v. Iceland), *The International Court Debates in the Storting of Justice,* The Hague, 1986, 99; also Minister of Maritime Law, Jens Evensen, (St.f.) 29 January 1975. Norway conducted negotiations with the Soviet Union, the United Kingdom, the Federal Republic of Germany, and France.

20. This so-called ladder was agreed to internally in Norway's Fisherman Association in 1988 (Sagdahl 1993). Depending on the size of the total quota, the conventional gear fleet gets between 65 and 75 percent of the quota.

21. In recent times pollution and habitat destruction have made the implementation of fisheries management regimes even more difficult. The predictive accuracy of existing population dynamics models will decrease to the extent that these influences change the underlying parameters. This will necessitate more and broader based research programs and regulation programs.

22. The problems of interjurisdictional management between adjacent waters of the states in federal systems, such as the United States, are very similar to the case under discussion in this chapter.

23. Accurate record keeping is important not only to ensure compliance, but also as a critical part of the fish stock monitoring and research program. Falsified data can make the problem of estimating stock size and potential effects of various regulation programs even more difficult.

24. In addition to these two categories, Finland and Sweden were given preferential treatment in the "special relationship" agreements negotiated with them; however, these agreements covered no areas north of 62°N.

25. As a consequence of growing European Union quotas in Norwegian waters, the third-country share is now again on the rise.

26. Because the Coast Guard cannot require catch reports or on-board inspections in international waters, estimation of catches is largely based on visual observation from Coast Guard vessels operating in the area and therefore necessarily somewhat imprecise.

27. Twenty-odd vessels have recently been purchased by Icelanders and Faroese from the crisis-ridden Canadian Atlantic industry; Icelandic owners have intentional agreements for even more (Director of Landsdelsutvalget, Harald Bolvåg, cited in *Aftenposten*, 20 August 1994, 2.

28. See *Fiskeribladet*, 5 August 1992, 4. This quota arrangement is based in Avtale mellom Norge og Grønland/Danmark om gjensidige fiskeriforbindelser (Copenhagen, 9 June 1992; in force 4 March 1994; provisionally implemented 24 September 1991, prior to adoption), *Overenskomster med fremmede makter*. Oslo: Ministry of Foreign Affairs, 1994, 1500–3.

29. Shortly after reaching agreement on the contents of the 1992 framework agreement, negotiations between Norway and Greenland on the annual quota broke down over Greenlandic linkage of Loophole engagement and quotas from Norway (Bjarne Myrstad of the Norwegian Ministry of Fisheries to *Fiskaren*, 23 August 1991).

30. See Protocol 22/1993, p. 13; Protocol 23/1994, 14; and Protocol 24/1995, 13.

31. The incident is reported in *Fiskaren*, 16 September 1992, 3.

32. *Nordlys*, 8. October 1993, 13, reports that the Icelandic Fisheries Minister was rebuked by his Russian counterpart on an official visit to Murmansk.

33. *Fiskaren,* 6 May 1994, 5, notes that the Russian Fisheries Minister threatened to sever cooperative relations with Iceland; and in the 1 July 1994 issue, that the Russian party encouraged by the Russian Fisheries Committee, had broken industry-level negotiations on direct deliveries to Iceland.

34. According to Icelandic imports statistics, Russian landings were somewhat reduced in 1994 compared to the two preceding years, but still reached almost 11,000 tons (Nils Torsvik, "Mindre russisk torsk til Island" (Less Russian Cod to Iceland), *Fiskaren,* 7 March 1995, 15.

35. Chairman of Norway's Fisherman Association, Einar Hepsø, referred in *Fiskeribladet,* 10 May 1994, 3. So far, such a measure has not materialized; it might interfere with domestic and international competition rules.

36. Minister of Maritime Law, Jens Evensen, in Debates in the Storting (St.f.) 9 March 1978.

37. Recommendation S. of the Standing Commitee on Foreign Affairs and the Constitution (Innst. S.) 190, 1977-78; and Debates in the Storting (St.f.), 9 March 1978. These concerns were shared also by key players in the government, including the defense minister; see Brundtland (1997), 354.

38. Moscow's line has long been that Norway does not have unilateral management authority in the Svalbard zone, hence prohibiting captains to acknowledge such authority by complying with Norwegian reporting procedures.

39. Director General Kåre Bryn of the Norwegian Ministry of Foreign Affairs to *Fiskeribladet,* 9 September 1997, 10.

40. On the significance of the measurement program on nuclear contamination, also involving the Norwegian MRI, see Stokke (1998).

41. Director of the MRI, Roald Vaage, to *Fiskaren,* 11 February 1998, p. 5; Vaage emphasizes that both Russian fisheries authorities and PINRO are actively trying to remove these new barriers to the joint research program.

42. In the Soviet Union, the Ministry of Fisheries was the only financial source until 1989; in Norway, the Marine Research Institute received from 75 to 95 percent from the Ministry of Fisheries (Annual Reports of the IMR 1984–90).

43. Annual reports of the IMR for the years 1984–1990. Until 1988, the IMR was a part of the Fisheries Agency, which sorts, with a certain autonomy, under the Ministry.

44. PINRO (1992); the currency rate used in the program is that of 25 November 1992: 447 rubles to the dollar.

45. Sevrybpromrazvedka, the research unit of Sevryba, was merged with PINRO into Sevrybpoisk; after PINRO had been removed from that organization, the former is referred to both as Sevrybpoisk and Sevrybpromrazvedka. See interview with General Director Gennady Storoshev, referred in Landsdelsutvalget (1993), appendix 1, 7–8.

46. *Fishing News International,* December 1994, 2.

47. The former director of PINRO, Georgy Luka (pers. comm. 29 July 1992), notes that the staff had been cut from 700 to less than 400 since 1989.

48. Steinar Olsen of the IMR to *Fiskaren,* 27 January 1993, p. 8.

49. In 1993, this covered the costs of some 50 percent of total activities (Director of PINRO, Fyodor Troyanovsky, referred in Davidsen et al. 1994, 7).

50. Research Director Arvid Hylen, MRI, pers. comm. 28 July 1993. In 1993, the sum was NOK 3 million, and in 1994, NOK 2 million. These funds were granted by the Ministry of Foreign Affairs as a part of the Norwegian program to support the former socialist states in Europe.

51. Steinar Olsen of the IMR, pers. comm, 26 April 1995.

52. Valery Shleinik to *Fiskeribladet,* 20 April 1995, 6.

53. For examples of critical assessments published by Soviet nondepartmental research institutes, see Matishov (1989, 1990), Anon. (1991), Anon. (1990b), Anon. (1990c).

54. Report to the Storting (St.meld.) 58, 1991–92, 28.

55. Proposition to the Storting (St.t.prp.) 74, 1976–77, 1; our translation.

56. For an assessment of the balance of this exchange, see Stokke and Hoel (1991).

57. Unlike the trawler-based Russian industry, as much as two-thirds of the Norwegian cod harvest in the Barents Sea is taken by small and medium-sized vessels with few alternative targets.

58. Foreign Minister Knut Frydenlund, Foreign Policy Statement in the Storting (St.f), 15 November 1978; our translation.

59. *Ressursoversikten* 1988.

60. Joint Commission Protocol 1982–1986.

61. Eivind Bolle in the Storting (St.f), 8 April 1981.

62. *ICES Cooperative Research Report* 1980, 222; 1981, 245. The ACFM recommend enlargements to 135 mm for cotton, hemp, polyester and polyamid and 155 mm for other materials: the Norwegian proposal (1982) and subsequent unilateral regulation (1983) is 135 mm, up from 125, which is still the agreed measure today.

63. Joint Commission Protocol, November 1981, 4, repeated in 1982–88.

64. Note of 22 April 1982 from the government of the Union of Soviet Socialist Republics to the government of the Kingdom of Norway.

65. Joint Commission Protocol, November 1982, 5.

66. When Norway in 1990 unilaterally sharpened her minimum size regulations for cod and haddock from 42 to 47 mm and from 39 to 44 mm, respectively, the Soviets did not complain about the Norwegian unilateralism but made it clear that they would not follow suit (Joint Commission Protocol, November 1989, 4).

67. Joint Commission Protocol, November 1989, 4.

68. In this context, a former Norwegian commissioner notes that scientific cooperation has contributed significantly to a positive negotiations climate in the

bilateral commission (Gunnar Gundersen to the Norwegian fisheries daily, *Fisker-ibladet*, 26 November 1987).

69. This assumption is not without problems, one of them being that various fishers might have widely different levels of risk aversion.

70. We have controlled for the problem that Soviet and Russian vessels in the Svalbard zone invariably receive written warnings from the Norwegian Coast Guard because they refuse to sign the inspection papers. This is controlled for by disregarding warnings given to Soviet vessels in this zone for the entire time period; almost all of these warnings result from this sovereignty-related rather than fisheries-related disobedience.

71. *Extract of the Report of the Advisory Committee on Fishery Management to the North-East Atlantic Fisheries Commission. Introductory Items. Cod, Haddock, Saithe, Redfish and Greenland Halibut in Sub-Areas I and II*, Copenhagen: ICES, October/November, 1993.

72. Torstein Myhre of the Coast Guard, referred in *Nordlys*, 7 May 1992.

73. The report, presented as confidential, is referred in *Nordlys*, 18 November 1992.

74. Pavel Latishev referred in *Fiskaren*, 23 June 1994, 4.

75. Aleksandr Rodin, at the conference Fisheries Development in the Barents Region, Tromsø, 4–5 October 1994.

76. *Rybnoe Khozjajstvo* 1990.

77. Norwegian Coast Guard materials 1984–91.

78. Georgy Luka, former director of PINRO, pers. comm. 29 July 1992.

79. While a common fine at home would be 500 rubles, depending on the severity, violations in foreign EEZs resulted in fines of 10,000 rubles (Georgy Luka, former Director of PINRO, pers. comm.)

80. Several Norwegian dailies reported that Faroe exports of cod in 1991 were twice as high as the reported catches would permit (*Fiskaren*, 26 August 1992). While the accuracy of these reports were later questioned, they nevertheless drew considerable political attention.

81. Director General and Norwegian representative in the Joint Commission, Gunnar Kjønnøy in the Norwegian Ministry of Fisheries to *Fiskaren*, 12 August 1992.

82. *Fiskeribladet*, 28 August 1992.

83. See *Rapport fra den norsk-russiske*, 1993.

84. Norwegian Commissioner Gunnar Kjønnøy, on the Conference on Fisheries Development in the Barents Region, in Tromsø, 4–5 October 1994.

4

Acid Rain in Europe and North America

Don Munton, Marvin Soroos, Elena Nikitina, and Marc A. Levy

Introduction

Overshadowed by developments on global environmental issues such as ozone depletion has been an equally extraordinary regime change over recent decades regarding the regional and transboundary issue of acid rain. In the early 1970s, no governments had policies in effect explicitly to reduce the emissions that lead to acid rain. Indeed, few even had scientific research programs under way to investigate the problem, and existing environmental policies to reduce ambient air pollution were probably contributing to a worsening of acid rain (through the increasing use of tall stacks). By 1980, new norms were emerging in the form of the 1979 Convention on Long-Range Transboundary Air Pollution (LRTAP) in Europe and the 1980 Canada-U.S. Memorandum of Intent (MOI). By 1991, emission reduction protocols had been concluded under the LRTAP convention, a new North American accord—the 1991 Canada-U.S. Air Quality Agreement—had been signed, and most industrial countries had instituted acid rain control programs. New and stronger international environmental regimes had thus come into effect in both Europe and North America.[1]

The aim of this chapter is to assess whether or not the development of two regimes, based on the 1979 LRTAP convention and the 1980 MOI, had a positive impact on the management of the acid rain problem during the 1980s, and, if so, how this impact was transmitted. The chapter begins with a brief description of the acid rain problem and the interests affected. It also lays out the policy and diplomatic responses, emphasizing the two regimes under study.

The task then shifts from description to explanation. The explanatory puzzle is highlighted by contrasting the acid rain problem as it stood in the late 1970s with the situation that emerged by the early 1990s. This "causal narrative" section assesses what contribution the international regimes made to bringing about this transformation. The evolution is examined both from the perspective of those who led the effort to control acid rain and of those laggard countries that resisted, for awhile, the emergence of the new regime. The impact, if any, on particular regional acid rain conflicts is also considered.

Section three focuses on the causal pathways identified in chapter 1. We thus retain the emphasis on causality but shift from a historical to a theoretical perspective. Our task here is to formulate a different type of explanation of what impact the LRTAP convention and MOI made, one that frames causes and effects in terms of discrete causal mechanisms rather than specific events, countries, and regions. The rationale here is to render conclusions comparable to the other case studies in the book and to move from the idiosyncratic to the general. Not surprisingly perhaps, certain of the causal mechanisms or pathways appear to have been more important than others, and certain ones appear to have been more or less important here than in the other two cases considered in previous chapters.

There are two broad reasons for examining two cases rather than just one in this chapter—reasons of comparison and of contrast. First, the ecological problem of acidification was basically the same in Europe and North America. While different countries responded to different impacts of acidification, the same set of sources and impacts are to be found in both settings. And, while distinct as instruments, the efforts to build the two regimes both created and responded to what became a common pool of scientific research on the sources, transport and deposition of acid rain. Moreover, the United States and Canada were both signatories to the LRTAP Convention, as well as to the MOI, thus linking two otherwise separate diplomatic and political developments. Comparison of the two regimes also underscores the fascinating fact that regulations to reduce the emissions causing acidification were brought into effect in most major countries on both sides of the Atlantic by 1990. This point has been underemphasized in existing studies on acid rain.[2] Secondly, the impact of the individual causal pathways was somewhat different in the two cases. Thus there are different lessons to be learned from the two cases about the effectiveness of international environmental regimes.[3]

Behavioral Complex

The Environmental Problem of Acidification

The term "acid rain" has come to stand for a complex set of physical and chemical phenomena by which gases, especially sulfur dioxide and nitrogen oxides (SO_2 and NO_x), are emitted as a result of combustion and other processes, transformed into acidic compounds while being transported through the atmosphere, and ultimately deposited on land and water surfaces.[4] Acidic deposition has been shown to damage aquatic resources (lakes and streams as well as fish) and terrestrial ecosystems, though much debate continues on the extent of the impact of acid rain, per se, on trees, crops and structures.[5]

From the outset, the focus in the acid rain debates was mostly on sulfur dioxide emissions. Nitrogen oxides also cause acidification, but they entered the political agenda after sulfur because of the early Scandinavian preoccupation with sulfur emissions and freshwater acidification, and because of scientific hunches that nitrogen oxides were a less significant factor in acidification. Volatile organic compounds (VOCs) came onto the political agenda in the latter half of the 1980s, with increased scientific appreciation for the role of ground-level ozone in ecosystem damage. In an effort to understand the damage acid rain may do to terrestrial ecosystems, especially forests, researchers came to realize that most terrestrial impacts are not traceable to a single cause, but rather to a host of interacting stresses. These stresses include climatic variation, disease, and other natural causes. Ground-level ozone (or tropospheric ozone, as opposed to stratospheric ozone) is chief among the anthropogenic stresses that combine with traditional acid rain to harm plants, materials, and human health. Ozone is a potent oxidant, causing corrosion of materials and cellular damage to living organisms. The principal ingredient in urban smog, ozone itself does not travel long distances because of its high reactivity, but its precursors (NO_x and VOCs) are capable of traveling across borders.

If acid rain were ever "discovered" in the usual sense, that discovery occurred roughly a century and a half ago. What is recent is a reasonably full, scientifically based understanding of the origins, nature, extent, and impact of this exceedingly complex and subtle problem. Unlike the problem of marine oil pollution, for example, scientific research and knowledge were critical to the emergence of acid rain as an international issue. Unlike marine oil pollution, acid deposition can only be detected reliably with scientific instrumentation. Although some acidification effects can be ascertained by ordinary observation (such as a decrease in fish populations or crown dieback in trees), these impacts can easily be ascribed, and often have been ascribed, to other causes (e.g., overfishing or disease). Moreover, given its nature, the cumulation of knowledge about the acid rain problem required the integration of theory, data, and methods from diverse areas of physics, chemistry, engineering, meteorology, limnology, zoology, biology, plant pathology, agricultural science, and numerous other specialized fields.

The history of acid rain research has a number of scientific threads, developed largely independently of each other.[6] Some of these threads related to air and atmospheric processes, some to vegetation and soils, and others to aquatic systems. The modern "discovery" of acid rain represents a bringing together of these scientific threads. If we take as given the fundamental experiments that provided the basic knowledge of the nature of the atmosphere, of aquatic systems and of plants, then the earliest thread in the acid rain story was the observation and confirmation of the simple fact that pollutants from human activity took the form of acids, particularly in areas near major combustion sources. Acidic rainfall as a local, short-range phenomenon was observed in industrial parts of England as early as the mid-1800s, and it was noted again in the latter 1800s and early 1900s (Smith 1852; Lawes 1854; Smith 1872; Lawes, Gilbert, and Warington 1883; Crowther and Ruston 1911). Following invention of the pH scale in the early 1900s, measurements of precipitation acidity became both more precise and more frequent. By the 1950s discoveries of low pH (highly acidic) rain had become common in Scandinavia, Canada, and the United States (Barrett and Brodin 1955; Herman and Gorham 1957; Junge and Gustafson 1956; Cogbill and Liken 1974).

Scientific studies of the impact on vegetation of sulfur fumes provided a second and only somewhat related thread. Although this impact was almost certainly in part an acidic deposition phenomenon, the focus here was on the deleterious effect of fumes in gaseous form, especially from sulfide ore smelters, on the vegetation of surrounding areas (Haywood 1904, 1910; U.S. Department of Interior 1915). Relevant studies here included some carried out in connection with the Canada-U.S. Trail smelter controversy of the 1920s and 1930s (Canada, National Research Council 1939). The deposition of heavy metals from industrial operations was also noted in some of the earliest studies and monitored more intensively later on (Kramer 1973; Hutchinson 1974). Another, closely related thread was the discovery that the atmosphere was a source of nitrogen, sulfur, and other nutrients for agricultural land (Way, cited in Cowling 1982; Lawes 1854; Shutt 1910, 1914, 1917, 1925). These studies were generally done by agricultural scientists who usually considered these airborne substances beneficial (i.e., fertilizers) rather than harmful pollutants.

This view was challenged by a fourth thread in the scientific literature. Zoologists and biologists demonstrated that acidic lakes and streams were harmful to fish. Pioneering discoveries came early in the 20th century, but did not make it into the scientific mainstream (Dahl 1927). The speculations and evidence of others about acidification effects remained largely ignored (Gorham 1955; Gorham and Gordon 1960, 1963; Dannevig 1959). A number of researchers, working largely independently of each other, contributed to the emergence in the 1970s of concern about the aquatic impacts of acidic deposition in North America (Beamish 1970; Beamish and Harvey 1971, 1972; Beamish 1976; Bird 1972; Likens, Bormann, and Johnson 1972; Likens and Bormann 1974). Similar work was underway in Europe (for example, Braekke 1976).

These concerns were sometimes, although not always, related to the simple observation that pollution could be caused by distant sources as well as ones close at hand. The source of "dust rain" experienced in Europe in 1875, for example, was identified as a volcanic eruption in Iceland, "smudsig snefeld" (dirty snow) in Norway in the late 1800s was attributed to industrial Britain, and studies at the turn of the twentieth century suggested "colored rain" in the Mediterranean and "red dust" deposits in England to be from the Sahara desert (Eriksson 1952; Cowling 1982). The much discussed phenomenon of fallout from nuclear weapons tests in the 1950s and 1960s is yet another example of the long-range transport of air pollution. Indeed, observations back to at least the seventeenth century suggest that pollutants could travel long distances (Evelyn, cited in Gorham 1981). Some of the earliest acid rain studies confirmed that it was not merely a local problem, affecting only the near vicinity of major pollution sources. Perhaps the first to suggest this was Eville Gorham who in the 1950s showed the considerable extent of acid rain in a rural area of Nova Scotia, "an agricultural district not much subject to [local] industrial air pollution" (Herman and Gorham 1957).[7] Other research by Gorham pointed to long-range transport into the English lake district, and from the nickel smelters outside Sudbury, Ontario (Gorham 1955; Gorham and Gordon 1960). Gorham, an ecologist by training, provided no precise meteorological data, however, and was basically investigating site-specific deposition.[8]

The meteorological thread in understanding what we know as acid rain was demonstrated conclusively by studies incorporating data on wind patterns and an improved understanding of atmospheric chemistry. The first person to integrate meteorological data with deposition studies was the Swedish scientist, Svante Odén. As early as 1961–62 Odén began analyzing the chemistry of rain storms along the Swedish coast and correlating these results with data on wind trajectories.[9] His results pointed clearly to sources in Britain and continental Europe. Odén's findings and conclusions were published in a Swedish scientific bulletin in 1968 (Odén 1968, 1976; *Environmental Research* 1967). The first acid rain related studies providing meteorological data on North America would not appear for another fifteen years (Summers and Whelpdale 1976; Cogbill 1976).

Based on a unique set of precipitation data for Scandinavia going back to the early 1950s, Odén also showed, for the first time, that precipitation was becoming more acidic, and that the extent of the area affected by acidic deposition was growing. Moreover, based on data from a water quality monitoring network in Sweden and Finland, he had accumulated strong evidence by the mid-1960s that surface waters in Sweden were generally becoming increasingly acidic, alarmingly so given the lack of buffering capacity in the country's rock-bound lakes and thin soils. With these discoveries, he provided the last two pieces of the puzzle and offered the first more or less complete synthesis of the problem of acid rain. Odén and his work directly inspired a number of the North American researchers, particularly Gene Likens (cited above), Ellis Cowling (1980, 1982), and David Schindler (1985, 1986, 1988, 1989).

As had Gorham, Odén also noted or hypothesized a range of damaging effects from acidification. Unlike Gorham, he made his concerns public. He warned of damage to lakes and rivers, fish (including the spring melt "acid shock" effect), soils, plants, forest growth, man-made structures, and human health. Odén also warned of the related problem of the emission and deposition of heavy metals. This aspect of long-range transport was subsequently very much overshadowed by that of acid rain, but re-emerged on the international agenda by the late 1980s (UNECE 1989b). Unlike many of his more traditional colleagues, Odén was unwilling to be bound by certain scientific norms against popularizing science; he became a policy advocate (Odén 1967). He accused Sweden's neighbors of fighting an "insidious chemical war," and pushed for the acid rain issue to be taken up internationally (Lee 1970). As a result, Sweden took its concerns to the Organization for Economic Cooperation and Development (OECD) and then highlighted acid rain in its report to the 1972 UN environment conference in Stockholm (OECD 1972; Sweden 1971; Sweden 1972). Subsequent calls for action came from, for example, the 19th Congress of the International Association of Limnology, held in Winnipeg, Canada, in 1974 (Odén 1976). Between 1968 and the early 1970s, acid rain moved fairly quickly from the scientific to the policy arena.

The Actors

Like most environmental issues, acid rain has featured a battle among governments, industry, labor, and environmentalists. Governments came under pressure from scientists and environmental groups to stop acid rain, although only after the scientific community had brought the issue to public attention. Certain industries were quickly fingered as the chief culprits. The primary sources of emissions that are precursors of acid rain were never really in doubt—particularly smelters and those electric utilities that burn coal, especially high-sulfur coal, to produce their power. The companies that mine the coal had similarly strong but slightly different corporate interests, as did the labor unions representing the miners whose jobs depended on the use of coal. Behind them, concerned but not leading the charge against acid rain controls, were those business and other groups with reasons to oppose the increases in electricity rates expected to result from the imposition of regulatory measures. These opposition coalitions, sometimes informally and sometimes formally organized (as through the Edison Electric Institute and the National Coal Association in the United States), adopted a more or less common strategy across countries. They first denied the reality of acid rain or denied they were its cause, attacking the mounting scientific evidence on various grounds. When the basic facts could no longer be challenged credibly, they switched to arguing costs. Acid rain controls, they insisted, were too expensive and the benefits uncertain or minimal. The economic and political strength of the opponents and the potential costs of emission reductions were so great that, unlike the MARPOL case, action on acid rain was not forthcoming from industry itself.

These battle lines formed in most countries, including Britain, Germany, Canada, and the United States (Munton 1983; Yanarella and Ihara 1985; Schmandt and Roderick 1985; Regens and Rycroft 1988; Boehmer-Christiansen and Skea 1991; Howard and Perley 1991). At the same time, some important divergences of interests emerged within the pro and con coalitions, divergences that were ultimately of much political relevance. There were differences, particularly important in America, between the economic interests ultimately pursued by the electric utilities (wanting to keep their costs down) and the coal companies and miners (wanting to continue mining and selling coal, whatever the price of acid rain controls). There were also subtle but significant differences in the perspectives of those companies engaged in mining high-sulfur coals and those specializing in low-sulfur coals. The latter understandably opposed any subsidy or advantage that might be given to the former, and vice versa. There was also a basic difference in the interests of the miners who worked in the high-sulfur mines and those who produced low-sulfur coal, although worker solidarity constrained open expression of this difference.

There were also obvious and strong policy differences across countries. Initially (as of the late 1970s), only Sweden, Norway, Finland, and Canada were persuaded that acid rain was a significant policy problem. Each of these countries had economically and often culturally important freshwater ecosystems that were vulnerable to acid rain. Moreover, these countries were all net importers of acid rain caused by others; they all had lower sulfur emissions than their neighbors, and were significantly less a source of acid rain to their neighbors than their neighbors were to them. Their emergence as early proponents of acid rain controls was thus driven both by their ecosystem vulnerability and by the fact that they were more victims of transboundary acid rain than perpetrators. Their advocacy owed little if anything to domestic pressure. Those countries less in favor tended to be big producers and major exporters, but not significant importers (such as Britain and the United States). Others, particularly Germany, were significant producers, exporters, and importers. They came to support acid rain control somewhat later than the leaders, but joined the campaign well before the laggard states.

Data for selected European countries on production, importing and exporting of SO_2 and similar data for North America are presented in table 4.1. As shown there, most of the sulfur deposited in Sweden and Norway is imported while most in Britain is domestic in origin. Germany is in between; it produces slightly less than half of the sulfur deposited in the country and thus significant amounts of German deposition come from elsewhere. (This type of table came to be known within EMEP circles as a "blame" matrix, for obvious reasons.) With respect to North America, most of the sulfur deposited in the United States is domestic in origin; little of it comes from Canada. Much of that deposited in Canada, however, comes from the United States. For Canada and for the Nordic countries, therefore, acid rain is more of an international problem than it is for Britain and the United States. The largest transboundary flow anywhere is across the U.S.-Canadian border. The amount of sulfur originating in the United States and deposited in Canada (about 2500

Table 4.1a
Sources and transboundary flows of sulfur
Atmospheric sulfur budget for Europe, 1980 (*kilotonnes of sulfur per year*)

Emission receivers	Emission sources							
	U.K.	FRG	Sweden	Norway	Other Europe	Total Europe	Unknown sources	Total
U.K.	810	25	—	—	95	930	87	1,017
FRG	87	673	—	—	960	1,720	96	1,816
Sweden	42	42	100	24	223	431	136	567
Norway	48	24	12	10	124	217	89	306
Other Europe	510	970	67	9	17,125	18,682	2,574	21,256
Total Europe	1,497	1,734	179	43	18,527	21,980	2,982	24,962
Residuals	1,063	82	96	34	5,793	7,068		
Total emissions	2,560	1,816	275	76	24,320	29,048		

Notes: (1) "Other Europe" includes the western part of the Russian Federation; (2) "Residuals" includes deposition at sea, outside Europe, and contribution to "unknown sources." Sources: Based on a table presented by Boehmer-Christiansen and Skea, 1991, using EMEP data. The figures have been converted to kilotonnes of sulfur (from kilotonnes of SO_2). Totals may not add up due to rounding.

Table 4.1b
Atmospheric sulfur budget for Eastern North America, 1980–82 (*kilotonnes of sulfur per year*)

Emission receivers	Emission sources		
	Eastern U.S.	Eastern Canada	Total
United States	3,700	200	3,900
Canada	2,500	900	3,400
Residual (outflow eastward)	[4,000]	[900]	[4,900]
Total for North America	10,200	2,000	12,200

Notes: Data include only anthropogenic sources. Sulfur originating in the western parts of both countries is not shown. Figures for the residual eastward flow are calculated from other data in the chart.
Sources: Table compiled by the authors from data presented in Canada, Federal Provincial Research and Monitoring Coordinating Committee, 1986, which was based on Fay et al. 1985, Galloway and Whelpdale 1980.

kilotonnes per year) far exceeds that originating, or deposited, in any single European country, although deposition levels are higher in parts of Europe (Shaw 1993, 109). See tables 4.1a and 4.1b.

At the same time, and consistent with the distinction between exporters and importers, there were also corresponding divergences among jurisdictions within countries. The domestic battle within the United States pitted states that were major suppliers of high-sulfur coal and staunchly opposed to controls, such as Ohio, Illinois, and West Virginia, against recipient states such as Vermont and Maine, that advocated them. New York joined the latter group when it became clear that its Adirondacks area was being severely affected by acid rain (Schofield 1965, 1976; Baker et al. 1991, 1993). Within Canada, the province of Nova Scotia was for many years a reluctant participant in the Canadian campaign to reduce transboundary acid rain and a holdout on the domestic policy front. Though a downwind recipient (as Gorham's work in the 1950s had showed), it is also a coal-producing and coal-burning province. Over the 1980s, the three Canadian westernmost provinces (like the U.S. western states) took little part in the movement toward acid rain controls, arguing that deposition from their less substantial emissions had no negative impact on the well-buffered soils of the Canadian prairies.

Governments were pressured, sometimes successfully and sometimes not, by interest groups concerned with air pollution and acid rain. In Britain the fight was led by the National Society For Clean Air, the Council for the Protection of Rural England, and Friends of the Earth. The Federation of Citizens' Groups for Environmental Protection and other groups allied with the German Green Party played a similar role, as did the Swedish NGO Secretariat on Acid Rain. In the United States the cause was taken up both by local groups and by the established national environmental organizations such as the National Wildlife Federation and the National Clean Air Coalition. Environmental groups in Canada banded together to form the Canadian Coalition on Acid Rain, which lobbied not only in Canada but, at least for awhile, in the United States as well. The influence of these various groups, while not negligible, does not appear to have been decisive in any country, except perhaps in the case of the United States.

Acid Rain Regimes

Convention on Long-Range Transboundary Air Pollution

The Nordics led the way in seeking international action to deal with acid rain. It is often reported that acid rain made its international debut at the 1972 Stockholm Conference (Fraenkel 1989; Levy 1993). In fact, Sweden and Norway took the problem to the OECD three years before that historic gathering. A 1969 meeting organized by the OECD's Air Management Sector Group concluded that "there has been a significant increase in the atmospheric content of sulfur compounds and that there are atmospheric processes giving rise to transport of these compounds over long distances" (OECD 1972, 2). The risk of acid precipitation and long-range transport of sulfur compounds thus entered the agenda of international institutions as a problem that, it was agreed, "required continuing study." Cooperative monitoring of SO_2 emissions began in 1972 (OECD 1972, 1–1; Ottar 1976). Technical work continued over the 1970s (OECD 1977). In 1978 the OECD's monitoring and transport modeling activities were consolidated under the auspices of the Cooperative Programme for the Monitoring and Evaluation of the Long-Range Transmission of Air Pollutants in Europe (EMEP).

While the movement toward regime formation began with this Scandinavian initiative at the OECD, it was given, through a curious twist of Cold War politics, a strong push by the Helsinki process that emerged from the Conference on Security and Cooperation in Europe (CSCE). Acid rain ended up lodged in an often ignored body, the United Nations Economic Commission for Europe (UN ECE). In 1975 Soviet premier Leonid Brezhnev called for cooperation between east and west on issues of "environment, energy, or transport." The main motivation was to further the détente process in the wake of the 1975 Helsinki accords, creating a forum that could yield more cooperation than the combative Helsinki process, while still giving the Soviets the aura of international legitimacy they desired. The ECE, a UN body with membership virtually identical to the CSCE, considered the different options. Ruling out energy and transport as overly sensitive, it looked at alternative areas for environmental cooperation. Acid rain fit the multiple agendas in play at the time. The eastern bloc countries, led by the Soviet Union, were concerned more about process than substantive issues, wanting to further east-west cooperation in the form of a treaty (Chossudovsky 1988; McCormick 1989; Lammers 1991).[10] The Nordics (Sweden, Norway, and Finland) were concerned about substance—reducing the long-range transport of air pollution—which meant binding cuts to reduce SO_2 emissions in neighboring states. Denmark and the Netherlands supported controls as well. Others, like France, appeared indifferent. The blocking coalition, staunchly opposed to controls, but willing to accept a convention that did not specify controls, was led by Britain, Germany, and the United States. Negotiations proceeded. The momentum from the Helsinki process and the OECD's acid rain program was sufficient to keep talks going. The Soviet Union reportedly applied pressure at times to sustain western interest (Jackson 1990).

The result was a framework agreement, what became known as the Convention on Long-Range Transboundary Air Pollution, or LRTAP accord, signed in November 1979 by thirty-three states, including the United States and Canada, and the European Commission (Convention on Long-Range Transboundary Air Pollution 1979).[11] The LRTAP convention is historic in two ways beyond being the first international accord dealing explicitly with acid rain. It has been called the first multilateral treaty explicitly addressing atmospheric environment matters and the first international environmental treaty between east and west (Fraenkel 1989).[12]

At its center, the convention had no mandatory controls on emissions but simply a call for states to reduce transboundary air pollution as much as economically feasible. The LRTAP Convention also called on states to report their efforts to reduce transboundary pollution flows. This provision had more impact than might have been expected. Major reviews of national policies and strategies are conducted every four years, and updates are provided annually.[13] Most importantly, the convention also created mechanisms for collecting and disseminating information on pollution flows, effects, and mitigation options. The existing EMEP program was folded into the LRTAP organizational umbrella and provided much of the scientific data for this collaborative effort. These processes proved to be the guiding force of the LRTAP dynamic. Beginning with technical and scientific matters, the parties slowly began to work on protocols governing emissions of sulfur dioxide, nitrogen oxides, and volatile organic compounds—the "sox, nox, and vocs" talks (Levy 1991a).

Under LRTAP auspices, EMEP generated annual sulfur "budgets" every year since 1980 and NO_x budgets since 1988. EMEP relies primarily on self-reporting of member governments, but engages in well-established practices to unearth potential anomalies, and it requests revisions where appropriate. EMEP has compiled emissions data for OECD countries since 1980. Impact assessment programs were also successively established for rivers and lakes, forests, crops, and materials. The lakes and rivers program created a large data base and developed sensitivity maps showing the susceptibility of acidification of waters in Europe and North America. Another critical element in the ECE/EMEP process of reaching consensus among the countries involved was the development of a common computer model, dubbed "RAINS," linking emissions and impacts on a continental basis, and its subsequent widespread use (Alcamo, et al. 1991).

SO_2 Protocol

When the LRTAP Convention entered into force in 1983, following the requisite number of ratifications, the Nordics began to push for a follow-up sulfur protocol that would have the "targets and timetables" on which there had been no agreement in 1979. The joint proposal called for a 30 percent reduction in sulfur emissions by 1993, with 1980 as the base year. An alternative proposal from Austria, Germany, and Switzerland that called for adopting the best available pollution-reduction technology was eventually abandoned in favor of the Nordic approach. Canada hosted a ministerial meeting in Ottawa in February 1984 at which the so-called 30 percent club was established. Thirteen countries committed themselves to this reduction in SO_2 emissions.[14] A follow-up, joint expert-ministerial meeting held in Munich in August 1984 broadened support. Ultimately, twenty-one LRTAP convention parties signed or acceded to the first SO_2 emissions protocol in Helsinki in July 1985. The most important holdouts were Britain and the United States, but Poland, Spain, and a few other countries also did not sign.

Under the 1985 sulfur protocol, states agreed to reduce emissions, or their transboundary fluxes, by 30 percent by 1993 (using 1980 as a base year). The option to reduce fluxes instead of total emissions was inserted at the insistence of the Soviet Union. Reducing transboundary flows from its territory would be easier, or less costly, than reducing emissions within it. Only the "European" part of the country, west of the Urals, is bound by LRTAP rules; thus, for LRTAP regime purposes, what happens environmentally east of the Urals is irrelevant. (The only other country to which this technicality applies is Turkey.) The Soviet Union, which was not at the time particularly concerned about acid rain, per se, was thus able to join the sulfur protocol knowing it could focus on those emission sources west of the Urals that were mostly responsible for westward transboundary flows.

LRTAP Convention members reached agreement on a new sulfur protocol in 1994. The first sulfur protocol was basically a lowest common denominator agreement, used primarily as a proselytizing tool in which the terms were established early on by a small group of leaders who then campaigned for accession among a group of reluctant states. In more recent talks, states sought to create a genuine collective regulatory instrument. The targets were not simply reflections of what states would achieve anyway, but constituted real mutual sacrifice for the sake of a common good. This protocol is based not on flat rate reductions, but on "critical loads," a measure of the amount of sulfur deposition that individual ecosystems and organisms can tolerate without damage.[15] It specifies individual reduction targets for each signatory, based on the sensitivity of the regions where emissions are deposited and on the abatement costs within the emitter country.

NO_x Protocol

By the mid-1980s, there was agreement among the activist governments that NO_x was also a sufficiently important source of ecosystem damage to warrant a separate protocol to the LRTAP Convention. Negotiations thus began on NO_x as soon as the sulfur protocol was signed in 1985. Differences emerged among those who favored reductions, those who favored a freeze on emissions, and those who preferred no action. States such as Austria, Switzerland, and West Germany, which were only beginning to control vehicle emissions, favored a straightforward 30 percent reduction (from 1985 levels), as was used in the sulfur protocol. A second group, including Canada and the United States, favored a freeze as many of them had already moved to regulate NO_x emissions and would get no credit for having done so under such a cut. Some states advocated particular technology-based control programs, while others supported allowing emission increases. More than a few were either unable or unwilling to stem what they anticipated would be mounting emissions, especially from ever-increasing numbers of automobiles on their roads. An extended debate also raged about the criterion to underlie the cuts, if any. As there was never enough support for cuts, the most that could be done was an agreement calling for a freeze of emissions (or their transboundary fluxes) by 1995, using 1987 as a base year. The protocol was signed by twenty-seven countries in Sofia, Bulgaria, in November 1988. A group of states that favored reductions also chose to issue a separate declaration committing themselves to 30 percent cuts by 1998.

Attention then turned to VOCs. A protocol was negotiated between 1989 and 1991 that allows three options for regulating emissions. Countries were permitted to bind themselves to a 30 percent reduction, to a freeze, or to a 30 percent reduction only in designated areas.[16] Like the first NO_x protocol, the VOC protocol calls for its successor to be based on critical loads. Because VOCs and NO_x are both precursors of tropospheric ozone, serious regulation based on the critical loads approach requires that their emission reductions be negotiated jointly in the future. As of the late 1990s, work is under way to pursue this ambitious and complex regulatory strategy.

Canada-United States Memorandum of Intent

The second case of an acid rain regime begins with the Canada-U.S. Memorandum of Intent (MOI) signed in August 1980. This accord reflected mounting Canadian concerns about the long-range transport of air pollution, particularly acid rain, and American interest in more specific and local transboundary air pollution problems, a concern emanating especially from the U.S. Congress. The MOI built upon a report by a binational scientific advisory committee, the Bilateral Research Consultation Group (BRCG), appointed by Ottawa and Washington. This group concluded that acid rain was a serious problem in North America, that "irreversible acidification" was occurring in sensitive aquatic ecosystems, and, although the evidence was less clear, that there were "reasons to be concerned that forests and some crops may be damaged with continued pollutant loadings" (Canada–United States, Research Consultation Group 1979).

Negotiation of the MOI was preceded in mid-1979 by the issuing of a general statement of principles (and therefore nonbinding in legal terms) on which a formal air quality agreement might be based. The Joint Statement on Transboundary Air Quality affirmed that Canada and the United States "share a determination to reduce or prevent transboundary air pollution which injures health and property on the other side of the boundary." This concept and phrasing were taken directly from the 1909 Boundary Waters Treaty, for decades the basis of cooperative efforts to deal with water pollution. This mimicking of the key terminology of the 1909 accord highlighted the fact that no similar statement of relevant principles and commitments existed in the area of air pollution, and it was intended to begin to fill that void. The Trail Smelter arbitration, well-known by international lawyers, had in 1941 set out the basic principle that "no State has the right to use or to permit the use of its territory in such a manner as to cause injury by fumes in or to the territory of another or the properties or persons therein, when the case is of serious consequences and the injury is established by clear and convincing evidence" (Trail Smelter Arbitral Tribunal 1941; Read 1963; Dinwoodie 1971; Murray 1972). Despite subsequent local transboundary air quality problems (especially in the Detroit-Windsor area), no further joint effort had been made to develop a regime for air quality corresponding to that developed on water quality. And the Trail Smelter case provided an insufficient precedent for solving problems like acid rain, where there were many potential sources of pollutants rather than just one specific source.

In the 1979 joint statement, Canada and the United States specifically agreed that a future bilateral agreement on air quality should encompass: (1) preventing and reducing deleterious transboundary air pollution, (2) control strategies, including the limitation of emissions, (3) expanded notification and consultation on matters involving a risk or potential risk of transboundary air pollution, (4) expanded scientific exchanges and increased research and development cooperation, (5) expanded monitoring and evaluation efforts, (6) cooperative assessment of long-term environmental trends, (7) institutional arrangements and equal access, nondiscrimination, and liability and compensation, and (8) measures to implement an agreement. Agreement on these principles was seen as a first step toward a formal accord. Even these generalities and modest steps were too much for those in Washington already concerned about the costs imposed by existing United States air pollution laws, including officials in the Department of Energy and the Office of Management and Budget (OMB). They opposed going further but ultimately lost this first of many battles on the acid rain issue waged in Washington. (They did not lose many others over the next decade, however.)

The Canada-U.S. Memorandum of Intent was signed on 5 August 1980. Both in structure and content, it closely paralleled the 1979 LRTAP convention. Both provided for information exchange and research cooperation through technical working groups. Borrowing from the LRTAP convention model and from the successful process that led to the Great Lakes Water Quality Agreement of 1972, the MOI established five technical-level working groups to further this exchange and cooperation. It also committed both countries to "vigorous enforcement" of existing standards "in a way which is responsive to the problems of transboundary air pollution"—a provision sought more by Canada than the United States. The LRTAP convention similarly called on its signatories to "develop the best policies and strategies including air quality management systems" and "control measures compatible with balanced development." Neither accord contained commitments to specific reductions in emissions; there were no targets and timetables.

Unlike the LRTAP convention, the MOI explicitly committed both countries to the negotiation and conclusion of a bilateral air quality agreement to deal broadly with transboundary air pollution.[17] These negotiations were to begin by June 1981. The view even of proponents in Pierre Trudeau's Ottawa and in Jimmy Carter's Washington, however, was that the MOI was all they would have for some time to come. None of those involved expected a quick conclusion to any negotiations. With the election of Ronald Reagan, the goal of concluding an accord to reduce acid rain was not so much significantly delayed as not moved any closer. The new administration agreed to continue doing research on acid rain but refused to consider any control actions, and it maintained this position through its two terms in office. The first casualty was the MOI process.

The joint working groups encountered continual disagreements and much change of personnel, particularly on the American side. Those charged with examining possible regulations and regulatory approaches never got off the ground. Although the joint efforts had been preceding reasonably well on scientific aspects of the MOI process, American officials decided in the latter stages of the studies that they could not support Canadian scientists' proposal for a target of no more that 20 kg per hectare per year of wet sulfate deposition to protect sensitive aquatic ecosystems—a target that the Canadian government had, perhaps unwisely, publicly tied to a 50 percent reduction in SO_2 emissions. Eventually, Canadians charged that Reagan administration officials had interfered with the work of American scientists on the key groups, unilaterally restricted their mandates, and replaced group members judged too favorable toward emission controls (Robinson 1982; BNA 1982).

The negotiations were suspended by Canada in June 1982 in the face of Washington's outright refusal to consider control measures. The acrimony that followed was eventually replaced by the "good neighbor" policy of the Mulroney government after the 1984 Canadian election, but neither the new team nor the new approach met with any more success on acid rain. The mid-1980s saw a series of presidential–prime ministerial summits, a special report from two high-level envoys (Lewis and Davis 1986), and a few rounds of informal discussions, but no change in the Reagan administration's position.[18] No real progress was made until after the election of George Bush in 1988 and until after Congress in 1989 finally took on the task of amending the U.S. Clean Air Act to deal, among other pollution problems, with acid rain (Cohen 1992; Bryner 1993).

1991 Canada-United States Air Quality Agreement

The Canada-United States Air Quality Agreement (AQA) was ultimately signed by Prime Minister Mulroney and President Bush in Ottawa in March 1991 in the aftermath of the Gulf War (Canada and United States 1991). Formal bilateral negotiations began in the summer months of 1990 and ended in December. The negotiators had begun their work even before the final votes on the new U.S. Clean Air Act, the legislation that gave Washington its first clear authority to deal with acid rain. Informal bilateral talks the previous year had produced an agreed list of elements to be included in the prospective accord. This so-called "elements paper" was in turn based on the 1980 Memorandum of Intent and the 1979 Statement of Principles (Smith and Biniaz 1991). The preamble to the 1991 agreement specifically cites the MOI and the 1986 envoys report as well as the 1979 LRTAP Convention and the Trail smelter arbitration.

The first-ever, general Canada-U.S. agreement on air quality features SO_2 and NO_x commitments to reduce emissions by roughly 50 percent in the eastern parts of the continent. Unlike the LRTAP SO_2 protocol, this agreement deals with emissions only, not with transboundary fluxes, let alone environmental deposition or effects. The United States had refused to make any explicit commitments to reducing the flows of pollution across its boundary or to achieving any specific deposition targets. The 1991 accord also provides for continued coordination on research and monitoring, for strengthened processes of prior notice and consultation, and for the establishment of a bilateral coordinating group, the Canada-United States Air Quality Committee. Not limited to acid rain, or even to long range transport, it provides a framework within which other, emerging transboundary air pollution problems might be addressed. Canada and the United States agreed to conduct periodic public reviews of the progress being made in acid rain control programs, consult with each other on new bilateral air quality issues (within thirty days of the submission of a formal request by one of the governments), negotiate with each other on unresolved bilateral air quality issues (within ninety days of the submission of a formal request by one of the governments), and refer any issues not solved through negotiations to an agreed third party.

Canadian and American scientists and officials meet under the auspices of the 1991 AQA to conduct coordinated monitoring and emission inventories, as they previously had done through less formal structures. Fiscal restraints imposed on governments in recent years, however, have both significantly reduced personnel in key government departments and reduced funds for monitoring, especially in the province of Ontario, which in the 1980s had led the charge against acid rain among the provinces.

The governments' joint reports on implementation of the accord suggest that significant progress is being made and that commitments are being kept (Canada–United States 1992, 1996).

Causal Narrative

The concerns and promises of the 1979 LRTAP and the 1980 MOI became the firm commitments of the sulfur and nitrogen protocols of 1985 and 1988 and the Canada-United States AQA of 1991. Subsequent steps toward the implementation of these accords represented substantial shifts in the policies of most countries involved in the regimes from what those policies had been in the 1970s and early 1980s. Before examining the policy directions and shifts of some of the key participants, it would be useful to note both the pattern of legal accession to the regimes and the pattern of emission reductions brought about under, though not necessarily, because of, the regimes. Table 4.2 shows the dates states signed and ratified the various LRTAP conventions or acceded to them. It thus represents the minimum political impact of the regime. Table 4.3 shows both the extent to which states have reduced their emissions of sulfur and nitrogen oxides, and the overall percentage reductions achieved between 1980 and 1994. It thus portrays quantitatively the acid rain-related behavior of these states at the time the LRTAP and MOI regimes were inaugurated and a decade and a half later. This table thus suggests the maximum possible degree of impact of the developing regimes on states. This is not to suggest, however, that the cuts shown here are entirely or solely due to the regimes themselves.

The effectiveness of the MOI and LRTAP regimes in environmental terms is less clear and much less easy to assess. Preliminary indications, however, are promising. Presumably because of emission reductions in Canada and the United States, airborne SO_2 has decreased, the total area in eastern Canada subjected to high deposition of sulfates has shrunk, and some aquatic ecosystems appear to be recovering (Environment Canada 1997). One-third of the lakes in southeastern Canada monitored since the 1980s had lower acidity levels as of the late 1990s. A majority of the lakes in central Ontario showed similar trends, a result attributed largely to emission reductions from the smelters outside Sudbury. There is no

Table 4.2
Signatories to and ratification of 1979 LRTAP and protocols

	LRTAP		EMEP		SOX–1		NOX		VOCs		SOX–2	
	Signed or acceded	Ratified*	Signed or acceded	Ratified	Signed or acceded	Ratified	Signed or acceded	Ratified	Signed or acceded	Ratified	Signed or acceded	Ratified
Austria	13 Nov 79	16 Dec 82	dns	4 June 87	9 July 85	4 June 87	1 Nov 88	15 Jan 90	19 Nov 91	23 Aug 94	14 June 94	27 Aug 98
Belarus	14 Nov 79	14 May 80	28 Sept 84	4 Oct 85	9 July 85	10 Sept 86	1 Nov 88	8 June 89				
Belgium	13 Nov 79	15 July 82	25 Feb 85	5 Aug 87	9 July 85	9 June 89	1 Nov 88		19 Nov 91		14 June 94	
Bosnia	dns	1 Sept 93	dns	1 Sept 93								
Bulgaria	13 Nov 79	9 Jun 81	4 Apr 84	26 Sept 86	9 July 85	26 Sept 86	1 Nov 88	30 Mar 89	19 Nov 91	27 Feb 98	14 June 94	
Canada	13 Nov 79	15 Dec 81	3 Oct 84	4 Dec 85	9 July 85	4 Dec 85	1 Nov 88	25 Jan 91			14 June 94	8 Jul 97
Croatia	dns	8 Oct 92	dns	8 Oct 92							14 June 94	
Cyprus	dns	20 Nov 91	dns	20 Nov 91								
Czech Republic	dns	30 Sept 93	dns	1 Jan 93	dns	30 Sept 93	dns	1 Jan 93	19 Nov 91	1 Jul 97	14 June 94	19 Jun 97
Denmark	14 Nov 79	15 July 82	28 Sept 84	29 Apr 86	9 July 85	29 Apr 86	1 Nov 88	1 Mar 93	19 Nov 91	21 May 96	14 June 94	25 Aug 97
Estonia					dns							
Finland	13 Nov 79	15 Apr 81	7 Dec 84	24 June 86	9 July 85	24 June 86	1 Nov 88	1 Feb 90	19 Nov 91	11 Jan 94	14 June 94	8 Jun 98
France	13 Nov 79	3 Nov 81	22 Feb 85	2 July 87	9 July 85	12 Mar 86	1 Nov 88	20 July 89	19 Nov 91	12 Jun 97	14 June 94	12 Jun 97
Germany	13 Nov 79	15 July 82	26 Feb 85	7 Oct 86	9 July 85	3 Mar 87	1 Nov 88	16 Nov 90	19 Nov 91	8 Dec 94	14 June 94	3 Jun 98
Greece	14 Nov 79	30 Aug 83	dns	24 June 88			1 Nov 88	29 Apr 98	19 Nov 91	10 Nov 95	14 June 94	24 Feb 98
Hungary	13 Nov 79	22 Sept 80	27 Mar 85	8 May 85	9 July 85	11 Sept 86	3 May 89	12 Nov 91	19 Nov 91		9 Dec 94	
Iceland	13 Nov 79	5 May 83										
Ireland	13 Nov 79	15 July 82	4 Apr 85	26 June 87			1 May 89	17 Oct 94			17 Oct 94	4 Sep 98
Italy	14 Nov 79	15 July 82	28 Sept 84	12 Jan 89	9 July 85	5 May 90	1 Nov 88	19 May 92	19 Nov 91	30 June 95	14 June 94	14 Sep 98
Latvia	dns	15 July 94		18 Feb 97								

Country												
Lichtenstein	14 Nov 79	22 Nov 83	dns	1 May 85	9 July 85	13 Feb 86	1 Nov 88	24 Mar 94	19 Nov 91	24 Mar 94	14 June 94	27 Aug 97
Lithuania	dns	25 Jan 94										
Luxembourg	13 Nov 79	15 July 82	21 Nov 84	24 Aug 87	9 July 85	24 Aug 87	1 Nov 88	4 Oct 90	19 Nov 91	11 Nov 93	14 June 94	14 Jun 96
Moldova	dns	9 June 95										
Netherlands	13 Nov 79	15 July 82	28 Sept 84	22 Oct 85	9 July 85	30 Apr 86	1 Nov 88	11 Oct 89	19 Nov 91	29 Sept 93	14 June 94	30 May 95
Norway	13 Nov 79	13 Feb 81	28 Sept 84	12 Mar 85	9 July 85	4 Nov 86	1 Nov 88	11 Oct 89	19 Nov 91	7 Jan 93	14 June 94	3 July 95
Poland	13 Nov 79	19 July 85	dns	14 Sept 88			1 Nov 88				14 June 94	
Portugal	14 Nov 79	29 Sept 80	dns	19 Jan 89					2 Apr 92			
Romania	14 Nov 79	27 Feb 91										
Russia	13 Nov 79	22 May 80	28 Sept 84	21 Aug 85	9 July 85	10 Sept 86	1 Nov 88	21 June 89			14 June 94	
San Marino	14 Nov 79											
Slovakia	dns	28 May 93	dns	28 May 93	dns	28 May 93	dns	28 May 93			14 June 94	1 Apr 98
Slovenia	dns	6 July 92	dns	6 July 92	dns						14 June 94	7 May 98
Spain	14 Nov 79	15 June 82	dns	11 Aug 87			1 Nov 88	4 Dec 91	19 Nov 91	1 Feb 94	14 June 94	7 Aug 97
Sweden	13 Nov 79	12 Feb 81	28 Sept 84	12 Aug 85	9 July 85	31 Mar 86	1 Nov 88	27 July 90	19 Nov 91	8 Jan 93	14 June 94	19 July 95
Switzerland	13 Nov 79	6 May 83	3 Oct 84	26 July 85	9 July 85	21 Sept 87	1 Nov 88	18 Sept 90	19 Nov 91	21 Mar 94	14 June 94	23 Jan 98
Turkey	13 Nov 79	18 Apr 83	3 Oct 84	20 Dec 85								
Ukraine	14 Nov 79	5 June 80	28 Sept 84	20 Aug 85	9 July 85	20 Oct 86	1 Nov 88	24 July 89	19 Nov 91		14 June 94	
United Kingdom	13 Nov 79	15 July 82	20 Nov 84	12 Aug 85			1 Nov 88	15 Oct 90	19 Nov 91	14 June 94	14 June 94	17 Dec 96
United States	13 Nov 79	30 Nov 81	28 Sept 84	29 Oct 84			1 Nov 88	13 July 89	19 Nov 91			

Source: Produced by Ronald Mitchell, 1997 with data from Consortium for International Earth Science Information Network (CIESIN). 1996. Environmental Treaties and Resource Indicators (ENTRI) [on-line]. University Center, Mich. URL: http://sedac.ciesin.org/pidb/
dns = did not sign prior to coming into force (but may have acceded).
*Ratified: includes ratification, succession, accession, or acceptance.

Table 4.3
Emissions of sulfur and nitrogen oxides (1000 tons a year)

	Sulfur			Nitrogen Oxides (as NO$_2$)		
	1980	1994	% Reduction	1980	1994	% Reduction
Albania	60	60	0	30	30	0
Austria	198	37	81	246	177	28
Belarus	370	190	49	234	2,073	−786
Belgium	414	147*	64	442	350*	21
Bosnia and Herzegovina	240*	240*	0	54	54	0
Bulgaria	1,025	742	28	416*	327	21
Croatia	75	44	41	83*	59	29
Czech Republic	1,128	635	44	937	369	61
Denmark	226	78	65	274	272	1
Estonia	138	70	49	72	43	40
Finland	292	58	80	295	283	4
France	1,669	565*	66	1,823	1,521*	17
Georgia	81	81	0	188	188	0
Germany[1]	3,758	1,498	60	3,657	2,872	21
Greece	200	255*	−28	306*	306*	0
Hungary	816	370	55	273	183	33
Iceland	3	12	−300	13	22	−69
Ireland	111	78*	30	73	122*	−67
Italy	1,900	745*	61	1,480	2,050*	−39
Kazakhstan	70	70	0	76	76	0
Latvia	58	58	0	93	93	0
Lithuania	111	111	0	158	158	0
Luxembourg	12	6	50	23	21	0
Macedonia[2]	5	5	0	2	2	0
Moldova	46	46	0	35	35	0
Netherlands	245	74	70	583	526	10
Norway	70	18	74	184	225	−22
Poland	2,050	1,302	36	1,229	1,105	10

Table 4.3 (continued)

	Sulfur			Nitrogen Oxides (as NO_2)		
	1980	1994	% Reduction	1980	1994	% Reduction
Portugal	133	136	−2	96	254	−165
Romania	881*	280*	68	369*	443*	−20
Russian Federation[3]	3,580	1,492	58	1,734	1,995	−15
Slovakia	390	119	69	197*	173	12
Slovenia	118	88	25	48	66	−38
Spain	1,660	1,036*	38	950	1,227*	−29
Sweden	254	48	81	454	392	14
Switzerland	58	16	72	170	140	18
Turkey[3]	430	177*	59	175	175	0
Ukraine	1,924	858*	55	1,145	568	50
United Kingdom	2,452	1,359	45	2,319	2,219	4
Yugoslavia[4]	203	212	−4	47	52	−10
Biogenic sea emissions	360	360	0	0	0	0
Volcanic	285	285	0	—	—	—
Total	28 644	14 607	—	21 718	19 942	—

The table shows national official data received at the ECE Secretariat. Percentage reductions are shown as positive figures; increases in emissions between 1980 and 1994 are therefore shown as negative figures. Key: *Interpolated data (no data have been officially submitted). 1. Includes East Germany in 1980 figure. 2. Former Yugoslavia republic of Macedonia. 3. Part within the EMEP area of calculation. 4. Former Yugoslavia, excluding Slovenia, Croatia, Bosnia and Herzegovina, and Macedonia. Table compiled and percentage reductions calculated by the authors, based on EMEP sources.

evidence yet of recovery of North American lake biota, however. In Europe, reduced levels of sulfates have been observed both in the atmosphere and in precipitation (EMEP 1996, 72–3). Monitoring of surface water chemistry at selected European sites has revealed declining sulfate concentrations (Norwegian Institute for Water Research 1997). Moreover, the drop in acidity has been greater in the 1990s than in the 1980s. Lake alkilinity levels (in effect, their buffering capacities) have also increased and at some monitoring sites there has also been improvement in invertebrate fauna—both signs of ecosystem recovery. The forest damage situation remains mixed but monitoring is continuing (UNECE 1997). On the other hand, consistent with the smaller reductions of NO_x emissions, the deposition of nitrogen compounds has generally not declined. Some scientists are concerned that nitrates may become a more important element of acidification as sulfate levels drop.

New scientific evidence suggests that the existing SO_2 emission reduction programs do not go far enough. Coupled with the modest ecosystem impact of reductions to date, this evidence has given rise to calls for a further round of emission controls in Canada and the United States (Acidifying Emissions Task Group 1997).

The essential task here is to explain the role the regimes had in moving from the first snapshot to the second; that is, the role played by the LRTAP convention and the U.S.–Canadian MOI in both changing state behavior and beginning to effect environmental improvements. In idealized terms, our mode of analysis is to construct causal explanations of the relevant changes. Because this is part of a study on the effectiveness of international regimes, we scrutinize those parts of the causal chain that involved regimes directly. Other important factors are looked at as well because they sharpen our arguments by identifying precisely where the regimes made a difference and where they did not. They also strengthen our arguments by serving as "control variables" or elaborate them by offering "intervening variables."

We believe regimes are likely to have different effects on laggard and leader states, and on those that move from the latter to the former position. Explanations are given on how interests and actions of the major laggard countries changed over time, emphasizing causal connections to international regimes. Did the LRTAP convention contribute to reevaluation of interests? Did it force action where none was desired? Did it provide critical knowledge? Did it promote internal political changes? Or did it have other impacts? A similar, but necessarily somewhat different, set of questions are asked about the leaders in the fight for acid rain regimes. Little effort is made to discuss the parts played, or not played, by those countries that were neither significant leaders nor significant laggards.

Finally, since there are two case studies, we will deal with each separately, or at least largely so. To be sure, there are strong similarities in the substantive content of the 1979 LRTAP and the 1980 MOI, and both resulted, by 1990, in formal agreements to reduce emissions. To this extent a comparison is appropriate. Our analysis departs from other analyses that have tended to contrast these two regimes (Shaw 1993). The international processes flowing from the 1979 and 1980 accords, however, remained relatively separate over the 1980s. Why? For one reason, acidification in North America and in Europe are only very slightly related as ecological phenomena. (That is, sources in the one region do not significantly affect the other.) In this sense, acid rain is a regional ecological problem not a "global" one. Equally important was the politics. The Euro-centered multilateral process was well underway before the bilateral one began. Moreover, many in Washington would have been happy to allow acid rain to be dealt with entirely by a multilateral process in a somewhat obscure European-based organization—as long as that process did not move much beyond the general exhortations and consultations of the 1979 convention. It soon did, however, in the form of the SO_2 protocol, and the United States, never a leader on the issue, began opting out. For different reasons, no one in acid rain–conscious Ottawa was content to leave it as a LRTAP convention issue.[19] It had too high a profile publicly. More generally, North American problems, environmental and otherwise, tend to be dealt with there. North American defense, for example, has always been handled in Washington and, when necessary, bilaterally, but almost never under NATO auspices. In much the same way, and for some of the same reasons, North American acid rain was handled, from the outset and over the 1980s, much more as a bilateral issue than as a multilateral one.

Nordics Lead the Way

The view of the Nordic countries—Norway, Sweden, and Finland—toward the LRTAP regime has been shaped by geography, science, and politics. Since contemporary scientific understanding of long-range transport and acid rain was originally synthesized by scientists from Sweden and Norway, policymakers in these two states knew earlier than others of the threat involved. Nordic scientists were the first to study rainfall chemistry systematically, to prove the acid deposition in their countries was largely the result of pollutants transported over great distances, and to begin assessing the widescale environmental effects of acidification. Wind patterns and the location of these countries made them victims of acid deposition originating largely from pollutants emitted in other countries, in particular the British Isles, central and eastern Europe, and the former Soviet Union. Topography meant their aquatic systems were especially vulnerable to acidification. Nordic countries as a result needed little convincing of the need for international solutions.

While their impact on the LRTAP regime is clear, its impact on them is less so.[20] After having failed to gain consensus for emission reductions in the 1979 LRTAP convention, Norway, Sweden, and Finland continued their quest within the LRTAP process, joined other like-minded countries in Ottawa in 1984 to form the "30 percent club," and helped persuade a growing number of countries to accept this goal, which became the centerpiece of the 1985 sulfur protocol. With efforts already begun to reduce sulfur emissions, the Nordic countries were in compliance with the protocol by the time it came into force in 1987. By 1993 they had made substantial progress toward achieving substantially deeper reductions. Sweden set the trend, unilaterally committing itself to an 80 percent reduction. Norway followed. Both have been extremely successful in cutting back sulfur emissions, having achieved actual reductions of 81 and 74 percent, respectively, for the period 1980–1994 (see table 4.3). Finland exceeded its own goal of a 50 percent reduction in SO_2 emissions by 1995, having achieved a reduction of 67 percent by 1991. It then announced a new goal of reducing sulfur emissions by 80 percent (from 1980 levels) by 2000 and actually met that goal by 1994 (see table 4.3).

The means by which these reductions were accomplished varied. Norway restricted the sulfur content of coal in 1976 and 1983. More significantly, Sweden and Finland responded to the first round of international oil price increases in 1973–74 by undertaking a restructuring of their national energy policies in ways that would limit their need for imported oil. Lacking significant domestic sources of fossil fuels, Sweden and Finland opted for the construction of nuclear power plants. These came on line by the early 1980s. Norway supplemented its traditional reliance on hydroelectric power with the development of North Sea oil resources.

Was the LRTAP regime a significant factor in the remarkable reductions of sulfur emissions within the Nordic countries? There can be little doubt that a substantial decline in sulfur emissions would have taken place there over the 1980s even without the LRTAP regime and the sulfur protocol. The ambitious reduction efforts were at least partly attributable to domestic factors. Environmentally minded publics were kept well aware by the media of the damage acid deposition was causing to the lakes, and perhaps to some forests and crops. Moreover, relatively large proportions of the Norwegian and Swedish populations engage in outdoor recreation, including many of their leaders. These people were especially alarmed about the disappearance of game fish in freshwater lakes, streams, and rivers. Noting the reports of forest damage in central Europe, Finns feared acid damage to their forests would undermine the health of the forest products industry that is so critical to their national economy.

At the same time, no strong domestic opposition to reducing sulfur emissions arose in any of the Nordic countries. Their relative prosperity and high technological capacity made it possible for industries to reduce air pollution dramatically without major economic sacrifices and disruptions. Even the major polluting industries appeared to accept the need for strong governmental policies. The Finnish electric power utility, in contrast to its counterparts in other countries, viewed the rising concern over acid deposition as a favorable situation because it wanted to develop nuclear power.

The impressive cutbacks in sulfur emissions of the Nordic countries were thus driven more by domestic considerations than by any direct pressures from other states to abide by international standards. Since none of these countries exported significant acid rain elsewhere, there was little enough interest abroad in the Nordics' reductions. But it does not follow that the controls imposed and accomplished were completely unrelated to the existence of the LRTAP regime. As heavy importers of transboundary pollutants, the Nordic countries have an interest in ensuring the compliance of other LRTAP convention countries with internationally mandated reductions of air pollution and in strengthening these regulations. In short, they have a strong stake in the effectiveness of the LRTAP regime. They realized any reluctance on their part to abate their own domestic sources of acid deposition, no matter how small a proportion of the overall problem these might be, would be seized upon by other countries as an excuse for inaction. Going well beyond the 30 percent reduction specified by the sulfur protocol was viewed by the Nordic countries as an essential tactic for moving the LRTAP process forward and, more specifically, to persuade the laggard LRTAP convention parties to cut their sulfur emissions and to undermine any contention that a 30 percent reduction was not feasible on economic or technological grounds. In this sense, the LRTAP regime appears to have created a momentum among the Nordic and other leader countries to make increasingly bold commitments to reduce sulfur emissions.

The LRTAP regime has thus served as an instrument for exerting pressure internationally. In its absence, the Nordics would have lacked an institutional mechanism for influencing the environmental policies of other states, either by calling attention to their own accomplishments or by exhorting their counterparts. Nordic representatives have used numerous LRTAP forums to seek new, stronger rules and to scrutinize and criticize what they considered less than satisfactory efforts by other countries to limit air emissions. They responded to excuses for inaction by calling attention to the best available technologies, what they can achieve, and what they will cost. Internationally adopted numerical goals thus not only give signatory countries specific goals to shoot for but also give other states legitimate grounds for lodging complaints when they are not achieved. The regime thus both influenced the means adopted and increased their impact.

Not content to rely solely on intergovernmental contacts to publicize the acid deposition problem and to influence heavily polluting states, the Swedish government latched upon the idea of stimulating contact between NGOs, which would not be limited to the conventions of diplomatic behavior. The agriculture and foreign ministries provided funds to set up the Swedish NGO Secretariat on Acid Rain in Goteborg in 1982. This group attempted to mobilize NGO activity on acid deposition in the countries most responsible for the problem in Sweden, and it used various LRTAP forums as avenues for its lobbying efforts. Attention was directed first at West Germany and the United Kingdom, but starting in the mid-1980s contacts were made with Poland as well as the former Czechoslovakia and East Germany and more recently with Russia, Belarus, Ukraine, and the new Baltic states. It appears doubtful that such an organization would have been set up in the absence of the LRTAP regime. Without the regime lending international legitimacy to its cause, it is unlikely that the secretariat would have been as successful in securing supplemental funding for its projects or as influential.

The LRTAP regime has even been used by certain Nordic countries against others. The Norwegian government initially resisted taking action against a major smelting operation located in Bodo, Norway, near the Swedish border. The labor unions as well as the company wanted to keep it open. Citing LRTAP regulations, Sweden prevailed upon Oslo to close the smelter, and it eventually did so in 1986 (Lykke interview).

The story is similar with respect to NO_x. While the Nordic countries declared their intention to go beyond the Sofia protocol and reduce NO_x emissions by 30 percent, they found meeting NO_x emission reduction targets more difficult than those for SO_2. Their NO_x emissions actually rose during the 1980s.[21] None achieved the 30 percent reduction of NO_x emissions by 1998 called for in the separate declaration, although Sweden may attain it by 2000. Norway became a party to the nitrogen protocol and, with substantial reluctance, agreed to the declaration only after Sweden, Denmark, and environmental NGOs strongly criticized Norway for holding out on a commitment to reduce NO_x emissions (Soybe 1988, 4–5). In Norway, the commitments made in signing the Sofia declaration, as well as other international environmental agreements, have provoked something of a backlash.[22] Critics in Finland and especially in Norway contend that politicians were too anxious to maintain their countries' reputations as environmental leaders and, consequently, gave in to pressure without having adequately investigated whether the NO_x emissions reductions were feasible.[23]

The 30 percent NO_x cutback has provided an ambitious goal, which serves some of the same purposes as the unilaterally declared goals regarding sulfur emissions. The impact of the declaration appears to be greater, moreover, by virtue of its being an internationally agreed-upon standard, albeit a nonbinding one. Achieving this goal became a matter of national pride for Sweden and important to its strategy of demonstrating to other countries that emissions of acid forming pollutants can be reduced significantly if appropriate policies are adopted. In adopting its own plan for reducing NO_x emissions, Finland appears to have been driven to minimize its embarrassment in failing to comply fully with the terms of the Sofia declaration. Thus, while domestic factors were more important than international pressures in the adoption of sulfur emission controls in the Nordic countries, the opposite was the case in the reduction of NO_x.

Germany under LRTAP

Germany was a convert to limiting acid rain and a vital one. Until 1982 its leadership was skeptical about the problem and opposed controls. Germany, however, became as strong a supporter of acid rain controls as the Nordic countries.[24] Its initial opposition was largely attributable to the fact that it was a major producer of SO_2, and thus faced potentially high domestic control costs, and to the absence at the time of any noticeable acidification damage within Germany. Despite the warnings of Gorham, Odén, and other scientists, acid rain was still seen as largely a threat to aquatic, not terrestrial, ecosystems. Then in 1981 forest dieback, or *Waldsterben,* was discovered in Germany. It quickly became a major issue. One of the key scientists involved was Bernhard Ulrich (1979). Media reports about this discovery created a sense of national alarm in Germany. Large swaths of the Black Forest and other areas were believed threatened with severe damage, and acid rain was widely seen as the culprit (Wetstone and Rosencranz 1983; Schutt and Cowling 1985). Suddenly, acid rain loomed large on the agendas of citizen groups and political parties. Following national elections in 1982 in which each major party competed to strike the strongest environmental stance, and in which the Green Party made major gains, policy shifted irrevocably. Germans also realized that while the country produced much of its own acid rain, a considerable proportion was imported from its neighbors (see table 4.1). Subsequently, forest damage was discovered also in Switzerland, Italy, Netherlands, East Germany, Czechoslovakia, and other countries (Fraenkel 1989; Hajer 1995).

German support for strict international norms to reduce sulfur emissions and for ambitious domestic measures was announced at a 1982 acidification conference in Stockholm, held on the tenth anniversary of the original Stockholm environment conference (Hileman 1983). Germany's move was a critical addition to the procontrol alliance. The conventional view, however, is that the German conversion was not connected to the LRTAP regime. To be sure, Germany was under pressure from the proponents of controls, as were others. But the conversion of 1982 is thought by most analysts to have come about as a result of German scientific research and domestic political forces (Levy 1993). In fact, there was a direct connection to the regime or at least to developments that were an intrinsic part of the regime if not to the regime itself as codified in the 1979 convention. Essential to Bernhard Ulrich's work on *Waldsterben* was SO_2 data collected and published as part of the 1970s OECD phase of the LRTAP process.[25] Less clear, but likely of some consequence in fueling the German debate, were NGO contacts with the Nordic countries.

The LRTAP Convention quickly became, for Germany, a vehicle for proselytizing its European friends and neighbors. Germany committed resources to promoting European-wide forest health surveys, held workshops to train monitors, and funded data collection and interpretation. More importantly, Germany lobbied for adoption of 30 percent sulfur reduction targets and NO_x reduction targets. In 1984, to help put pressure on the reluctant, it hosted a high-level conference in Munich on acid rain, attended by experts and ministers, that set the stage for the sulfur protocol the next year. The final communiqué of the conference made explicit reference to the draft protocol and urged its adoption. The connection with the LRTAP process could not be more clear: the conference report appeared under the UNECE logo.

Germany freely used the LRTAP regime to further its foreign environmental policy objectives. The regime appears to have had less direct influence on the content of its domestic acid rain policies. Germany has resisted the concept of framing regulations about critical loads, preferring instead to stick to issuing strict technology standards. Whereas some of its Nordic allies have started to feel the bite of the LRTAP regime because of difficulty meeting the NO_x reduction targets, Germany's ambitious NO_x reduction program has placed it on a comfortable schedule.

Although an importer as well as a source of emissions, Germany has less of an environmental stake in the LRTAP process than the Nordic countries. Unlike the Nordics, it had access in the 1980s to a far more powerful institution—the European Community. Immediately following its conversion, Bonn sought EC-wide regulations that mirrored its own domestic response to acid rain calling for steep reductions in sulfur and nitrogen emissions from large power plants. Britain, Spain, and other countries opposed these measures. As is usual within what is now the European Union, a compromise solution was ultimately reached. The 1988 Large Combustion Plant Directive designating specific reduction targets for SO_2 and NO_x for each EC member became the vehicle for the concrete regulations implementing the general LRTAP objectives (Boehmer-Christiansen and Skea 1991). Germany also succeeded eventually in obtaining EC directives requiring strict automobile emissions reductions. Domestically it reduced its emissions from stationary sources through a combination of retrofitting scrubbers on power plants and converting to low-sulfur coal.

Russia

The LRTAP Convention was a benchmark in the evolution of Soviet attitudes toward participation in international contacts between East and West. Traditionally rather uncooperative and reserved with respect to international commitments during the Cold War, Moscow became an enthusiastic supporter of the LRTAP process in the latter 1970s. It even favored the unsuccessful Nordic initiative to include in the convention binding commitments for reductions in emissions causing transboundary air pollution in the European region, though its support cooled somewhat later.

Two fundamental facts of Russian environmental geography are of importance here. First, it was a net importer of transboundary air pollution. Prevailing west-to-east winds carried five to ten times more sulfur and nitrogen pollutants into the country from Western Europe than flowed in the opposite direction (Insarov and Fillipova 1981). The primary foreign sources in the 1970s were Poland, Czechoslovakia, Hungary, East Germany, West Germany, and Finland. Although the former USSR sent more SO_2 into some countries than it received from them—especially Finland, and to a lesser extent, Sweden and Norway—it was on the whole more a victim than a cause of acidic deposition.[26] Secondly, the Asian part of the former USSR, east of the Urals, was not included within the purview of the European-based LRTAP regime. By securing agreement of the other parties that LRTAP control provisions would take into account either reductions of national emissions *or* reductions of transboundary fluxes, the USSR made its compliance much less onerous. Given that only a small percentage of its emissions are transported to other LRTAP countries, reducing transboundary fluxes was a considerably less onerous and less costly undertaking than reducing national emissions by a similar percentage would have been. Russia thus focused on those industrial sources of air pollution that posed the greatest problem for neighboring countries, namely those located in a 300-kilometer belt along its western border.

To a significant extent these reductions were accomplished by a set of actions, the net effect of which was to move a significant portion of Russia's heavy polluting industries eastward, beyond the Urals. Other, more conventional measures included reducing emissions at plants that particularly contributed to transboundary flows. Flue gas desulfurization facilities (scrubbers) were installed on power stations in the Leningrad, Donbass, and Dnieper regions—areas where the major sources of transborder fluxes to the West were located. Several nonferrous metallurgy enterprises adopted new low-sulfur technologies for smelting, pollution control equipment was introduced, and some sulfuric acid production plants were constructed using captured SO_2. Much of this was carried out under the first national Law of Air Protection, adopted in 1980, and the more stringent air quality standards and norms for air emissions that it introduced. A number of changes were also made in energy policies over the 1980s. Greater emphasis was placed on the development and use of natural gas (rather than coal), on increasing nuclear power production (especially west of the Urals), on development of an energy complex in Siberia, and on increased use of low-sulfur coals. Overall, the former Soviet Union reported a 29 percent reduction in sulfur emissions in the European region during the period of 1980–1990, although those in the Asian part of the country increased by 12 percent during the latter 1980s (Obzor Zagriaznenia 1991; Varnavsky et al. 1989). By 1993 Russia was reporting "overcompliance" with the SO_2 protocol; emissions from European Russia had decreased fully 52 percent from their 1980 levels. Although some of these cuts were the result of industrial and energy policy changes and of the economic crisis Russia was experiencing, the impact of LRTAP on both environmental and energy policy is also evident.

The former USSR signed and ratified the NO_x protocol, but was rather reserved in the process of its negotiation. Like the Nordics and Canada, the Russians probably suspected, and later found, that reducing NO_x emissions was more difficult than reducing sulfur discharges. While NO_x emissions from all sources in European Russia had nevertheless decreased by 14 percent from 1987 levels by 1992, this decrease was mainly the result of a reduction in discharges from stationary sources caused by the decline in industrial production. Mobile source emissions continue to grow despite measures adopted to control them. Since the early 1990s, the major emphasis in air protection policies has been on control of emissions from cars, especially in the most polluted cities. One plan was to provide nonethylene gasoline to Moscow, St. Petersburg, other large cities, and resort areas, and to provide service stations along international roads to allow replacement of gasoline with compressed and liquid gas.

The timing of these developments could suggest that the 1979 convention and later protocols had a tremendous impact on Russian air pollution and energy policies. A closer examination of the historical context, however, suggests a somewhat different conclusion. While it was certainly true that domestic environmental considerations and priorities at the time were of relatively minor importance in the decisions to take these various measures, there were other essentially domestic factors at work. The restructuring of the energy sector was encouraged by the declining resource base in the European region, expansion of nuclear power, and the development of abundant fossil fuels in Siberia. The shutdown of numerous inefficient and environmentally antiquated factories, after the breakup of the Soviet Union in the early 1990s, also had the side effect of reducing air pollution emissions from industrial sources. Declining levels of industrial production, as a result of the economic crisis in Russia from the early 1990s, had a similar effect. (And, therefore, SO_2 and NO_x emissions may increase in the near future once the economy recovers from the current recession.) But the LRTAP was not inconsequential. The conclusion of one study was that about one-third of the total reductions by Russia under the sulfur protocol can be attributed to this factor (Kotov and Nikitina 1996). Thus, while some developments were taken quite independently, the LRTAP regime must ultimately be given credit for a significant part of the changes within Russia.

The regime also led to bilateral environmental agreements in the late 1980s and 1990s between the USSR, on the one hand, and Finland, Norway, and Sweden, on the other. Under the 1985 environmental agreement with Finland, for example, the two countries adopted an action program for reducing air pollution emissions in the border areas by 50 percent by 1995 (relative to 1980 levels). A follow-up 1992 agreement between Finland and Russia extends the commitment to reduce transborder flows in this region. The LRTAP convention and bilateral processes became closely interlinked. The same scientists participated in the LRTAP working groups and the scientific activities of the bilateral arrangements. EMEP data on background levels of wet and dry acidic deposition, in addition to information from specially established monitoring stations along the Russian-Norwegian border, are used by a joint expert group to model transboundary flows. Essentially the same research methods are employed at the multilateral and bilateral levels. Beyond scientific cooperation, however, the results have been meager.

The Nordic countries were particularly concerned about the substantial emissions from northwestern Russia on the Kola peninsula near the borders with Finland and Norway. The two largest sources of air pollution in this region are the Pechenga and Severo nickel mining and smelting complexes of Norilsk Nickel—the largest nonferrous metals company in Russia. Emissions from these two smelters amounted to about 364,000 tons of SO_2 in 1993, and their annual SO_2 emissions exceeded the total releases of Norway, Sweden, and Finland combined. For Russia, however, controlling pollution fluxes from the Kola peninsula presents a more difficult problem than controlling those from other areas, even when international support is offered.[27] Various attempts to solve this problem both by domestic and international efforts have failed. One project with a price tag of (U.S.) \$270 million to refurbish Pechenga's obsolete plant involved Scandinavian companies and financial assistance from both the Norwegian and Russian governments. The new processes would have removed 97 percent of the sulfur (Nikitina 1991; Tennberg and Vaahtoranta 1991; Shmiganovsky 1990). The project did not go ahead, in part due to economic difficulties in Russia (Kotov and Nikitina 1996). Another round of negotiations between Norilsk Nickel and other possible actors was under way at the end of the 1990s. Even without this project, however, there has been a reduction in emissions from the Kola facilities, mostly due to production decreases, of about 38 percent from their 1980 level. A corresponding reduction of transborder fluxes in general to the Nordic countries resulted (EMEP 1992). For this the LRTAP regime and bilateral agreements can take no credit, but they may yet lead to the desired reduction in emissions from the Kola smelters and in transboundary fluxes in the region.

Eastern Europe

LRTAP regime processes took a different course in the politics of the Eastern European countries. Obliged to sign the 1979 LRTAP convention by the Cold War politics of the day, they entered the post-USSR, post-Cold War era with their own interests much more at stake. Poland had the strongest environmental movement and the most concern over domestic environmental damage, yet it refused to sign the 1985 sulfur protocol. The reason its negotiators gave was that government calculations showed that it would be impossible to achieve 30 percent reductions, and they did not want to sign an agreement with which they could not comply.

For Czechoslovakia and East Germany the LRTAP Convention had been a small pawn in the grand Cold War strategy against the West. These governments never took acid rain seriously even though their regions were the most seriously affected in all of Europe. Both signed the 1985 sulfur protocol without intending to comply. In Hungary acid rain politics were not salient on either environmental or political grounds. Domestic damage was moderate, and sulfur emissions were declining co-incidentally due mostly to increased use of natural gas.[28]

At lower levels of the government bureaucracies, especially among the scientific community, the LRTAP process had more meaningful effects. Without the inducement of furthering the goals of the Helsinki process, it is difficult to imagine that the former Soviet Union, Czechoslovakia, East Germany, and Hungary would have participated as actively and as consistently as they did in the research programs coordinated by LRTAP. All of these governments were seeking to suppress knowledge of environmental damage, yet were lured into creating it because of their entanglement in the LRTAP regime. East European researchers collecting domestic acidification data were routinely blocked from publishing such data directly in their home countries. But if they supplied their results to LRTAP working groups, which published these data in UN publications, it was then much easier for the same scientists to publish the data domestically. The LRTAP regime was a moderately high political priority in most of Eastern Europe, and it would have been difficult to censure LRTAP publications. LRTAP research programs permitted East European researchers to refute their governments' claims that they were not suffering significant pollution and do so without being prosecuted.

In the radically different political environment of Central Europe in the 1990s, the LRTAP regime has become no less important, partly for symbolic reasons. Without any significant exception, the central European governments are committed rhetorically to the LRTAP convention's protocols.[29] They wish to show that they are worthy partners for political and economic integration in Europe, and they have calculated that supporting the LRTAP process is a good way to demonstrate this worthiness. There is, however, little evidence of a deeper commitment than the symbolic. Given the turbulent changes under way, it is impossible to say how deeply the regime's effects actually extend. Many of these countries signed the 1994 sulfur protocol, for example, without any sense of what implementation measures would be required or how much such measures would cost. Thus the final verdict on the effect of the LRTAP regime on Eastern Europe is unclear.

Britain Accepts Controls

The United Kingdom is the largest emitter of sulfur in western Europe, and the fourth largest in all of Europe. Having refused to sign the 1985 sulfur protocol, it was branded the "dirty man of Europe." As a result, the country was buffeted by a wide variety of political pressures, both from within and especially from without. Succumbing to this pressure, the British government did an about face, ordering national sulfur reduction measures in 1986. The most significant of these plans included the installation of desulfurization equipment on three large coal-burning power stations (Boehmer-Christiansen and Skea 1991). The precise extent of promised British desulfurization fluctuated since that point, sometimes rising and sometimes falling. Although the commitment has never reached the 30 percent target of the 1985 protocol, the British government ultimately adopted a policy of sulfur reductions that fell just short of its requirements.

It is highly unlikely, absent the LRTAP process and sulfur protocol, that these measures would have been adopted.[30] British desulfurization policies were seen at first more as a foreign policy concern than a domestic issue.[31] Britain exports about 65 percent of its sulfur emissions and suffers relatively little acid damage within its own territory compared to what occurs in the countries where much British sulfur falls. Norway especially suffers from British emissions, and for that reason it has been particularly active in trying to cajole and pressure the government in London. About 16 percent of its deposition nationwide was traceable to British emissions, and the figure approached 40 percent in southern Norway where many very sensitive ecosystems are located (see Table 4.1). The 1986 decision to scrub the three large power plants emerged on the heels of a joint British-Scandinavian research project (funded by Britain's nationalized utility industry, the Central Electricity Generating Board) that provided conclusive proof that acid deposition was killing fish in southern Norway.

Acid rain effects in Scottish and Welsh aquatic systems have also been observed, and British forest surveys in the latter 1980s revealed extensive damage that may be in part attributable to acidification. Until the 1990s, however, these local effects did not generate nearly as much domestic political attention as the transboundary effects.[32] Moreover, it was only later that Britain became bound by the 1988 European Community directive governing emissions from large power plants, which forced stricter standards than those adopted during the wrangling with the Scandinavians in the mid-1980s.

The sulfur dioxide protocol figured prominently in the political pressure placed on the British government. Beginning in 1984 with the 30 percent club meeting in Ottawa, a wide range of domestic actors referred to the LRTAP negotiations in efforts to embarrass the government. From this date on, the opposition parties consistently promised to join the 30 percent club if elected. Elements of the ruling Conservative party also urged the government to sign the protocol, and a prominent House of Commons Environment Committee report in 1984 proposed that the government join other Europeans and sign (Levy 1991b). The emerging LRTAP regime thus served as a landmark that exerted a profound influence on the domestic debate: it was virtually impossible to find a supporter of acid rain controls in the U.K. who did not also favor signing the sulfur protocol. Some players also believe international scientific work under the emerging regime played a critical, and direct, role in persuading key decision makers of the need to control.[33]

The evidence for the regime's influence on the British nonetheless remains somewhat murky. To argue that it did not play a role in Britain's limited desulfurization policies, one would have to argue that the Norwegian and Swedish pressure alone would have been sufficient to bring about the same policy changes. This is plausible, but unconvincing. The Nordics would have had a much harder time without the protocol. LRTAP meetings (regularly attended by British NGOs) provided a chance for domestic and international opponents to embarrass the British government, and they regularly forced the issue onto the agendas of the government, political parties, and environmental activists. The British government eventually committed itself in principle to adopting even stricter emission reduction standards, toward the goal of achieving "critical loads," deposition levels which in theory will leave sensitive ecosystems unharmed (United Kingdom 1990, 149).

The British were willing to sign the 1988 NO_x protocol because they calculated the country could achieve the mandated emissions freeze without any change in existing policy. During the negotiations to revise the SO_2 protocol based on critical loads, Britain again was criticized for opposing needed cuts in SO_2 emissions by environmental groups such as Friends of the Earth. While this sort of criticism is now somewhat dated, it once again reflects an instance of the LRTAP regime entering domestic politics via pressure groups. Britain has agreed under the 1994 revised sulfur protocol to undertake stringent new domestic reductions—50 percent by 2000 and 80 percent by 2010.

Canada Joins In

Canada's situation vis-à-vis both the MOI and LRTAP regimes resembles that of the Nordics. It needed little convincing that acid rain was a problem, partly because of its status as a heavy net importer of transboundary flows, partly because of its own sensitive ecosystems (which are very much like those in Sweden and Norway), and partly because of its attentiveness to the scientific evidence. But the MOI legacy, more than the MOI process, had a clear impact on domestic policy decisions.

Acid rain had arrived on the Canadian agenda in June 1977 when federal environment minister Romeo LeBlanc became the first politician in North America to call attention to it.[34] To ensure the call to arms was noticed, his speechwriters came up with some colorful language, labeling acid rain "an environmental time bomb" and "the worst environmental problem [Canada has] ever had to face" (Howard 1977). LeBlanc's speech also described the acid rain falling in Canada as resulting from "a massive international exchange of air pollutants." Although he noted that neither the United States nor Canada was "free of guilt," it was made clear to the covering media that most of the acid rain originated in the United States. Canada's response to this threat was thus, from the outset, very much conditioned by the transboundary character of the phenomenon. LeBlanc called for negotiations with the United States to "draw up new rules which could allow one nation to tell the other to turn off the pollution at the source."

In also predicting that these negotiations would commence in a few weeks, the minister was overly optimistic. It was not weeks but years before formal Canadian–American negotiations began, and then almost a decade and a half before new pollution control regulations came into effect in all of North America. While negotiated reductions were years away, the governments did form a bilateral scientific advisory group, the BRCG, which studied and reported twice on the problem, in 1979, and, after some delays, in October 1980. The BRCG work, in turn, did lead to the MOI. There is no evidence that these bilateral scientific reports did little directly, or at first, to change American policy, though they did raise concern about the effects of acid rain in the United States. Paradoxically, they may also have helped to set back the U.S. policy process by fanning the flames of opposition. As part of the MOI legacy, they certainly became an important stimulus for mounting public concern in Canada (Howard and Perley 1980; Weller et al. 1980; House of Commons 1981), and an important peg on which subsequent Canadian efforts in Washington were hung.

After negotiations with the United States started and then stalled in the early 1980s, a new Canadian domestic dynamic set in. Sometimes lost in the often heated Canadian rhetoric about America's SO_2 onslaught against the Canadian environment was the fact that fully 50 percent of the acidic deposition in Canada emanated from domestic sources. The Ontario government had for decades done its best to ignore a long series of scientific studies of, and continuing complaints and proposals about, the "fumes" originating with the smelters near Sudbury—from farmers, from nearby municipalities, and even from its own officials.[35] Although emissions had been reduced over the 1960s and 1970s, the single most prominent measure taken, after the abandonment of open-pit roasting of ores in the 1930s, was the construction by International Nickel Co. (Inco) of its famous 380m "super-stack" in the early 1970s which merely had the effect of spreading the SO_2 emissions further and over a wider area. For Canada, as for the Nordics, a combination of public pressures to deal with the acid rain problem, the need to set an example, and the need to deflect American criticism that Canada was asking the United States to do what it had not done itself, eventually drove Canadian governments to take unilateral action. The only way to respond to the critics, within and without, was to put together a domestic control program of the sort envisaged by the MOI.

Discussions between Ottawa and the provinces had begun early on. Such consultations were unavoidable since pollution is constitutionally a shared jurisdiction in Canada. The federal government normally sets nonmandatory national air quality standards and guidelines, except in the case of new motor vehicles, where it has regulatory authority. The laws responsible for reducing emissions are normally enacted by provincial legislatures and enforced by provincial ministries. Ontario was thus responsible for regulating the emissions from the smelters near Sudbury and those of its provincially owned utility, Ontario Hydro.[36] Even taking federal–provincial coordination difficulties into account, however, moving against acid rain was easier in Canada than in the United States. The major polluting provinces—Ontario and Quebec—were also the most vulnerable to acidification and hence had a self interest. In the United States, the major sources of pollutants were located in states relatively unaffected by acid rain and with a strong vested economic interest in coal production and coal burning.

In February 1982, the federal and provincial governments had agreed that Canada would seek a 50 percent reduction of emissions of SO_2 (based on 1980 levels) from the relevant parts of Canada and the United States.[37] No understanding was reached at this time about how the additional Canadian reductions would be apportioned among the provinces, however, and the Canadian offer was conditional on adoption of a similar U.S. program. When a modest American control proposal being developed by EPA was decisively turned down within the Reagan White House in late 1983, Canadian governments decided to proceed unilaterally. Although it would be highly unusual, for example, in trade negotiations, to go into talks already having made unilateral tariff cuts, that is analogous to what Canada (and the Nordics) did in the case of acid rain. Given American intransigence, Canadian governments were trapped by the need, in effect created by the MOI, to demonstrate their commitment up front.

At yet another federal–provincial meeting in March 1984, just prior to the 30 percent club meeting, agreement was reached on a unilateral 50 percent reduction in SO_2 emissions by 1994.[38] This time, the deal was not contingent on American action. The following year saw specific commitments by individual provinces and offers of federal money to help finance SO_2 controls. In the end, federal funding only went to assist modifications in one smelter in Quebec. Inco proceeded with an extensive set of process changes at its smelter near Sudbury, Ontario, without, in the end, accepting any government assistance. Ontario Hydro emissions were also reduced. Although two provinces, New Brunswick and Nova Scotia, held out for over two years before signing formal agreements with Ottawa, Canada had more or less met its obligations as a member of the 30 percent club, and its commitment to the LRTAP sulfur protocol, by early 1985. If the Canadian prime minister could not then meet his good friend, the president of the United States, as he claimed, with "clean hands," he could do so, at least, with cleaner hands (*Toronto Star* 1985, A3).

NO_x reductions were a different story for Ottawa. With its own scientists at odds over the significance of NO_x in environmental acidification, the federal government decided to control NO_x emissions for other reasons. New motor-vehicle NO_x standards were established in 1985 that were expected to reduce emissions by the year 2000 by around 45 percent. (As usual, these changes followed similar changes within the United States.) In addition, a 10 percent reduction in stationary source emissions of NO_x was included in the pollution control measures for Ontario Hydro power plants. Because Canada had already taken these actions, negotiation of the LRTAP NO_x protocol found Ottawa in the somewhat embarrassing position of resisting proposals for 30 percent reductions. For those states that had not yet taken any action against NO_x, initial cuts of 30 percent would have been relatively easy; for Canada, an additional 30 percent reduction appeared much less easy. Moreover, the environmental impact of the relatively low concentrations of NO_x found in Canada was assumed to be less serious than that of the much higher concentrations found in parts of Europe (Doern 1993). Under fire from some NGOs for rejecting the proposed new NO_x 30 percent club, and from some industry sources for going too far, Ottawa supported the eventual protocol compromise of a freeze. It did not avail itself of the opportunity to sign the separate Sofia declaration, even though that pledge allowed signatories to select, for the 30 percent cuts, any base year between 1980 and 1986.

Although complaining mightily about the difficulties of further cuts during the Sofia process and at the protocol signing ceremony, Canada was soon to undertake just such cuts. As a result of U.S. pressure during negotiation of the 1991 AQA, the federal government tightened mobile-source NO_x standards for vehicles produced after the 1996 model year, thus bringing Canada into line, once again, with new American regulations.

America Shifts, Finally

Although the United States signed the LRTAP Convention in 1979, it was, along with the United Kingdom, the major "refusenik" on the 1985 SO_2 protocol. It signed the MOI with Canada in 1980 but then, for the duration of the Reagan administration, repeatedly refused to adopt or to negotiate controls. Yet, under the Bush Administration in 1990 it adopted new legislation domestically to reduce the emissions that lead to acid rain. How did this happen?

The LRTAP regime never figured as prominently in American acid rain debates as it did in some European countries. The United States could without much concern sign the 1979 convention and thus be involved as a great power in an east-west political initiative because the convention was largely toothless. Washington did sign the NO_x protocol, but that imposed no requirements beyond what the United States already had done domestically or was planning to do. American officials participated in LRTAP scientific programs for intellectual more than political reasons. The LRTAP process never received much attention in Washington, unlike most other capitals. The LRTAP convention can thus be discounted as a direct causal agent in changing American policy. Whether or not the LRTAP and MOI had any indirect impact on the shift in U.S. policy that came about in 1990 is another matter. The short answer is that the American government tried but was unable to ignore the MOI entirely. It tried to ignore the broader LRTAP enterprise, but here again the effort was ultimately unsuccessful. The case can thus be made (and is explored more fully in the next section) that both regimes were effective to a degree in a more subtle and indirect way.

A major coal producer and coal user, the United States had much more substantial emissions of SO_2 than Canada. Successive versions of the U.S. Clean Air Act had since 1970 addressed these emissions as a local, ambient air-quality problem, but they were not generally regarded circa 1980 as sources that had, or could have, an impact on remote areas. Most of the long-range deposition from U.S. SO_2 sources had little or no effect due to well-buffered soil conditions in the immediate downwind regions. The areas that were vulnerable (mainly upstate New York and the New England states) were smaller and less significant on a national political scale than affected areas in Canada (particularly Ontario and Quebec), which are the political heartland of that country. Equally important, the coal-burning electric utilities that were the largest U.S. sources of SO_2 were a vital part of America's industrial structure. It would be expensive to clean up (or so they argued at the time), and the rates they charged their customers were of considerable political interest. Moreover, the political clout of both the utilities and the coal industry was considerable. Their view was that if midwestern power plants did, in fact, send some damaging pollution into New England or across the border into Canada—something that had to be proved—then any damage caused would have to be balanced against all these facts, and especially against the expected costs of the cleanup.

If the Canadian interest was clearly to press for controls on acid rain, the overall American interest (as defined during the 1980s) was to oppose them. Canada pushed for the MOI, and once that was in place pushed for an agreement with control provisions. The United States approached the MOI very cautiously (as it did the LRTAP Convention), insisted on more and better evidence about the causes and effects of acid rain, and resisted for some time the pressures from Canada to undertake domestic controls and to negotiate a bilateral accord with targets and timetables. That resistance, and a considerable (but not total) immunity to any MOI influence, was evident for the tenure of the Reagan administration.

The MOI regime did not lead in the short term to a change in the American government's environmental policy or to any reduction in the emissions of the private-sector actors who were the major causes of acid rain. That policy changed in 1990, however, after amendments to the Clean Air Act in 1990 mandated the necessary reductions from these sources. In the United States, the decade following the conclusion of the 1980 Canada-USA MOI was dominated not by any significant discussion of the 1979 LRTAP Convention or the MOI, or even of the on-going bilateral conflict with, or any responsibilities to, Canada.[39] Rather, it featured a long and often bitter and apparently unresolvable domestically focused debate over American environmental policies and over who would bear the burden of new controls. While the concerns of Canada and the problem of transboundary air pollution were not completely ignored, they played a modest role in this debate.

From the outset, the Reagan administration felt relatively free to ignore not only the spirit but also, in some respects, the letter of the MOI commitments made by its predecessor (Canadian Institute of International Affairs 1981). And it did so despite a promise by President Reagan himself, made to the Canadian prime minister in early 1981, that the United States would honor these commitments. The administration not only refused to negotiate controls but also tried to relax domestic SO_2 standards, including those for plants affecting Canada, in direct violation of the MOI commitment to "promote vigorous enforcement of existing laws and regulations" to respond to transboundary air pollution. The United States also failed on various occasions to inform Canada of proposed policy or regulatory changes, thus violating MOI requirements to provide advance notification and consultation. It largely ignored the BRCG and MOI bilateral scientific groups when it embarked on its own study of acid rain, the National Acid Precipitation Assessment Program (NAPAP) process.[40] (For that matter, the NAPAP reports virtually ignored the transboundary aspects of acid rain.) Administration appointees also departed significantly from the spirit of the MOI as well as that of long-standing bilateral traditions by interfering with the scientific work being carried out in the MOI work groups from 1981 through 1983. Scientists on the working groups who thought the United States should respond to acid rain were replaced with others who were more skeptical. One working group was not allowed to do a critical part of its mandated task. And drafts of the working group reports were vetted and revised by senior policy officials who were nonscientists (Robinson 1982).

To be sure, the United States never repudiated the MOI explicitly,[41] nor did the Reagan administration feel free to ignore it completely. Either action would certainly have entailed some costs politically, costs that the administration did not want to face and, to some extent, did not have to face. When confronted with criticism that they were violating its principles, administration officials such as EPA administrator Anne Gorsuch staunchly maintained they were acting in accordance with the MOI. The administration, or at least the State Department, carefully maintained and continually expressed an interest in meeting and talking with Canadian counterparts. At various points after the formal negotiation process had been suspended by Canada in 1982, American officials proposed that it be restarted. In part this position and the earnest declarations of interest ensured that the United States was meeting its international obligation under the regime to "negotiate." In this sense, given that the U.S. administration could have ceased all talks with Canada, absent the MOI, it helped ensure U.S. interest in minimally maintaining communication.

While the Reagan administration could with reasonable impunity refuse to sign the 1985 LRTAP sulfur protocol, stall the MOI process, and refuse to negotiate "targets and timetables" with Canada, it did find it difficult to ignore international developments entirely. Its uneasiness about being on the outside of the international movement toward acid rain controls, while maintaining it was a world leader on environmental policy, was evident on various occasions. Though unwilling to pay the price of admission to the "30 percent club," the Reagan administration did insist on being invited as an observer to its founding in February 1984—an event that Canada intended to use to put pressure on the United States. The senior EPA official who came received an intense grilling at a U.S. embassy–arranged press conference. He subsequently branded the Ottawa meeting as "Without a doubt, a hanging in effigy of the American policy" (Green 1985, 136).

The same American uneasiness also led a few months later to an almost comical set of diplomatic exchanges prior to the follow-up August 1984 Munich conference. Before deciding to send EPA head Ruckelshaus to the gathering, Washington insisted that Germany, Canada, and other participants promise they would not use the conference to embarrass the United States. To be sure, it is doubtful that these international events influenced American policy directly. The Reagan administration never seriously wavered over the next four years from its opposition to further controls and its position that "more research needs to be done."[42] At the same time, the fact that American officials were so worried about the head of EPA being embarrassed in Munich, and went to some lengths to prevent it, suggests strongly that they perceived themselves politically vulnerable on the issue—internationally and at home. They knew then they were (along with the British) the odd ones out. Such perceptions, in turn, indicate that the changing climate of international opinion on acid rain induced by the LRTAP Convention and MOI regimes was having some impact on Washington. It became increasingly difficult for the American political process to ignore the fact that the evidence on acid rain and the movement toward controls was building.

In its fundamental antipathy to acid rain controls if not to the MOI, the Reagan administration had an abundance of powerful allies—the American coal industry as well as the mine worker unions, coal-producing and coal-burning states, the electric utility industry, and the private sector in general. These interests had highly influential allies within Congress, including Senator Robert Byrd of West Virginia and Representative John Dingell, the powerful chair of the House Energy and Commerce Committee. Any bill aimed at dealing with acid rain was ensured a slow, sometimes even quick, death—at least until the late 1980s. Absent Ronald Reagan, progress was thus unlikely. Had the Carter administration been reelected in 1980, it is arguably the case that years would have passed before new legislation with significant controls on acid rain could have been adopted and any meaningful bilateral agreement could have been concluded.[43]

This political stalemate began to loosen in the late 1980s. The longer the legislative roadblock lasted, the more overdue revision of the U.S. Clean Air Act (CAA) became. Pressures and support for tightening American air pollution laws mounted. Recognizing that the time had come to move, presidential candidate George Bush committed himself to revising the CAA in early 1988 in the acidic snows of the New Hampshire primary, a state where support for such action had become an obligatory political stance. As president, Bush quickly made good on his campaign pledge. He proposed sweeping changes to the existing CAA in July 1989, including new controls on SO_2 emissions. It was by then taken for granted by environmental groups, officials, and legislators alike that any process of amending the act had to include measures to counter acid rain. The eventual amendments (CAAA) mandated a near 50 percent reduction in SO_2 over ten years and stringent new regulations on mobile sources of NO_x. To reduce the costs of the SO_2 cuts, the bill allowed electrical utility companies to take whatever control measures would be least costly, and it introduced an innovative emissions trading scheme. The new act received congressional approval and presidential signature in November 1990. By the late 1990s, the mandated cuts were well under way. The vast majority of power plants opted to switch to cheap low-sulfur coal rather than fit existing plants with expensive scrubbers. The United States had finally joined the ranks of those committed to substantial reductions of the precursors of acid rain.

Analytic Assessment

It is clear that the LRTAP and MOI regimes did not effect changes in the critical environmental decisions of all involved states. Some, like the Nordics and Canada, were committed for powerful reasons of self-interest to the reduction of emissions well before the regimes came into being. Others, particularly Germany, adopted similar policies for reasons that seem to have had little to do with the respective regime. Still others, such as certain East European states, became more aware of the acid rain problem through participation in LRTAP but did not have the means to afford the clean-up measures that were, and are, required. On the other hand, the emerging regimes appear to have encouraged the control programs eventually adopted by the former Soviet Union and the two regime holdouts—Britain and the United States—at least in an indirect way and to have had some impact on certain aspects of the behavior of others.

The question to be addressed in this section is: how did this occur? What were the causal pathways through which the regimes exerted whatever influence they did? This question will be answered by applying the models identified in chapter 1 and explored in the other cases. Regimes can effect changes by modifying utilities, enhancing cooperation, bestowing authority, facilitating learning, redefining roles, and facilitating internal realignments. Of the six pathways, there is some evidence for all, but more for some than for others. Illuminating these pathways means necessarily taking another cut at the same empirical evidence. To avoid duplicating what has already been discussed, this second cut will be less a rehashing and more a peeling back of further layers of the analytical onion.

Regimes as Utility Modifiers: LRTAP

A number of the impacts that the LRTAP convention had on state behavior constitute a modification of utility calculus, as suggested by the foregoing causal narrative. This was most straightforward in the case of the former Soviet Union, though a degree of utility modification can be observed in some other countries as well.

From the creation of the LRTAP convention in 1979 the former Soviet Union consistently viewed the acid rain issue as a moderately high foreign policy agenda item. The USSR changed its policy in line with regime objectives, funded and participated in collaborative research ventures, and joined the Scandinavians in applying often severe diplomatic pressure on European neighbors to reduce emissions. Without the LRTAP regime, Soviet interest in acid rain as a matter of foreign and domestic policy would have been quite low. There was no significant domestic constituency behind such actions, and foreign pressure was rather low as well. Russian emissions were less important to the leader states than emissions in Britain, Germany, and Poland, with the not insignificant exception of those from the Kola peninsula. Absent LRTAP, the Soviet Union would almost definitely have simply ignored the whole issue.

The LRTAP regime's primary influence on the Soviet Union was thus one of modifying foreign policy utilities. The Russians responded measurably to the LRTAP regime, but they did so in a way that made clear they were mainly interested in acid rain for broad foreign policy reasons, not for domestic reasons. The Soviet Union's actions strongly suggest a strategy of seeking to be a leader within the LRTAP process without actually undertaking costly reduction measures. In formulating treaty commitments it sought to ensure that whatever measures were agreed to would entail as close to zero cost as possible. The clearest reflection of this was the successful Soviet ploy to secure the clause in the 1985 SO_2 protocol that counted a reduction in transboundary fluxes as equivalent to a reduction in total emissions. LRTAP had the effect of raising the issue on the Soviet foreign policy agenda and of altering the calculus by which decision makers settled on a course of action. The emission reduction measures undertaken did not reflect a concern for domestic acidification. (That such a concern never really arose also suggests that learning was not an important mechanism.)

The LRTAP regime had these utility-modifying effects on the USSR because of Soviet desires to use the regime to serve broader interests in East-West relations. In the late 1970s the Soviets wished to embed the West in a trans-European treaty. They calculated that doing so would further their goal, pursued in the Helsinki process, of securing legitimization of the Soviet and East European governments. As détente soured, Moscow continued to utilize the LRTAP process as a vehicle for portraying the members of the Soviet bloc as responsible environmentalists while prominent western states (chiefly the United States and Britain) played the role of renegades. It is quite clear that in this linkage between acid rain and broader foreign policy goals the latter figured far more prominently in Soviet calculations than did acid rain, per se. It is also clear that Soviet decision makers realized that they had to take the LRTAP regime seriously if they were to reap any linkage benefits.

Others in the eastern bloc also responded to the LRTAP regime in ways that suggest a utility-modification impact. East Germany and Czechoslovakia, for example, signed the 1985 sulfur protocol although there were no significant domestic constituencies arguing for sulfur reductions. They were clearly following the policies of the Soviet Union by linking acid rain policies to broader foreign policy concerns. The point here should not be exaggerated. The impact of the regime was not sufficient to bring about compliance with the reduction promises they made. (And, as small, centrally located countries, they could not avail themselves of the "transboundary fluxes" loophole used by Russia.)

For Britain, the LRTAP regime had a more muted utility-modification effect that was intertwined with effects at the level of domestic political realignment and authority bestowment (to be discussed below). While these different impacts were linked in practice, it is possible to isolate the utility-modification effect for the purposes of exposition. Once specific regulatory targets were announced within the LRTAP process, with the negotiation of the SO_2, NO_x, and VOC protocols, these targets became de facto standards for judging British action. For sulfur, U.K. actions lagged behind these standards until the 1990s. British decision makers were therefore faced with a continuous stream of criticism aimed at U.K. sulfur emission policies, criticisms that would have been more diffuse in the absence of these clear LRTAP benchmarks. The "dirty man of Europe" label coined by NGOs was picked up by the press and political parties. Prime Minister Thatcher encountered direct criticism from other heads of government during the 1980s, especially from German Chancellor Helmut Kohl. While this LRTAP-induced pressure was not decisive, it contributed to a recalculation of utilities by the U.K. government and to the British shift in policy. That foreign pressure mattered is made clear by the timing of the shift. When reductions were first announced in 1986, there was no serious concern about acidification damage within the United Kingdom. The initial reductions were thus driven almost entirely by foreign-policy concerns which had been influenced in turn by the LRTAP regime.

Regimes as Utility Modifiers: MOI

The MOI, per se, had little impact on Canadian assessments of costs and benefits. From Minister LeBlanc's 1977 "time bomb" speech on, Ottawa was officially, resolutely, and permanently on record as favoring controls on emissions that led to acid rain. Canada's utility calculations were driven from the outset by the known science and by the realization that, like Sweden and Norway, it received much of its acid rain from transboundary flows of air pollution, contributed rather little to its neighbors, and had wilderness regions and economic interests highly vulnerable to acidic deposition. The utility calculations were admittedly crude. Anything more than ballpark estimates of the environmental costs of acid rain were at the time yet to be determined, and the benefits were never really calculated precisely. That there would be significant benefits from controlling acid rain, however, was never in doubt in Ottawa. As a consequence, the necessity of controlling emissions both in Canada and the United States was a given, as was the desirability of a bilateral agreement to cement the commitments to those controls. Thus the MOI reflected and confirmed but did not influence the basic Canadian objectives. The policy objective preceded the regime rather than followed it.

The MOI and LRTAP, translated in part through Canadian efforts, probably played a modest part in changing American utility calculations. The Reagan administration, though perhaps not Reagan himself, remained throughout two terms opposed, as a matter of policy and of ideology, to controlling emissions from those industries that were the major sources of acid rain. In this objective, they were joined by key congressional allies like Byrd and Dingell. The administration's major concern about the bilateral process with Canada was that it might induce a reexamination of domestic air pollution regulations—something to be avoided strenuously and at whatever cost to bilateral relations. Canadian complaints were not to undermine in any way the administration's position in the debate on acid rain, its plans to reform (i.e., to weaken) the Clean Air Act and, more broadly, the viability of its overall domestic program.

After eight years of Reagan, different assessments about the desirability of addressing acid rain emerged in the executive branch. Unlike their predecessors, George Bush and his advisors saw the political benefits of support for a broadening and strengthening of America's most important environmental legislation, the Clean Air Act, if not the environmental benefits of actually doing so. They also believed that the economic costs, especially of acid-rain controls, could be reduced by adopting a market mechanism approach. Utilities had clearly changed. The question is why.

In this significant policy shift, more credit can be given to years of Canadian pressure than to the distant developments of the LRTAP or the by-then almost forgotten MOI. But international considerations in general were overshadowed by the electoral and domestic political calculations that almost always dominate policymaking in Washington. If so, where is the regime influence, if any? There is some empirical evidence, in addition to anecdotal evidence, that Canada exerted a significant, if less than sufficient, influence on America's transition to acid rain controls.[44] Canadian influence was clearly more on the agenda-setting process than on the ultimate policymaking or legislative process, but was no less important for that. (A more detailed discussion of Canada's "public diplomacy" is presented in the discussion below of regimes as authority enhancing mechanisms.) Assuming Canadian efforts had some impact on America's acid rain policy shift, Canadian behavior then becomes a relevant intervening factor between the regime and American behavior. To the extent that the MOI and LRTAP regimes had an impact on Canadian policy, they may also have had an indirect impact, through Canadian behavior, on aspects of American policy. To come back to the question of American utility calculations, the argument here is that the regimes did have a modest indirect influence. The nature of the impact of the regimes on Canadian policy is a matter to which we will return. The emerging regimes played a part in changing domestic alignments on the acid rain issue. And this domestic realignment played a part in the new U.S. administration's different perception of American policy utilities.

Moving away from the basic U.S. decision to accept emission controls, the MOI did affect utilities in a more modest way. Even after passage of the Clean Air Act, it served to encourage an American view of the desirability of negotiating a bilateral accord, and thus to push the process of resolving the acid rain issue and strengthening the bilateral regime for air quality. Amending the U.S. Clean Air Act in 1990 provided the legislative basis for controlling acid rain in the United States and provided the constitutional basis for concluding the bilateral agreement long sought by Canada, and it did so with little extra cost. The new act sufficed legislatively and domestically, but it did not suffice for the purposes of bilateral politics. Negotiation of an air-quality agreement was necessary, in the words of one American official, because only such an accord could finally bury the often hostile rhetoric over acid rain and "get this issue off the agenda" of Canadian–American relations. The most concrete symbol of the issue as a long-standing agenda item was the promise in the MOI by the United States as well as Canada to negotiate an agreement. Had the MOI never been signed, some sort of bilateral agreement may still have been necessary in Canada for domestic political purposes but would have been much less important in the United States. Given the MOI was signed, its presence made more compelling for the United States the benefits of concluding a bilateral accord.

Regimes as Enhancers of Cooperation: LRTAP

The LRTAP regime's cooperation-enhancing effects, and especially its ability to induce consensus and reduce fears about cheating, stemmed largely from EMEP. The collective emissions data, while relying on national reports, were considered highly reliable because they were regularly evaluated by scientists in the context of the creation of transport models. Erroneous national reports would have been detected in the course of modeling because of the anomalous results they would have generated. In fact, there are reports that the Czech government considered submitting false reports in the 1980s but opted not to precisely because it believed that the subterfuge would be detected through EMEP. While the LRTAP convention lacked enforcement powers, EMEP's ability to uncover potentially embarrassing misinformation or violations appears to have increased the willingness of states to set emission targets collectively.

The LRTAP regime also made it possible for states to improve the quality of the bargains they struck by creating an institutional home for the sharing of information and the creation of novel forms of cooperation. There is little doubt that the institutions and process established by the 1979 LRTAP convention contributed to the cooperative spirit in which, and the ease with which, the protocols were negotiated. Those involved in these negotiations, especially from the Nordic countries, were impressed by the important role played by the collective EMEP figures on emissions and deposition. Another illustration of this dynamic can be seen in the adoption of the critical-loads approach. LRTAP bodies provided a unique function in promoting the acceptance of harmonized methodologies for measuring and mapping critical loads; for disseminating authoritative, comprehensive assessments of critical loads; for spreading consideration of the approach across Europe; and finally for encouraging states to set collective policy based on critical loads. The contrast with the European Union (formerly the European Community) is instructive in this regard. While EC/EU directives on power plant and automobile emissions clearly had more impact in achieving emission reductions by states that otherwise would not have sought them, it is striking how crude such measures are compared to those under the LRTAP regime. These directives simply mandated targets and technologies without encouraging—in fact, while actively discouraging—creative innovation; they created winners and losers and bred resentment. LRTAP regime initiatives, by contrast, led states to discover mutually profitable ways to solve common problems.

It might be noted that the early LRTAP protocols entailed little or no direct cost for the states that implemented them. Many had already moved on SO_2 and NO_x to the extent required. Many states signed the 1991 VOC protocol, however, before they fully knew what domestic measures would be required to implement it. And the revised 1994 sulfur protocol committed signatories to measures that in many cases moved beyond prior domestic requirements. These latter examples of cooperation are attributable in part to LRTAP success, if not at finding that fabled Pareto frontier, then minimally at building consensus, reducing fears about cheating, and improving the ability of states to discover mutually profitable zones of agreement.

The LRTAP regime's origins in the Helsinki process, combined with the awareness that the continent's acidification problem required special attention to the economic problems in eastern and central Europe, leads to the question: what impact did the LRTAP regime have in promoting effective East-West collaboration to reduce acid rain? Here the record is quite poor. LRTAP never made it possible for eastern and central European countries to get their concerns on the political and negotiating agenda, and it never promoted any serious discussion of how to promote fruitful financial transfers to implement reduction measures in the East. Because it is virtually impossible to imagine an effective solution to Europe's acid rain problem that does not involve mutually beneficial East-West bargains, it is unfortunate that LRTAP regime was unable to play a positive role in this regard (Levy 1995, 65–66).

Regimes as Enhancers of Cooperation: MOI

Given the rather sorry history of the Canada–United States MOI work groups in the early 1980s, it is difficult to find the same degree of cooperation-enhancing impact in the case of the MOI. This is clearly one case that sorely tried and, for most of a decade, defeated what has been termed the problem-solving "diplomatic culture" of Canadian-American relations (Holsti 1971). Indeed, as noted earlier, the MOI work groups themselves became a source of conflict. Canada probably made a mistake opting for a process where a specific report was requested of work groups explicitly tied to the treaty negotiation process, rather than embarking on a LRTAP-like, open-ended process of scientific exchange and cooperation. Once the MOI work groups had submitted their reports, and the MOI-mandated bilateral negotiations hit an impasse, the necessary level of bilateral scientific collaboration largely came to an end. Other efforts, however, were made.

A later round of joint scientific cooperation emerged in 1987. Some Canadian officials felt the resulting discussions limited the damage to their cause from an interim report out of the U.S. NAPAP program that had downplayed the seriousness of acid rain (NAPAP 1987). An earlier, and undoubtedly more effective, joint effort was the 1986 report of two special envoys appointed by the president and prime minister (Lewis and Davis 1986). In enhancing mutual cooperation, the major contribution of this report was to secure Ronald Reagan's acknowledgment, for the first time, that acid rain was, in fact, a problem in need of a solution. None of the protagonists in the domestic American debate had previously achieved that end. The president's public acceptance of the envoys' report eliminated an important constraint and moved the two countries somewhat closer to joint action. These examples of cooperation in the mid-1980s were not explicitly a part of the MOI process, but they were attempts to keep it going in another way and under another name.

In a different manner, the MOI also enhanced cooperation by facilitating the process—once it began—of agreeing on the structure of the 1991 Air Quality Agreement. The MOI provided the model for what became known as the "elements paper" on which agreement was reached in 1989–90, prior to the commencement of formal negotiations. The elements paper in turn served as both an outline and a preliminary table of contents for the eventual bilateral agreement. As noted earlier, the MOI itself contained most of the major provisions eventually included in the formal agreement with the vital exception of the specific emission-reduction commitments. Officials in both countries had more than enough time to become familiar and comfortable with the MOI provisions and this clearly facilitated the ultimate negotiations.

Overall, however, the cooperation enhancement pathway appears to have been more important in the case of LRTAP than of the MOI. Why should this be?

One possible reason concerns the numbers of actors. Other things being equal, one may assume that the larger the number of actors, the greater the likelihood of cheating and of defections and the higher the transaction costs. On the other hand, with fewer actors there would be less concern about cheating and defections, and lower transaction costs. As a result, mechanisms to deal with these problems are likely to be less important to the actors involved and hence less critical to regime effectiveness. The simple difference in the number of signatories to the LRTAP Convention and the MOI may thus help explain why this pathway appears more significant in the former case than in the latter.

Second, the importance of cooperation enhancement may vary with the character of the original ecological problem. Contrary to common assumption, not all international environmental issues are straightforward common-property problems. Some clearly are, including ozone depletion, global warming or climate change, and pollution of the atmosphere from nuclear testing. But there are also international environmental problems that, by their physical and ecological nature, have less effect on ecosystems held in common (such as the stratosphere) than on ecosystems within the territories of particular states. Cases where emissions from one country cross a boundary to affect an ecosystem in another country would include the famous Trail smelter case, pollution of the Rhine River, and the problem of acid rain. There may be no difference in environmental terms between the deterioration of ecosystems claimed by no one state and that of those under the sovereign control of particular states. There are, however, fundamentally important differences in political terms. And these political differences become more important to the extent that the environmental problem at issue is a transboundary, upstream-downstream one with a predominant source state and a victim state, as opposed to one where most or all states contribute and all suffer the effects.

Regimes where common-property issues predominate and those where asymmetrical, transboundary effects predominate should logically differ in the extent to which collective action constraints impose themselves. The cooperation enhancing effects of a regime should decrease in importance the more the environmental problem at issue is a transboundary rather than commons problem. The acid rain problem has some of the elements of a commons problem, in that the pollutants move through the atmosphere. (This aspect was emphasized in the European case by the continentwide EMEP emission/deposition data, as noted above.) On the other hand, acid rain can also exhibit the characteristics of a classic upstream-downstream problem, particularly so in the case of acid rain in North America. There are states that are major sources of the pollutants in question (i.e., the United States) and states that are key recipients (i.e., Canada). Only trace effects of Canadian emissions are felt in the United States.

That there was less cooperation enhancement under the MOI than the LRTAP Convention may thus be due in part to the fact that the former dealt with a problem that was more transboundary in nature than it was a commons problem. With respect to the other issues covered in this volume, and indeed with environmental issues in general, the cooperation-enhancement pathway may well be less important in regimes relating to transboundary problems such as acid rain than it is for regimes that have more of a common-property resource character, such as marine pollution or climate change.

Regimes as Bestowers of Authority: LRTAP

Regimes can bestow authority. They encourage actors to comply with rules because they are legitimate, whether or not following the rules is in their self interest in terms of costs and benefits. Some of the LRTAP Convention's influence can be traced to its ability to induce states to treat its norms and outputs as authoritative, beyond simple calculation of interest. This causal mechanism can be observed operating in the United Kingdom, in eastern and central Europe, and in the former Soviet Union.

In the United Kingdom the 30 percent sulfur reduction target acquired a level of legitimacy and authority that bears no relationship to scientific merit or economic interest. By the end of the 1980s the United Kingdom was on a trajectory to achieve a reduction in the 25 to 29 percent range, against a baseline that, unlike most of the rest of Europe, reflected significant reductions over the 1960s and 1970s. The gap between what Britain was going to do and the 30 percent target was arguably trivial. Nonetheless, numerous actors, both within Britain and abroad, took the gap as evidence of a serious breach that required extraordinary measures to rectify. This phenomenon is most readily understandable as a function of LRTAP bestowing on the 30 percent figure a level of legitimacy and authority that it otherwise would have lacked.

The same phenomenon repeated itself during 1993 when Britain was negotiating its targets under the revised sulfur protocol. According to the accepted principle based on critical loads, Britain should have aimed for reductions of 80 percent, but its negotiators were only willing to commit to 76 percent. Britain received some flak for this. At one point Norway's environment minister publicly, and somewhat undiplomatically, called his British counterpart a "shitbag." Clearly the anxiety over these few percentage points was out of proportion to real interests, yet the degree to which the critical loads concept had acquired authority prompted a heated response. In the end, a face-saving measure was adopted whereby Britain accepted the 80 percent target with a later target year.

In post-1989 eastern and central Europe, LRTAP Convention norms were treated as authoritative by the new governments that replaced communist predecessors. In large part this was directly connected to a particular utility-based calculation: these governments desperately wanted to join the European Community and they thought that complying with LRTAP norms would help, or even be necessary, to achieve this goal. Yet the independent impact of the norms as an authority mechanism is less than clear. There are many things a new regime in the East could have done to demonstrate worthiness to the West, and few EC members were concerned about transboundary air pollution from the East. Perhaps it was the LRTAP Convention's status as a legal treaty that explains how seriously formal support for it was taken (Levy 1993). The desire to integrate with the West was what motivated the East to adopt green intentions, but LRTAP's authority helped shape what form those green intentions took.

The importance of the authoritative status of the LRTAP regime norms should not be overestimated. No state has undertaken actions to reduce emissions that can be explained by this phenomenon. Rather, this mechanism shaped the nature of public debate in Britain and the form of public promises in the East. It did not generate action that would not have otherwise occurred.

Somewhat more important was the LRTAP regime's ability to bestow authority on information and knowledge. The high degree of acceptance of emissions and transport models owes a great deal to EMEP's status as an international institution. Joint research programs organized under LRTAP's Working Group on Effects elicited greater national participation than can be explained simply by national research priorities or calculations of interest. This impact is most observable in those countries where scientific knowledge about emissions, transport, and damage was most threatening, especially in the East. These governments consistently enacted measures aimed at suppressing such knowledge, and they offered pronouncements downplaying the seriousness of air pollution and acid rain; yet they treated contradictory data and conclusions from the LRTAP process with deference. It appears that LRTAP authority in the East helped push these governments to release information that they would rather have kept hidden.

Regimes as Bestowers of Authority: MOI

Similar to the process unfolding in Europe, the MOI helped legitimize and popularize in the United States the critical idea of reducing emissions by half. The proposal to do so first emerged in the context of the MOI process and was given significant scientific support by the work group reports, even though the American scientists involved did not, in the end, specifically support the 50 percent goal. In succeeding years, this objective was adopted by virtually all of the U.S. environmental NGOs active in the acid rain and Clean Air debates and became the conventional yardstick by which control proposals were measured. Accordingly, in 1989, 50 percent was accepted by the Bush administration as the appropriate reduction target, or at least the politically necessary one, when it came to draft the Clean Air Act Amendments. Although the MOI process did not ensure this result, it bestowed considerable early authority to the 50 percent target.

As well as encouraging actors to comply with rules because they are legitimate, even if self-interest would suggest they should not do so, regimes also encourage actors who *are* complying to pressure those who are not. As shown above, complying with both the letter and the spirit of the MOI was very much in Canada's interest as the recipient of considerable American pollution. The perceived legitimacy of the norms enshrined in the MOI, however, gave Canadian diplomacy both a weapon and a certain hard-edge aggressiveness. Not content merely to comply with the regime, Canada pushed it as hard as deemed possible. This was political and environmental policy intervention with an attitude. And the effort met with some success.

Whatever the effectiveness of the MOI as an environmental regime, it certainly did not suffer from disuse. The Canadian government employed it early, often, and in a variety of contexts. Barely a month after the MOI was signed, Ottawa referred to it in a diplomatic note concerning Washington's plans to reassess regulations governing power plant fuels. From then on, and for the next four years, it was invoked in ministerial public statements and private meetings with American counterparts, in formal notes and frequent ambassadorial letters, and in officials' statements and arguments at bilateral negotiation meetings. It also served as one basis (along with the LRTAP Convention) of the text of innumerable Canadian drafts of what eventually became the bilateral 1991 AQA. The findings and conclusions of the scientific reports generated by the MOI working groups were continually marshaled to buttress political and diplomatic efforts. In short, while the MOI did not change the perception of Canadian interests, and its use by Canada may not have had much direct impact on the United States, it was unquestionably a useful weapon in the Canadian political arsenal. Environmental regimes, if not sufficient to defeat the strong, at least serve to arm the weak.

The MOI also had an impact on the style of Canadian behavior and the way in which its case was presented to the United States. Breaking with the long-standing tradition of conducting "quiet diplomacy," officials in Ottawa and at the Canadian embassy in Washington adopted a more public diplomacy, bypassing the State Department and carrying their arguments more often and more directly to the U.S. Congress, to U.S. opinion leaders, and to the American public. A considerable public information campaign was mounted, and the embassy became the source of an endless stream of newsletters, factsheets, posters, newspaper articles, and letters-to-editors. Key parts in this campaign were played by two Canadian government–sponsored films about acid rain, one of which was labeled "foreign propaganda" by the U.S. Department of Justice, a notoriety that ensured a high demand for it in U.S. environmental circles. The counselor for environmental affairs at the embassy and other Canadian officials at consulates across America were made available to any U.S. group who wanted a speaker and to some who did not know they wanted one. Cabinet ministers, and even the prime minister, were called in when the occasion warranted a high-level speaker. Acid rain tours to Canada were arranged for politicians, congressional staffers and journalists to see first-hand the damage caused by acid rain. Ottawa also broke precedent and supplied Canadian government scientists to testify at U.S. congressional hearings on the Clean Air Act. Even Canadian customs officers were enlisted in the battle; they handed out "stop acid rain" brochures to American tourists driving into Canada.

This activity did not go unnoticed. It was the source of considerable chagrin to some American officials, most notably Anne Gorsuch, the first head of the EPA during the Reagan administration. The public activity was also a sore point for, among others, Ohio coal producers, whose association president lambasted the prime minister in a personal letter, accusing Canada of launching a "PPPB" program, exporting "pollution, power, propaganda, and booze." But Canada's propaganda efforts also received considerable support, particularly from those Americans, inside Washington and outside, who came to agree that something must be done to curb acid rain.

More than mere comfort was gained from this support. The "in-your-face" element of the information campaign was continually and carefully weighed both by Ottawa and especially by the Canadian embassy in Washington. Generally the campaign's effects were seen as positive. The cries of wounded outrage from opponents were taken by the Canadians for the most part as signs that the information was having its effect and the pressure was being successfully applied.

Underlying the campaign was a clear if usually unstated sense that Canada had the moral high ground through the 1980s. This view of the Canadian position was shared by many of the proponents of acid rain controls in the United States. (Indeed, this point was conceded by one U.S. official who later claimed, in an interview with one of the authors, that the United

States had finally taken the moral high ground in 1990 with the passage of the Clean Air Act.) To put the matter in a counterfactual manner, had the MOI not existed and had acid rain developments internationally not been what they were, Canada's position would have been sorely weakened and its public diplomacy campaign might never have been mounted let alone pursued as confidently and aggressively as it was. Thus, if Canada's influence in the American policy arena was indeed exerted more through this public effort than through backroom lobbying, then the MOI and LRTAP regimes can be given a share of the credit for the adoption of U.S. controls.

In the end, however, regimes do not have an unlimited shelf life as bestowers of authority. At some point, their continued use against an intransigent opponent can become politically dysfunctional, even counter-productive. Over-use can engender annoyance and damage the working relationships essential to an on-going diplomacy. This may have happened in the case of the MOI. Suggestions by Canadian officials that the United States was not living up to its provisions gave rise to fierce protests of innocence in Washington, by EPA administrator Gorsuch in particular. Canadian officials eventually stopped invoking explicitly the original 1980 accord. In fact, the diplomatic records suggest that the MOI was rarely mentioned internally and never invoked bilaterally by Canada after the fall of 1984. There was, however, more to this abrupt break in what had become a clear rhetorical pattern than a desire not to continue rankling the Americans. In the Canadian election of October 1984 the Progressive Conservatives under Mulroney replaced the Liberal government that had negotiated and signed the MOI. From that point on, civil servants in Ottawa, wise in the sensibilities of politicians and governing parties, likely decided that discretion was advisable. They chose, at least as much for reasons of governmental politics as of bilateral diplomacy, to cease referring explicitly to the MOI. Thus, changes in governing parties can reduce the usability of a regime commitment even when it might be employed to a country's advantage.

Regimes as Learning Facilitators: LRTAP

Possibly unique among international environmental regimes, LRTAP has developed a base of scientific information that has significantly facilitated learning, both about the environmental problem of acid rain and about the need for solutions. Some of this scientific base has emerged from the EMEP program. (Much of it has also come from scientific work in Canada and the United States.) Over the years, EMEP expanded the number of air pollution monitoring stations in Europe and standardized the instruments and processes used for making measurements. Its synthesizing centers in Oslo and Moscow gather and compile the data from the network and issue a variety of reports; they also develop models of the flow of pollutants from emission and deposition data and meteorological reports.

EMEP is perhaps best known for its annual tables that report how much of each country's acid deposition originates in each of the other countries, and, conversely, where each country's emissions go (see table 4.1). The quality of EMEP data has been upgraded over the years, largely through efforts made to standardize observations and upgrade the instruments and skills used in the poorer and less technologically advanced countries of southern and eastern Europe. Scientists representing EMEP make periodic visits to monitoring stations to critique the operators on whether they are correctly implementing EMEP's procedures. In some cases, new instruments are tested at several of the stations for possible use throughout the network. Some problems remain in the availability and validity of the emission figures from certain countries, but procedures have been developed to cross-check data.

Learning takes a variety of paths. The most important of these begins with the exchanges of information taking place through contacts among scientists. Scientists from eastern Europe and the former Soviet Union especially benefited from contacts with their western counterparts, which for decades had been discouraged or prohibited. The scientists then took what they have learned about the acid deposition problem to political officials, who were then better informed when they entered into negotiations on international agreements. Another learning path involves NGOs, such as the Swedish Acid Rain Secretariat. It has played a significant role in disseminating information generated by EMEP and other LRTAP bodies throughout the region by means of its widely read publication, *Acid News,* and its mobilization of NGOs in other countries.

Learning also occurs, as noted in chapter 1, both with respect to understanding the environmental problem of acid rain and developing policies and negotiating agreements among parties to the problem. The LRTAP regime undoubtedly played a critical role in raising consciousness throughout Europe of the seriousness of the acidification problem and the long-distant transport of air pollutants. Beyond Norway and Sweden, where awareness of the acid deposition problem first emerged, appreciation in other European countries of the magnitude of the problem has grown by the dissemination of basic knowledge gained through the EMEP program. Much more has since been learned about the consequences of acidification. The LRTAP regime has also been an incubator for new approaches to address the acid deposition problem, in particular in the emergence of the critical loads concept. In contrast to the across-the-board reductions approach, the cornerstone of the first LRTAP sulfur and nitrogen protocols, the critical loads approach incorporated into the revised sulfur protocol of 1994 establishes individualized emission ceilings for each country that take into account the scientifically determined impacts of pollutants where they are deposited.[45] The continuing availability of data on the transboundary movement of air pollutants is also an essential input into assessing compliance with the protocols.

The learning impact has been felt not only on the available stock of scientific and substantive understanding, but also on political and diplomatic processes. While considerable knowledge is disseminated through official reports, such as those of EMEP, officials who have participated in LRTAP negotiations and working groups either as diplomats or scientists stress the importance of networks of communication that develop in the numerous meetings of LRTAP groups through which participants exchange information, insights, and experiences in an informal manner. Participants learn about what other countries are doing to address the acid deposition problem and receive suggestions on emission reductions as well as estimates on how much they will cost. National officials and negotiators have accepted EMEP figures and the models developed for these, such as the "RAINS" model, as a basis for drafting agreements—despite being aware that the data had technical shortcomings, especially during the program's early years. Some involved in these processes suggest that the specific reductions mandated by the sulfur and nitrogen protocols were not as important as the impact of the overall LRTAP process. As one interviewee observed, "you can't look at the effect of LRTAP from a snapshot perspective; it is the process that is important."[46] Some would go so far as to argue that without the EMEP data it would have been impossible to negotiate the protocols on sulfur and nitrogen emissions.

Scientific developments, promoted by the Nordics under what later came to be called the EMEP process, also influenced the German conversion. Technical data on sulfur deposition produced by the OECD in the 1970s played a critical role in the work of Bernhard Ulrich, the scientist whose report to the German environment ministry touched off the *Waldsterben* debate. That, in turn, led to the significant change in Bonn's policies in 1982. Learning processes had an impact on Germany.

Overall, the wide availability of scientific and policy information, especially that collected and reported by EMEP and the OECD during the 1970s, had a profound effect not only on the creation but also the strengthening of the LRTAP regime.

Regimes as Learning Facilitators: MOI

The LRTAP experience suggests that international institutions can facilitate individual and social learning. Regime-generated processes can make it more difficult for states to maintain there is no problem requiring action, and they can serve to educate states about the nature of the problem and the ways in which it can be solved. Various official and semiofficial scientific reports on acid rain in North America, starting with those of the BRCG and the MOI work groups, served to broaden understanding about the phenomenon. Data on the problem of acid rain in Europe were part of Canadian assessments but less important in the United States. Nevertheless, information about the LRTAP process had some impact in the latter. For example, around the time of his confirmation as EPA administrator, William Ruckelshaus read and was impressed by a report from an American think tank focused largely on European developments (Wetstone 1983). The extent of learning as a result of the MOI regime has already been discussed here, particularly in terms of an influence on public and NGO thinking. The learning mechanism played a pervasive role, including interacting with and having a particular impact on other pathways such as domestic realignment. It is nevertheless clear that its potential impact on Washington was lessened by the views of key officials in the Reagan administration.

Regimes must be seen as fragile rather than all-powerful institutions. Reluctant governments can frustrate the enhancement of learning. They can ignore evidence they do not like and fasten on the slimmest of contrary evidence. Such inclinations and activities can weaken the process of implementing and extending a regime. The Reagan administration, for one, certainly did what it could to ensure that the MOI process did not lead to acid rain controls. When it decided that it did not like the content of the emerging MOI work group reports, it did its best to water down the message (for example, by insisting its scientists withdraw from supporting emission cuts). It then ignored the reports themselves. When a panel established under the president's own science advisor to review these reports confirmed that acid rain was a problem requiring action, the Reagan administration buried that report, too (OSTP 1984). When EPA determined that action was necessary and its head proposed a limited control program, this initiative was killed internally (EPA 1983). And when the president's personal envoy concluded with a Canadian counterpart that acid rain was, indeed, a problem requiring action, this conclusion was formally accepted by the president but soon countered by a contrary preliminary report out of the major national study into acid rain (Lewis and Davis 1986; NAPAP 1987).

Regimes as Agents of Role Redifinition: LRTAP

Not much empirical support appears in the acid rain case for the idea that acid rain regimes brought about any significant change in state roles and identities. That the issue of acid rain was to some extent socially constructed there can be little doubt, especially in the way in which it was placed on the international agenda. That the interests and roles of some states changed is also clear. Most of the leader countries, however, went from an agnostic position to that of ardent believer and proponent prior to the conception let alone the formal establishment of the regimes. Germany is perhaps the prominent exception. In the early 1980s Germany moved from identifying itself as a skeptic, or even an opponent, to seeing itself as a victim to some extent. It began to support the LRTAP regime in part because it had become convinced (by hard data and Ulrich's theory about environmental impacts) of the need for its neighbors to control emissions as well as itself. While there were other and perhaps more important causal pathways at work here, the change in roles cannot be overlooked.

Regimes as Agents of Internal Realignment: LRTAP

If we relax the assumption that actors are unitary, an assumption often but not always made in the above-noted pathways, then another causal mechanism can be seen to operate. Regimes can also affect behavior by causing internal realignments, shifting the power balance among domestic groups.

The LRTAP regime played a modest role in realigning domestic politics in some countries. The most significant manifestation of this mechanism in real emission reductions was in the United Kingdom, but it also appears in the German case. Other manifestations of this mechanism, while having less impact on the environmental bottom line, are worth elaborating for analytical purposes.

For Germany, the *Waldsterben* debate, fueled by Ulrich's use of the OECD data, led undoubtedly to a significant political realignment on the acid rain issue. The German policy conversion was prompted by more than mere learning at the expert and official levels. Acid rain controls and support for the MOI were very much prompted by critical political movements, including the sudden success of the Green Party in national German elections.

Within Britain, the impact is less obvious and clear-cut. Three distinct ways exist in which the LRTAP regime altered domestic political alignments. First, it raised the salience of the acid-rain issue sufficiently so that a variety of political actors concerned about Britain's political position in Europe actively sought a shift in the British position. These actors included members of Margaret Thatcher's cabinet (William Waldegrave) and political party elites across the entire spectrum. Prior to 1983, when negotiations began on the sulfur protocol, Sweden and Norway had tried hard to bring about a shift in Britain without ever awakening domestic political interest. The LRTAP process thus helped achieve what Nordic diplomacy alone could not.

Second, the LRTAP regime was able to weaken the control that the U.K. Forestry Commission had on assessing the state of Britain's forests, by making such assessments take place under LRTAP auspices, following harmonized methodology, with the results being publicly released annually. The Forestry Commission is a rather conservative body with a long history and entrenched methods and biases. It denied that British forests were vulnerable to acidification damage and resisted pleas to join in a Europeanwide assessment of forest health. When Germany promoted such a program of assessment, though, it became very difficult for the United Kingdom to resist. In the mid-1980s Friends of the Earth carried out its own assessment of British forests using LRTAP process methodologies and released results indicating serious damage. This embarrassed the Forestry Commission and it questioned the report's validity. By 1985, however, the commission was participating, albeit reluctantly, in the LRTAP forest assessments. While there is a reasonable argument to be made that British forests are not as damaged as some rather simple methods suggest, annual release of these results was reported in the press, used by NGOs, and in general added to the pressure to reduce emissions.

Another significant impact on domestic politics has been the result of the emergence of critical loads as the guiding management tool within the LRTAP regime. The British government adopted critical loads as its own guiding principle in 1990. This quite clearly would not have happened absent the LRTAP process. The United Kingdom participated actively in the LRTAP effort to map critical loads. A British government scientist was named chair of the Working Group on Effects, which oversaw the mapping effort—quite a change from the United Kingdom's earlier "dirty man of Europe" period. In the course of carrying out the measurement and mapping exercises, it was discovered that Britain contains a significant area that is among Europe's most vulnerable to acidification. This conclusion, which hit the British press around 1992, radically transformed the domestic debate about acid rain. The constituency supporting acid rain controls expanded from environmental activists and elites concerned about the standing of Britain abroad to include those worried about the fate of the British countryside—a far larger group. By 1993 when the new sulfur protocol was being negotiated, Britain was voluntarily pursuing policies aimed at reductions on the order of 70 percent. It had effected reductions of about 45% by 1994 (see table 4.3).

This is not meant to exaggerate the LRTAP regime's impact. During this period Britain was undergoing an across-the-board "greening"; its policies were changing on a number of issues, including ozone depletion and climate change, not just on acid rain. Politics within the European Community and within Britain itself were probably more instrumental in this general greening than LRTAP. At the same time Britain was privatizing its power industry, thereby breaking a monopoly that had resisted acid rain controls quite strongly, and allowing private utilities to switch from coal (politically popular because of union politics) to natural gas (economically efficient because of lower costs).

Another manifestation of the domestic realignment pathway affected several countries in 1988 when the NO_x protocol was signed. The initial negotiating position of the lead countries had been a 30 percent reduction of NO_x emissions. Negotiations eventually focused on a freeze in emissions. NGOs saw this as a defeat and they mounted a campaign to pressure countries to sign a separate pledge at the signing ceremony promising to reach 30 percent reductions. No government really wanted to sign this pledge. The very reason the leaders had retreated from 30 percent reductions to a freeze was that they had determined reductions were going to be more costly than they had initially estimated. Twelve countries ended up signing the pledge, however, out of fear of being embarrassed by the NGO campaign. It is clear that NGOs seized a window of opportunity at the NO_x protocol signing ceremony, where environment ministers were all present and press coverage was guaranteed, which gave their campaign a major boost. It is hard to imagine these governments falling prey to such a campaign in the absence of the protocol's signing ceremony.

Regimes as Agents of Internal Realignment: MOI and LRTAP

Regimes can bring about internal realignment by creating new constituencies and new forces. Another way is by facilitating the political armament or disarmament of existing groups. Regimes can provide these groups new ammunition to use against their opponents and can take away or counter the ammunition used by those opponents. This sort of process unfolded in both Canada and the United States, albeit in different ways.

The internal realignment in Canada was less extensive than in the United States but nonetheless notable. The MOI provision that Canada and the United States would "develop a bilateral agreement . . . to combat transboundary air pollution" had a measurable effect not only on the Reagan administration, which felt compelled to continue negotiations even when opposed to taking any domestic action to reduce transboundary air pollution, but also on Canadian governments, which a decade later could still settle for nothing less. Although a prominent NGO (the Canadian Coalition on Acid Rain) argued that a bilateral agreement was irrelevant once the U.S. Clean Air Act had been passed, Ottawa could not so easily escape from this MOI commitment. If nothing else, it needed the symbolic closure of an international agreement. Solving the acid rain problem took a back seat for awhile to negotiating the Canada–United States Free Trade Agreement, but it could not be forgotten. The MOI commitment also had an impact on Canada's provincial governments. Though neither signatories to the 1980 accord nor consulted during its negotiation, they had come to accept the need for the promised bilateral accord. Negotiation of the 1991 agreement tested that commitment and revealed its extent.

During the 1990 negotiations, the United States insisted on certain improvements in Canadian environmental policies. These demands stemmed less from a concern about the impact of Canadian emissions on the United States than from the need in Washington to be seen, especially by Congress, to gain something politically from the negotiations. The most prominent quid pro quo sought by Washington was for Canada to commit itself in the agreement to a national cap on SO_2 emissions, similar to that in the emerging American law. The existing Canadian SO_2 reduction plan placed a 2.3 million ton emissions limit only on the seven eastern provinces. The three western provinces had adamantly rejected both any limits on their emissions and the concept of a national cap, pointing to the minimal environmental impact of western emissions on the eastern acid rain problem. Faced with this new American bargaining position in the fall of 1990, however, the federal government went back to the provinces arguing that the long sought acid rain accord was hanging in the balance. The western provinces grudgingly fell into line, and a Canadian national cap of 3.2 million tons thus became part of the 1991 bilateral accord. Ottawa's willingness to accept the U.S. demand can be partly explained by Environment Canada's long-standing interest in just such a national cap, but this objective had previously been a frustrated one.

Pursuit of the agreement called for by the MOI thus strengthened tempo-
rarily the hand of the federal government vis-à-vis its provincial governments.

For the United States, however, internal realignment had a considerably more important impact. To gauge the extent to which the emerging
international regimes on acid rain had a role in this process of political
armament and disarmament and the extent to which other factors, especially domestic factors, were responsible, more historical detail on the
American realignment is provided here.

The shift, from opposing to legislating acid rain controls came about
gradually rather than suddenly, largely through coalition building and
coalition disintegration. Support for greater controls on SO_2 grew, albeit
slowly, in the years following the MOI. The bilateral reports out of the
MOI process itself, additional investigations for the National Academy
of Sciences and the president's own science advisor, and even the contro-
versial NAPAP interim report, steadily added evidence of the reality of
the problem and the need to act (United States–Canada MOI 1983;
NAPAP 1987; NAS 1981, 1983, 1985, 1986; U.S. OSTP 1984; U.S. OTA
1984). As the issue of acid rain became better understood and better covered in the American media, an increasing number and array of environmental groups added this item to their list of demands (Boyle 1981;
Luoma and Shaw 1987). Wilderness and conservation groups concerned
about the effects of acid rain on lakes, forests, and wildlife were joined
by groups concerned about the health effects of ambient air quality, who
embraced the issue of acid rain, either for its own merits or often as a
hook on which to peg demands for controlling further the SO_2 emissions
that also affected urban air pollution levels. Pressure to deal more broadly
with air quality also mounted. During the 1980s, opponents of acid rain
controls and stiffer auto emission standards had used, as a way of achieving their objectives, the tactic of blocking any attempt in Congress to
undertake the long-overdue review of the U.S. Clean Air Act. This strategy, however, while successful for a number of years, ultimately ensured
growing and broader support from a wider constituency for just such a
review. And, more generally, the proponents of acid rain controls were
given some boost by the widespread dissatisfaction in the United States
over the Reagan administration's neglect of environmental issues. By the

time there was a supportive administration in the White House, acid rain controls had become one of the accepted necessities in a new act.

Over roughly the same period there was a gradual but equally important disintegration of the opposition forces. The formidable and solid front comprising the investor-owned utility companies, most coal companies, the coal miners union, the midwestern coal states, and their political representatives in Washington that prevailed politically for most of the 1980s was by the end of the decade no longer a united force. Like many coalitions its members had somewhat different interests. The electric power industry consistently opposed any and all bills, but especially those that required general use of expensive pollution control measures, such as the scrubbers imposed on new plants by the existing legislation. The coal producers wanted to ensure that power plants continued to burn coal but had much less concern about the costs imposed on the utilities. But what kind of coal? A "renegade" faction of low-sulfur coal producers emerged in the early 1980s with the aim of preventing a repeat of the congressional political deal of 1978 that had strongly favored the use of high-sulfur coal by effectively requiring the installation of scrubbers.[47] This group argued that there were other less expensive options, specifically, wider use of low-sulfur coal. Some high-sulfur companies, sensing that growth in the industry was going to be in low-sulfur production, began acquiring low-sulfur deposits, thus further weakening the opposition camp. In 1987, correctly reading the writing on the political wall, the high-sulfur coal mine–dominated United Mine Workers of America (UMWA) and some of the high-sulfur coal companies, working with Senator Robert Byrd, broke from the utilities. They came out in support of the sort of control measures they had previously opposed, arguing for forced retrofitting of generating plants with the expensive scrubbers. That, in turn, would allow continued use of high-sulfur coal. There were still other key defections. Politicians in certain of the most affected coal states, such as Ohio, also offered compromise solutions in an attempt to head off congressional action even more unfavorable to them.

By the late 1980s the opposition coalition was thoroughly fractured. Into this disarray stepped the Bush administration determined to give

America the long-awaited new Clear Air Act, but concerned about the costs of doing so. In the end, the amendments to the act required reductions but not scrubbers and allowed the electric utilities to adopt whatever measures were least costly. When most of the utilities met the new regulations by switching to low-sulfur coal, they did so at costs far below any of the estimates the companies themselves and most analysts had made over the 1980s (Munton 1998).

Tracing the causal links in any complex social system is, of course, difficult. Assessing and demonstrating the impact of the LRTAP and MOI regimes on domestic U.S. realignment is particularly difficult. Participants in the process tend not to point to the regimes or to factors outside of the domestic realm, preferring instead to highlight elements of the internal U.S. political battle with which they were most familiar. It appears arguable, however, that there was an impact from the regimes. The LRTAP and MOI were part of the context in which the American domestic debate ran its course. The development of the LRTAP protocols and the MOI inspired Canadian programs undoubtedly affected the thinking of some participants in the American debate. Relatively early on in that debate, studies and some media coverage focused on the growing gap between the LRTAP-bound Europeans and the anticontrol position of the United States (Wetstone and Rosencranz 1983, and, for example, Tye 1983). American politicians at both the federal and state level and their staffers began making fact-finding treks to Europe (BNA 1984; Fay 1984) as well as to Canada. European scientists were invited to the United States (Cowling 1982; Cowling and Odén 1980; *Arkansas Democrat* 1985). Later in the 1980s, key actors in the clean air debate noted pointedly at congressional hearings that the United States was the only industrial state that had still not adopted controls.[48]

The influence Canada had on American thinking would be easy to exaggerate, as has been done by observers on both sides of the border. There appears to be little doubt, however, that Canada exerted some. In particular, it helped place acid rain on the U.S. domestic policy agenda and define the policy options. And one of the key weapons in the Canadian arsenal up to 1984 was the MOI. Its central proposition, that the acid rain problem was real and required policy attention, was supported by most of the scientific evidence gathered over the 1980s in the United States and elsewhere. That proposition was accepted, eventually, by most of those involved in the American policy process, as it had been elsewhere.

The impact of the international regimes as they developed over the 1980s can be seen perhaps most clearly by a counterfactual analysis. Suppose history had unfolded differently. Suppose that the drive behind the LRTAP regime in Europe and the MOI in North America had steadily withered through the 1980s as new scientific evidence generated by these accords pointed to a lack of actual damage and, instead of confirming suspicions, raised serious questions about the importance of SO_2 to acidic deposition. Suppose also that the LRTAP protocols of the 1980s had never happened and that the movement started by the Nordics toward national control programs had collapsed over the course of the mid-1980s instead of gathering steam. In such a situation, it is hard to imagine the opposition to acid rain controls in the United States following the path toward decline that it did. Instead, the opponents would have maintained the upper hand. They would not have allowed the domestic debate to shift from the issue of whether or not acid rain was a problem to the matter of how it should be handled. They would have much more strenuously and successfully resisted calls for controls. And they would not, one by one, have begun to adjust first to the likelihood and then to the certainty of congressional action. Opponents almost certainly would have pointed to the lack of SO_2 control measures in other countries as evidence that they were not necessary in the United States, and they would have pointed to those countries that had backed away from controlling emissions as proof that such policies were a mistake.

But the acid rain regimes did develop. And they offered encouragement to the proponents and no solace for the opponents of controls. Although it is difficult to find direct and concrete evidence here of the regimes' active impact—to find the proverbial smoking gun—it is also difficult to avoid ascribing to the growth and persistence of the regimes an important part of the opponents' loss both of credibility and of will.[49] The regimes were effective, in a passive sense, just by being there. Their continuance and evolution made increasingly untenable a whole range of argument that might otherwise have justified inaction.

Conclusion

As did the regimes concerned with marine oil pollution and the Barents' fisheries, the acid rain regimes that emerged over the course of the 1980s and 1990s had identifiable impacts on state behavior as well as on the environment. The acid rain case, however, was a somewhat more complicated one in the sense that there were two primary pollutants (SO_2 and NO_x), a tortured scientific debate, and two distinct though related processes (LRTAP and MOI). As well, the regime impacts varied from country to country. In particular, the leaders of the acid rain campaign were affected by the regimes differently from the laggards.

As with the other two cases examined in this volume, there can be no doubt that the acid rain regimes were partly responsible for changing political behavior—deeds as well as words. Most importantly, they contributed to reducing European and North American emissions of SO_2 and, to a lesser extent, of NO_x. The reductions (shown in table 4.3) would not have happened to the extent they did in the absence of the LRTAP and the MOI. Whether or not the regimes and the changes in behavior have solved or even begun to solve the environmental problem is another matter. Just as it is difficult to assess the environmental effects in the oceans of the reduced loadings of oil from shipping, it is difficult at this point to assess how many lakes or trees have been or will be saved by reductions in acidic deposition. Emerging scientific evidence is suggestive of ecosystem improvement, particularly for certain lakes and streams, but it is not conclusive. What is clear is that terrestrial and inland aquatic ecosystems, like marine ecosystems, are now being less buffeted by anthropogenic sources.

It is extremely difficult to judge which of the two regimes was more effective. Obviously, the LRTAP regime was the more effective in the case of the European countries. The MOI regime had an impact not only on the United States but also on Canada. If the LRTAP regime was more responsible for the U.S. shift than the MOI, then in some sense it was probably the more influential of the two. We would suggest, however, that the question of relative potency is ultimately not the important one. To repeat: both were effective to a measurable extent and particularly so in the matter of SO_2 emissions. What is clear is that the degree to which the policy changes responsible for the emission reductions and the reduced sulfate loadings were themselves the result of the regimes varied from country to country. The regime impacts were more important in the cases of laggard countries, especially the United Kingdom and the United States, where they helped bring about a shift to controls. They were less important substantively but still significant to the policies adopted by the leader countries, such as Sweden, Norway, and Canada, and by Germany, the most important convert.

What conclusions can be drawn from the LRTAP and the MOI cases about the ways in which regimes can be effective? It is abundantly clear that regimes work in complex and indirect ways, rather than in simple and direct fashion. There are, as often is the case in the realm of political and social behavior, many factors at work. It is the rare occasion when any state's leadership adopts a course of action simply because a new regime is coming into shape. More often, critical decisions about changing modes of behavior will be influenced by a variety of factors working through a maze of political forces. This means that causal pathways are more often subtle and intricate than straightforward. It is possible, even likely, that if regimes were more forceful, blunter instruments, they would evoke even more entrenched opposition in response. The tendency of regimes toward subtlety and deftness is, ironically, perhaps a source of their strength and effectiveness.

The importance of the causal pathways was found to vary across actors. Indeed, this pattern was a distinctive element of the acid rain case in comparison with the marine oil pollution and Barents Sea fisheries cases. As the previous section discussed effectiveness pathway by pathway, it is useful here to proceed country by country.

The adoption of acid rain controls by the USSR can best be explained in terms of utility modification. Absent LRTAP, the Soviet Union would almost certainly have simply ignored the acid rain issue. The opportunity for linkage to East-West politics provided by LRTAP altered the benefits of environmental action. Given the terms of the LRTAP regime, Moscow's interest in furthering East-West cooperation could be served without costly reduction measures. Once this utility calculus was clear, it became and remained a strong supporter of the regime. While perhaps most of the Russian reductions were not the result of LRTAP, some were, particularly those cuts to sources along its western border.

The support initially provided by the East European countries also reflected utility calculations concerning the same broader foreign-policy agenda and, of course, the necessity at the time of agreeing with Moscow. In later years, after the collapse of communism, they were keen to demonstrate their commitment to "Europe" as part of their effort to prove themselves worthy of membership in what was then becoming the European Union. The LRTAP regime also encouraged their cooperation by the legitimacy of the scientific and technical information gathered under EMEP and on the processes by which it was gathered. These processes also went beyond being a source of information; they disseminated knowledge and understanding both about the science and the policy options, a particularly valuable contribution for the East Europeans who started with relatively little expertise and technical backup. Indeed, LRTAP's success in enhancing cooperation, bestowing authority, and facilitating learning is perhaps unique among international environmental regimes. Given the post-transition economic distress of these countries, however, they faced much more difficulty in implementing the LRTAP targets than did the West European countries or the Russians. Reductions beyond those resulting from the retiring of old, inefficient plants were very costly, and by and large were not pursued. In this respect, the LRTAP regime was not ultimately effective.

The most prominent pathway in the case of Britain was perhaps the extent to which the LRTAP regime enhanced the authority and legitimacy of the emerging environmental norms. The specific LRTAP regulatory targets for sulfur, NO_x, and VOCs became the de facto standards for judging British action. The criticisms that British decision makers received both from within and without would have been much less effective in the absence of these clear LRTAP benchmarks. The developing regime also had a utility-modification effect on Britain as well as facilitating some domestic realignment. In these respects, however, the regime mechanisms were joined by other factors. The behavioral change was thus both less and less clearly a function of the regime, per se. The British case does provide a good example of how regimes interact with other influences to facilitate or even force behavior changes.

The MOI and the LRTAP regimes had some impact on the United States through bestowing authority, especially on Canadian public diplomacy, and through some occasional (rather than continuous) successes at enhancing cooperation. Both regimes played a more significant role in realigning American domestic politics, albeit an indirect one. Indeed, the continued development of the regimes and their viability over the 1980s was arguably a necessary though not sufficient condition behind America's shift toward SO_2 controls. Absent those developing regimes, opponents of acid rain controls in the United States would have continued to question the science and the seriousness of the problem and would have much more strenuously and successfully resisted calls for controls. The U.S. experienced a significant change in utility calculations from the opposition of the Reagan administration to the support of the Bush forces for amending the Clean Air Act. The changing perceptions of costs and benefits came about largely because of internal political factors, including the environmental neglect of the 1980s, but was facilitated by the regimes through the authority bestowing and domestic realignment pathways.

For Germany, the convert, the regime appears to have exerted influence through learning processes, through a redefinition of its international role in the issue-area, and most importantly through a fostering of a domestic realignment. Given Germany's key role in the debates and developments after 1982, this case alone offers significant testimony to the effectiveness of those developments that we have summarized as the LRTAP regime.

For the leaders, the impact of the regimes was less dramatic. As to Sweden, Norway, and Canada, they were from the outset supportive of the controls eventually adopted and they proceeded in some respects in advance of the regimes. Our analysis suggests, however, that it would be a mistake to assume therefore that the respective regimes had no impact on them or on Germany. On the contrary, regime effectiveness is revealed in at least two key ways. The regimes bestowed a certain international authority on the leaders' efforts (including those of Germany after 1982) to persuade others—and each other—to adopt and implement the policies that would begin to solve the acid-rain problem. Both regimes also played a part in ensuring the leaders' rhetoric was turned into action, increasing their determination to proceed and perhaps moving up the timing of their policy adoptions. As would-be leaders, they were vulnerable to the criticism that their efforts to pressure others were not matched by their own actions. The mechanism here has some relationship to the notion of regimes as role definers, in the sense that it is a socially constructed one and arises in part out of role conceptions. It differs from that notion (as set out in chapter 1) in that the operative influence here is not a regime-induced change in an actor's role but the politics of others' expectations and of ideas.

Regimes work in diverse ways. The question of why different countries were influenced through different pathways is largely beyond the scope of the present chapter. Taken most generally, this is a question of what kinds of countries, or groups of countries, are more susceptible to what kinds of regime influences. Or, what are the interaction effects between problems, actors, and regimes as they combine to influence behavior? One example of such an interaction effect was noted earlier. The cooperation-enhancing effects of the LRTAP regime were greater than those for the MOI, and we attributed this to the stronger common-property character of the environmental problem in the former and the larger number of actors involved there.

This chapter yields two final insights of a somewhat different character. One picks up on the point about numbers of actors. The other focuses on the ideas manifested by the regime. First, a comment on the numbers issue. The LRTAP countries could and did move ahead, and they negotiated and signed the 1985 sulfur protocol without key potential signatories such as the United States and United Kingdom. They could then employ that new norm against holdouts like Britain and employ it quite effectively. Canada, on the other hand, could only move ahead unilaterally and certainly could not, without the United States, negotiate and sign a similar accord. The regime norms Canada could wield were the much weaker, largely procedural norms of the original MOI. Contrary to arguments suggesting cooperation and momentum are more difficult to obtain with a larger number of actors, comparison of the two acid rain regimes suggests the opposite may well be the case in international environmental affairs, at least sometimes. There are some advantages to larger numbers as well as certain disadvantages. These sorts of questions and possibilities should be explored in studies of regime effectiveness in other environmental issues and other issue areas.

The matter of ideas introduces a new element into an analysis of the causal pathways. The argument that the LRTAP and MOI regimes facilitated domestic realignment in the United States and the United Kingdom suggests an important factor lying behind this particular causal mechanism, and perhaps behind some of the others. Indeed, this comparison of the LRTAP and MOI cases suggests an additional pathway or causal mechanism, distinct from the six that are the focus of this volume. There was clearly a change of thinking on acid rain brought about by the mounting scientific evidence and the growing movement toward controls—a change in the social and political climate. More than the mere existence of the scientific basis and assumptions of the LRTAP and MOI regimes, it was the persistence or the *viability* of the ideas enshrined in the regime that was critical in promoting a reassessment, by key actors, of the political dynamics of the acid rain issue in the United Kingdom and the United States. The cumulation of scientific research and the continuing movement toward adoption of control policies by other governments made it increasingly untenable to argue against the need for acid rain controls, and gave powerful ammunition to the proponents of action. The late 1980s argument that the United States was the only industrial state that had still not adopted controls was also telling.

In such ways regimes may thus play an ideational role. The LRTAP and MOI served both to create and to reinforce new climates of opinion not only about scientific but also about policy matters. This appears to be a process broader than learning, conventionally defined. It is more sociological than psychological in nature, involving an element of social pressures and social conformity. The processes involved may thus represent an additional, distinct pathway to the six considered in this volume, and one that merits further exploration in other cases. It might be called, at the risk of some confusion, the "climate effect" mechanism.

The present analysis of these two regimes touches on but unfortunately does not offer a conclusive answer to one of the strategic questions often debated both in the international environment literature and in the halls of diplomacy: Is it "better" to accept agreement in the short term on a relatively weak regime, in the hope that it will be strengthened in the future, or to set one's sights resolutely on a strong regime and accept nothing less even if it takes longer to reach consensus? The analysis of the LRTAP case suggests incrementalism works. Relatively weak regimes effectively utilizing various mechanisms identified here can become stronger in a relatively short period. Analysis of the MOI case suggests two conclusions. First, incrementalism can be thwarted for a significant period of time by a determined player. Evolution of weak regimes can be frustrated in the short term by their major opponents. Second, and more optimistically, international regimes can over the medium to longer term facilitate the domestic changes necessary to secure support for and compliance with their norms.

There is perhaps no single answer to the sort of "tortoise versus hare" debate implied in the question above. With respect to acid rain, moreover, this debate tends to obscure one of the most important general observations to be made about this case. Acid rain gave rise to conflicting views and differing domestic policies in the early and mid-1980s. Nevertheless, the policy differences had become negligible in broad terms as of the early 1990s. Despite differences in national situations, national cultures, national approaches, and national priorities, emission controls had been adopted by all of the key industrial countries of Western Europe and North America by the end of the decade. Some credit for that must go to the international environmental regimes created and developed to address the problem of acid rain.

Notes

The authors are indebted to Geoffrey Castle and Wendy Leanne Marks for assistance in the researching of this chapter. They are also grateful to a large number of participants in the acid rain issue from both Europe and North America who willingly gave of their time for interviews, to people in the Russian Federation State Committee on Environmental Protection for their assistance and insights, and to officials in the Norilsk Nickel office in Moscow. Sonja Boehmer-Christiansen attended two of our meetings, provided a wealth of information and answered numerous questions. Guy Fenech of Environment Canada provided both material and technical assistance. We are in debt to four anonymous reviewers, selected by MIT Press, for their criticisms and suggestions. Catherine Lu also read the manuscript in various stages and offered both comments and encouragement. In addition to the financial support provided to the project of which this chapter is a part, support for our work has come in a variety of forms from the Canada-United States Fulbright Fellowship Program, the University of Northern British Columbia, North Carolina State University, and the Norwegian Research Council.

Don Munton is professor of international studies at the University of Northern British Columbia. Marvin Soroos is professor of political science at North Carolina State University. Elena Nikitina is senior researcher at the Institute of World Economy and International Relations, Russian Academy of Sciences. Marc Levy is lead project scientist for the Socioeconomic Data and Applications Center (SEDAC) at CIESIN within the Columbia University Earth Institute.

1. Prior to the 1980s, the existing international regime for transboundary air pollution in North America was largely defined by the famous Trail smelter case and arbitration of the 1930s and 1940s. American farmers and then the American government complained about the deleterious effects of SO_2 "fumes" from the Cominco smelter at Trail, B.C., near the Canada-U.S. border. (In fact, the ecosystem problem was largely acidification.) Following an investigation by the International Joint Commission (IJC) and subsequent arbitration, the company was required to pay compensation and to reduce drastically its emissions of sulfur dioxide (SO_2). The now well-known principle in international law established by the tribunal (subsequently elaborated as Principle 21 of the 1972 Stockholm Declaration) is discussed in a later section of this chapter. The development, although not the effectiveness, of the international legal regime in Europe for the long-range transboundary air pollution is traced by Fraenkel 1989.

2. Two of the most thorough existing analyses of domestic acid rain policymaking, those by Boehmer-Christiansen and Skea 1991 and Hajer 1995, both tend to emphasize the differences in policy and process among countries grappling with this problem. The former contrast Britain and Germany, while the latter contrasts Britain and Netherlands. The essence of the argument in this chapter, on the other hand, is that there was a significant degree of commonality in the policies eventually adopted by most industrial countries by the end of the 1980s.

3. Levy's (1993) analysis of the LRTAP convention focuses on whether or not it had an impact on the European signatories to that regime. The present chapter, with its focus on the causal pathways or mechanisms through which regimes are effective, pushes that earlier analysis in new directions. Adding the MOI case allows a comparison of the two regimes and of the situations in Europe and North America. Being able to contrast the pathways involved in the two cases allows the present analysis to extend further our understanding of emerging international environmental norms and rules.

4. While the term "acid rain" is a misnomer in at least two senses, and while it is often wrongly equated with the phenomenon of long-range transport, its use is acceptable here as long as we recognize that the acidification problem involves more than merely rain and is part of a general phenomenon of the movement of pollutants through the air and over long distances. Since rainfall is normally slightly acidic (because it combines with atmospheric carbon dioxide to form dilute carbonic acid), "acid rain" actually refers to precipitation that is more acidic than normal. Scientists have also shown that much acidic deposition occurs in dry as well as wet form, so more than "rain" is involved. The term "acid rain" also should not be seen as synonymous with "long-range transport of air pollu-

tion" (LRTAP). While much of what becomes acidic deposition is transported long distances, so also are such pollutants as pesticides, herbicides, heavy metals (like mercury), and other toxins. LRTAP is thus a general phenomenon that is broader than "acid rain."

5. On the related problems of arctic haze and acid fogs, see Soroos 1996 and Hileman 1983.

6. The following discussion focuses on major themes in the scientific history of acid rain, rather than following a straightforward chronological approach (for example, Cowling 1982). It is based on Munton 1981, using Holt-Jensen 1973; Likens, Wright, Galloway, and Butler 1979; Cowling 1979, 1982, and the presentations of Ellis Cowling and Svante Odén to a 1980 Congressional hearing on acid rain (United States 1980). For a different approach, see Kowalok (1993).

7. It is clear from this article and his Lake District work that Gorham recognized acid rain originated with distant sources, although he did not actually investigate meteorological patterns. Kowalok (1993) and his source (Cowling 1982) are thus incorrect in stating that Gorham assumed acidic precipitation was caused by local sources.

8. James Kramer, a geochemist, did extensive monitoring of SO_2, sulfates, and heavy metals in the region around Sudbury during the early 1970s and used local meteorological data. He concluded (erroneously, it turns out) that the high sulfate deposition in the region was due entirely to the Sudbury area smelters and not to long-range or transboundary sources (Kramer 1973). Subsequent analyses showed that most of the sulfates deposited in the region originated in the United States. This first became apparent from monitoring studies conducted during and after a shut-down of the largest smelter.

9. Since it had long been recognized that substances could be transported great distances through the atmosphere (see above discussion), the phenomenon of long-range transport was not exactly "news." What was new was the concept of long-range transport as a normal rather than unusual phenomenon. One important basis for Odén's demonstration of the source-receptor link—a theoretical understanding of atmospheric chemistry—had been provided during the 1950s by two Swedish pioneers in this field, Carl Gustav Rossby and Erik Erickson (Cowling 1982).

10. The terminology adopted in this chapter with respect to what is now Russia is as follows: "Soviet Union" or USSR is used in reference to an action taken or a statement made prior to the dissolution of that entity, while "Russia" is used in reference to events since dissolution.

11. The title of this convention is sometimes confused. The "T" in the LRTAP convention is the term "transboundary"; on the other hand, the phenomenon is usually described as the long-range "transport" of air pollutants.

12. This characterization by Fraenkel and others is arguably incorrect, but certainly needs to be qualified. It can be argued that the 1963 Partial Test Ban Treaty (PTB) stands as the first in both respects, in that it was prompted by some

environmental concerns and brought about the reduction of atmospheric radio-nuclides (see Soroos 1997), even though it was cast at the time and has been seen since as an arms control agreement. The PTB arguably had more effect on the atmospheric environment than it did on controlling nuclear arms; nuclear testing proceeded apace after 1963, albeit underground.

13. On the LRTAP and EMEP structures and processes, see: Andersson 1989; Fraenkel 1989; and Levy 1993. Major reviews have been published in various UNECE reports: ECE/EB.AIR/27 (1991) and ECE/EB.AIR/14 (1987); annual updates have appeared in ECE/EB.AIR/22 (1989) and ECE/EB.AIR/25 (1990).

14. The 30 percent figure was a compromise. While several European countries, especially Sweden and Norway, were prepared to agree to a figure of 50 percent or higher, Canada was unable to meet a national 50 percent reduction in SO_2. The Canadian SO_2 control program was based on a 50 percent reduction of emissions (from a 1980 base level) in the seven eastern-most provinces only. Taken on a national basis, the Canadian reduction was actually about 35 percent, and even that required some generous assumptions about the 1980 base case. While the Canadians argued that the western Canadian emissions were of little environmental consequence (which is true), the Europeans pressed for national targets. Eventually, a 30 percent national cut was agreed upon.

15. Beginning in 1986, LRTAP meetings began promoting the measurement and mapping of critical loads, defined as: "a quantitative estimate of an exposure to one or more pollutants below which significant harmful effects on specified sensitive elements of the environment do not occur according to present knowledge" (Nilsson and Grennfelt 1988, based on the definition agreed by the UN-ECE Working Group on Nitrogen Oxides, February 1988). See also UNECE 1989a, part two, 17–28.

16. For more detailed information, see Soroos 1997, 131–2.

17. One perhaps curious feature of the MOI as a document is the near absence of explicit references to "acid rain." This appears to have been due to American concern to avoid acknowledging the acid rain problem before it had been further studied.

18. Ironically, the Reagan administration moved extremely quickly in late 1986 and early 1987 to conclude an international air quality agreement with Mexico. Why the contrast? The fundamental difference between the Canada-U.S. and Mexico-U.S. cases is that in the latter the United States is the recipient of transboundary pollution. The problem along the Mexican-American border was a new, very large, Mexican smelter that threatened to send air pollution into the United States. This was a problem about which the Reagan administration, perhaps not surprisingly, felt little research was needed and on which international action was taken immediately.

19. Another reason why efforts in the LRTAP and MOI arenas were less closely linked than one might expect was bureaucratic. This was particularly the case in the Canadian Department of External Affairs, where the United States Bureau

and the embassy in Washington paid relatively little attention to what was transpiring under LRTAP in Europe, largely leaving that arena to the International Affairs Branch of Environment Canada and staff in Geneva. A reflection of the U.S. view of LRTAP as a scientific rather than regulatory process is that the chief American LRTAP negotiator is currently based at Research Triangle Park in North Carolina rather than in Washington at EPA headquarters.

20. The information in the following paragraphs and subsequent sections on Nordic views and policies is based on the following interviews conducted by Marvin Soroos in 1993: Eija Lumme, Helsinki, Finland, April 26; Pekka E. Kauppi, Helsinki, Finland, April 26; Matti Pohjola, Helsinki, Finland, April 26; Ygnve Brodin, Solna, Sweden, April 27; Eva Thornelof, Solna, Sweden, April 27; Göeran Persson, Stockholm, Sweden, April 28; Christor Ågren, Göteborg, Sweden, April 29; Gun Loeveblad, Göeteborg, Sweden, April 29; Eric Lykke, Oslo, Norway, May 1; Anton Eliassen, Oslo, Norway, May 1; Per Bakken, Oslo, Norway, May 4; Harold Doveland, Lillestrøm, Norway, May 4.

21. Reducing NO_x emissions poses a significantly different challenge for Norway. As the negotiations on the Nitrogen protocol were coming to a conclusion, Norwegian officials were surprised to learn that their country's NO_x emissions were nearly twice as high as had been thought. Previous statistics had not taken into account the emissions from Norway's large coastal fleet, which it was now realized accounted for approximately 40 percent of Norway's total NO_x emissions (Elliason interview). Retrofitting the existing fleet to reduce NO_x emissions would be very expensive. Furthermore, since ships generally stay in service much longer than cars (the average life of a fishing boat is 40 years), it would be decades before the fleet would turn over. Pollution control regulations imposed only on new vessels would thus have little short-term effect (Elliason interview).

22. Questions were raised within the Labor Party and various ministries of the Norwegian government about whether sufficient attention was given to the economic interests of Norway, in particular those associated with the health of the country's shipping and petroleum industries. It was believed in some quarters that the prime minister and environment ministry had been given too free a hand in determining Norway's position in international negotiations on air pollution. Other ministries, in particular the finance ministry, became more assertive in determining Norwegian positions at LRTAP negotiations, in particular on VOCs. Some critics of this shift in Norway's orientation toward LRTAP protocols complain that the country has aligned more with the United Kingdom and the United States in recent negotiations than with the Nordic countries and other leader states (Lykke interview). All of this weakened the unity and camaraderie that the so-called Nordic mafia had maintained since the first LRTAP negotiations (Thornelof interview).

23. The Nordic countries signed the Sofia declaration in the belief that new regulations on automobile exhausts going into effect in 1990 would achieve much of the 30 percent reduction. The effect of the laws was to require that new cars be equipped with catalytic converters and to make unleaded gasoline more readily

available. It soon became apparent, however, that these laws would accomplish less than had been initially anticipated. The number of automobiles and road miles driven began to increase rapidly and many cars that predate the law will not be phased out during the 1990s (Brodin interview).

24. This section and the subsequent sections on eastern Europe and Britain are based in part on earlier work by Marc Levy 1991a, 1991b, 1993.

25. Personal communication, Bernhard Ulrich to Don Munton, June 1998.

26. As of the early 1990s, Russia imported more NO_x from Finland, Norway, and Sweden than it exported to them—about eight to fifteen times as much (EMEP/MSC-E, Moscow 1994, p 31).

27. Interview with Dr. A. Pressman, WSC-E 1987.

28. These and subsequent arguments on East European policies are based on interviews conducted by Marc Levy with Hungarian, Polish, and Czech officials in Geneva (January–February 1991) and in Warsaw and Prague (June–July 1991). Czech researchers would often publish EMEP data as soon as they were released by LRTAP, writing small articles in domestic journals.

29. Levy interviews (see above). See also Hungary 1990; Poland 1990, 12–15, 19–20; and Moldan et al. 1991, 37–39 and 89–93.

30. Some private industry in Britain has "matched" this record of government action. One British manufacturer replaced the sulfur in its safety matches with ferrophosphorus. It was estimated that match users in the United Kingdom release about 100 tonnes of SO_2 into the atmosphere every year (*Vancouver Province* 8 January 1993). What part of this contributes to long-range transport or to acidic deposition is apparently not known.

31. These and subsequent arguments on British policymaking are based on interviews conducted by Marc Levy with British officials in Department of the Environment July–August 1991, London.

32. Levy interviews (see above). See also Boehmer-Christiansen and Skea 1991, especially 205–229. For an opposing view that attributes much greater impact to local effects and domestic politics in the United Kingdom, see McCormick 1989, 91–113. Hajer's discourse analysis (1995) curiously tends to ignore the LRTAP process and its impact, but it does make the case that the view of the U.K. Forestry Commission about forest damage only shifted in the latter 1980s (132–38).

33. One of the proponents of controls within the Thatcher cabinet (William Waldegrave, quoted by Hajer 1995, 149) has noted that "it was a very high priority for me to get the prime minister to visit Scandinavia. The influence on her of her visit to Norway was important." Visits by Dutch politicians to view German forest damage appear to have had a similar impact (Hajer 1995, 209).

34. The analysis here and in subsequent sections on Canadian and American policies is based in part on earlier work by Don Munton (1980–81, 1983) but extends that work considerably. The present discussion has been informed by extensive interviews in Canada and the United States conducted in 1992–5 and

some research into official documents. An interview list and specific dates are available on request.

35. On this history, see Munton 1998.

36. In November 1969 the Ontario government had ordered Falconbridge, the Sudbury-area's smaller nickel producer, to half its 932 tons per day of SO_2 emissions by 1975. In July 1970 the government placed a similar control order on Inco, the area's and the world's largest nickel producer, requiring its smelter to reduce SO_2 emissions from 5200 tons/day in 1971 to 750 tons/day by 1978. Inco did not meet the latter target. The first SO_2 controls in Canada, at the Cominco Smelter in Trail, in the 1930s, were mandated by the federal government.

37. Canada's "national" totals for the purpose of regulating sulfur dioxide emissions were those emitted in the seven provinces east of the Saskatchewan-Manitoba border. The western provinces contribute about 30 percent of total Canadian emissions, most of which are emitted by sour gas wells in the province of Alberta. It was assumed western sources did not contribute to the acid rain problem in eastern North America since the deposition is safely neutralized when deposited on the calcium rich soils of the Canadian Prairies. The same situation prevails in the United States where cuts were made in emissions east of the Mississippi.

38. The SO_2 reduction agreed to by the provinces was not a 50 percent cut in actual emissions. The 1980 base figure used was the emissions allowable under the existing SO_2 regulations and not the *actual* emissions, which were at the time much lower. In real terms, the reductions agreed to by the provinces amount to only a 35 percent reduction from actual 1980 emissions. Critics, especially American opponents of acid rain controls, characterized this as a reduction of "phantom" emissions (McMahon 1988). Environment Canada officials argued that an economic downturn left 1980 emissions much lower than their normal levels, thus using actual 1980 emissions was an inappropriate yardstick.

39. By the mid-1980s, Canadian officials were referring to the "collapse" of the MOI process.

40. The duplicity of the Reagan administration over acid rain may have reached its height in the series of events surrounding the release of the long-awaited National Acid Precipitation Assessment Program (NAPAP) interim report of 1987. Comprising over 800 pages, ten substantive chapters, and four volumes, the first of which was an executive summary largely written by the White House-appointed NAPAP director, Dr. J. Lawrence Kulp, the report was accompanied by an administration-prepared press release. In general, the summary and the press release left the impression that the damage due to acidic deposition was largely unproven, slight and not widespread where proven, and probably not getting worse. Release of the interim assessment was greeted with what one industry journal termed "a crescendo of criticism" (Ember 1987; Roberts 1987). Canada's environment minister, Tom McMillan, reacted quickly and angrily. He called a press conference the day after the NAPAP assessment was released and branded it "voodoo science."

41. Senior administration officials implicitly questioned its basic premise. At a bilateral ministerial meeting in the fall of 1983, for example, Canadian environment minister Charles Caccia referred to the MOI, and Secretary of State George Shultz responded by arguing that before you agree to act on a problem you must agree there is a problem. The preamble to the MOI, however, begins by noting that the two countries "share a concern about actual and potential damage resulting from transboundary air pollution . . . including the already serious problem of acid rain."

42. This was the conclusion of Charles Caccia, the Canadian environment minister who hosted the 30 percent club meeting and took his turn in the mid-1980s trying to budge Washington (Caccia interview with Don Munton 1991).

43. This judgment was confirmed by one of the senior officials in the Carter EPA, David Hawkins (interview with Don Munton April 1992).

44. Elite surveys conducted in 1989 and 1991 found that a strong majority of those interviewed, Americans as well as Canadians, thought that "Canada's public relations efforts to influence U.S. policy [had] been successful" (Alm 1993). The proportion answering positively was notably as high among congressional staffers as in the sample overall. When asked to compare factors accounting for the successful passage of the 1990 Clean Air Act, the survey respondents placed "Canadian lobbying" behind White House and congressional personnel changes, environmental group lobbying and public concern, but ahead of the selection of William Reilly as the new head of EPA. When asked to indicate which American actors had been influenced by Canada, most of those surveyed pointed to the U.S. media and public.

45. The Canada–United States AQA is a somewhat more complicated case. While it embodies commitments to reductions of emissions within both the United States and Canada of around 50 percent, the respective reduction programs involved are not national programs in the geographic sense since they target particular sources in the eastern part of each country responsible for most of the acidic deposition damage. Sources in western Canada and the United States were by and large not targeted because their emissions do little damage to sensitive areas. Thus the Canada-U.S. accord incorporates, implicitly, some of the thinking behind the critical loads approach.

46. Per Bakken, Soroos interview May 1993.

47. One of the factors behind the emergence of this low-sulfur coalition was the publication of the book *Clean Coal / Dirty Air* by B. A. Ackerman and W. T. Hassler (1981), which documented the economic irrationality of mandating installation of scrubbers on power plants under the 1977 Clean Air Act.

48. David Hawkins of the Natural Resources Defense Council (and former deputy assistant administrator of the EPA), for example, noted in his testimony to a Senate committee on 24 March 1987 that since both Germany and the United Kingdom had announced control programs, the United States was the only western industrialized country refusing to act on acid rain.

49. The force of this argument is substantiated, for example, by comments (reported by Fay 1984) during one European fact-finding mission by American politicians. The delegation was told in the United Kingdom that, at that time (i.e., prior to the conclusion of the joint U.K.-Norwegian study, referred to above), British experts disputed the deposition effects of acid rain claimed by their Scandinavian counterparts; nevertheless, "if the U.S. were to undertake a control program, the U.K. would certainly review its present policy" (p. 10). The delegation was also told by officials of the European Community that the large combustion plant directive then being prepared would receive a political boost "if the U.S. were to adopt a similar program" (Fay 1984, 6).

5

Regime Effectiveness: Taking Stock

Oran R. Young
(with the assistance of the project team)

There is no simple test available to those seeking to gauge the proportion of the variance in collective outcomes at the international level that can be explained by the presence and operation of social institutions. Accordingly, there will always be an element of judgment in efforts to assess the effectiveness of international regimes. That said, however, analytic tools do exist that are useful in constructing persuasive arguments about the role of institutions. This concluding chapter distills the principal findings of this project regarding the study of effectiveness and, in the process, makes the case for employing a number of analytic tools in combination to provide a basis for evaluating the effectiveness of specific regimes.

At the outset, we can state without hesitation that regimes do matter in international society, so that there is nothing to be gained from perpetuating the debate between neoinstitutionalists and neorealists about the "false promise of international institutions" (Mearsheimer 1994–1995). At the same time, there is considerable variation in the extent to which specific institutions shape collective outcomes at the international level or, in the terminology of this study, in the effectiveness of international regimes. As a result, the proper concern at this juncture focuses on the factors that make institutions more or less effective as mechanisms for altering the behavior of actors in international society and, in the process, for solving or alleviating a variety of problems.

There are complex, interactive relationships among institutions, ideas, and material conditions that make it virtually impossible to arrive at simple conclusions about the relative importance of each of these classes of determinants of collective outcomes in specific situations, and these relationships ensure that the efforts of those seeking to demonstrate the primacy of one or another set of determinants are doomed to failure. Yet it can be interesting and important to focus attention on the roles that regimes play in these interactive processes. Because institutions are generally more malleable than ideas or material conditions, the policy process exhibits an understandable tendency to direct attention toward institutional solutions. But it is equally important to bear in mind that a strategy of modifying existing institutions or creating new ones without taking into account the impact of ideas and material conditions has led to a long line of policy failures in efforts to solve specific problems at the international level as well as the domestic level.

In the course of our work, we have devised a three-stage procedure for evaluating the effectiveness of specific international regimes. We begin in each case by taking snapshots that document differences in the relevant behavioral complex before and after the introduction of the regime and that serve as a means of delineating the range of its potential effects. We then deploy a battery of analytic techniques designed to demonstrate causal connections between the operation of the regime and the changes we have documented, a process that narrows the focus of our analysis and spotlights changes deserving further consideration. This paves the way for an assessment of the behavioral mechanisms or pathways underlying these links, a final step that moves the discussion beyond measures of association and raises the possibility of developing usable knowledge about the success of international institutions. We discuss each of these stages of analysis in this chapter, using examples drawn from the case studies presented at length in the preceding chapters. The chapter concludes with some observations on the generalizability of our findings, the relevance of intervening variables, and the implications of our work for institutional design.

Delineating the Field of Potential Effects

In our case studies, we have adopted the procedure of taking before-and-after snapshots as a means of delineating the range of effects that may be attributable to the operation of an international regime. To illustrate, we started by describing the status of the Barents Sea fisheries and, more generally, the state of Soviet/Russian–Norwegian relations in northern Europe in the period preceding the establishment of the bilateral regime in the mid-1970s. Then we proceeded to take a second snapshot covering the same issues at the present time. In cases where the regime has experienced one or more watershed changes, it is helpful to repeat the procedure of taking before-and-after snapshots several times to allow for the possibility of differentiating among phases or stages of a regime's development regarding the matter of effectiveness. In the case of oil pollution, for example, we took one set of snapshots for the period from the inception of the regime in the early 1950s to the watershed of the mid-1970s and another set covering the period from the negotiation of MARPOL to the present. In each case, the basic idea is the same. We use before-and-after snapshots as a technique for identifying changes in the relevant behavioral complexes to be investigated further through the application of analytic techniques designed to disentangle the causal force of institutional drivers from that of other social drivers at work at the same time.

Behavioral Effects

It is immediately apparent that none of the regimes we have studied in depth has succeeded in providing a quick and decisive solution to the problem that motivated its creation. The world's oceans are certainly not free of oil or immune to the ecological damage caused by oil pollution, although it is only fair to observe that there is a good deal of controversy in scientific circles about the long-term effects of discharging oil into marine ecosystems. The cod, haddock, and capelin stocks of the Barents Sea area are not all thriving, although considerable uncertainty remains about the role of human harvesting as a determinant of the condition of these stocks. Europe's lakes, forests, and urban habitats are not acid free, and the emerging concept of critical loads raises questions about the earlier practice of focusing on individual pollutants in efforts to control transboundary fluxes in this region.

The snapshots we have taken do bring into focus a wide range of significant developments in the behavioral complexes associated with these three cases. The expectations of owners and operators of oil tankers have changed dramatically during the period following the watershed change in the oil pollution regime in the 1970s. Whereas virtually everyone now acknowledges the need to conform to equipment standards (for example, building segregated ballast tanks into new tankers), violations of the discharge standards relied on prior to the negotiation of MARPOL were widespread. The shift from discharge standards to equipment standards in dealing with vessel-source oil pollution is a particularly dramatic case. But experience with the operation of many regimes has led to experiments with new policy instruments in an effort to solve transboundary problems. Another striking illustration from these cases centers on the shift from best available technology (BAT) requirements to standards based on the concepts of critical loads and incentive systems in dealing with transboundary fluxes of airborne pollutants.

In the process of retrofitting existing tankers to make use of crude oil washing (COW) and building new ships to meet standards requiring segregated ballast tanks (SBT), the world's tanker owners and operators succeeded in retiring old ships and shaking down the tanker fleet to meet sharp shifts in the demand for the transport of oil by sea. Thus, the creation or evolution of an international regime can provide the impetus for participants in the behavioral complex to undertake measures that will enhance their welfare in the long run but that for one reason or another they find difficult to initiate in the short run.

In the Barents Sea, the shift from an atmosphere of tension in the mid-1970s due to jurisdictional conflicts between Norway and the former Soviet Union regarding the delineation of the maritime boundary in the central Barents Sea to the routinized cooperation associated with the joint management system now in place is a striking development. Among other things, it demonstrates that the resolution of jurisdictional problems is not a necessary condition for the development of institutionalized management practices. The experience with the Barents Sea regime has also contributed to the general realization that older management systems based on the concept of maximum sustainable yield (MSY) must give way to new practices incorporating tools like multispecies management (MSM) in dealing with fisheries in areas such as the Barents Sea. Additionally, a growing awareness of linkages among fish stocks and other elements of large marine ecosystems (e.g., the presence of radioactive contaminants in the Barents and Kara Seas) has made it clear that whole-ecosystems approaches are in order as a means of managing fish stocks effectively.

For its part, transboundary air pollution proposed during 1977–1978 as a focus for cooperation within the context of the CSCE process, precisely because it was regarded as somewhat obscure and unlikely to prove politically sensitive, has become a matter of high politics in Europe. A similar evolution has occurred in Canadian–American relations in North America. Governments now devote considerable resources to activities undertaken under the aegis of the LRTAP regime and the North American Air Quality Agreement of 1991.

Starting in the mid-1970s as a problem of dealing with the deposition of sulfur dioxide in Scandinavian lakes, transboundary air pollution is widely understood today as a problem encompassing a range of pollutants affecting many ecosystems across all of Europe. Ecosystems models incorporating the idea of critical loads have replaced pollutant-by-pollutant approaches to thinking about the scope of the problem and about the relative merits of different ways of combating air pollution. With the operation of the Environmental Monitoring and Evaluation Programme (EMEP) and the negotiation of substantive protocols on sulfur dioxide, nitrogen oxides, volatile organic compounds, and persistent organic pollutants, moreover, the parties to the LRTAP regime have become enmeshed in a set of programmatic activities that has taken on a life of its own. Although actual behavior varies from country to country, everyone understands that there is no going back to old ways in this issue area.

These cases demonstrate, as well, that individual actors have reacted quite differently to the specific regimes we have studied. Whereas there is good evidence to suggest, for example, that LRTAP stimulated significant behavioral changes in Great Britain, Germany might well have taken the steps it did during the 1980s with or without the impetus provided by this regime. For their part, the Scandinavians have often exceeded requirements articulated in the LRTAP protocols as a means of setting a good example and, in the process, exerted pressure on others to meet various agreed-upon targets relating to transboundary air pollution. Much the same can be said of the development of reception facilities by port states in conformance with the requirements of the oil pollution regime. By contrast with the almost universal acceptance of the MARPOL equipment standards, considerable variance remains in the extent to which the world's major ports are outfitted with the reception facilities called for under the terms of this regime.

Other Consequences

Throughout, the analyses have been guided by a concept of effectiveness starting with problem solving and emphasizing efforts to redirect the behavior of those whose actions give rise to international environmental problems. To this, we have added emphasis on effects that are internal to the behavioral complex under consideration, direct in the sense that the causal chain leading from regime to problem solving is short, and positive in the sense that the effects operate to ameliorate rather than to exacerbate the problem at hand. There is no reason to alter this approach as a result of the case studies carried out by the members of our research team. Whatever the merits of studies that focus on implementation, compliance, and goal attainment, we are ultimately concerned with problem solving—eliminating vessel-source oil pollution, sustaining fish stocks, and abating transboundary fluxes of airborne pollutants. There is no way to come to terms with these problems without addressing the behavior—individual, corporate, governmental—that causes or gives rise to them.

Even so, the work we have done suggests the need to extend the domain of effectiveness to consider several additional types of effects, without losing track of our primary interest in problem solving (Levy, Young, and Zürn 1995). In some cases, these additions pertain to the character of the original behavioral complex. Thus, the process of creating and operating an international regime can sharpen the definition of the problem at stake or, in some cases, lead to a substantial redefinition of the problem to be solved. Clearly, the understanding of long-range air pollution acquired through experience with the regime articulated in the Geneva convention of 1979 and its subsequent protocols has added greatly to our knowledge of air pollution as a pervasive by-product of advanced industrial systems. It seems undeniable, as well, that this increasingly sophisticated understanding of the problem has played a role in the ongoing process of regime development by energizing the movement leading to the protocols on sulfur dioxide, nitrogen oxides, and volatile organic compounds and, in the process, incorporating the idea of critical loads into management strategies in this area. Experience with the oil pollution regime, by contrast, has contributed to the growing realization that land-based pollutants in contrast to vessel-source pollutants are major determinants of the health of large marine ecosystems. This does not mean that vessel-source pollutants are unimportant, and it should not be interpreted as a failure of the regime itself. But it does illustrate the role that regimes can play in shaping international agendas on matters extending beyond their proximate concerns.

Similarly, the establishment and operation of international regimes can have the effect of alleviating or even resolving conflicts among participants, whether or not they eliminate the environmental problems that trigger their formation. As the study of the Barents Sea fisheries regime makes clear, this arrangement has not prevented sharp swings in the condition of important fish stocks (although a case can be made that these fluctuations would have been more severe in the absence of the regime). Nonetheless, the regime has been quite effective in dealing with Norwegian–Russian conflicts concerning both jurisdictional issues and the allocation of allowable catches. By treating the area known as the Grey Zone as a management unit and differentiating it from the area of the Barents Sea subject to conflicting jurisdictional claims, the regime encourages cooperation that avoids the hardening of jurisdictional claims. Similarly, the use of fixed keys to guide the initial division of shared stocks has served to decouple conservation and allocation, thus rendering the work of the joint commission more effective. Conflict resolution in the absence of problem solving obviously leaves a good deal to be desired. But given the time, energy, and resources consumed in dealing with conflicts at the international level, the role that regimes can play in resolving or at least managing conflicts is far from trivial.

Beyond this, regimes can empower a variety of nonstate actors and contribute to the development of unofficial communities that include a mix of experts and policymakers who can function as pressure groups, sources of institutional innovations, and watchdogs in the day-to-day operations of regimes. In these cases, the clearest example of this type of effect involves LRTAP where the programmatic activities of the regime have brought together a transnational group of individuals who are knowledgeable about the impact of acid rain on European ecosystems and who have developed analytic devices like the RAINS model that have clearly played a role in the evolution of the regime (diPrimio 1996). Similar occurrences are prominent in cases examined by others, like the water quality regime established under the terms of the Great Lakes Water Quality Agreement of 1972 as extended in 1978 and amended in 1987 (Botts and Muldoon 1996).

Demonstrating Causal Connections

Delineating the range of potential effects is an important step, but it constitutes only the first stage in the effort to assess the effectiveness of international regimes. The next stage involves an effort to determine which of the changes captured in the before-and-after snapshots can be attributed, wholly or in part, to the operation of the regimes we have studied. In this area, our most significant conclusions involve the development of methods or analytic techniques for demonstrating causal connections. Specifically, the case studies have illuminated a distinction between two modes of reasoning that figure prominently in this stage of our enquiry: variation finding analysis and tendency finding analysis. In our judgment, these approaches to understanding complement and reinforce one another, though the authors of several of the case studies show a propensity to favor one or the other mode. Thus, we treat these modes of reasoning as tools to be deployed in tandem in the effort to produce persuasive conclusions regarding the effectiveness of international regimes. Because the two modes differ sharply in methodological and even epistemological terms, however, we are now convinced that it is important to distinguish them clearly and to evaluate explicitly the contributions of each to efforts to understand the role of institutions as determinants of collective outcomes in international society (we include a more extended discussion of these matters in an appendix entitled "Notes on Methodology").

As David Dessler points out, variation finding analysis seeks to answer the question "under what conditions will international regimes be effective" and proceeds to respond to this question by framing hypotheses linking various factors to anticipated levels of effectiveness (Dessler 1992). The product of this sort of analysis is a set of propositions in which institutional effectiveness is treated as the dependent variable and a variety of factors (or combinations of factors) are singled out as independent variables. Thus, we may anticipate that effectiveness will vary as a function of the level of consensus within the membership group regarding both the causes of the problem to be solved and the appropriate methods for solving the problem. Or we may hypothesize that the effectiveness of institutional arrangements will depend on the presence of a dominant actor willing to contribute disproportionately to solving the problem as a kind of public good, so that the set of actors concerned with the relevant problem form a privileged group (Olson 1965). Clearly, many hypotheses of this general type are possible and worthy of exploration on the part of those seeking to understand the effectiveness of institutions at the international level.

Variation finding analysis works best in situations featuring large universes of cases that resemble one another as closely as possible. Under these conditions, it is feasible to draw representative samples and to deploy the techniques of statistics, including multivariate analysis, to measure the strength of the association among dependent variables and any of a number of independent variables. Unfortunately, these conditions are seldom present when it comes to the analysis of institutional arrangements in international society. In this setting, we ordinarily deal with small numbers of cases, and there are often good reasons to suspect that individual cases differ from one another in significant ways. Even so, the fundamental logic of variation finding analysis remains the same (King, Keohane, and Verba 1994). We are still interested in identifying "the conditions of institutional effectiveness" and framing hypotheses in which specific independent variables are linked to effectiveness treated as the dependent variable. Understandably, those who use variation finding analysis to study institutional effectiveness in situations where universes of cases are small are apt to favor hypotheses that state necessary or sufficient conditions. Because such hypotheses are expected to apply without exception, every case constitutes a critical test of the expected relationships as long as it belongs to the relevant universe of cases.

Tendency finding analysis, by contrast, highlights what is often called genetic explanation (Nagel 1961). Those who adopt this approach ask "how is it possible to solve problems in international society" and then seek to understand the roles that institutions play in such processes (Dessler 1992). This approach leads directly to a search for the mechanisms or pathways through which regimes can affect the behavior of their members. Such efforts do not yield generalizations asserting regular relationships between independent and dependent variables. Rather, they lead to insights concerning the mechanisms through which institutions influence the behavior of their members under a variety of conditions. Thus, we may expect the establishment and operation of an institution to drive up the costs of a certain type of behavior by making it a violation of regime rules and taking steps to maximize the likelihood that such violations will be publicized. Similarly, we may see regimes affecting the behavior of individual members by strengthening the hand of those policymakers and administrators who support courses of action compatible with regime rules.

Unlike variation finding analysis, tendency finding procedures seek to identify the particular combinations of forces at work in specific situations and to show how these combinations account for the outcomes that occur. Individual cases may be unique in the sense that the particular combinations of forces at work do not occur in any other cases. Yet the causal tendency associated with each of the individual forces may be similar from case to case. As a result, the testing of genetic explanations does not require a comparison of hypothesized regularities with empirical evidence relating to a collection of comparable cases. Instead, those who engage in tendency finding analysis often examine individual cases in depth, seeking to construct persuasive narrative accounts or stories using procedures they describe as process tracing or thick description.[1] The objective here is to develop detailed accounts of individual cases rather than to assemble data sets of the sort required to test the hypotheses flowing from variation finding analyses.

Revisiting the Behavioral Models

Demonstrating the existence of causal connections between the operation of regimes and the content of collective outcomes is an impressive achievement. Yet it does not tell us how institutions work to produce outcomes or impacts measurable in terms of problem solving, a fact that not only leaves lingering doubts about the effectiveness of regimes in many cases but also makes it difficult to design effective institutional arrangements for the future. The effort to take this final step and, in the process, to remove any vestigial doubts about whether regimes matter constitutes the third stage in the analytic procedure developed in connection with this project. Because regimes are not actors in their own right and because solving international problems requires guiding or channeling the behavior of those who are actors—including individuals and nonstate actors as well as governments—in the relevant behavioral complexes, the next step in our analytic strategy is to examine behavioral pathways leading from the creation and operation of international regimes to the behavior of key actors. This is a complex subject marked by differences of opinion on the underlying sources of the behavior of relevant actors that recapitulate diverging views regarding behavioral mechanisms prevalent throughout the social sciences.

A number of factors make it difficult to separate out the effects of different behavioral mechanisms operating at the same time, even though they are relatively easy to differentiate in analytic terms. The signals generated by some mechanisms are weak either because these mechanisms account for only a small proportion of the variance in actor behavior or because they are masked by other signals that are more apparent to the outside observer. Individual mechanisms not only operate simultaneously but they also interact with each other in complex ways, a fact that makes it difficult to assign weights to the significance of various mechanisms on an individual basis. The mechanisms shaping the behavior of actors who are formal members of regimes—usually national governments—may differ substantially from those mechanisms that come into play as determinants of the behavior of the ultimate subjects of regimes—often nonstate actors such as tanker owners, fishers, and industrial plants emitting airborne particulates. The roles different mechanisms play also vary across regime types and what we call behavioral complexes in this project. Mechanisms that work to induce actors to take regulatory standards (e.g., the equipment standards of the oil pollution case) seriously, for instance, are apt to differ from those that lead actors to participate in collective-choice procedures (e.g., arrangements for setting allowable catch levels in the Barents Sea fisheries on an annual basis) and to accept the outcomes these procedures produce.

Even so, our project has yielded some preliminary conclusions about the mechanisms through which international regimes influence actor behavior. At the most general level, we now believe that all the mechanisms described in chapter 1 have some role to play in making regimes effective. But their significance is not uniform across the set of international regimes, and their operation in specific cases is often more complex than simple models would lead one to believe. This is not good news for those whose main concern is the pursuit of parsimony in explaining or predicting social phenomena. Yet it should not be treated as evidence that it is impossible to build cumulative knowledge of how regimes work and what it is likely to take to achieve effective results in specific cases.

Rational Utility Maximizing

The first two models we have considered (regimes as utility modifiers and as enhancers of cooperation) share the assumption that actors are unitary decision makers operating in a utilitarian mode that features calculations of costs and benefits. Examples of this type of behavior are easy to spot in these case studies. Equipment standards proved effective in the case of oil pollution, for example, because they increased dramatically the costs associated with building noncompliant vessels. It is not difficult to detect violations of key equipment standards; retrofitting tankers to correct violations once they have been detected is extremely costly, and the resale value of tankers failing to meet the standards is low. Moreover, it requires a firm commitment on the part of only a few important members of this regime to make the equipment standards compelling. These are classic utilitarian considerations. Turning to the case of acid rain, on the other hand, we find evidence that regimes can affect the cost-benefit calculations of some actors more than others and that they often do so by manipulating intangible costs in contrast to material costs. Thus, we have found that LRTAP played a much more significant role in shaping the behavior of the United Kingdom than of Germany and especially the Scandinavian countries. What is more, one of the main forces at work in the case of

Britain was the rising political embarrassment stemming from the growth of the country's reputation as the "dirty man" of Europe.

Regimes also regularly help actors to do what they would ultimately prefer to do by overcoming collective-action problems that make such steps seem risky or costly. A classic case emerges from the account of the Barents Sea fisheries regime. In effect, the regime both promotes transparency by making it increasingly difficult for fishers and processors to cheat and reduces transaction costs through the establishment and operation of a decision-making procedure that now operates on a routine basis without any need for constant attention on the part of policymakers. Yet it is important to recognize that these standard utilitarian considerations cannot account entirely for the effects of this regime. A mechanism of great importance in this case centers on the redefinition of roles that arose from the growing acceptance of fishery conservation zones and, more recently, exclusive economic zones (EEZs) and that allowed Norway and Russia acting as coastal states to phase out fishing by third parties in the area covered by the regime. Nor is this more complex pattern of behavioral drivers in any way unusual. On the contrary, it illustrates one of our major conclusions. Although there is no denying that utilitarian considerations are important sources of effectiveness, almost every successful regime presents us with a complex dynamic in which several types of mechanisms operate in tandem to produce the behavioral effects that we observe.

Other Unitary Actor Models

As a result, we now believe that there is a clear need to pay more attention to the operation of our next three models (regimes as bestowers of authority, as learning facilitators, and as role definers), which retain the unitary actor assumption but emphasize sources of behavior that are difficult or impossible to interpret in utilitarian terms. These models are not as highly developed or as tractable in analytic terms as the familiar rational-choice models of utilitarian analyses. Yet there is ample evidence in these cases of the roles nonutilitarian forces play as drivers of behavior associated with the operation of regimes. In several cases, the mechanisms we have characterized as bestowing authority and redefining roles have interacted with each other to produce significant effects. A major development in the oil pollution case, for example, arose from the expanded roles of port states in contrast to flag states in dealing with vessel-source pollution. But this development was made possible through broader shifts in the allocation of authority among coastal, flag, and port states with respect to a wide range of marine issues. Similar comments are in order about the important new roles accorded to classification societies and insurance companies in enforcing compliance with equipment standards that apply to tankers. These new roles have proven essential to the success of the equipment standards, but they would have amounted to nothing if the members of the oil pollution regime had refused to recognize the legitimacy of assigning such important roles to nonstate actors. Yet another case involves the expansion of the regulatory authority of coastal states over living resources located in marine areas adjacent to their coastlines. There can be no doubt that this development was critical to the ability of Norway and Russia to set up a bilateral management system for the Barents Sea and to phase out third-party fishing. But it is equally clear that this move derived its legitimacy from a broader shift in the allocation of authority over marine areas. Without the enhanced authority derived from this broader shift, Norway and Russia would have had great difficulty imposing their bilateral regime for the Barents Sea fisheries.

Our cases also yield clear evidence of the role of social learning in the evolution of regimes. Sometimes social learning is fundamentally a matter of devising new means with which to pursue unchanging objectives. The introduction of equipment standards as a method of getting around the basic problems afflicting discharge standards in oil pollution is a clear case in point. Much the same can be said of the growing interest in the concept of multispecies management (MSM) as a means of dealing with the shortcomings of maximum sustainable yield (MSY) from individual species in the Barents Sea fisheries. A more far-reaching form of social learning, on the other hand, occurs in cases where the operation of a regime leads to major changes in how the problem a regime addresses is understood and, as a result, in ideas about how to cope with it. There is clear evidence of such a dynamic at work in the case of LRTAP. When the parties signed the Geneva convention of 1979 initially launching this regime, their understanding of the nature of acid rain and its effects on ecosystems was relatively primitive. In considerable part as a result of activities sponsored by the regime, however, sophistication regarding the nature of this problem has grown markedly. This is reflected in developments like the emergence of the concept of critical loads which has led in turn to significant growth in the scope and strength of the regime and in the nature of the behavioral changes required of its members.

These observations do not demonstrate that regime analysis should turn away from models that assume utility maximizing behavior on the part of unitary actors. What we are discovering, instead, is a need to explore nonutilitarian sources of behavior capable of accounting for important developments that utilitarian analyses are poorly equipped to explain (Wendt 1992) and that often interact in complex ways with utilitarian calculations in actual cases. Although this conclusion may appear troubling to those concerned with parsimony, we are convinced that this is not as serious a problem as it may seem at first. In essence, analysts may start with familiar utilitarian models and proceed to supplement them with models pointing to factors like authority, role definitions, and learning to produce satisfactory accounts of the full range of behavior associated with the operation of regimes in international society. Because the utility-maximizing models are far more highly developed in analytic terms, however, we now believe that there is a need to accord some priority to the clarification and strengthening of the nonutilitarian models to provide analysts with an adequate tool kit for tackling the next phase of research on the effectiveness of international regimes.

Disaggregating Complex Actors

The case studies included in this project also lend credence to our final model (regimes as agents of internal realignments) in the sense that they have turned up unambiguous evidence of links among domestic politics and the operation of regimes. In the oil pollution case, the regime helped to level the playing field in countries like the United Kingdom and the United States between a powerful and highly organized industry on the one hand and a much larger but more diffuse public concerned with marine pollution on the other. Ultimately, the industry bowed to pressure to accept equipment standards mandating segregated ballast tanks, despite evidence that this solution is not an efficient one in purely economic terms. The regime for the Barents Sea fisheries has served both to subject the actions of bureaucratic managers to greater public scrutiny and to institutionalize the role of scientists as contributors to the decision-making process established by the regime. As the case study points out, this offers no guarantee that the regime's conservation goals will be fulfilled. But it does open up the regime and increase the transparency of efforts within member countries regarding the management of these marine resources. For its part, LRTAP and its North American counterpart have empowered domestic critics of prevailing environmental policies in countries like the United Kingdom and the United States and, in the process, helped to create domestic constituencies capable of bringing pressure to bear on relevant government agencies.

While our case studies do not exhaust the range of variation in these terms, several general observations about the role of internal forces do emerge from our work. Interactions between regimes and domestic politics are likely to vary greatly from one country to another and, probably, from one type of regime to another. In some cases, regimes may become entangled as well in internal political processes within nonstate actors who are important players in a given behavioral complex. The role of the oil pollution regime as a force affecting the inner workings of shipbuilders, classification societies, insurance companies, and corporate owners of tankers, for example, is a topic deserving more careful scrutiny in the future. Beyond this, one of the most important processes at work here centers on the role of regimes in empowering and legitimizing various interest groups—some would call them communities—seeking to influence the behavior of governments on the issues that regimes address. In the case of LRTAP and its North American counterpart, for example, environmental forces working in legislative settings and in broader forums aimed at influencing the evolution of public opinion were able to exploit these regimes as a means of building political coalitions and exerting pressure on groups opposed to more stringent efforts to control air pollution.[2]

Overall, these cases do not justify any move toward a wholesale rejection of unitary actor models in favor of analyses centered on the dynamics of domestic politics. Yet there is clear evidence of the role that such forces play, especially in situations of the type represented by the case of long-range transboundary air pollution. As with nonutilitarian sources of behavior, our conclusion here is that we need to add a concern with domestic politics to the tool kit available to those who are concerned with understanding the dynamics of existing regimes or who are charged with the task of devising new regimes to cope with problems currently coming into focus on the international political agenda.

Identifying Distinctive Mechanisms

The case studies have also drawn our attention to the roles played by behavioral mechanisms that loom large in specific cases but that do not map onto one or another of our analytical models in any simple fashion. Partly, this is a matter of emerging mechanisms that exhibit elements of two or more analytically distinct behavioral pathways at the same time. In part, it is a reflection of the fact that behavioral mechanisms are often situation specific in the sense that they are closely tied to certain characteristics of the particular behavioral complexes within which they operate. There are substantial costs to carrying this contextualizing line of thought too far. In the extreme, it would require us to treat every case as a completely unique situation. Yet it is important to remain alert to the operation of situational factors that tie regimes to the behavioral complexes within which they operate.

The distinctive mechanisms that emerge from this line of thought are not incompatible with the behavioral models that have guided this project. They merely remind us that these models are based on analytic distinctions, whereas actual behavior is often an amalgam of more than one distinct type of behavior or tied to situational factors. To make these observations concrete, we offer a few illustrations drawn from the cases examined in this project.

Coercing Compliance

Regimes can set standards or spell out requirements that subjects have to meet to do business profitably or even to do business at all. In effect, such regimes work more by eliminating opportunities to violate regulative prescriptions than by increasing incentives to comply with rules. The case of equipment standards relating to vessel-source oil pollution is instructive here. In effect, the regime grants authority to or, better yet, deputizes classification societies and insurance companies to police these standards by refusing to certify or insure ships that fail to conform to equipment standards like the rules pertaining to segregated ballast tanks. This procedure is effective because some of the key members of the regime are willing to ban noncomplying tankers from their ports or even to impound tankers caught in violation of the equipment standards. From the point of view of tanker owners and operators, however, the situation is clear. Unlike the case of discharge standards where operators can decide whether or not to comply while engaged in transporting oil, owners and operators are effectively barred from transporting oil by sea if they are unprepared to accept the requirements of the equipment standards. Despite the fact that the equipment standards mandate outcomes that are economically inefficient in some cases, tanker owners and operators have no choice but to conform to the MARPOL standards. In effect, the equipment standards work because they coerce a variety of nonstate actors to play by the rules of the regime, thereby avoiding the manipulative tactics that so often accompany regulatory efforts at the national level.

Enmeshing States
Regimes often launch programmatic activities—in contrast to laying down regulatory prescriptions—that are uncontroversial at the time of their initiation due to the seeming unimportance of the activities involved. Over time, however, they become more and more influential as the issues achieve political prominence and the evolution of the regime itself enmeshes the participants in a web of institutionalized activities from which they cannot easily extricate themselves. A process of this sort figures prominently in the case of LRTAP. The 1979 Geneva convention is almost devoid of explicit rules, a fact that makes it of no more than marginal interest to ask about compliance with the rules of this regime. Even the substantive protocols added in subsequent years tend to specify overall goals (e.g., a 30 percent reduction in sulfur emissions by an agreed-upon date) rather than to articulate well-defined rules. But the LRTAP regime lends credence or authority to a set of broader principles (e.g., the polluter pays principle and the precautionary principle) and mandates a process centering on the work of EMEP that keeps the issue of transboundary air pollution before national policymakers in a politically po-

tent manner. None of this would have had significant impacts on behavior in the absence of mounting evidence concerning the seriousness of air pollution and growing public concern about such matters. Yet given these developments, which LRTAP itself helped to foster, the regime has served to draw governments—more so in some member states than in others—into a normatively grounded social practice that they can no longer ignore in political terms.

Shaping Expectations

Regimes can influence current behavior by shaping the expectations of various parties about rules and procedures likely to be adopted in the future, even when they do not mandate specific actions at the time of their creation. This is particularly true where key actors must make investment decisions involving the commitment of large sums of money to production facilities or research and development initiatives with extended amortization schedules. Because investments in tankers are large and retrofitting costly, for instance, tanker owners and operators need to make concerted efforts to foresee probable developments in equipment standards over periods of several decades at a time. Similar concerns arise for chemical manufacturers facing choices about long-term investments in the production of alternatives to chlorofluorocarbons. Inevitably, this gives rise to problems of decision making under uncertainty and necessitates judgment calls on the part of those responsible for investment decisions. But assessments of ongoing and future trends in the development of international regimes dealing with issues like vessel-source marine pollution and the protection of stratospheric ozone undoubtedly constitute important elements in the decisions of important actors. Conversely, trends in the equipment choices made by those ordering new tankers or in the production decisions of chemical companies may influence the thinking of those responsible for the operation of the relevant regimes. The decision of tanker owners and operators to adopt the technology of segregated ballast tanks appears to have reflected an assessment on their part of the probable evolution of the rules governing marine pollution. This decision has served to reinforce the commitment to equipment standards that has marked the evolution of the international regime dealing with vessel-source pollution in recent years.

Stepwise Processes

Regimes can also set in motion social practices that initiate stepwise processes leading toward desired results over time. The case of the Barents Sea fisheries regime exemplifies this pattern. At its inception, this regime reflected the conventional approach to fisheries management based on the pursuit of conservation through the use of analytic techniques associated with the concept of maximum sustainable yield (MSY). But the results flowing from this bilateral regime made it clear early on that this approach was inadequate to solve the problem of managing these fisheries effectively. Although compliance with the regime's rules and prescriptions on the part of fishers was relatively high, the fish stocks remained subject to dramatic fluctuations and severe depletions. This experience produced a growing awareness of interdependencies among fish stocks and a rapid growth of interest in the idea of multispecies management (MSM). But this development, too, fails to offer a surefire means of solving the underlying problem. Accordingly, we are witnessing today a growing interest in ideas involving large marine ecosystems and marine conservation biology that would lead to management based on holistic or ecosystems perspectives (Sherman 1992; Norse 1993). To be sure, this development poses complex methodological problems. But it does allow for both a consideration of links among distinct human activities (e.g., fishing and the dumping of various wastes at sea) and an assessment of the relative importance of anthropogenic forces (e.g., fishing) and nonanthropogenic forces (e.g., changes in water temperature) as determinants of the status of fish stocks. As the case study suggests, this process has not yet resulted in an ability to solve all the problems of managing fisheries in the Barents Sea area. But there is no mistaking the role the regime has played in encouraging the stepwise process that has occurred here.

Generalizing the Behavioral Models

To what extent are the conclusions reached generalizable to other environmental regimes and beyond that to the larger universe of international regimes operative in other issue areas? The answer to this question lies in a consideration of the role of the behavioral mechanisms we have discussed rather than in any effort to construct overarching propositions spelling out necessary or sufficient conditions for the achievement of effectiveness. Broadly speaking, we are convinced that the behavioral mechanisms we have examined in this project are generic in that each of them comes into play in a variety of settings, though it is no doubt true that individual mechanisms are particularly prominent in some domains and less significant in others. At the same time, our work on behavioral mechanisms has led us to conclude that there is a major division between two broad categories of processes through which regimes affect the behavior of subjects and through them the content of collective outcomes in international society. We have labeled them collective-action processes and social practices.

Mechanisms intended to solve collective-action problems, which are the focus of mainstream thinking in international relations, rest on utilitarian premises in the sense that they treat the actors in international society as coherent units possessing well-defined utility functions and seeking to promote their own interests through a process of weighing the benefits and costs associated with alternatives or options in situations featuring interactive decision making. Regimes, on this account, are regulatory arrangements created to avoid or ameliorate social dilemmas (Dawes 1980, Keohane 1984). Behavioral prescriptions—rules, norms, principles—are the essential elements of regimes, and efforts to implement them and elicit compliance with their requirements are critical to their success. The central link in this chain is clear: the role of regimes is to alter incentives in such a way as to prevent individualistic behavior likely to lead to collective-action problems in situations involving strategic interaction. Recently, an interesting debate has arisen among those who think in these regulatory terms about the extent to which the achievement of compliance is better understood as a matter of management rather than a matter of enforcement. The issue here involves the relative importance of sanctions in contrast to various forms of debate, exhortation, and capacity building as sources of behavior (Chayes and Chayes 1995; Downs, Rocke, and Barsoom 1996; Mitchell 1998). But this does not alter the fact that the focus of arrangements designed to solve collective-action problems is on factors that affect the extent to which the behavior of subjects conforms to the requirements of regulatory arrangements.

The social-practice perspective, by contrast, approaches regimes as arrangements that affect behavior through nonutilitarian mechanisms like inducing actors to treat prescriptions as authoritative, enmeshing actors in communities that share a common discourse, or stimulating processes of social learning. Such practices may even affect the identities of actors by influencing the way in which they see their roles in social interactions (Wendt 1994). This way of thinking treats institutions as "cognitive, normative, and regulatory structures and activities that provide stability and meaning to social behavior" (Scott 1995: 33). It directs attention to processes through which actors become participants in complex social practices that influence their behavior more through de facto engagement and through their impact on the discourse in terms of which these practices are conducted than through conscious decisions about compliance with prescriptive rules (Litfin 1994). The LRTAP regime offers a striking case in point. Even with the addition of substantive protocols pertaining to sulfur dioxide, nitrogen oxides, volatile organic compounds, and persistent organic pollutants, this regime is relatively short on regulatory content. Yet the regime has played a role of considerable importance in raising the priority accorded to transboundary air pollution as an issue on the international political agenda, changing the discourse in terms of which this issue is addressed and drawing its members into an increasingly complex social practice that has altered responses to long-range air pollution over a period of several decades.

What are the implications of this contrast between collective-action and social-practice perspectives on the effectiveness of international regimes? The key point is that they direct the attention of students of international institutions to different research agendas. The research puzzles in the collective-action perspective center on utilitarian assessments of the behavior of regime members about matters like compliance with institutional commitments, the relative merits of different policy instruments available for use in conjunction with specific regimes, and the problems of avoiding or resolving differences on the application of rules to particular circumstances. Those who think in terms of the social-practice perspective, by contrast, pose different research puzzles. Issues that loom large on their horizons involve the sources of behavioral change in general in contrast to compliance more specifically, the prospects for socializing actors to conform to rules without making conscious calculations concerning the benefits and costs of doing so, and the processes through which regimes integrate individual actors into communities engaged in practices that are not governed by utilitarian calculations (Botts and Muldoon 1996).

Is one of these research agendas right while the other is wrong? Certainly not! Each points to a particular set of questions that arise from different perspectives on the mechanisms through which regimes affect the behavior of participants and that command increased attention among students of international institutions. Is this bifurcation, which is easy enough to understand once we grasp the differences among the behavioral mechanisms through which regimes affect outcomes, a good thing or a bad thing in terms of its implications for the enhancement of our understanding of the effectiveness of international institutions? We are convinced that it can and will emerge as a healthy development, so long as we treat the collective-action and social-practice perspectives as complementary points of departure that can serve to enrich our thinking rather than as competing analytic platforms to be defended by committed adherents. Although the development of a unified theory of institutions should remain a long-term goal, further explorations of the relative importance of the behavioral mechanisms we have examined in this project can play an important role during the foreseeable future in clearing up some of the persistent sources of confusion that have plagued efforts to conceptualize and operationalize the determinants of regime effectiveness.

Adding Intervening Variables

The study of behavioral mechanisms is destined to loom increasingly large in regime analysis, especially among those who desire to go beyond explaining the consequences of existing arrangements to the design of effective regimes to handle newly emerging problems. Even so, focusing on behavioral mechanisms alone is not sufficient to explain all the variance in the effectiveness of international regimes. Clearly, at this stage, a number of intervening variables also enter the equation in specific cases, so that effectiveness is a matter of linkages or interactions among the institutional properties of regimes and the sources of actor behavior on the one hand and various features of the behavioral complex on the other. Successful regimes guide the behavior of participants in ways that are well-suited to the circumstances in which they operate. Unsuccessful regimes typically involve a mismatch among the institutional arrangements created and key features of the relevant behavioral complexes. To make this point easier to understand, we offer some examples drawn from our cases.

Problem Structure

Specific features of the human endeavors giving rise to international problems commonly affect the character of the regimes required to solve them. In the case of vessel-source pollution, for instance, the fact that ships must be able to enter ports in a variety of countries makes it both feasible and appropriate to authorize port states to act as enforcers of equipment standards for tankers. Significantly, this means that a strategy of relying on equipment standards can prove effective even when many regime members do not make a sustained effort to enforce them. As long as a relatively small number of key port states take the standards seriously, tanker owners and operators will be motivated to incorporate the required equipment into the initial design of their ships. Compare this situation with the case of transboundary air pollution, where there are often striking asymmetries among emitters and recipients, and victims cannot acquire jurisdiction over those responsible for the problem in the same way that port states can exercise jurisdiction over tankers even if they are registered in other countries. Under these circumstances, there is no substitute for persuading public authorities in states where the polluters are located to make a sustained effort to regulate their own subjects, a tall order given the fact that such issues are often perceived in distributive terms by the affected parties. This may help to explain the striking differences between the oil pollution regime with its explicit rules pertaining to such matters as equipment standards and reception facilities and the LRTAP regime with its tendency to establish overall goals and to leave the fulfillment of such goals to the discretion of member states exercising authority within their own jurisdictions. Note also that problem structures can change over time in ways that have important consequences for the effectiveness of regimes. The Soviet system for verifying compliance with fisheries regulations at the time of off-loading catches in port, for example, became entirely inadequate during the late 1980s when Soviet trawlers were permitted to land larger and larger portions of their catch in Norwegian rather than Soviet ports.[3]

Members and Subjects

Another feature of the behavioral complex that stands out as important on the basis of our studies concerns relationships among national governments and those whose behavior is responsible for the problem to be solved. A striking feature of many—though by no means all—international institutions is that there is a clear separation between those actors who are the formal members of regimes and those whose behavior has given rise to the problem. Whereas the actual members of regimes are typically states, those who are subject to regime rules and procedures are often nonstate actors like tanker owners and operators, private and sometimes quasi-public fishing companies, municipal utilities and corporations burning fossil fuels, and even the millions of individuals who operate private automobiles. It follows that a major determinant of regime effectiveness in many cases is the willingness and the ability of national governments to translate regime rules, procedures, and programmatic commitments into practices that succeed in directing the behavior of the right set of subjects. This observation raises a host of questions about regulatory politics within the domestic systems of member countries, the relative merits of different policy instruments as tools for the pursuit of regulatory goals, and the circumstances in which public agencies come under the influence of those they have been established to regulate. Not surprisingly, the results of these regulatory processes can and do vary greatly not only from issue to issue but also from country to country, a fact that has led us to examine the fate of regime requirements on a country-by-country basis in evaluating the effectiveness of the LRTAP regime and, to a lesser extent, the other cases we have studied.[4]

Other Nonstate Actors

We have found, as well, that behavioral complexes differ markedly with regard to the presence and importance of a variety of nonstate actors, other than those whose behavior is the source of the problem itself. In some cases, these are nongovernmental organizations (NGOs) ranging from prominent scientific establishments like the International Council for the Exploration of the Sea to advocacy groups like Greenpeace. In other cases, they are intergovernmental organizations (IGOs) like the International Maritime Organization, the Organization for Economic Cooperation and Development, and the UN Economic Commission for Europe. In still other cases, they are quasi-nongovernmental organizations (QUANGOs), like the World Conservation Union (formerly known as the International Union for the Conservation of Nature and Natural Resources). The evidence does not support any simple generalization that regimes involving the active participation of these nonstate actors are more effective than those in which such actors play a more marginal role. Yet it is hard to understand what has happened in the case of oil pollution, for example, without a careful examination of the role of the IMO or in the case of transboundary air pollution in Europe without an assessment of the part played by advocacy groups and green political parties. To the extent that those who stress the rising significance of nonstate actors are correct, students of the effectiveness of international regimes will need to pay closer attention to the place of these actors in the behavioral complexes they examine (Lipschutz 1996; Wapner 1996). Certainly, our studies suggest that these actors have acquired a prominent place in the realm of international environmental issues.

Designing Effective Institutions

Insofar as we conclude that the operation of institutions accounts for a significant proportion of the variance in collective outcomes at the international level, it becomes relevant to think about designing regimes in such a way as to maximize their contribution to solving specific problems in international society. Much has been written about the constraints on institutional design attributable both to the limits of our knowledge about the operation of complex social practices and to the nature of the bargaining process leading to the establishment of regimes; there is no need to repeat these warnings here (Young 1989). Yet we do have several observations about this subject of a more specific nature that arise from the research conducted in connection with this project.

There is no reason to assume that international institutions—or any other social institutions—will be equally effective (or ineffective) across space, time, and issue areas (Ostrom 1990). Many debates about the significance of neoliberal institutionalism in international relations take the form of blanket assertions to the effect that international regimes are all epiphenomena (Strange 1983; Mearsheimer 1994–1995) or, conversely, that international activities are largely composed of rule-governed behavior (Henkin 1968; Chayes and Chayes 1995). We do not find this way of framing the problem helpful. It appears that the significance of institutions as determinants of collective outcomes varies considerably from issue area to issue area, from case to case, and even from time to time in connection with the same regime. Some of this variance is attributable to the character of the institutions that have been put in place in different issue areas. But it also appears undeniable that some circumstances are more conducive to the operation of institutions than others (Wettestad and Andresen 1991). Although the cases here all deal with environmental matters, it is by no means clear that the critical division separates environmental issues from security or economic issues or what some writers describe as "low" politics in contrast to "high" politics (Young 1997). Clearly, there is much more to be learned about the determinants of institutional effectiveness in international society. But our current understanding of this matter leads us to look as much to the capacity of international rules to embed themselves in the internal political dynamics of member states as to the traditional distinctions that students of international relations propound among substantive issue areas.

That said, it is important to ask what we have learned about the attributes or properties of international regimes themselves that appear to be associated with success. Given the small size and internal variability of our collection of cases, it is obviously dangerous to generalize about such matters. Even so, we offer several observations regarding this subject. In general, our analysis lends weight to a number of recent arguments derived from an analysis of interactive behavior among regime members treated as unitary actors. Thus, the need to be concerned with compliance is far less important in situations where there is at least one Pareto optimal equilibrium (for instance, battle of the sexes) than in situations where there is no equilibrium or the equilibrium is suboptimal for all concerned (for example, chicken or prisoner's dilemma) (Downs, Rocke, and Barsoom 1996). Transparency is clearly an important factor in eliciting compliance in cases where actors have incentives to violate rules (Chayes and Chayes 1995). The difference between discharge standards and equipment standards in the oil pollution case is a dramatic example of this proposition. The capacity of a regime to contribute to an improved understanding of the problem to be solved and to evolve to handle new tasks is surely a significant determinant of effectiveness in many cases. The story of the regime for transboundary air pollution illustrates this proposition clearly.

Perhaps the most important contribution of this project to our understanding of design principles, however, comes from the level of analysis associated with the use of causal models. An important implication of this argument is that regimes are often effective in solving international problems when they can redirect the interplay of political forces within the domestic policymaking arenas of key members. This is especially true of arrangements involving large numbers of members, like the air pollution and oil pollution regimes, as well as certain individual members whose actions are critical to the success of the whole arrangement, like Germany and the United Kingdom in the air pollution case. Partly, this is a matter of finding ways to influence the policy processes that take place within governmental arenas. Here, too, the changes that occurred in German policy on transboundary air pollution in the early 1980s and in British policy in the same issue area during the late 1980s are particularly instructive cases to examine. In part, it is a matter of strengthening both the capacity and the willingness of government agencies to channel the behavior of major private actors, like oil companies, chemical producers, and fishers. It is hardly necessary to look to developing countries to find instances in which government regulators have been captured by those they were created to regulate; lesser forms of influence on the part of the targets of public regulations abound. As the case of oil pollution suggests, moreover, well-financed private actors sometimes have a considerable capacity to escape regulations (e.g., by using flags of convenience in operating oil tankers) or to bargain effectively with government agencies on the content of standards (e.g., automobile fuel efficiency requirements).

Certainly, it is hard to generalize about the role of international regimes as forces in the domestic politics of individual members. In the transboundary air pollution case, for example, our evidence suggests not only that the regime played some role as a determinant of the behavior of the Soviet Union–Russia and, especially, Great Britain in this issue area but also that the role of the regime was quite different in the two countries. Those responsible for designing international regimes will not find it easy to formulate rules in such a was as to deal effectively with the domestic political dynamics of a number of leading members at one and the same time. Nor are there any simple rules of thumb or design principles that negotiators can turn to in the search for optimal sets of rules in this connection. Nonetheless, our research suggests that an ability to design regimes in such a way as to maximize their force in a number of different domestic political settings is an important determinant of regime effectiveness. This is a lesson that is not likely to be lost on those who become leaders in the establishment of international regimes.

Conclusion

Do international regimes or, more broadly, institutional arrangements in international society matter in that their operation accounts for a significant proportion of the variance in collective outcomes? Our research has convinced us that the answer to this question is a clearcut "yes." At the same time, we are now in a much better position to deal with variations in effectiveness within and among regimes and to respond to the analytical challenges facing those who wish to contribute to our understanding of regime effectiveness. For starters, there is no simple and straightforward way to define effectiveness treated as a dependent variable or target of analysis. The indirect measures often employed in studies of regime consequences (e.g., measures of the implementation of regime rules on the part of responsible public authorities or of compliance with these rules on the part of subjects) are severely limited as indicators of effectiveness. Yet effectiveness in the direct sense of problem solving often appears as a shadowy or moving target. In the final analysis, we have concluded that the most productive approach is to focus on the behavior of actors giving rise to problems, bearing in mind the need to think hard about the extent to which behavioral change serves to alleviate the problems under consideration.

To obtain a clear picture of the effectiveness of regimes, moreover, it is necessary to draw causal inferences about the connections among regime operations and collective outcomes. We have found it useful here to employ a battery of techniques of analysis featuring a combination of variation-finding analysis and tendency-finding analysis. Bringing these tools to bear on these cases, we have sought to disentangle the driving forces at work in the realm of international cooperation, showing in the process that institutions are significant forces in their own right but that they almost always interact in complex ways with other drivers involving ideas and material conditions.

The demonstration of causal connections between institutions and collective outcomes is a major achievement. Yet we cannot conclude our investigation of regime effectiveness here. To show how regimes become causal agents and to open up the prospect of generating usable knowledge, we have turned to a study of causal models. In effect, this means reconstructing the behavioral pathways through which the operation of regimes influences the behavior of those actors whose activities have given rise to the problems to be solved. We have taken some significant steps toward framing and deploying a series of models to show how institutions work to channel behavior, steps that clearly point to the need to supplement the simple utilitarian models that inform much conventional thinking about international relations. Even so, one of our principal conclusions is that students of international regimes will need to devote much more attention to the identification of behavioral mechanisms as we seek to build a coherent body of knowledge about the roles institutions play as determinants of collective outcomes at the international level. Only then will we be able to realize the full potential of regime analysis as a means of developing both analytic insights and usable knowledge about the effectiveness of institutions in international society.

Notes

1. Although the ideas of process tracing and thick description are somewhat difficult to pin down, they highlight the search for understanding through the development of detailed and typically chronological narratives (Geertz 1973).

2. For a study of the Great Lakes Water Quality Agreement (GLWQA), which illustrates a somewhat different political dynamic, see Botts and Muldoon (1996).

3. For efforts to devise more generic approaches to the idea of problem structure, see Rittberger and Zürn (1991) and Andresen and Wettestad (1995).

4. These observations account for the recent increase in studies dealing with the domestic implementation of international commitments. See Jacobson and Weiss 1995; Victor, Raustiala, and Skolnikoff 1998; Weiss and Jacobson 1998; and Hanf and Underdal forthcoming.

Appendix: Notes on Methodology

The major findings of this project include methodological as well as sub-stantive matters. We introduced the distinction between variation-finding analysis and tendency-finding analysis in the body of chapter 5. But to avoid breaking the flow of the argument, we have reserved a fuller ac-count of the problems and prospects of using these two types of analytic procedures for this methodological appendix. Each of these sets of tech-niques has its distinctive advantages and disadvantages; we would not recommend relying exclusively on one or the other. Used in tandem, we are convinced that these techniques can take us some distance toward the goal of revealing the nature of the causal links between regimes and significant changes in the behavioral complexes within which they operate.

Applying Variation-Finding Techniques

Variation-finding analysis is subject to two types of errors, both of which require careful attention in studies of the sort we have undertaken in this project. Perhaps the most easily understood of the two arises from the danger of spurious correlation. The fact that the establishment of an inter-national regime is followed by the amelioration of the problem that moti-vated its creation or significant changes in the behavior of relevant actors does not justify the conclusion that the regime played a causal role in these developments. We cannot assume, for example, that the move to segregated ballast tanks following the introduction of equipment stan-dards under the oil pollution regime is a product pure and simple of this shift in the regime's rules. Nor can we be confident that the rapid

expansion of efforts to curb transboundary flows of certain airborne pollutants would not have occurred in the absence of the long-range transboundary air pollution regime. It is possible that these behavioral changes
were driven by other forces, so that agreement on the content of new
regime rules is properly understood as a side effect or byproduct of the
operation of these other forces.

Although somewhat less familiar, the other type of error that arises
with variation-finding analyses is equally important. This is the danger
of failing to detect causal links between regimes and actor behavior where
they actually exist. In the typical case, this failure involves a multivariate
relationship in which offsetting factors mask the effects of an institutional
arrangement. The fact that major fish stocks of the Barents Sea have experienced sharp swings in recent years, for example, suggests to some observers that the Norwegian–Russian regime for these resources has been
largely ineffective as a conservation measure. Yet it is worth considering
the possibility that physical forces, like changes in water temperature,
have played a key role in causing fluctuations in the condition of relevant
stocks, and that these fluctuations would have been even greater in the
absence of the management efforts associated with the Norwegian–Russian regime. Somewhat similar issues arise in cases where there are significant lag times between the creation of a regime and its impact on the
problem to be solved. In general, the longer the elapsed time between
regime creation and impact, the harder it is to demonstrate convincingly
the existence of the causal link. In cases like transboundary air pollution
and especially ozone depletion where prior emissions are apt to reside
in the atmosphere for some time, this problem may become particularly
difficult to overcome in a satisfactory manner.

These difficulties, known to the statistically inclined as type 1 and type
2 errors, have been a focus of considerable attention among those who
conduct quantitative studies of social phenomena. Though no procedure
is foolproof, many statistical techniques have been developed to minimize
the danger of falling into one or the other of these traps. Unfortunately,
this line of attack cannot solve the problems of avoiding spurious correlations and overlooking masked effects for students of international institutions. The universe of cases is almost always too small to support the use
of statistical procedures in a meaningful fashion. Equally important, the

members of our small universe of cases vary considerably among themselves. Of course, those familiar with statistical procedures will think to cope with this latter problem by dividing the universe of cases or, more likely, the sample drawn from the universe into two or more smaller subsets. But in a realm in which the overall universe is too small to support statistical procedures to begin with, this approach to the problem of variability among cases is obviously not workable.

What can those engaged in variation-finding analyses of institutional effectiveness do to overcome these problems? One response is to rely on natural experiments featuring variation on the independent variable. This method involves identifying two or more situations that resemble each other closely except for the presence or absence of an international regime or the character of the regimes in operation. If a series of these experiments yields the conclusion that progress toward solving the relevant problems is markedly greater in those cases featuring the presence of an international regime, this would count as evidence in support of the proposition that regimes do matter. Similar observations are in order on the conduct of natural experiments focusing on different types of regimes. Our case studies did not lend themselves particularly well to the use of this analytic technique. Each case-study team concentrated on its own case; the teams did not attempt cross-case comparisons. In each instance, moreover, the team focused on the performance of existing regimes; they did not compare their cases with other instances where no regime exists. Even so, some opportunities arose here to take advantage of natural experiments. In the case of LRTAP, for example, we were able to exploit the fact that the geographical domain of the regime stops at the Ural Mountains to compare Soviet–Russian behavior in the area covered by the regime with behavior regarding air pollution in the part of the country not covered by the regime. Similarly, the oil pollution case offered an opportunity to compare results before and after the shift from discharge standards to equipment standards.

Two other procedures show promise in realizing the potential of variation-finding analysis. One centers on the systematic assessment of what we have termed rival hypotheses. The idea here is to make a concerted effort to explain links that appear to stem from the impact of institutions in terms of the impact of other variables. The oil pollution team, for example, investigated the possibility that tanker owners and operators would have moved toward segregated ballast tanks for purely economic reasons, whether or not the regime's preexisting discharge standards had been replaced with equipment standards. Similarly, the air pollution team explored the extent to which domestic political developments, in contrast to the international regime dealing with transboundary air pollution, constituted the real driving forces in this area during the years following the negotiation of the 1979 Geneva convention. It is apparent from these efforts that the assessment of rival hypotheses is by no means cut-and-dried. Some behavioral changes are clearly overdetermined. In other cases, it is hard to decide how much of the variance to attribute to institutional forces in contrast to other factors like shifting economic calculations. Even so, this procedure is a promising one. In the hands of the case-study teams, its use has resulted in both a paring down of exaggerated claims for the effects of international institutions and a solidification of the argument that some of the variance in collective outcomes is in fact attributable to the operation of social institutions.

Further, there is the procedure of focusing on hard cases as a means of avoiding plausible but facile claims about the effects of institutional arrangements (Young 1992). A hard case, in this context, is one in which various features of the situation militate against institutions affecting the content of collective outcomes. This may be a consequence of extreme asymmetries in the structural power of the members, as in the case of Norway and Russia in the Barents Sea regime; sharp differences in the nature of the behavioral changes required of different members, as in the case of transboundary air pollution, or any of a number of other factors that cast doubt on the capacity of institutions to redirect behavior and, in the process, to solve or ameliorate the problems that motivate their establishment. Although the argument is not logically conclusive, a striking correlation between the creation of a regime and progress in problem solving will carry greater weight in connection with a hard case than similar correlations in cases where the nature of the problems makes it relatively easy to find solutions with or without the aid of an explicit regime. Here, too, the evidence from our cases is suggestive. It indicates that there is an irreducible core of institutional effectiveness at the international level, even while justifying the skepticism of many regarding the casual claims that are sometimes made by those who have embraced the new institutionalism in international relations (Young 1994).

Deploying Tendency-Finding Procedures

Whatever its general merits as an analytic tool, variation-finding analysis is not sufficient to answer all questions about the effectiveness of international regimes in a convincing manner. It is not surprising, therefore, that we witness today a striking growth of interest in the potential of tendency-finding analysis as an additional means for illuminating the role of institutions as determinants of collective outcomes in international society. The hallmarks of tendency-finding analysis include not only a concern with constructing detailed narratives focusing on individual cases but also an interest in a level of disaggregation that highlights efforts to reconstruct the forces at play in the decisions of individual regime members (and other relevant actors) at critical turning points in their participation in processes set in motion under the terms of a given regime. Whereas a variation-finding analysis may seek to generalize about the distribution of structural power among regime members or the transparency of regime rules and the performance of regimes in solving problems, for example, tendency-finding analyses endeavor to construct convincing narratives that delineate the pathways that lead actors to respond to the dictates of international regimes. In many cases, this will involve an effort to reconstruct in some detail the decision-making processes within individual regime members as they endeavor to come to terms with the behavioral requirements embedded in a regime's rules or programmatic activities.

Not surprisingly, it is easier to call for analysis of this type than to carry it out in specific cases. Although there is no easy recipe for the development of such narrative accounts, we have found several procedures distinctly helpful as methods for reconstructing the dynamics of individual cases. One is the method often described as process tracing or thick description (Geertz 1973). While these phrases are far from self-explanatory, they refer to efforts to reconstruct the forces at work in shaping the behavior of key actors at critical moments in a regime's development. Why, for example, did tanker owners and operators accept the transition from discharge standards, which are relatively easy to evade, to equipment standards, which are virtually impossible to evade, during the 1970s? Why did Germany change from being a relatively lukewarm supporter of the transboundary air pollution regime to being a pusher for increasingly stringent rules in this issue area during the early 1980s? Why did Norway, which had a policy of shying away from bilateral arrangements with the former Soviet Union due to the asymmetry between the two countries in terms of power, embrace the idea of the Barents Sea fisheries regime in the late 1970s? How did the Barents Sea regime operate to create a binational community of actors with a strong mutual interest in the perpetuation of this arrangement, even in the wake of drastic changes in the political and economic circumstances of the member states? The goal, on this account, is to construct detailed stories or narratives that answer these questions by depicting the outcomes as the final stages of identifiable developmental sequences and delineating the earlier stages of the sequences leading to these outcomes. The result of the analysis, as Dessler puts it, "is a set of claims as to *causal pathways* that led from the initial stage in the narration (environmental problem) to the final phenomenon to be explained (environmental action)" (Dessler 1992, emphasis in original).

Another procedure we have found helpful involves the use of counterfactuals. Treated as thought experiments, counterfactuals require the analyst to answer questions about what would have happened in the absence of an international regime (Fearon 1991). Would tanker owners and operators have proceeded to incorporate segregated ballast tanks into new ships even in the absence of an international rule requiring them to do so? Would Norway and Russia have been able to avoid jurisdictional disputes in the central Barents Sea even in the absence of the Grey Zone Agreement? Would sulfur dioxide emissions in Europe have declined even in the absence of the 1985 protocol on sulfur dioxide? The use of counterfactuals cannot constitute a test of proposed explanations for collective outcomes in any formal sense; this method involves only a comparison of the world as it is with a hypothetical alternative. Like the examination of rival hypotheses in variation-finding analyses, however, the use of counterfactuals forces us to show how institutional arrangements operate to influence the behavior of those involved in a given issue area. To the extent that it is difficult to come up with a plausible explanation of a pattern of behavior without reference to the operation of a regime, arguments that point to the causal role of the institution in question gain force. As Thomas Biersteker has argued, there is a world of difference between rigorous and sloppy uses of the method of counterfactuals (Biersteker 1993). But treated properly, this method adds yet another tool to the arsenal of those who seek to make sound judgments about the role that institutions play in accounting for variations in collective outcomes at the international level.

References

Acidifying Emissions Task Group. 1997. *Towards a National Acid Rain Strategy.* Report submitted to the National Air Issues Coordinating Committee, October.

Ackerman, B.A., and W.T. Hassler. 1981. *Clean Coal / Dirty Air.* New Haven, CT: Yale University Press.

Alcamo, Joseph, Roderick Shaw, and Leen Hordijk, eds. 1991. *The Rains Model of Acidification.* IASSA Executive Report 18, January 1991.

Alm, Leslie R. 1993. "The Long Road toward Influence: Canada as an American Interest Group." *Journal of Borderlands Studies* 8(2) (June): 13–32.

Andersson, Catharina. 1989. "A European Monitoring System." *Acid Magazine* 8 (September): 4.

Andresen, Steinar, and Jorgen Wettestad. 1995. "International Problem-Solving Effectiveness: The Oslo Project So Far." *International Environmental Affairs* 7: 127–149.

Anonymous. 1990. "Cleaner Oceans: The Role of IMO in the 1990s." *IMO News* 3: 6–12.

Anonymous. 1990. *Ecologia i biologicheskaya productivnost Barentseva moria* (Ecology and biological productivity of the Barents Sea). Moscow: Nauka.

Anonymous. 1990. *Ecologia, vosproizvodstvo i okhrana bioresursov morei severnoi evropy* (Ecology, reproduction and protection of biological resources in the North European seas). Murmansk.

Anonymous. 1991. *Ecological Situation and Conservation of the Barents Sea Fauna and Flora.* Apatity: Kola Science Center, USSR Academy of Sciences.

Anonymous. 1990a. *Natural Resources of the Kola North: Assessments, Planning, Management, Utilization* (in Russian). Apatity: Kola Science Center, USSR Academy of Sciences.

Anonymous. 1990b. "Seven Nations' Aircraft to Fly Patrol to Search for Ships Polluting Baltic Sea." *International Environment Reporter* 13(8) (8 August): 328–329.

Anonymous. 1990c. "Tanker Orders Contribute to Pollution." *International Environment Reporter* 13(11) (10 October): 428.

Anonymous. 1993. "1991 MARPOL Amendments Enter into Force." *IMO News* 2: 2.

Anonymous. 1996. "Circular issued on reception facilities." *IMO News* 1996(2): 3.

Arkansas Democrat. 1986. "Scientists to Discuss Dangers Acid Rain Poses to Arkansas." 9 April.

Ausubel, Jesse, and David Victor. 1992. "Verification of International Environmental Agreements." *Annual Review of Energy and the Environment* 17(1): 1–43.

Axelrod, Robert, and Robert O. Keohane. 1986. "Achieving Cooperation under Anarchy: Strategies and Institutions." Pp. 226–254 in Kenneth A. Oye, ed., *Cooperation under Anarchy*. Princeton, NJ: Princeton University Press.

Babich, Harvey, Devra Lee Davis, and Guenther Stotzky. 1980. "Acid Precipitation: Causes and Consequences." *Environment* 22 (4): 6–13, 40.

Baker, J.P., W.J. Warren-Hicks, J. Gallagher, and S.W. Christensen. 1993. "Fish Population Losses from Adirondack Lakes: The Role of Surface Water Acidity and Acidification." *Water Resources Research* 29(4): 861–874.

Baker, L.A., A.T. Herlihy, P.R. Kaufmann, and J.M. Eilers. 1991. "Acidic Lakes and Streams in the United States: The Role of Acidic Deposition." *Science* 252: 1151–1154.

Barnes, R.A. 1979. "The Long Range Transport of Air Pollution: A Review of the European Experience." *Journal of the Air Pollution Control Association* 29: 1219–1235.

Barnett, James K. 1974. "United States and Canadian Approaches to Air Pollution Control and the Implications for the Control of Transboundary Pollution." *Cornell International Law Journal* 7: 148–170.

Barrett, E., and G. Brodin. 1955. "The Acidity of Scandinavian Precipitation." *Tellus* 7(2): 251–257.

Baskakov, V. 1993 "Stock-holding—an Important Stage of Transition to Market Relations (in Russian)." *Rybnoye Khoziastvo* (3): 8–12.

Bates, D.V., and R. Sitzo. 1983. "Relationship between Air Pollution Levels and Hospital Admissions in Southern Ontario." *Canadian Journal of Public Health* 74: 117–122.

Beamish, R.J. 1970. "Factors Affecting the Age and Size of the White Sucker *Catostomous Comersoni* at Maturity." Ph.D. dissertation, University of Toronto.

Beamish, R.J., 1976. "Acidification of Lakes in Canada by Acid Precipitation and the Resulting Effects on Fish." *Water, Air, and Soil Pollution* 6: 501–514.

Beamish, R.J., and H. Harvey. 1971. "Why Trout Are Disappearing in La Cloche Lakes." *Globe and Mail*. July 26.

Beamish, R.J., and H. Harvey, 1972. "Acidification of the La Cloche Mountain Lakes, Ontario, and Resulting Fish Mortalities." *Journal of the Fisheries Research Board of Canada* 29(8): 1131–1143.

Bergmeijer, Pieter. 1990. "The International Convention for the Prevention of Pollution from Ships." Paper presented at the Pacem in Maribus XVII Conference in Rotterdam, The Netherlands. June.

Biersteker, Thomas. 1993. "Constructing Historical Counterfactuals to Assess the Consequences of International Regimes: The Global Debt Regime and the Course of the Debt Crisis of the 1980s." In Volker Rittberger, ed., *Regime Theory and International Relations*. Oxford: Clarendon Press, 315–338.

Bird, D. 1972. "Rise in Acid Found in Rainfall Study." *New York Times*. January 30.

BNA. 1982. "Canadian Official Accuses Administration of Manipulating Acid Rain Scientific Work." *BNA Environment Reporter* 13(23): 782.

BNA. 1984. "Three Democratic Governors Leave for Europe on NGA-backed Trip to Study Acid Rain Issue." *BNA Environment Reporter* 15: 1290.

Boehmer-Christiansen, Sonja, and Jim Skea, 1991. *Acid Politics: Environmental and Energy Policies in Britain and Germany*. London: Belhaven.

Bolin, B. et al. 1972. *Air Pollution across National Boundaries*. Swedish Ministry for Foreign Affairs and Ministry of Agriculture. Case study for the United Nations Conference on the Human Environment, Stockholm, Sweden: Norstadt and Sons.

Botts, Lee, and Paul Muldoon. 1996. *The Great Lakes Water Quality Agreement: Its Past Successes and Uncertain Future*. Hanover: Institute on International Environmental Governance.

Boyle, Robert H. 1981. "An American Tragedy." *Sports Illustrated* 55(13) (21 September) 68–82.

Braekke, F.H. 1976. "Impact of Acid Precipitation on Forest and Freshwater Ecosystem in Norway." SSNF Project Research Report FR6/76, Oslo, Norway.

Breitmeier, Helmut C., Marc A. Levy, Oran R. Young, and Michael Zürn. 1996. "International Regimes Database (IRD): Data Protocol." IIASA WP–96–154.

Brosset, Cyril. 1973. "Air-Borne Acid." *Ambio* 1(1): 2–9.

Brundtland, Gro Harlem. 1997. *Mitt liv: 1939–1986*. Oslo: Gyldendal, 1997.

Bryner, G.C. 1993. *Blue Skies, Green Politics: The Clean Air Act of 1990*. Washington, DC: Congressional Quarterly, Inc.

Burke, William T., Richard Legatski, and William W. Woodhead. 1975. *National and International Law Enforcement in the Ocean*. Seattle, WA: University of Washington Press.

Børsting, Georg, and Olav Schram Stokke. 1995. *International Cooperation in Fisheries Science: Research Effectiveness and the Barents Sea Fisheries Regime*. Lysaker: Fridtjof Nansen Institute, report no. 2.

Campbell, Donald T., and Julian Stanley. 1966. *Experimental and Quasi-Experimental Designs for Research.* Chicago: Rand McNally.

Camphuysen, C.J. 1989. *Beached Bird Surveys in the Netherlands, 1915–1988: Seabird Mortality in the Southern North Sea Since the Early Days of Oil Pollution.* Amsterdam, The Netherlands: Werkgroep Noordzee.

Canada, Acidifying Emissions Task Group. 1997. *Towards a National Acid Rain Strategy.* Report submitted to the National Air Issues Coordinating Committee, October 1997.

Canada, Environment Canada. 1997. *1997 Canadian Acid Rain Assessment.* Ottawa, volumes I–V.

Canada, Federal Provincial Research and Monitoring Coordinating Committee. 1986. *Assessment of the State of Knowledge on the Long-Range Transport of Air Pollution and Acidic Deposition: part 2, Atmospheric Sciences.* Ottawa.

Canada, House of Commons, Sub-committee on Acid Rain of the Standing Committee on Fisheries and Forestry. 1981. *Still Waters.* Queen's Printer: Ottawa.

Canada, National Research Council. 1939. *Effect of Sulphur Dioxide on Vegetation.* NRC no. 815, King's Printer, Ottawa.

Canada and United States. 1991. *Agreement between the Government of Canada and the Government of the United States of America on Air Quality.* Ottawa. Environment Canada.

Canada–United States. 1992. Canada–United States Air Quality Agreement, *Progress Report.* March 1992.

Canada–United States. 1996. Canada–United States Air Quality Agreement, *Progress Report.*

Canada–United States Research Consultation Group on the Long-Range Transport of Air Pollutants. 1979. "The LRTAP Problem in North America: A Preliminary Overview." Ottawa and Washington.

Canadian Institute of International Affairs. 1981. *Political and Legal Implications of a Canada–United States Air Quality Accord.* Proceedings of a Conference, Don Munton and Susan Eros, eds. December, Toronto.

Chayes, Abram, and Antonia Handler Chayes. 1995. *The New Sovereignty: Compliance with International Regulatory Agreements.* Cambridge: Harvard University Press.

Chossudovsky, E. 1988. *East–West Diplomacy for Environment in the United Nations: The High Level Meeting within the Framework of the ECE on the Protection of the Environment, A Case Study.* New York.

Churchill, Robin R., and Geir Ulfstein. 1992. *Marine Management in Disputed Areas: The Case of the Barents Sea.* London: Routledge.

Clark, William C., Nancy Dickson, Ellis Cowling, Jenny Craig, Karl Irving, Diana Roth, Roderick Sheer, Susan Subak, and Joshua Tosteson. 1993. "Acid Deposition and Long-Range Transport of Air Pollutants: A Historical Perspective of

Risk Management in the United States." Unpublished manuscript, August 1993, Harvard University.

Clarkson Research Studies, Limited. 1990. *The Tanker Register*. London: Clarkson Research Studies, Ltd.

Cogbill, C.V. 1976. "The History and Character of Acid Precipitation in Eastern North America." *Water, Air, and Soil Pollution* 6: 407–413.

Cogbill, C.V. and G.E. Likens. 1974. "Acid Precipitation in the Northeastern United States." *Water Resources Research* 10(6): 1133–1137.

Cohen, R.E. 1992. *Washington at Work: Back Rooms and Clean Air*. New York: Macmillan Publishing Company.

Collins, Michael David. 1987. "The Tanker's Right of Harmless Discharge and Protection of the Marine Environment." *Journal of Maritime Law and Commerce* 18:2 (April): 275–291.

Convention on Long-Range Transboundary Air Pollution. 1979. UN/ECE/GE 79–42960 (reprinted in *Environmental Law and Policy* 6(1980): 37–40.

Cowley, James. 1988. "IMO and national administrations." *IMO News* 4: 6–11.

Cowley, James. 1990. "Regulatory and Environmental Aspects of Marine Pollution." In *IMAS 90: Marine Technology and the Environment*. London: Institute of Marine Engineers, 3–15.

Cowling, E.B. 1980. "Acid Precipitation and Its Effects on Terrestrial and Aquatic Ecosystems." Pp. 540–555, in T.J. Kneip and P.J. Lioy, eds., *Aerosols: Anthropogenic and Natural, Sources and Transport*. New York: NY Academy of Sciences.

Cowling, E.B. 1982. "Acid Precipitation in Historical Perspective," *Environmental Science & Technology* 16(2): 110A–123A.

Cowling, E.B. November 1979. "From Research to Public Policy: Progress in Scientific and Public Understanding of Acid Precipitation and Its Biological Effects." Proceedings of the Action Seminar on Acid Precipitation. Toronto, Ontario, Canada, 38–59.

Cowling, Ellis, and Svante Odén (joint presentation). 1980. United States House of Representatives Committee on Inter-State and Foreign Commerce, Subcommittee on Oversight and Investigations Hearings on Acid Rain, 96th Cong., 2d Sess., Washington: US Government Printing Office, February 26 and 27, serial no. 96–150.

CRISTAL. 1971. "Contract Regarding an Interim Supplement to Tanker Liability for Oil Pollution (14 January 1971)." Reprinted in 10 I.L.M. 137 (1971).

Crowther, C., and H.G. Ruston. 1911. "The Nature, Distribution, and Effects upon Vegetation of Atmospheric Impurities in and Near an Industrial Town." *Journal of Agricultural Science* 4: 25–55.

Cummins, Philip A., Dennis E. Logue, Robert D. Tollison, and Thomas D. Willett. 1975. "Oil Tanker Pollution Control: Design Criteria vs. Effective Liability Assessment." *Journal of Maritime Law and Commerce* 7(1) (October): 169.

Curtis, Jeff B. 1985. "Vessel-Source Oil Pollution and MARPOL 73/78: An International Success Story?" *Environmental Law* 15(4) (Summer): 679–710.

CCE Technical Report. 1991. Mapping Critical Loads for Europe. No. 1, July, A168–71.

Dahl, K. 1927. "The Effects of Acid Water on Trout Fry." *Salmon and Trout Magazine* 46: 35–43.

Dannevig, A. 1959. "The Influence of Precipitation on the Acidity of Water Courses and on Fish Populations" (title translated from the Norwegian). *Jeger og Fisker* 3: 116–118.

David L. Coffin, and John H. Knelson. 1976. "Acid Precipitation: Effects of Sulphur Dioxide and Sulphate Aerosol Particles on Human Health." *Ambio* 5(5–6): 239–42.

Davidsen, Trond. 1992. *'Sevryba'—fiskerigigant i nord. Endringer i den sovjetrussiske fiskerinæringen* (Sevryba—fisheries giant in the North. Changes in the Soviet–Russian Fisheries Industry). Tromsø: FORUT/NORUT.

Davidsen, Trond, and Anatoly Vasilyev. 1994. *Fiskerinæringen i Nordvest-Russland: selskaper og organisering* (The fisheries industry in northwest Russia: companies and organization). Tromsø: NORUT Samfunnsforskning, SN 17.

Davison, Ellis H., II. 1984. "Legislative/Administrative Mechanisms for Ensuring that Adequate Reception Facilities Are Provided in Ports." Proceedings of IMO/UNDP international seminar on reception facilities for wastes. London: IMO/UNDP.

Dawes, Robyn. 1980. "Social Dilemmas." *Annual Review of Psychology* 31: 169–193.

Dempsey, Paul Stephen, 1984. "Compliance and Enforcement in International Law—Oil Pollution of the Marine Environment by Ocean Vessels." *Northwestern Journal of International Law and Business* 6:2 (summer), 459–561.

den Boer, Marja, Sipke Havinga, Henk Hazelhorst, Marja Holsink, Liesbeth Meijer, Rob Splint, Guy van Spronsen, and Hans Zwijnenberg. 1987. *Loos'-alarm: Afvalolie van de scheepvaart in de Waddenzee.* Groningen, The Netherlands: Werkgroep Eemsmond van de Landelijke Vereniging tot Behoud van de Waddenzee.

Dessler, David. 1992. "The Architecture of Causal Analysis." Paper presented at the Center for International Affairs, Harvard University.

Dinwoodie, D.H. 1971. "The Politics of International Pollution Control: Trail Smelter Case." *International Journal* 27: 219–235.

diPrimio, Juan Carlos. 1996. "Monitoring and Verification in the European Air Pollution Regime." Working Paper WP–96–47, International Institute for Applied Systems Analysis.

Doern, G. Bruce. 1993. *Green Diplomacy: How Environmental Policy Decisions Are Made.* Policy Study 16, C. D. Howe Institute, Toronto.

Downs, George W., David M. Rocke, and Peter N. Barsoom. 1996. "Is the Good News about Compliance Good News about Cooperation?" *International Organization* 50 (summer): 379–406.

Drewry Shipping Consultants, Ltd. 1981. *The Impact of New Tanker Regulations.* London: Drewry Shipping Consultants, Ltd.

Drewry Shipping Consultants, Ltd. 1985. *Tanker Regulations: Enforcement and Effect.* London: Drewry Shipping Consultants, Ltd.

Ember, Lois. 1987. "Acid Precipitation Program Head Resigns." *Chemical and Engineering News,* October 12, 15.

EMEP. 1996. *Transboundary Air Pollution in Europe.* MSC-W Status Report, Oslo.

EMEP. 1992. *Calculated Budgets for Airborne Acidifying Components in Europe. 1985, 1987, 1988, 1989, 1990, and 1991.* MSC-W Technical Report, Oslo.

EMEP. 1991. *Estimation of Airborn Transport of Oxidised Nitrogen and Sulphur in Europe—1988,* 1989. MSC-E, Moscow.

Engesæter, Sigmund. 1993. "Scientific Input to International Fishery Agreements." *International Challenges* 13(2): 85–107.

Environmental Research. 1967. Statens Offentliga utredninger, 43.

Environmental Protection Agency. 1983. "Acid Deposition: Current Knowledge and Policy Options." Briefing document for the administrator by the Acid Deposition Task Force, 1 August.

Erdman L., I. Dedkova, et al. 1994. Transgranichnyi Perenos Soedinenyi Sery i Azota v 1992 Godu na Territorii Rossiiskoy Federacii, Ukrainy, Belarusy, Moldovy, Kazahstana, Stran Baltii, Zakavkazya i Sredney Azii. Report no. 12, EMEP Meteorological Synthesizing Center—East, Moscow, Russia.

Eriksson, Erik. 1952. "Composition of Atmospheric Precipitation." *Tellus* 4(4): 280–303.

Fay, James A. 1984. "European Views on Controlling Acid Rain." MIT Energy Laboratory Report no. MIT-EL 84–002, February.

Fay, J.A., D. Golomb, and S. Kumar. 1985. "Source Apportionment of Wet Sulphate Deposition in Eastern North America," *Atmospheric Environment* 19: 1773–1782.

Fearon, James. 1991. "Counterfactuals and Hypothesis Testing in Political Science." *World Politics,* 43 (January): 169–195.

Ferenbaugh, R.W. 1975. "Acid Rain Biological Effects and Implications." *Environmental Affairs* 5: 745–755.

Finland, Ministry of the Environment, Environmental Protection Department. 1989. Air Quality Management in Finland, 2d edition, Booklet 15.

Fraenkel, Amy A. 1989. "The Convention on Long-Range Transboundary Air Pollution." *Harvard International Law Journal* 30(2): 447–476.

Franck, Thomas M. 1990. *The Power of Legitimacy among Nations*. New York: Oxford University Press.

French, Hilary F. 1997. "Lessons from the Ozone Experience." Pp. 151–171 in Lester R. Brown et al., *State of the World 1997*. New York: W.W. Norton 1997.

Galloway, J.N., and D.M. Whelpdale. 1980. "An Atmospheric Sulphur Budget for Eastern North America." *Atmospheric Environment* 14: 409–417.

Geertz, Clifford. 1973. *The Interpretation of Cultures: Selected Essays*. New York: Basic Books.

GESAMP (IMO/FAO/UNESCO/WMO/WHO/IAEA/UN/UNEP Joint group of experts on the scientific aspects of marine pollution). 1990. *The State of the Marine Environment*. New York: United Nations.

Glazov, S.F. 1979. "Zagryaznennost' Mirovogo okeana i bor'ba za chistotu morskoi sredy (Pollution of the world's oceans and the struggle to clean up the marine environment)," in *Ekonomicheskaya geografiya Mirovogo okeana* (*Economic geography of the world's oceans*). Leningrad.

Goldstein, Judith, and Robert O. Keohane, eds. 1993. *Ideas and Foreign Policy: Beliefs, Institutions, and Political Change*. Ithaca: Cornell University Press.

Gorham, E. 1955. "On the Acidity and Salinity of Rain." *Geochimica et Cosmochimica Acta* 7: 231–239.

Gorham, E. 1957. "The Chemical Composition of Lake Waters in Halifax, Nova Scotia." *Limnology and Oceanography* 2: 12–21.

Gorham, E. 1981. "Scientific Understanding of Atmosphere-Biosphere Interactions: A Historical Overview." In National Research Council, *Atmosphere-Biosphere Interactions*. Washington, DC: National Academy Press.

Gorham, E., and A.G. Gordon. 1960. "Some Effects of Smelter Pollution Northeast of Falconbridge, Ontario." *Canadian Journal of Botany* 38: 307–312.

Gorham, E., and A.G. Gordon. 1960. "The Influence of Smelter Fumes Upon the Chemical Composition of Lake Waters Near Sudbury, Ontario, and Upon the Surrounding Vegetation." *Canadian Journal of Botany* 38: 477–487.

Gorham, E., and A.G. Gordon. 1963. "Some Effects of Smelter Pollution Upon Aquatic Vegetation Near Sudbury, Ontario." *Canadian Journal of Botany* 41: 371–378.

Gray, William O. 1978. "Testimony," In *Oil Tanker Pollution—Hearings*. Ed. by U.S. Congress, House Committee on Government Operations, Government Activities and Transportation Subcommittee, 95th Cong. 2d sess. Washington, DC: GPO.

Green, Fitzhugh. 1985. "Public Diplomacy and Acid Rain." *Toledo Law Review* 17: 133–137.

Green, Fitzhugh. 1986. "Acid Rain and U.S.–Canadian Relations." *Washington Quarterly* 9: 103–108.

Grolin, Jesper. 1988. "Environmental Hegemony, Maritime Community, and the Problem of Oil Tanker Pollution." Pp. 13–44 in Michael A. Morris, ed., *North-South Perspectives on Marine Policy*. Boulder, CO: Westview Press.

Haas, Ernst B. 1990. *When Knowledge Is Power: Three Models of Change in International Organizations*. Berkeley: University of California Press.

Haas, Peter M. 1989. "Do Regimes Matter? Epistemic Communities and Mediterranean Pollution Control." *International Organization* 43 (summer), 377–403.

Haas, Peter M. 1993. "Epistemic Communities and the Dynamics of International Environmental Cooperation." Pp. 168–201 in Volker Rittberger, ed., *Regime Theory and International Relations*. Oxford: Oxford University Press.

Haas, Peter M., Robert O. Keohane, and Marc A. Levy, eds. 1993. *Institutions for the Earth: Sources of Effective International Environmental Protection*. Cambridge: MIT Press.

Hajer, Maarten. 1995. *The Politics of Environmental Discourse*. Oxford, Clarendon Press.

Hambling, P. 1984. "Summary of the Approach Taken in the United Kingdom to the Implementation of MARPOL 73/78 Reception Facility Requirements." Proceedings of IMO/UNDP international seminar on reception facilities for wastes. London: IMO/UNDP.

Hamre, Johannes. 1991. "Barentshavets fiskeressurser—utvikling og potensiale (Barents Sea fisheries resources—development and potential) in N.C." Pp. 231–242 in N. Stenseth, N. Trandem, and G. Kristiansen, eds., *Forvaltning av våre fellesressurser. Finnmarksvidda og Barentshavet i et lokalt og globalt perspektiv*. Oslo: Ad Notam.

Hanf, Kenneth, and Arild Underdal, eds. *The Domestic Basis of International Environmental Agreements*. Aldershot: Ashgate, forthcoming.

Hart, H.L.A. 1961. *The Concept of Law*. Oxford: Oxford University Press.

Harvey, Harold H., and Richard J. Beamish. 1972. "Acidification of the LaCloche Mountain Lakes." *Journal of the Fisheries Research Board of Canada* 29: 1131–1143.

Hasenclever, Andreas, Peter Mayer, and Volker Rittberger. 1997. *Theories of International Regimes*. Cambridge: Cambridge University Press.

Havforskningsinstituttets årsmelding. Annual. (annual report of the Marine Research Institute). Bergen: Norwegian Marine Research Institute.

Haywood, J.K. 1904. *Injury to Vegetation by Smelter Fumes*. U.S. Department of Agriculture, Bulletin 89.

Haywood, J.K. 1910. *Injury to Vegetation and Animal Life by Smelter Wastes*. U.S. Department of Agriculture, Bulletin 113.

Henkin, Louis. 1968. *How Nations Behave: Law and Foreign Policy*. New York: Praeger.

Herman, F.A., and E. Gorham. 1957. "Total Mineral Material, Acidity, Sulphur, and Nitrogen in Rain and Snow at Kentville, Nova Scotia." *Tellus* 9(2): 180–183.

Hersoug, Bjørn. 1992. "Norsk fiskerinæring: Landanalyse" (The Norwegian fisheries industry: country study). Pp. 231–287 in B. Hersoug, ed., *Fiskerinæringens hovedtrekk: Landanalyser av Danmark, Færøyene, Grønland, Island og Norge* (Main features of the fisheries industry: country studies of Denmark, the Faroe Islands, Greenland, Iceland, and Norway). Copenhagen: Nord-REFO report no. 30.

Hersoug, Bjørn and Alf Håkon Hoel. 1992. *Hvem tok fisken?* (revised version, September 1991). Tromsø: Fiskeriforskning/Norges Fiskerihøyskole, Skriftserie, rapport 10.

Hileman, Bette. 1983. "1982 Stockholm Conference on Acidification of the Environment." *Environmental Science and Technology.* 17: 15A.

Hileman, Bette. 1983. "Acid Fog." *Environmental Science and Technology* 17(3): 117A–120A.

Hoel, Alf Håkon. 1994. "The Barents Sea: Fisheries Resources for Europe and Russia." Pp. 115–130 in O.S. Stokke and O. Tunander, eds., *The Barents Region: Cooperation in Arctic Europe.* London: Sage Publications.

Hoel, Alf Håkon. 1993. *Researching the Barents Sea Fisheries Resources: Widening the Agenda?* Lysaker: Fridtjof Nansen Institute, note no. 2.

Holdway, P. 1986. "A Circumnavigational Survey of Marine Tarm." *Marine Pollution Bulletin* 17:8 (August): 374–377.

Holsti, K.J. 1971. "Canada and the United States." In S. Spiegel and Kenneth N. Waltz, eds., *Conflict in World Politics.* Cambridge: Winthrop, 375–396.

Holt-Jensen, Arild. 1973. "Acid Rain in Scandinavia." *Ecologist* 3(10): 378–382.

Hønneland, Geir B. 1998. "Autonomy and Regionalisation in the Fisheries Management of Northwestern Russia." *Marine Policy* 22(1): 57–66.

Hønneland, Geir B. 1994. *Regionalisering og autonomi i nordvest-russisk fiskeriforvaltning* (Regionalization and autonomy in northwest Russian fisheries management). Tromsø: NORUT Samfunnsforskning, report no. 30.

Hønneland, Geir B. 1993. *Fiskeren og allmenningen; forvaltning og kontroll. Makt og kommunikasjon i kontrollen med fisket i Barentshavet* (The fisherman and the commons; management and control. Coercion and communication in the control of the Barents Sea fisheries). Tromsø: Hovedoppgave, Institutt for samfunnsvitenskap, University of Tromsø.

Howard, Ross. 1977. "Industrial Pollutants 'Time Bomb' LeBlanc Warns." *Toronto Star.* 21 June, B2.

Howard, Ross, and Michael Perley. 1980. *Acid Rain: The North American Forecast.* Toronto: Anansi.

Howard, Ross, and Michael Perley. 1991. *Poisoned Skies*. Toronto: Stoddart.

Hungary. 1990. Report to the September 1990 UN Meeting on Industrial Co-operation for Air Pollution Control Technology, ECE/UNDP/AP/15/R.5 (29 August).

Hutchinson, T.C., and L.M. Whitby. 1974. "Heavy-Metal Pollution in the Sudbury Mining and Smelting Region of Canada." *Environmental Conservation* 1(2): 123–32.

ICES Cooperative Research Report. annual. Copenhagen: ICES.

IJlstra, Ton. 1989. "Enforcement of MARPOL: Deficient or Impossible." *Marine Pollution Bulletin* 20(12) (December): 596–597.

IMCO, OP/CONF/2. 1961. *Views of Contracting Governments on the Working of the International Convention for the Prevention of Pollution of the Sea by Oil, 1954.* London: IMCO.

IMCO. 1964. *Pollution of the Sea by Oil.* London: Inter-Governmental Maritime Consultative Organization.

IMCO, SCOP I/21. 1965. *"Load-on-Top" System.* London: IMCO.

IMCO. 1968. *Resolution A.153(ES.IV).* London: IMCO.

IMCO. 1973. *Facilities in Ports for the Reception of Oil Residues.* London: IMCO.

IMCO. 1976. *Facilities in Ports for the Reception of Oil Residues.* London: IMCO.

IMCO. 1977. *Resolution A.391(X).* London: IMCO.

IMCO. 1979. *Resolution A.412(XI).* London: IMCO.

IMCO. 1980. *Facilities in Ports for the Reception of Oil Residues.* London: IMCO.

IMCO. 1981. *Resolution A.499(XII).* London: IMCO.

IMO. 1984. *Facilities in Ports for the Reception of Oil Residues.* London: IMO.

IMO. 1989. *Strategy for the Protection of the Marine Environment.* London: IMO.

Insarov, G., and L. Fillipova. 1981. "Model Vlyania Fonovyh Concentraciy Sernistogo Angidrida na Rastenia." *Problemy Ekologicheskogo Monitoringa i Modelirovania Ecosystem.* Leningrad, vol. 4, 235–250.

International Conference on Pollution of the Sea by Oil. 1954. *General Committee: Minutes of 3rd meeting held on 30 April 1954.* London: IMCO.

Izrael, Yu. 1984. *Ekologia i Control Sostoyania Prirodnoy Sredy.* 2d ed., Moscow, Gidrometeoizdat.

Jackson, C. Ian. 1990. "A Tenth Anniversary Review of the ECE Convention on Long-Range Transboundary Air Pollution." *International Environmental Affairs* 2(3): 217–226.

Jacobson, Harold K., and Edith Brown Weiss. 1995. "Strengthening Compliance with International Environmental Accords: Preliminary Observations from a Collaborative Project." *Global Governance* 1: 119–148.

Jørgensen, Henning Peter. 1993. "Interaction between Multispecies Research, Management and Administration." Pp. 17–29 in J.R. Nielsen and T. Helgason, eds., *Multispecies Fisheries Management.* Nordic Council of Ministers, report no. 3.

Junge, C.E., and P.E. Gustafson. 1956. "Precipitation Sampling for Chemical Analysis." *Bulletin of the American Meteorological Society* 37: 244.

Kaitala, V., M. Pohjola, O. Tahvonen. 1991. "An Analysis of SO_2 Negotiations between Finland and the Soviet Union." *Finnish Economic Papers* 14(2).

Keohane, Robert O. 1984. *After Hegemony: Cooperation and Discord in the World Political Economy.* Princeton, NJ: Princeton University Press.

Keohane, Robert O., ed. 1986. *Neorealism and Its Critics.* New York: Columbia University Press.

Khristenko, S.I. 1983. *Transport i okruzhayushchaya sreda (morskie nefteperevozki)* [Transport and the environment (marine oil transportation)]. Kiev: Naukova dumka.

King, Gary, Robert O. Keohane, and Sidney Verba. 1994. *Designing Social Inquiry: Scientific Inference in Qualitative Research.* Princeton: Princeton University Press.

Kirby, J.H. 1965. "Background to progress." *The Shell Magazine* 45(697) (January): 24–27.

Kirby, J.H. 1968. "The Clean Seas Code: A Practical Cure of Operational Pollution." *Oil Pollution of the Sea: Report of Proceedings of the Third International Conference on Oil Pollution of the Sea, Rome, 7–9 October.* Winchester, England: Warren and Son, 201–212.

Korelsky, V. 1993. Main Directions and Modes of Change in the Fisheries of Russia (in Russian). *Rybnoye Khoziastvo* (3): 3–7.

Kotov, V., and E. Nikitina. 1996. "Norilsk Nickel: Russia Wrestles with an Old Polluter." *Environment* 38(9): 6–11.

Kotov V., and E. Nikitina. 1997. "Transboundary Air Pollution: A Problem for Murmansk Oblast." UNDP Project on Environmental Capacity Building, Action Plan for Murmansk Region, report no. 1.

Kowalok, M.E. 1993. "Research Lessons from Acid Rain, Ozone Depletion, and Global Warming." *Environment* 35(6) (July/August): 12–20, 35–38.

Kramer, James. 1973. "Atmospheric Composition and Precipitation of the Sudbury Region." *Alternatives* (spring): 18–25.

Lammers, J. 1991. "The European Approach to Acid Rain." In D. Barstow, ed., *International Law and Pollution.* Philadelphia: Magraw.

Lawes, J.B. 1854. "On the Amount of, and Methods of Estimating Ammonia and Nitric Acid in Rainwater." *British Association Reports:* 70–71.

Lawes, J.B., J.H. Gilbert, and R. Warington. 1883. "New Determinations of Ammonia, Chlorine, and Sulphuric Acid in the Rain Collected at Rothamsted." *Journal of the Royal Agricultural Society* 19: 313–331.

Lee, J.M. 1970. "Pollution Defies Europe's Borders." *The New York Times.* 11 June.

Levy, Marc A. 1993. "European Acid Rain: The Power of Tote-Board Diplomacy." Pp. 75–132 in Peter M. Haas, Robert O. Keohane, and Marc A. Levy, eds., *Institutions for the Earth.* Cambridge: MIT Press.

Levy, Marc A., Oran R. Young, and Michael Zürn. 1995. "The Study of International Regimes." *European Journal of International Relations.* 1 (September): 267–330.

Levy, Marc A. 1991a. "SO_x, NO_x, and Talks: The Role of International Institutions in Reducing European Acid Rain." Manuscript, Harvard University.

Levy, Marc A. 1991b. "The Greening of the United Kingdom: Assessing Competing Explanations." Paper presented to annual meeting of American Political Science Association, Washington, DC.

Levy, Marc A. 1993. "East-West Environmental Politics after 1989." In Stanley Hoffmann, Robert O. Keohane, and Joseph P. Nye, Jr., *After the Cold War: International Institutions and State Strategies in Europe, 1989–91.* Cambridge: Harvard University Press, 310–341.

Levy, Marc A. 1995. "International Cooperation to Combat Acid Rain." *Green Globe Yearbook* 4: 59–68.

Lewis, Drew, and William Davis. 1986. *Joint Report of the Special Envoys on Acid Rain.* Washington and Ottawa, January.

Likens, G.E., and F.H. Bormann. 1974. "Acid Rain: A Serious Regional Environmental Problem." *Science* 84: 1176–1179.

Likens, G.E., F.H. Bormann, and N.M. Johnson. 1972. "Acid Rain." *Environment* 14(1): 33–39.

Likens, G.E., Richard F. Wright, James Galloway, and Thomas J. Butler. 1979. "Acid Rain." *Scientific American* 241(4): 43–51.

Lipschutz, Ronnie. 1996. *Global Civil Society and Global Environmental Change.* Albany, NY: SUNY Press.

Litfin, Karen T. 1994. *Ozone Discourses: Science and Politics in Global Environmental Cooperation.* New York: Columbia University Press.

Lumme, E. 1992. "Acidification Policy in Finland." In T. Schneider, ed., *Acidification Research, Evaluation, and Policy Applications.* Amsterdam: Elsevier Science Publications, 185–188.

Luoma, J.R., and J. Shaw. 1987. "Forests Are Dying, but Is Acid Rain to Blame?" *Audubon* 89(2): 36.

Luzin, G.P., ed. 1992. *Social and Economic Development of the Murmansk Area in the Period of Transition: Current State and Forecasts.* Apatity: Kola Science Center, RAN.

M'Gonigle, R. Michael, and Mark W. Zacher. 1979. *Pollution, Politics, and International Law: Tankers at Sea.* Berkeley: University of California Press.

MARPOL 73/78. 1978. "International Convention for the Prevention of Pollution from Ships (2 November 1973)." Reprinted in 12 I.L.M. 1319 (1973), 2 I.P.E. 552, and "Protocol of 1978 relating to the International Convention for the Prevention of Pollution from Ships (17 February 1978)." Reprinted in 17 I.L.M. 1546 (1978), 19 I.P.E. 9451.

Matishov, G. 1992. *Anthropogenic Destruction of the Ecosystems of the Barents and Norwegian Seas* (in Russian). Apatity: Murmansk Marine Biology Institute, Kola Science Center.

Matishov, G. 1989. *Ecologicheskaya situacia i problemy okhrani bioresursov v moriakh severnoi Evropy, na primere Barentseva moria* (Ecological situation and problems of protection of biological resources of the North European Seas: The Barents Sea case). Apatity: Murmansk Marine Biology Institute, Kola Science Center.

McCormick, J. 1989. *Acid Earth: The Global Threat of Acid Pollution.* 2d ed. London: Earthscan.

McGinnis, Michael, and Elinor Ostrom. 1992. "Design Principles for Local and Global Commons." Paper presented in Bloomington, Indiana. April 23–25.

McKenzie, Arthur. 1978. *Letter to the Honorable John L. Burton.* Ed. by U.S. Congress, House Committee on Government Operations, Government Activities and Transportation Subcommittee. 95th Cong., 2d sess. Washington, DC: GPO.

McLoughlin, James, and M.J. Forster. 1982. *The Law and Practice Relating to Pollution Control in the Member States of the European Communities: A Comparative Survey.* London: Graham & Trotman.

McMahon, Michael S. 1988. "Balancing the Interests: An Essay on the Canadian–American Acid Rain Debate." Pp. 147–171 in John E. Carroll, ed., *International Environmental Diplomacy.* New York: Cambridge Press.

Mearsheimer, John. 1994–1995. "The False Promise of International Institutions." *International Security* 19: 5–49.

Mendelsohn, Robert, and Guy Orcutt. 1979. "An Empirical Analysis of Air Pollution Dose-Response Curves." *Journal of Environmental Health and Management* 6: 85–106.

MEPC, V/Inf.A. 1976. "Report on SBT and COW Usage." (27 April).

MEPC, VIII/17. 1977. "Reception Facilities." (14 December).

MEPC, IX/11/1. 1978. "U.S. Airborne Oil Surveillance System." (2 March).

MEPC, XI/14. 1979. "Report on the Feasibility Study on Reception Facilities for Selected Ports in a Special Area—Mediterranean." (April 25).

MEPC, XII/14. 1980. "Report of the Secretary-General." (3 January).

MEPC, XVI/Inf.2. 1981. "Petroleum in the Marine Environment: Inputs of Petroleum Hydrocarbon into the Ocean Due to Marine Transportation Activities." (November).

MEPC, 19/5/1. 1983a. "Provision of Reception Facilities: Reception Facilities in the Mediterranean." (7 October).

MEPC, 19/5/2. 1983b. "Questionnaire on the Adequacy of Facilities in Ports for the Reception of Oil Residues from Ships: Summary of Replies." (21 October).

MEPC, 20/19. 1984. "Responses from Brazil, Iceland, FRG, GDR, Norway, and the USSR on Inadequate Reception Facilities in Other States." (24 September).

MEPC, 22/8/2. 1985. "Questionnaire on the Adequacy of Facilities in Ports for the Reception of Oil Residues from Ships: Summary of Replies." (8 October).

MEPC, 26/Inf.23. 1988. "Provision of Reception Facilities." (5 August).

MEPC, 27/15/2. 1989a. "Intensified Control on Operational Requirements under MARPOL Annexes I and II." (3 February).

MEPC, 27/5/4. 1989c. "Provision of Reception Facilities: Reception Facilities and Recycling of Oily Wastes in the Marine Industry." (15 February).

MEPC, 30/17. 1990a. "Enforcement of Pollution Conventions: Violations of Conventions and Penalties Imposed." (20 July).

MEPC, Circ.234. 1990b. "Facilities in Ports for the Reception of Oil Residues." (13 August).

MEPC, 30/Inf.13. 1990c. "Petroleum in the Marine Environment: Update of Inputs of Petroleum Hydrocarbon into the Oceans Due to Maritime Transportation Activities." (19 September).

MEPC, 30/Inf.30. 1990d. "Questionnaire on the Adequacy of Facilities in Ports for the Reception of Oil Residues from Ships: Summary of Replies." (15 October).

MEPC, 32/14. 1991a. "Enforcement of Pollution Conventions: Violations of Conventions and Penalties Imposed." (13 November).

MEPC, 31/8/5. 1991b. "Oil Tanker Design and Pollution Prevention." (4 April).

MEPC, 32/10. 1991c. "Provision of Reception Facilities: Guidelines for the Provision of Reception Facilities for Oily Wastes." (15 August).

MEPC, 31/5/1. 1991d. "Uniform Interpretation and Amendments to MARPOL 73/78." (4 April).

MEPC, 38/Inf.22 1996. "Provision of Reception Facilities: Reception Facilities for Tankers, Submitted by INTERTANKO." (3 May).

M'Gonigle, R. Michael, and Mark W. Zacher. 1979. *Pollution, Politics, and International Law: Tankers at Sea.* Berkeley, CA: University of California Press.

Miles, Edward et al. Forthcoming. *Explaining Regime Effectiveness: Confronting Theory with Evidence.* Cambridge: MIT Press.

Mitchell, Ronald B. 1994. *Intentional Oil Pollution at Sea: Environmental Policy and Treaty Compliance.* Cambridge: MIT Press.

Mitchell, Ronald B. 1996. "Strategies of International Social Control: Changing Incentives, Opportunities, or Values." Paper presented at the annual meeting of the International Studies Association in San Diego, CA. 18–20 April.

Mitchell, Ronald B. 1997. "International Control of Nuclear Proliferation: Beyond Carrots and Sticks." *The Nonproliferation Review* 5:1 (fall): 40–52.

Mitchell, Ronald B. 1998a. "Adversarial and Facilitative Approaches to on Site Inspection in Arms Control and Environmental Regimes." Paper presented at the annual convention of the International Studies Association, March 1998.

Mitchell, Ronald B. 1998b. "Sources of Transparency: Information Systems in International Regimes." *International Studies Quarterly* 42(1) (March): 109–130.

Mitchell, Ronald B. 1999. "International Environmental Common Pool Resources: More Common than Domestic but More Difficult to Manage." In J. Samuel Barkin and George Shambaugh, ed., *Anarchy and the Environment: The International Relations of Common Pool Resources.* Albany, NY: SUNY Press.

Moguilevkin, I.M. 1982. *Biznes i more: Morskaya torgovlya i sudokhodstvo pri kapitalizme* (Business and the sea: Marine commerce and shipping under capitalism). Moscow: Mysl.

Moldan, Bedrich, et al. 1991. *Environmental Recovery Program for the Czech Republic.* Prague: Academia.

Montfort, C.L. 1984. "Presentation of the Outcome of the IMO/UNEP Feasibility Study on Reception Facilities in a Special Area—Mediterranean (1979)." Proceedings of IMO/UNDP international seminar on reception facilities for wastes. London: IMO/UNDP.

Moss, James E. 1963. *Character and Control of Sea Pollution by Oil.* Washington, DC: American Petroleum Institute, Division of Transportation.

Munton, Don. 1981. "Acid Rain and Basic Politics." *Alternatives* 10 (spring-summer): 21–28.

Munton, Don. 1980–81. "Dependence and Interdependence in Transboundary Environmental Relations." *International Journal* 36(1) (winter): 139–184.

Munton, Don. 1983. "Life, Liberty, and the American Pursuit of Acid Rain." *Alternatives* 11(2) (winter): 13–20.

Munton, Don. 1998. "Dispelling the Myths of the Acid Rain Story." *Environment* 40 (July/August), 4–7, 27–34.

Murray, Keith A. 1972. "The Trail Smelter Case: International Air Pollution in the Columbia Valley." *BC Studies* 15: 68–85.

Nagel, Ernest. 1961. *The Structure of Science: Problems in the Logic of Scientific Explanation.* New York: Harcourt, Brace and World.

National Academy of Sciences (NAS). 1975. *Petroleum in the Marine Environment.* Washington, DC: National Academy of Sciences.

National Academy of Sciences. 1981. *Atmosphere-Biosphere Interactions: Toward a Better Understanding of the Ecological Consequences of Fossil Fuel Combustion.* Washington, DC: National Academy Press.

National Academy of Sciences. 1983. *Acid Deposition: Atmospheric Processes in Eastern North America.* Washington, DC: National Academy Press.

National Academy of Sciences. 1985. *Acid Deposition: Effects on Geochemical Cycling and Biological Availability of Trace Elements.* Washington, DC: National Academy Press.

National Academy of Sciences, 1986. *Acid Deposition: Long-Term Trends.* Washington, DC: National Academy Press.

National Academy of Sciences and National Research Council (NAS/NRC). 1985. *Oil in the Sea: Inputs, Fates, and Effects.* Washington, DC: National Academy Press.

National Research Council of Canada. 1939. *Effects of Sulphur Dioxide on Vegetation.* no. 815, Ottawa.

Nikitina, E. 1991. "New Soviet Environmental Policy: Approaches to Global Change." *International Studies Notes* 16(1).

Nikitina, E. 1992. "Perestroika: How It Affects Soviet Participation in Environmental Cooperation." In M. Stewart, ed., *The Soviet Environment: Problems, Policies, and Politics.* Cambridge: Cambridge University Press.

Nikitina, Elena N., and Peter H. Pearse. 1992. "Conservation of Marine Resources in the Former Soviet Union: An Environmental Perspective." *Ocean Development and International Law* 23: 369–382.

Nilsson, J., and P. Grennfelt. 1988. *Critical Loads for Sulphur and Nitrogen.* Report from a UN-ECE and Nordic Council of Ministers workshop, Skokloster, Sweden, March 1988.

Norse, Elliott A., ed. 1993. *Global Marine Biological Diversity: A Strategy for Building Conservation into Decision Making.* Washington, DC: Island Press.

Norwegian Institute for Water Research. 1997. *The Nine Year Report: Acidification of Surface Water in Europe and North America—Long-Term Developments (1980s and 1990s).* Convention on Long-Range Transboundary Air Pollution, International Cooperative Program on Assessment and Monitoring of Acidification of Rivers and Lakes, Oslo, 1997.

Nye, Joseph S. 1987. "Nuclear Learning and U.S.–Soviet Security Regimes." *International Organization* 41 (summer): 371–402.

Obzor Zagriaznenia. 1991. *Okruizhauishei Prirodnoy Sredy v SSSR.* Moscow, Gidrometeoizdat.

Odén, Svante. 1967. *Dagens Nyheter.* 24 October.

Odén, Svante. 1968. "Acidification of Air Precipitation and its Consequences on the Natural Environment" (title translated from the Swedish). bulletin no. 1, *Ekologikommitten Statens Naturvetenskapliga Forskeningsrad.* Stockholm.

Odén, Svante. 1976. "The Acidity Problem—An Outline of Concepts." *Water, Air, and Soil Pollution* 6: 137–166.

OILPOL 54. 1954. "International Convention for the Prevention of Pollution of the Sea by Oil (12 May 1954)." Reprinted in 12 U.S.T. 2989, T.I.A.S. No. 4900, 327 U.N.T.S. 3 reprinted in 1 I.P.E. 332.

OILPOL 54/62. 1962. "1962 Amendments to the International Convention for the Prevention of Pollution of the Sea by Oil (11 April 1962)." Reprinted in 17 U.S.T. 1523, T.I.A.S. No. 6109, 600 U.N.T.S. 332 reprinted in 1 I.P.E. 346.

OILPOL 54/69. 1969. "1969 Amendments to the International Convention for the Prevention of Pollution of the Sea by Oil (21 October 1969)." Reprinted in 28 U.S.T. 1205, T.I.A.S. No. 8505 reprinted in 9 I.L.M. 1 and 1 I.P.E. 366.

Okidi, Charles Odidi. 1978. *Regional Control of Ocean Pollution: Legal and Institutional Problems and Prospects.* Alphen aan den Rijn, The Netherlands: Sijthoff and Noordhoff.

Olson, Mancur. 1965. *The Logic of Collective Action: Public Goods and the Theory of Groups.* Cambridge, MA: Harvard University Press.

O'Neil, William A. 1990. "In Defence of the Oceans." *Horizon* 1 (November): 1–8.

Organization for Economic Cooperation and Development. 1972. *Cooperative Technical Programme to Measure the Long-Range Transport of Air Pollutants.* Paris, OECD Environment Directorate.

Organization for Economic Cooperation and Development. 1977. *The OECD Programme on Long-Range Transport of Air Pollutants,* Paris.

Organization for Economic Cooperation and Development. 1977. *Control Strategies for the Long-Range Transport of Sulphur Compounds.* Paris, OECD Environment Directorate, ENV/AIR/77.13.

Organization for Economic Cooperation and Development. 1977. *Transfrontier Pollution of the Atmosphere by Sulphur Dioxide in the Context of the Recommendations of the OECD.* Paris, OECD Environment Directorate, ENV/AIR77.17.

Osborne, M.G., and J.M. Ferguson. 1990. "Technology, MARPOL, and Tankers—Successes and Failures." *IMAS 90: Marine Technology and the Environment.* London: Institute of Marine Engineers, 55–62.

Ostrom, Elinor. 1998. "A Behavioral Approach to the Rational-Choice Theory of Collective Action." *American Political Science Review* 92: 1–22.

Ostrom, Elinor. 1990. *Governing the Commons: The Evolution of Institutions for Collective Action.* Cambridge: Cambridge University Press.

Ostrom, Elinor, Roy Gardner, and James Walker. 1994. *Rules, Games, and Common-Pool Resources*. Ann Arbor: University of Michigan Press.

Ottar, Brynjulf. 1977. "International Agreement Needed to Reduce Long-Range Transport of Air Pollutants in Europe." *Ambio* 6(5): 262–269.

Ottar, Brynjulf. 1976. "Organization of Long-Range Transport of Air Pollution Monitoring in Europe." *Water, Air and Soil Pollution* 6: 219–229.

Oye, Kenneth A. 1986. "Explaining Cooperation under Anarchy: Hypotheses and Strategies." Pp. 1–24 in Kenneth A. Oye, ed., *Cooperation under Anarchy*. Princeton: Princeton University Press.

Parson, Edward A., and Owen Greene. 1995. "The Complex Chemistry of the International Ozone Agreements." *Environment* 37 (March): 16–20 and 35–43.

Parson, Edward A. 1993. "Protecting the Ozone Layer." Pp 27–74 in Peter Haas et al., *Institutions for the Earth: Sources of Effective International Environmental Protection*. Cambridge: MIT Press, 27–74.

Patin, S. A. 1979. *Vliyanie zagryazneniya na biologicheskie resursy i produktivnost' Mirovogo okeana* (Pollution impact on the biological resources and productivity of the World's oceans). Moscow: Pishchevaya promyshlennost.

Pearson, Charles S. 1975. *International Marine Environmental Policy: The Economic Dimension*. Baltimore, MD: Johns Hopkins University Press.

Peet, Gerard. 1992. *Operational Discharges from Ships: An Evaluation of the Application of the Discharge Provisions of the MARPOL Convention by its Contracting Parties*. Amsterdam, The Netherlands: AIDEnvironment.

Peterson, M.J. 1993. "International Fisheries Management." Pp. 249–305 in Peter M. Haas, Robert O. Keohane, and Marc A. Levy, eds., *Institutions for the Earth*. Cambridge: MIT Press, 1993.

Placci, C. 1984. "Report on the European Economic Commission/ENI-Snamprogetti (Italy) Technical and Economic Study on the Installation of Ballast Water Treatment Facilities at Mediterranean Ports and Oil Terminals." Proceedings of IMO/UNDP international seminar on reception facilities for wastes. London: IMO/UNDP.

Plaza, Fernando. 1997. "Port State Control: An Update." *IMO News* 4 (1997): 30–34.

Poland, Ministry of Environmental Protection, Natural Resources and Forestry. 1990. *National Environmental Policy*. Warsaw.

Powles, D. 1984. "Charter Party Provisions Applicable to Tankers Engaged in Trades Where Deballasting Facilities Are Not Available." Proceedings of IMO/UNDP international seminar on reception facilities for wastes. London: IMO/UNDP.

Primakov, E.M., ed. 1986. *Mirovoi okean: Ekonomika i politika (mezhdunarodnye problemy osvoeniya)* (The world's oceans: Economics and politics; international problems of development). Moscow: Mysl.

Pritchard, S.Z. 1978. "Load on Top: From the Sublime to the Absurd." *Journal of Maritime Law and Commerce* 9:2 (January): 185–224.

Pritchard, Sonia Zaide. 1987. *Oil Pollution Control*. London: Croom Helm.

Putnam, Robert D. 1988. "Diplomacy and Domestic Politics: The Logic of Two-Level Games." *International Organization* 42 (summer): 427–460.

Raymond, Gregory A. 1997. "Problems and Prospects in the Study of International Norms." *Mershon International Studies Review* 41: 205–245.

Read, John. 1963. "The Trail Smelter Dispute." *Canadian Yearbook of International Law*, vol. 1.

Regens, James, and Robert Rycroft. 1988. *The Acid Rain Controversy*. Pittsburgh: University of Pittsburgh Press.

Regional Marine Pollution Emergency Response Centre for the Mediterranean Sea. 1991. "Review of the Current Situation Concerning Reception Facilities for Ship-Generated Wastes in Mediterranean Ports (REMPEC/WG.3/Inf.5)." (7 November).

Reiss, Albert J., Jr. 1984. "Consequences of Compliance and Deterrence Models of Law Enforcement for the Exercise of Police Discretion." *Law and Contemporary Problems* 47:4 (fall): 83–122.

Rittberger, Volker, ed. 1993. *Regime Theory and International Relations*. Oxford: Oxford University Press.

Roberts, L. 1987. "Federal Report on Acid Rain Draws Criticism." *Science* 237: 1404–1406.

Robinson, Raymond M. 1982. "The Rule of Law Between Nations—An Acid Test." Address to National Academy of Sciences, Seventh Symposium on Statistics and the Environment, Washington, DC, 4–5 October.

Rosenau, James N., and Ernst-Otto Czempiel, eds. 1992. *Governance without Government: Order and Change in World Politics*. Cambridge: Cambridge University Press.

Sadler, P.G., and J. King. 1990. *Study on Mechanisms for the Financing of Facilities in Ports for the Reception of Wastes from Ships*. Cardiff, Wales: University College of Wales, Cardiff.

Sahrhage, Dietrich. 1989. "The Role of Science in International Management of Fish Resources." Pp. 207–220 in S. Andresen and W. Østreng, eds., *International Resource Management: The Role of Science and Politics*. London: Belhaven Press.

Sandler, Todd. 1997. *Global Challenges: An Approach to Environmental, Political, and Economic Problems*. Cambridge: Cambridge University Press.

Sasamura, Y. 1984. "Summary of the requirements of MARPOL 73/78, with Particular Reference to Reception Facilities in Ports," in *Proceedings of IMO/UNDP international seminar on reception facilities for wastes*. London: IMO/UNDP.

Sasamura, Y. 1990. "Oil in the Marine Environment." In *IMAS 90: Marine Technology and the Environment.* London: Institute of Marine Engineers, 27–32.

Schindler, D.W. et al. 1985. "Long-Term Ecosystem Stress: The Effects of Years of Experimental Acidification on a Small Lake." *Science* 228 (21 June): 1395–1401.

Schindler, D.W. et al. 1986. "Natural Sources of Acid Neutralizing Capacity in Low Alkalinity Lakes of the Precambrian Shield." *Science* 232 (16 May): 844–847.

Schindler, D.W. 1988. "Effects of Acid Rain on Freshwater Ecosystems." *Science* 239 (8 January): 149–157.

Schindler, D.W. et al. 1989. "Biological Impoverishment in Lakes of the Midwestern and Northeastern United States from Acid Rain." *Environmental Science and Technology* 23(5): 573–580.

Schmandt, Jurgen, and Hillilard Roderick, eds. 1985. *Acid Rain and Friendly Neighbors: The Policy Dispute between Canada and the United States.* Durham: Duke University Press.

Schofield, C.L. 1965. "Water Quality in Relation to Survival of Brook Trout, Salvelinus Fontinalis." *Transactions of the American Fisheries Society* 94(3): 227–235.

Schofield, C.L. 1976. "Acid Precipitation: Effects on Fish." *Ambio* 5: 228–230.

Schutt, P., and E.B. Cowling. 1985. "Waldsterben, a General Decline of Forests in Central Europe: Symptoms, Development, and Possible Causes." *Plant Disease* 69(7): 548–558.

Scott, W. Richard. 1995. *Institutions and Organizations.* Thousand Oaks, CA: Sage Publications.

Second International Conference on the Protection of the North Sea. 1987. *Quality Status of the North Sea: A Report by the Scientific and Technical Working Group.* London: Her Majesty's Stationery Office.

Secretariat of the Memorandum of Understanding on Port State Control. 1992. *Annual Report 1992.* The Hague, The Netherlands: The Netherlands Government Printing Office.

Shaw, Roderick. 1993. "Acid Rain Negotiations in North America and Europe: A Study in Contrast." In Gunnar Sjöstadt, ed., *International Environmental Negotiation.* Sage, London.

Sherman, Kenneth. 1992. "Large Marine Ecosystems." In *Encyclopedia of Earth System Science,* vol. 2. New York: Academic Press, 653–673.

Shutt, Frank T. 1910. "The Nitrogen Compounds in Rain and Snow." Transactions of the Royal Society of Canada, vol. VIII (III): 83–87.

Shutt, Frank T., and R.L. Dorrance. 1917. "The Nitrogen Compounds in Rain and Snow." Transactions of the Royal Society of Canada, vol. XI (III): 63–72.

Shutt, Frank T., and B. Hedley. 1925. "The Nitrogen Compounds in Rain and Snow." Transactions of the Royal Society of Canada, vol. XIX (III): 1–10.

Shmiganovsky, V. 1990. "Milliardy na Ekologiy." *Izvestia.* 10 October.

Simonov, A.I., ed. 1984. *Obzor sostoyaniya khimicheskogo zagryazneniya otdel'nykh raionov Mirovogo okeana za period 1980 1982* (Review of the state of chemical pollution in the selected areas of the world's oceans during the period of 1980–1982). Moscow: State Oceanographic Institute.

Simonov, A.I., and I.G. Orlova, eds. 1987. *Obzor sostoyaniya khimicheskogo zagryazneniya otdel'nykh raionov Mirovogo okeana za period 1983 1985* (Review of the state of chemical pollution in the selected areas of the world's oceans during the period of 1983–1985). Moscow: State Oceanographic Institute.

Simonov, A.I., and I.G. Orlova, eds. 1989. *Obzor sostoyaniya khimicheskogo zagryazneniya otdel'nykh raionov Mirovogo okeana za period 1986–1988* (Review of the state of chemical pollution in the selected areas of the world's oceans during the period of 1986–1988). Moscow: State Oceanographic Institute.

Smith, Robert Angus. 1852. "On the Air and Rain of Manchester." Memoirs of the Literary and Philosophical Society of Manchester, Second Series, volume tenth [sic], London, 207–217.

Smith, Robert Angus. 1872. *Air and Rain: The Beginnings of a Chemical Climatology.* London: Longmans, Green.

Smith, R.J. and S. Biniaz. 1991. "Beyond Dispute: An Air Quality Agreement in the Context of a Consultative Relationship." *Canada–United States Law Journal* 17: 421–429.

Smith, S.R., and A.H. Knap. 1985. "Significant Decrease in the Amount of Tar Stranding on Bermuda." *Marine Pollution Bulletin* 16(1) (January): 19–22.

Smit-Kroes, N. 1988. "Harmonisatie Noordzeebeleid: brief van de Minister van Verkeer en Waterstaat." *Tweede Kamer der Staten-Generaal* 17–408(43) (23 September): 1–6.

Snidal, Duncan. 1985. "The Limits of Hegemonic Stability Theory." *International Organization* 39(4) (autumn), 579–614.

Soroos, Marvin. 1993. "Arctic Haze and Transboundary Air Pollution." In Gail Osherenko and Oran Young, eds., *Polar Politics.* Ithaca, NY: Cornell University Press, 186–222.

Soroos, Marvin. 1997. *The Endangered Atmosphere: Preserving a Global Commons.* Columbia: University of South Carolina Press.

Soybe, Helen K. 1988. "Strange Attitude on Nitrogen Emissions." *Acid News* 1 (February).

Statistisk årbok. 1992. Annual. (Statistical yearbook). Oslo: Statistisk sentralbyrå (Statistics Norway).

Stokke, Olav Schram. 1996. "The Effectiveness of CCAMLR." In O.S. Stokke and D. Vidas, eds., *Governing the Antarctic: The Effectiveness and Legitimacy of the Antarctic Treaty System.* Cambridge: Cambridge University Press.

Stokke, Olav Schram. 1994. *Beauty and the Beast? Norway, Russia, and the Northern Environment*. Lysaker: Fridtjof Nansen Institute, report no. 1.

Stokke, Olav Schram. 1992. "Towards a Regional Fisheries Industry?" *International Challenges* 12(4).

Stokke, Olav Schram, and Alf Hakon Hoel. 1991. "Splitting the Gains: Political Economy of the Barents Sea Fisheries." *Conflict and Cooperation* 29: 49–65.

Stokke, Olav Schram, and Ola Tunander, eds. 1994. *The Barents Region: Cooperation in Arctic Europe*. London: Sage Publications.

Strange, Susan. 1983. "*Cave! hic dragones:* A Critique of Regime Analysis." Pp. 337–354 in Stephen D. Krasner, ed., *International Regimes*. Ithaca: Cornell University Press.

Summers, P., and D.M. Whelpdale. 1976. "Acid Precipitation in Canada." *Water, Air, and Soil Pollution* 6: 447–455.

Sutton, C.T. 1964. "The Problem of Preventing Pollution of the Sea by Oil." *BP Magazine* 14 (winter), 8–12.

Sweden, Preparatory Committee for the United Nations Conference. 1971. *Air Pollution Across National Boundaries: The Impact on the Environment of Sulphur in Air and Precipitation*. Stockholm.

Sweden. 1972. "Sulphur Pollution Across National Boundaries." *Ambio* 1(1): 15–20.

Tennberg, M., and T. Vaahtoranta. 1991. "Finland's Environmental Foreign Policy." In E. Liukkonen and M. Tennberg, eds., *Global Change and Finland: Seminar Report*. Helsinki, Finnish Institute of Foreign Affairs, 1991, 1–28.

Tetlock, Philip E., and Aaron Belkin, eds. 1996. *Counterfactual Thought Experiments in World Politics: Logical, Methodological, and Psychological Perspectives*. Princeton: Princeton University Press.

Toronto Star. 1985. "PM Decries Our Record on Acid Rain." 2 February, p. A3.

Tjelmeland, Sigurd. 1988. Fleirbestandsforskinga ved Havforskingsinstituttet— ei orientering (Multispecies research at the Institute of Marine Research—an orientation). *Fiskets Gang* 74(14–15): 5–9.

Tjelmeland, Sigurd (interview). 1992. *NFFR-Nytt*, 10, 6–7. Oslo/Trondheim: NFR/Research Council of Norway, 1992.

Tovalop. 1969. "Tanker Owners Voluntary Agreement Concerning Liability for Oil Pollution (7 January 1969)." Reprinted in 8 I.L.M. 497 (1969).

Trail Smelter Arbitral Tribunal. 1941. "Decision. Reported on March 11, 1941, to the Government of the United States of America and the Dominion of Canada, under the Convention signed April 15, 1935." *American Journal of International Law*: 684–734.

Tye, Larry. 1983. "U.S., Once a Leader, Trails Europe in Acid-Rain Action." Kentucky *Courier Journal*. 19 September.

Ulrich, B., R. Mayer, and P.K. Khanna. 1979. Deposition von Luftverunreinigungen und ihre Auswirkungen in Waldökosystemen im Solling. Schriften Forstl. Fak. Universität Gottingen, Sauerlander Verlag Frankfurt.

Underdal. Arild. 1998. "Explaining Compliance and Defection: Three Models." *European Journal of International Relations* 3: 5–30.

United Kingdom. 1990. *This Common Inheritance: Britain's Environmental Strategy.* Cm 1200. London: HMSO, September.

United Kingdom, Ministry of Transport. 1953. *Report of the Committee on the Prevention of Pollution of the Sea by Oil.* London: Her Majesty's Stationery Office.

United Kingdom, Royal Commission On Environmental Pollution. 1981. *Eighth Report: Oil Pollution of the Sea.* London: Her Majesty's Stationery Office.

United Nations, A/Conf.151/PC/103. 1992. "Survey of Existing Agreements and Instruments and Its Follow-up." (20 January).

United Nations, Economic Commission for Europe. 1989. *The State of Transboundary Air Pollution: Effects and Control.* Air Pollution Studies 5, Geneva, ECE/EB.AIR/22.

United Nations, Economic Commission for Europe, Working Group on Effects. 1989. "Effects of Some Heavy Metals Related to Long-Range Atmospheric Transport." Geneva, 26 April.

United Nations, Economic Commission for Europe and European Commission. 1997. *Ten Years of Monitoring Forest Condition in Europe.* Federal Research Centre for Forestry and Forest Products.

United Nations, Secretariat. 1956. *Pollution of the Sea by Oil.* New York: United Nations.

United States Congress. 1980. House Committee on Merchant Marine and Fisheries. 96th Cong., 2d sess. 1980. *Hearings on Protocol of 1978 Relating to the International Convention for the Prevention of Pollution from Ships, with Annexes and Protocols: Report to accompany H.R. 6665.* Washington, DC: GPO.

United States Congress. 1963. Senate. 88th Cong., 1st sess. 1963. *Message from the President: Amendments of the International Convention for the Prevention of Pollution of the Sea by Oil, 1954.* Washington, DC: GPO.

United States, Department of Interior. 1915. *Report of Selby Smelter Commission.* Bulletin 98.

United States, National Acid Precipitation Assessment Program (NAPAP). 1987. *Interim Assessment: The Causes and Effects of Acidic Deposition.* Washington, DC.

United States, Office of Science and Technology Policy. 1984. *Report of the Acid Rain Peer Review Panel.* William A. Nierenberg, Chairman. Washington DC.

United States Congress, Office of Technology Assessment. 1984. *Acid Rain and Transported Air Pollutants: Implications for Public Policy.* Washington, DC, OTA-O-204, June.

United States–Canada, Memorandum of Intent on Transboundary Air Pollution. 1983. "Executive Summaries, Work Group Reports." February.

UNLOSC (United Nations Law of the Sea Convention). 1982. UN doc. A/CONF.62/122; reprinted in International Legal Materials, vol. 21, 1982, 1261.

Vanhaecke, P. 1990. *Verontreiniging door schepen*. Antwerp, Belgium: ECOLAS (Environmental Consultancy and Assistance).

Varnavsky, V., B. Gromov, and J. Kovyliansky. 1989. "Teplofikacia i ee Rol v Reshenii Socialnyh i Ekologicheskih problem." *Elektricheskie Stancii* 8: 38–40.

Victor, David G., Kal Raustiala, and Eugene Skolnikoff, eds. 1998. *The Implementation and Effectiveness of International Environmental Commitments*. Cambridge: MIT Press.

W.W. Heck, O.C. Taylor, and D.T. Tingey, eds. 1987. *Assessment of Crop Loss from Air Pollutants*. London: Elsevier Applied Science. Proceedings of an international conference, Raleigh, NC.

Wapner, Paul. 1996. *Environmental Activism and World Civic Politics*. Albany, NY: SUNY Press.

Wardley-Smith, Jeffrey. 1969. "United Kingdom Ministry of Technology Work on Oil Pollution." Paper presented at the American Petroleum Institute's Joint Conference on Prevention and Control of Oil Spills in New York, 15–17 December.

Wardley-Smith, Jeffrey, ed. 1983. *The Control of Oil Pollution*. London: Graham and Trotman Publishers.

Waters, William G., Trevor D. Heaver, and T. Verrier. 1980. *Oil Pollution from Tanker Operations—Causes, Costs, Controls*. Vancouver, BC: Center for Transportation Studies.

Weiss, Edith Brown, and Harold K. Jacobson, eds. 1998. *Engaging Countries: Strengthening Compliance with International Environmental Accords*. Cambridge: MIT Press.

Weller, Phil, and the Waterloo Public Interest Research Group. 1980. *Acid Rain: The Silent Crisis*. Kitchener, Ontario: Between the Lines.

Wendt, Alexander. 1992. "Anarchy is What States Make of It: The Social Construction of Power Politics." *International Organization* 46: 391–425.

Wendt, Alexander. 1994. "Collective Identity Formation and the International State." *American Political Science Review* 88: 384–396.

Wetstone, Gregory, and Armin Rosencranz. 1983. *Acid Rain in Europe and North America: National Responses to an International Problem*. Washington, DC: Environmental Law Institute.

Wettestad, Jørgen, and Steinar Andresen. 1991. *The Effectiveness of International Resource Cooperation: Some Preliminary Findings*. Oslo: Fridtjof Nansen Institute.

Woodman, J.N., and E.B. Cowling. 1987. "Airborne Chemicals and Forest Health." *Environmental Science and Technology* 21(2): 20–126.

Yanarella, Ernest J., and Randal H. Ihara. 1985. *The Acid Rain Debate: Scientific, Economic, and Political Dimensions.* Boulder, CO: Westview Press.

Young, Oran R., and Konrad von Moltke. 1994. "The Consequences of International Environmental Regimes: Report from the Barcelona Workshop." *International Environmental Affairs* 6: 348–370.

Young, Oran R. 1992. "The Effectiveness of International Institutions: Hard Cases and Critical Variables." Pp. 160–194 in James N. Rosenau and Ernst-Otto Czempiel, eds., *Governance without Government: Order and Change in World Politics.* Cambridge: Cambridge University Press.

Young, Oran R. 1989. *International Cooperation: Building Regimes for Natural Resources and the Environment.* Ithaca, NY: Cornell University Press.

Young, Oran R. 1994. *International Governance: Protecting the Environment in a Stateless Society.* Ithaca, NY: Cornell University Press.

Young, Oran R., ed. 1997. *Global Governance: Drawing Insights from the Environmental Experience.* Cambridge: MIT Press.

Young, Oran R. 1991. "Political Leadership and Regime Formation: On the Development of Institutions in International Society." *International Organization* 45 (summer): 281–308.

Young, Oran R. 1989. "The Politics of Regime Formation." *International Organization* 43(3): 349–376.

Young, Oran 1983. "Regime Dynamics: The Rise and Fall of International Regimes." In Stephen D. Krasner, ed., *International Regimes.* Ithaca, NY: Cornell University Press, 93–113.

Zacher, Mark. 1978. "Testimony." In *Oil Tanker Pollution—Hearings.* ed. U.S. Cong., House Committee on Government Operations, Government Activities and Transportation Subcommittee. 95th Cong., 2d sess. Washington, DC: GPO.

Zilanov, K.V., S. Kovalyov, and G. Luka. 1991. "PINRO and Scientific Cooperation With Foreign Countries (in Russian)." Pp. 44–52 in *Complex Fishery Research of the PINRO* (in Russian). Murmansk: PINRO.

Zilanov, Viatcheslav K. 1988. "Edinstvo ekologicheskogo kompleksa severnych morei kak osnova razvitiia sotrydnichestwa Sovetskogo Soyuza i Norvegii v oblasti sokhranenia i optimalnogo ispolzovania morskikh jivykh resursov" (The unity of environmental complex of northern seas as the basis for developing cooperation in conservation and optimal utilization of marine living resources between the Soviet Union and Norway), in *Voprosy sotrudnichestwa SSSR i Norvegii v oblasti rybolovstwa* (Soviet–Norwegian cooperation in fisheries). Moscow: VNIRO.

Index

Academy of Sciences (USSR), 120
Acidification, acid rain, 11, 181, 208,
    238, 240–241n4, 246n48, 247n49,
    251, 253
  in Canada, 196–197, 218–219
  causes of, 157–158
  and Cold War, 166–167
  in Germany, 186–188
  impacts of, 156–157, 194–195,
    222, 223, 225–226
  industry and, 161–162
  intergovernmental negotiations on,
    167–175
  in Nordic countries, 160–161, 182–
    186
  reduction of, 155, 233, 254–255
  scientific evidence for, 231–232
  social learning about, 262–263
  Soviet Union and, 234–235
  as transboundary problem, 159–
    160, 163–165, 201, 241n7,
    244n26
Acid News (publication), 221
ACOPS. *See* Advisory Committee on
    Oil Pollution of the Sea
Adirondacks, 165
Advisory Committee on Oil Pollution
    of the Sea (ACOPS), 37
Air Management Sector Group
    (OECD), 166
Air pollution, 7, 13, 25, 155, 198,

243n22. *See also* Acidification,
    acid rain
  transboundary, 9, 159–160, 163–
    165, 171, 172–173, 182, 189,
    208, 214–215, 240–242nn1, 4, 9,
    12 , 242n18, 244n26, 253, 263,
    266–267, 270, 272, 274, 276,
    277, 286
Air Quality Agreement (AQA), 200,
    213, 218, 253
  implementation of, 174–175
  negotiation of, 173–174
Allocation: of fisheries, 103–104. *See*
    also Quotas
Amoco Cadiz, 37, 51
Antarctic Treaty System, 1–2
AQA. *See* Air Quality Agreement
Aquatic ecosystems: and acid rain,
    165, 171, 175, 180, 183, 194–
    195, 233
Arctic Commission (USSR), 119
Arkhangelsk, 95
Asia, 51
Authority, 23–24, 28, 142, 261, 262
  Canada-U.S. MOI and, 217–220
  under LRTAP, 215–217
  of oil pollution regime, 79–80

Baltic Sea, 46
Baltic states, 185
Barents Sea fisheries, 7, 8–9, 27, 91,

Barents Sea fisheries (cont.)
  149n1, 250–251, 252–253, 255,
    263–264
  as bilateral regime, 99–101
  boundary disputes in, 93–94, 98–99
  compliance control in, 147–148
  constituencies in, 144–145
  economy and, 94–95
  fishing fleets and, 11, 26
  jurisdiction in, 101–102, 108–112,
    138–139, 145–146
  management of, 92–93, 95–96,
    105–106, 112–115, 121, 122–
    132, 261, 262, 268, 282
  monitoring and enforcement in,
    106–107
  regulatory compliance in, 132–138,
    140–141
  Russian, 96–97
  scientific research in, 115–121,
    143–144, 146–147
  shared stocks in, 139–140
Bargaining powers, 104–105
Behavior
  mechanisms of, 259–260, 268–271
  and problem solving, 254–255
  and regime effectiveness, 19–22,
    260–261
Belarus, 185
Bierstaker, Thomas, 287
Bilateral Research Consultation
  Group (BRCG), 170, 197, 202, 223
Black Forest, 186–187
Black Sea, 46
Blame matrix, 163
Bodo (Norway), 185
Boundary disputes: in Barents Sea
  fisheries, 93–94, 98–99, 252
Boundary Waters Treaty (1909), 171
BRCG. *See* Bilateral Research Consul-
  tation Group
Brezhnev, Leonid, 166
Bush, George, 173, 200, 204–205,
  230–231, 236
Byrd, Robert, 204, 209, 230

CAA. *See* Clean Air Act
Canada, 165, 198, 242–243n19,
  246n44
  acidification in, 158, 162, 163–164,
    165, 170–171, 180, 196–200,
    205, 231–232, 234, 236, 242n14,
    245n38
  air pollution in, 7, 156, 159, 160
  Air Quality Agreement and, 173–
    175
  MOI and, 171–173, 201, 208,
    209–210, 213, 218–219, 220,
    227, 237
Canada-United States Air Quality
  Committee, 174
Canada-United States Free Trade
  Agreement, 228
Canada-U.S. Memorandum of Intent
  (MOI), 155, 156, 174, 196, 198,
    242n17, 246n41
  authority under, 217–220
  cooperation under, 212–215
  effectiveness of, 175–181, 208–210,
    233–239
  negotiation of, 171–173, 197
  politics of, 227–232
  recommendations for, 170–171
  social learning and, 223–224
  United States and, 200, 201–203,
    204
Canadian Coalition on Acid Rain,
  165, 228
Caribbean, 51
Carter, Jimmy, 44, 172
Central Electricity Generating Board
  (UK), 194
CFCs. *See* Chlorofluorocarbons
Chemical industry, 267
Chlorofluorocarbons (CFCs), 2, 267
Classification societies: oil transporta-
  tion industry and, 82–83
Clean Air Act (U.S.), 173, 174, 201,
  202, 209, 210, 217, 219, 228,
  229, 246n44
  Bush and, 204–205, 231, 236

Coal industry, 162–163, 162, 165, 183, 190, 201, 230, 246n47

Coastal states
boundary disputes between, 98–99
fisheries management and, 93, 262
jurisdiction of, 111–112, 142–143

Coast Guard (Norway), 98
and regulatory violations, 133–134
vessel inspections by, 132–133, 151n26

Coast Guard (Russia), 131

Cold War, 166–167, 193

Collective-action issues, 260, 261, 269

Collective action theory, 73–74, 214–215

Committee on Fisheries, 91, 92, 96

Committee on Law and Social Policy (U.S.), 37

Commons issues, 214–215

Compliance, 12–13, 151n23
coercion of, 265–266
with equipment standards, 70–72, 74–75
with fisheries regulations, 97, 98, 132–138, 140–141, 147–148, 272–273
with LRTAP, 175, 180–181
with oil pollution regulations, 49, 50, 57
reception facilities and, 76–77

Conference on Security and Cooperation in Europe (CSCE), 166, 253

Congress of the International Association of Limnology, 161

Conservation: of fisheries, 102–104, 130

Convention for the Prevention of Pollution of the Sea by Oil (OILPOL), 7, 33, 37, 40, 41–42, 50, 51, 53, 63
government monitoring under, 55–56

Convention of Antarctic Marine Living Resources, 139

Convention on Long-Range Transboundary Air Pollution (LRTAP), 9, 11, 14, 27, 155, 156, 167, 172, 174, 210, 232, 241n11, 242–243nn15, 19, 255–256, 270, 272, 273, 283
authority under, 215–217
behavior under, 260–261
cooperation and, 211–215
and Eastern Europe, 192–194
effectiveness of, 175–181, 233–239
Germany and, 187–188, 224–225
impacts of, 225–227, 253
nitrogen oxide protocol and, 169–170, 199
Nordic countries and, 182–186, 243n22
programmatic activities of, 266–267
Russia and, 188–192
signatories of, 176–177(table)
social learning and, 25, 220–223, 262–263
and Soviet Union, 17, 19, 206–207
sulfur protocol under, 168–169
United Kingdom and, 194–196, 207–208
United States and, 200–201, 203, 209, 231

Cooperation, 23, 166
fisheries management, 139–140, 151–152n33, 153–154n68
LRTAP and, 211–215
oil pollution regulations, 77–79
shared fish stocks and, 141–142
Soviet, 234–235

Cooperative Programme for the Monitoring and Evaluation of the Long-Range Transmission of Air Pollutants in Europe (EMEP), 14, 166, 167, 168, 211, 215, 217, 221, 222–223, 235, 253, 266

Corporations: oil pollution standards and, 42, 53

Costs and benefits: of regime adoption, 260–261

Council for the Protection of Rural
England, 165
Cowling, Ellis, 161
COW technology. *See* Crude oil
washing
Crude oil washing (COW), 22, 44,
70
adoption of, 71–73, 74, 81, 83, 89–
90n24, 252
CSCE. *See* Conference on Security
and Cooperation in Europe
Czechoslovakia, 185, 187, 189, 193,
211

Decision making, 260, 266–267
Denmark, 38, 52, 53, 167, 185
Dessler, David, 256
Development: regional, 103–104
Dingell, John, 204, 209
Dneper, 189
Donbass, 189

Eastern Europe, 192–194
and acid rain, 166–167, 185, 207,
235
East Germany, 185, 187, 189, 193.
See also Germany
Economics, 4–5
fisheries, 94–95, 96, 103–104
and oil tanker technologies adoption, 70–72, 81, 83
Ecosystems, 255
acid rain and, 175, 180, 262–263
fisheries management and, 252–
253
Edison Electrical Institute, 162
EEZs. *See* Exclusive economic zones
Electric power industry, 230
"Elements paper," 213
Embarrassment: enforcement
through, 137, 140–141, 147–148,
261
EMEP. *See* Cooperative Programme
for the Monitoring and Evaluation
of the Long-Range Transmission of

Air Pollutants in Europe (EMEP),
166
Emissions, 161–162, 178–179(table),
245n38. *See also* Nitrogen oxide
emissions; Sulfur dioxide emissions; Volatile organic compounds
Employment: in fishing industry,
113–114
Energy sources, 14, 183, 190
England: acid rain in, 158, 160. *See
also* United Kingdom
Environmentalism, 26
in Germany, 165, 187, 225
and oil pollution, 37, 79
in United Kingdom, 226–227
in United States, 229–230
Environmental Monitoring and Evaluation Program (EMEP), 14, 253
Environmental organizations, 119,
165. *See also by name*
Environmental Protection Agency
(EPA), 203–204
Environment Canada, 228, 245n38
EPA. *See* Environmental Protection
Agency
Equipment standards
adoption of, 74–75, 83, 260,
272
enforcing, 75–76, 265–266
and fleet countries, 52, 53
MARPOL, 27, 42–45, 85
meeting, 67–73
and oil pollution, 17, 48–49, 251–
252
and regulatory regime, 81–82
Europe, 89n15
air pollution in, 7, 156, 168, 180,
182, 222
LRTAP in, 215–216
oil pollution regulation in, 37–38,
51
sulfur dioxide emissions in, 163,
164(table), 165, 286
European Community, 94, 188, 195,
211, 216, 227

European Union, 109, 135, 151n25, 188, 211
Exclusive Economic Zones (EEZs), 26, 154n79
and Barents Sea fisheries, 91, 102, 108, 126–127, 135, 261
coastal states and, 145–146
Norwegian fishing industry, 97, 100
around Svalbard, 93–94, 149n2
vessel inspections in, 132–133
Exxon Valdez spill, 50

Faroese, Faroe Islands, 94, 135, 137, 154n80
Federation of Citizens' Groups for Environmental Protection, 165
Finland, 151n24, 183, 189, 191
acid rain reduction in, 160, 163, 167, 182, 186
Finnmark, 95
Fisheries, 27, 151n21. *See also* Barents Sea fisheries
interest groups and, 104–105
management of, 92–93, 97–98, 102–104, 105–107, 112–115, 121, 153nn57, 66, 255, 268
regulations, 122–132, 136–137, 150n11
regulatory compliance in, 132–138, 140–141
Russian management of, 96–97
scientific investigation of, 115–121
Fisheries Commission, 106
Fisheries Directorate (Norway), 98
Fisheries Ministry, 98, 121
Fisheries regimes, 2. *See also* Barents Sea fisheries
Fisherman Association (Norway), 97, 136, 150n20
Fishing fleets, 11, 26
Flag states, 262
discharge violations and, 56–57, 88n12
equipment standards and, 44–45, 52, 53, 67–68

tanker industry and, 38, 39–40, 82–83
Forestry Commission, 226
Forests: and acid rain, 183, 186–187, 195, 225–226, 244n32, 251
Framework Agreement: Barents Sea fisheries, 99
Framework Convention on Climate Change, 6
France, 52, 53, 85, 109, 150n19, 167
Friends of the Earth, 165, 226

Germany, 52, 88nn10, 12, 89n19, 109, 150n19, 226, 286
acid rain, 162, 163, 186–187, 205, 223, 234, 236, 253, 276
and LRTAP, 187–188, 224–225, 260
Gorham, Eville, 160, 186, 241n7
Gorsuch, Anne, 203, 219, 220
Great Britain. *See* United Kingdom
Great Lakes Water Quality Agreement (1972), 172, 256
Greece, 38, 52, 89n20
Greenland, 94, 109, 151n29
Green organizations, 26
Green Party (Germany), 165, 187, 225
Greenpeace, 119, 274
Grey Zone Agreement, 100, 110–112, 122, 132, 133, 138, 143, 145, 148, 255, 286

HCFCs, 13, 22
Helsinki accords, process, 166, 193, 207, 212
Hungary, 189, 193

Iceland, 94, 151–152nn27, 32–34
fisheries jurisdiction, 101, 108, 109, 110
overfishing by, 135, 137
ICES. *See* International Council for the Exploration of the Sea

ICS. See International Chamber of Shipping
IGOs. See Intergovernmental organizations
Illinois, 165
IMCO. See Inter-Governmental Maritime Consultative Organization
IMO. See International Maritime Organization
IMR. See Institute of Marine Research
Independent Tanker Owners Association (INTERTANKO), 38, 61
Industry, 161–162, 189
Institute of Marine Research (IMR), 105, 120, 121, 274
  and PINRO, 116, 118–119
  research by, 117–118
Institute of Oceanology (USSR), 120
Institute of Zoology (USSR), 120
Institutions
  effective, 274–277
  roles of, 25–26
Interest groups: bargaining power of, 104–105
Inter-Governmental Maritime Consultative Organization (IMCO), 40, 44, 55, 57, 63, 89n16
Intergovernmental organizations (IGOs), 37–38, 40, 105–106, 274
International Chamber of Commerce, 38
International Chamber of Shipping (ICS), 61
International Convention for the Prevention of Pollution from Ships (MARPOL), 7–8, 11, 33, 37, 41, 60, 89n23, 251, 252, 254, 266
  compliance with, 74–75
  discharge violations and, 56–57
  effectiveness of, 48–50
  equipment standards under, 27, 42–45, 67–73, 83, 85
  on reception facilities, 46–47, 63
  regulations of, 50–54

International Council for the Exploration of the Sea (ICES), 101, 121, 134, 144, 274
  fisheries management, 115, 116–117, 130, 147
  quota recommendations, 123–124
International law, 36–37, 53
International Maritime Organization (IMO), 8, 61, 62, 78, 90n25, 274
  authority of, 79–80
  on equipment standards, 68–69
  and pollution issues, 12, 38, 40, 43–44, 47, 50, 51, 57, 85–86, 88n5
International Nickel Company (Inco), 197
International Union for the Conservation of Nature and Natural Resources, 274
INTERTANKO. See Independent Tanker Owners Association
Investment, 13, 22, 117–118, 267
IOPP certificates, 67–68
Italy, 187

Jan Mayen, 133
Japan, 52, 53, 85
Joint Fisheries Commission, 99
Joint Statement on Transboundary Air Quality, 171
Jurisdiction, 272
  coastal state, 142–143
  over fisheries, 101–102, 108–112, 138–139, 145–146, 150n19, 255

Kara Seas, 9, 117
Karelia, 95
Kohl, Helmut, 208
Kola peninsula, 95, 191–192, 206

Labor unions, 185, 230
Lakes: and acid rain, 165, 175, 180, 183, 251, 253
Large Combustion Plant Directive, 188

Latin America, 51
Law of Air Protection (USSR), 190
Law of the Sea Convention (UNLOSC). *See* United Nations Law of the Sea Convention
Law on State Enterprise, 96
Learning: social, 24–25, 80–82, 220–224, 236, 261, 262–263
LeBlanc, Romeo, 196–197, 208
Leningrad, 189
Liberia, 38, 39, 46
Licensing: of fishing vessels, 126–127
Likens, Gene, 161
Load on Top (LOT), 42, 48, 53, 59, 70, 81, 89–90n24
Loophole, 94, 151n29
  jurisdictional issues over, 101–102, 105, 108–110, 146
LOT. *See* Load on Top
LRTAP. *See* Convention on Long-Range Transboundary Air Pollution

Maine, 165
Marine environment, 88n5, 262
  pollution and, 26, 35–36, 41, 54, 85–86, 151n21, 255
Marine Environment Protection Committee (MEPC), 40, 41, 67, 77
MARPOL. *See* International Convention for the Prevention of Pollution from Ships
Maximum sustainable yield (MSY), 252, 262, 268
Mediterranean, 46, 51
Memoranda of Understanding (MOUs): on oil pollution, 37–38, 68, 69, 80
MEPC. *See* Marine Environment Protection Committee
Meteorology, 160
Military: in Barents Sea, 92, 93, 116–117
Military Boundary Guard (Russia), 97

Miners, mining: coal, 162–163. *See also* Nickel industry
Mixed Fisheries Commission, 8
MMBI. *See* Murmansk Institute of Marine Biology
MOI. *See* Canada-U.S. Memorandum of Intent
Monitoring, 166
  acid rain, 174, 180
  fisheries, 106–107, 134–135, 138–139
Montreal Protocol (1987), 6
MOUs. *See* Memoranda of Understanding
MSM. *See* Multispecies management
MSY. *See* Maximum sustainable yield
Mulroney government, 173, 220
Multispecies management (MSM), 252, 262, 268
Multispecies modeling, 120
Murmanrybprom, 96
Murmanrybvod, 97, 131
Murmansk, 95, 105, 149n5
Murmansk County, 92
Murmansk Institute of Marine Biology (MMBI), 120
Mutual Access Agreement (1976), 100, 122, 127

NAPAP. *See* National Acid Precipitation Assessment Program
National Academy of Sciences, 229
National Acid Precipitation Assessment Program (NAPAP), 202, 213, 229, 245n40
National Clean Air Coalition, 165
National Coal Association of the United States, 162
National Society for Clean Air, 165
National Wildlife Federation, 165
Natural gas, 190
Netherlands, 53, 167, 187
New Brunswick, 199
New England, 201
New Hampshire, 204–205

New York, 165, 201

NGOs. *See* Nongovernmental organizations

Nickel industry, 175, 192, 197, 198, 245n36

Nitrogen oxides (NO_x), 157, 244n26
  reducing, 168, 169–170, 174, 178–179(table), 185–186, 187, 188, 190, 196, 199–200, 205, 208, 212, 227, 235, 243n21

Nongovernmental organizations (NGOs), 226, 274
  and acid rain, 165, 185, 187, 199–200, 221, 227, 228
  and oil pollution, 36, 37

Nordic countries, 205, 243–244n23. *See also* Finland; Norway; Sweden
  and LRTAP protocols, 182–186

Norilsk Nickel, 192

North American, 168. *See also* Canada; United States
  air pollution in, 159, 161, 170–171, 181, 215, 240n1
  sulfur dioxide deposition in, 163–164

North American Air Quality Agreement (1991), 9

Northeast Atlantic Fisheries Convention, 99

North Sea, 59

Norway, 87n2, 149n2, 243n22, 286
  acid rain in, 163, 166, 167, 194, 236
  and Barents Sea fisheries, 8–9, 26, 27, 91, 93–95, 105, 108–112, 142, 145, 251, 252, 255, 261, 262, 284
  emissions reduction in, 182, 183, 185–186, 225, 234, 242, 243n21
  fisheries management by, 97–98, 103–104, 112–117, 144, 150n20, 151n29, 153n57, 153n66
  fisheries regulations and, 122–132, 137, 140, 150nn12, 19, 152n38
  oil companies in, 38, 149n1

oil pollution regulations in, 52, 53
  regulation violations in, 133–135
  scientific research by, 117–118, 120, 139, 144, 152n42, 153n50
  and Soviet Union, 99–101, 115–116, 191
  vessel inspections by, 132–133

Norwegian Foundation for the Protection of Nature, 119

Norwegian Regulation Council, 121, 149n6, 150n9

Norwegian Sea, 93

Nova Scotia, 160, 165, 199

Nuclear energy, 117, 183, 190, 191

Oceans. *See also* Barents Sea fisheries; Marine environment
  fisheries, 92–93
  international law and, 36–37, 53
  oil pollution of, 47–49, 85–86

OCIMF. *See* Oil Companies International Marine Forum

Odén, Svante, 160–161, 186

OECD. *See* Organization for Economic Cooperation and Development

Ohio, 165, 230

Oil Companies International Marine Forum (OCIMF), 38

Oil industry, 89–90nn23, 24, 183

OILPOL. *See* Convention for the Prevention of Pollution of the Sea by Oil

Oil pollution, 6, 12, 35, 87n2, 251–252, 253–254, 255, 262, 263, 272, 276
  authority in, 79–80
  cooperation and, 77–79
  discharge standards and, 41–43, 54–59
  effectiveness of, 47–50
  equipment standards and, 17, 43–45, 265–266
  MARPOL convention and, 7–8
  reception facilities and, 45–47

regulations and, 33–34, 35, 40–42, 50–54
social learning and, 80–82
tanker regulations and, 38–39
variation-finding analysis in, 283–284
Oil Record Book (ORB), 52, 55
Oil tankers, 11, 80, 89nn18, 19, 21, 90n27, 267
discharge from, 33, 34–35, 41–43, 45–46, 54–59, 88nn6, 8–10
equipment standards for, 43–45, 48–49, 67–73, 74–76, 81, 85, 89n20, 251–252, 260, 265–266, 272
flag states and, 82–83
regulatory regime and, 38–39, 47–54, 88n7, 276
and spills, 37–38
Oil transportation industry, 73, 81. *See also* Oil tankers; Reception facilities
pollution regulation and, 38, 42, 43, 44, 48, 74–76
reception facilities and, 76–77
Ontario, 174, 175, 198, 245n36
Ontario Hydro, 198, 199
OPEC. *See* Organization of Petroleum Exporting Countries
ORB. *See* Oil Record Book
Organization for Economic Cooperation and Development (OECD), 63, 161, 166, 168, 223, 274
Organization of Petroleum Exporting Countries (OPEC), 47, 63
Overfishing: in Barents Sea, 124–126, 132, 134–136
Ozone, 2, 6, 13, 22, 157

Panama, 38
Pechenga Nickel, 192
Permanent Committee on Management and Control, 138
PINRO. *See* Polar Research Institute of Fishery and Oceanography

Poland, 168, 185, 189, 192
Polar Research Institute of Fishery and Oceanography (PINRO), 97, 105, 116, 118–119, 120, 121, 152nn41, 45, 47
Policy process, 250
Politics, 5–6, 137, 263, 277
of acid rain reduction, 181, 195, 203–205, 233, 261, 266–267
environmental, 14, 226–227
oil pollution regime and, 83–84
Pollution. *See* Air pollution; Oil pollution
Ports, 272
pollution control in, 88n4, 262
reception facilities in, 45, 46–47, 59–67, 89n17
Power plants, 188, 189, 194, 198, 199, 205, 230, 246n47
Private industry: regulation by, 85, 88n7
Problem solving, 277–278
approaches to, 4–6
behavioral mechanisms and, 254–255, 259, 268–269
Production plans, 124
Prosecution, 56–57
Public: and oil pollution regulation, 36, 89n22, 263

Quasi-nongovernmental organizations (QUANGOs), 274
Quebec, 198
Quotas
fisheries, 96–97, 100, 104, 109, 151n25, 154n80, 255
ICES recommended, 123–124
overfishing of, 124–126, 132, 134–136
shared, 129–130, 139–140, 141–142, 150nn17, 20

Radioactive pollution, 9
RAINS program, 168, 256
Reagan, Ronald, 172, 173, 229

Reagan, Ronald (cont.)
  and acid rain agreements, 201,
    202, 203–204, 209, 213, 219,
    223, 224, 236, 242n18, 245n40
Reception facilities, 88–89nn13–16,
    272
  industry adoption of, 76–77, 89n17
  for oil wastes, 45–47, 59–67
Regimes, 31n2
  actors in, 273–274
  behavioral mechanisms and, 251–
    254
  behavior models of, 21–28, 258–
    265, 268–271
  causal connections in, 256–258
  compliance in, 265–266
  direct and indirect effects of, 12–14
  effectiveness of, 1–2, 250–251,
    254–256, 274–277
  enmeshment by, 266–267
  good and bad effects of, 14–16
  problem solving of, 4–6, 10–11
  problem structure and, 272–273
  roles of, 22–28
Regulation Council (Norway), 98
Regulations, 259, 276
  fisheries, 106–107, 122–132, 136–
    137, 139–140, 150n11, 154n79
  oil transportation industry, 50–54
Roles
  institutional, 25–26
  regime definition of, 261–262
Royal Society for the Protection of
  Birds (RSPB), 37
Ruckelshaus, William, 203, 223
Russia, 149n1, 185, 244n26, 277
  Barents Sea fisheries, 8–9, 26, 27,
    105, 142, 145, 149n5, 255, 261,
    262, 284, 286
  boundary disputes with, 93–94
  compliance control, 140, 141, 148
  fisheries management by, 96–97,
    109–112, 116–117, 153n66
  fisheries regulations and, 122–132,
    134, 150n12, 152n38, 154nn70, 79

and Iceland, 151–152nn32–34
LRTAP and, 188–192
regulatory violations by, 134, 135,
  136, 137–138
scientific research by, 118–119,
  144, 152n41
Russo-Norwegian Environmental
  Commission, 121
Russo-Norwegian Fisheries Commission, 91

SBT technology. *See* Segregated ballast tanks
Scandinavia, 89n20, 157, 158, 161,
  244n33, 253, 260. *See also various
  countries*
Schindler, David, 161
Scientific research. *See also* Technologies
  on acidification, 158–159, 182,
    202–203, 208, 213, 217, 220–
    221, 223, 229, 231–232, 238
  of fisheries, 115–121, 131, 139,
    143–144, 146–147, 152nn41, 42,
    153–154nn50, 68, 282
  and regulations, 136–137
Scotland, 195
Secretariat on Acid Rain, 165, 185,
  221
Segregated ballast tanks (SBT), 22,
  43, 44, 52, 68
  adoption of, 70, 71, 72–73, 74, 81,
    82, 83, 89n20, 252
Severo Nickel, 192
Sevryba (North Fish), 95, 96–97,
  136, 152n45
Sevrybkholodflot, 96
Shared fish stocks, 129–130, 139–
  140, 141–142, 150n17
Shell Oil, 42, 53
Shipping, 88n3, 89n18. *See also* Oil
  tankers; Oil transportation industry
Siberia, 11, 190, 191
Smelters, 162, 175, 185, 192, 197,
  198, 245n36

Smog, 157
Social-practice perspective, 270–271
Sofia declaration, 185, 186, 200,
  243–244n23
Soviet Ministry of Fisheries, 95
Soviet-Norwegian Fisheries Commission. *See* Russo-Norwegian Fisheries Commission
Soviet Union, 76, 124. *See also* Russia
  acid rain and, 166–167, 182, 234–
  235
  air pollution and, 189–190, 277,
  286
  Barents Sea fisheries and, 91, 92,
  93–94, 95–96, 99–101, 108, 145,
  251, 252
  compliance control, 147–148
  fisheries regulations and, 126–129,
  130, 141, 154n70, 272–273
  LRTAP and, 17, 19, 169, 189–192,
  206–207
  and Norway, 115–116, 150n19
  regulatory violations by, 134, 135–
  136
  scientific research by, 119–120,
  139, 152n42
Spain, 168, 188
State Committee on the Environment,
  96, 121
Stepwise processes, 268
Sudbury, 175, 197, 198, 199, 241n8,
  245n36
Sulfur dioxide (SO_2) emissions, 11,
  157, 159, 166, 229, 232, 241n8,
  253
  LRTAP protocols and, 168–169,
  192–193, 207, 208, 212
  in North America, 163–165, 198–
  199, 200
  reducing, 167, 174, 178–179(table),
  182–184, 187, 189–190, 225,
  228, 235, 236, 242n14, 244n30,
  245n38, 246n47, 286
  in Soviet Union/Russia, 19, 189–
  190

in United Kingdom, 194, 195, 196,
  215–216
  and United States, 201, 205, 234
Surveillance
  of fisheries, 97, 151n26
  of oil discharge, 55–56, 57, 59, 73–
  74
Svalbard, 93–94, 133, 149n2,
  152n38, 154n70
Svalbard Treaty, 94, 150n12
Sweden, 15n24, 165, 183, 185, 191,
  225
  acid rain and, 160–161, 163, 166,
  167, 236, 242n14
  emissions reduction in, 182, 234
  oil pollution regulations and, 38,
  52, 53
Switzerland, 187

Tanker Safety and Pollution Preven-
  tion Conference, 37, 44
Technical-Scientific Fisheries Council,
  97
Technologies, 14, 22, 168. *See also*
  Scientific research
  fisheries, 97–98, 143, 153n57
  oil tanker, 42–45, 48, 70–71, 74–
  75, 81, 83, 252
Tendency-finding analysis, 257–258
  factors in, 285–287
Thatcher, Margaret, 208, 225,
  244n33
30 percent club, 195, 199, 242n14
Thought experiments, 18–19
Torrey Canyon spill, 37, 50
Trail Smelter, 159, 171, 214, 240n1,
  245n36
Tralflot, 96
Trudeau, Pierre, 172
Turkey, 169

Ukraine, 185
Ulrich, Bernhard, 186, 187, 223, 224
UMWA. *See* United Mine Workers of
  America

UN ECE. *See* United Nations Economic Commission for Europe, 166

United Kingdom, 37, 38, 87n2
acid rain, 162, 165, 182, 185, 188, 195, 235, 247n49
Barents Sea fisheries and, 108, 150n19
LRTAP and, 168, 194–196, 205, 207–208, 225–227, 253, 260, 261, 263
oil pollution, 7, 41
oil pollution regulation in, 51, 53, 78, 83, 88n10, 89n19, 90n27, 263
sulfur dioxide reduction in, 215–216, 234, 244n30
transboundary air pollution and, 276, 277

U.K. Forestry Commission, 225–226, 244n32

United Mine Workers of America (UMWA), 230

United Nations, 51, 60, 161

United Nations Conference on the Human Environment, 79

United Nations Economic Commission for Europe (UN ECE), 166, 188, 274

United Nations Law of the Sea Convention (UNLOSC), 91, 101, 108, 145

United Nations Fish Stocks Agreement, 94

United States, 89n21
acidification in, 158, 170, 180
air pollution and, 7, 156, 159, 163–165, 196–197, 198, 200–205, 213, 233–234, 238, 246nn45, 48
Air Quality Agreement and, 173–175
environmental politics in, 171–173, 208–209, 210, 218–220, 227–232, 236
LRTAP and, 168, 242–243n19

oil pollution regulation in, 37, 38, 43, 46, 50, 51, 52–53, 55–56, 70, 72, 76, 78, 83, 89n19, 263

UNLOSC. *See* United Nations Law of the Sea Convention

U.S. Pollution Incident Reporting System, 48

Ural Mountains, 17, 19, 169, 189, 283

Utilities, 162. *See also* Power plants

Variation-finding analysis, 256–257
application of, 281–285

Vermont, 165

Vienna Convention (1985), 6

VNIRO, 97

Volatile organic compounds (VOCs), 157, 243n22
reducing, 168, 170, 208, 212, 235

Waldegrave, William, 225, 244n33

Waldsterben, 186, 187, 225

Wales, 195

West Germany, 185, 189. *See also* Germany

West Virginia, 165

Working Group on Effects (LRTAP), 217, 226

World Conservation Union, 274

The Effectiveness of International Environmental Regimes:
Causal Connections and Behavioral Mechanisms
edited by Oran R. Young

To be effective, an international regime must play a significant role in solving or at least managing the problem that led to its creation. But because regimes—social institutions composed of roles, rules, and relationships—are not actors in their own right, they can succeed only by influencing the behavior of their members or actors operating under their members' jurisdiction.

This book examines how regimes influence the behavior of their members and those associated with them. It identifies six mechanisms through which regimes affect behavior and discusses the role of each through in-depth case studies of three major environmental concerns: intentional vessel-source oil pollution, shared fisheries, and transboundary acid rain. The behavioral mechanisms feature regimes as utility modifiers, as enhancers of cooperation, as bestowers of authority, as learning facilitators, as role definers, and as agents of internal realignments. The case studies show how these mechanisms can cause variations in effectiveness both across regimes and within individual regimes over time.

One of the book's primary contributions is to develop methods to demonstrate which causal mechanisms come into play with specific regimes. It emphasizes the need to supplement conventional models assuming unitary and utility-maximizing actors to explain variations in regime effectiveness.

Oran R. Young is Professor of Environmental Studies and Director of both the Institute on International Environmental Governance and the Institute of Arctic Studies at Dartmouth College.

Global Environmental Accord: Strategies for Sustainability and Institutional Innovation

"In the twenty-first century the world will confront the necessity of building effective international regimes to govern and manage multiple global commons. This volume brings together a group of thoughtful scientists to confront how to analyze these problems and propose tentative solutions. Scholars interested in large-scale environmental problems will find this book invaluable."
— Elinor Ostrom, Arthur F. Bentley Professor of Political Science, Indiana University

"This collection makes significant contributions to our understanding of how international regimes can influence the behavior that matters for conserving natural resources and protecting the environment, and hence what conditions can make for more effective international environmental management."
—Edward A. Parson, John F. Kennedy School of Government, Harvard University

The MIT Press Massachusetts Institute of Technology Cambridge, Massachusetts 02142
http://mitpress.mit.edu

YOUEP 0-262-74023-0

90000

9 780262 740234

Cover images: Top, oil tanker, bottom, fishing vessel; both from PhotoDisc, Inc., 1999.